Crafts
A Basic Survey

# Crafts
# A Basic Survey

## Virginia Irby Davis

*Lynchburg College, Virginia*

**wcb**
Wm. C. Brown Publishers
Dubuque, Iowa

Cover and interior design by Don P. Overmyer

Cover photo by © Bob Coyle

Copyright © 1989 by Wm. C. Brown Publishers. All rights reserved

Library of Congress Catalog Card Number: 87–72768

ISBN 0–697–00621–2

Printed in the United States of America by Wm. C. Brown Publishers
2460 Kerper Boulevard, Dubuque, IA 52001

10  9  8  7  6  5  4  3  2  1

*For Terry*

*But even if you have plenty of money to buy machinery . . . there still is a satisfaction in making a thing for yourself with your own hands that nobody can deny you.*

Comment of a southern highlands craftsman from *Handicrafts of the Southern Highlands,* by Allen H. Eaton, Russel Sage Foundation, New York, 1937.

# Contents

Preface    xi

Acknowledgments    xv


Part 1                    *Theoretical Aspects*    1

_____

1    Crafts and Society    3

*Working Definitions and Philosophy*    3

*Evolution of the Artist-Crafter*    4

*Crafts in America*    6

*Crafts Today*    8

2    Crafts and the Art Education Program    11

*Why Study Arts and Crafts?*    11

*Development of Art Education*    14

*Changes in Art Education*    15

*Objectives of Art Education in the Crafts*    15

3    The Arts-Crafts Teacher    19

*Qualifications of the Arts-Crafts Teacher*    20

*Teaching Art: Goals and Tasks of the Arts-Crafts Teacher*    20

*Standards of Achievement for the Crafts Student*    23

*Evaluation and Grading of Crafts Projects*    24

4    Crafts and Creativity    27

    *An Overview of Research in Creativity*    27

    *Characterizing Creativity and the Creative Individual*    29

    *Stages in the Creative Process*    30

    *Testing for Creativity*    30

    *Creativity and Crafts*    30

    *Current Trends in Creativity Research*    31

5    Basic Design for Crafts Students    33

    *Components of Art*    34

    *Elements of Art*    35

    *Principles of Organization*    47

    *Design in Crafts*    47

    *An Approach to Original Design*    49

6    Organizing a Crafts Program    51

    *General Considerations*    51

    *The Crafts Room or Workshop*    53

    *Tools and Equipment*    55

    *Materials and Supplies*    56

7    Crafts Today    57

      *Crafts in the Educational System*    59

      *Crafts as Recreation*    61

      *Crafts as Therapy and Rehabilitation*    63

      *Crafts for the Elderly and Handicapped*    64


Part 2                          *Procedural Instructions for Specific Crafts*    67

8    Coiled Basketry    69

9    Enamels on Metal    77

10    Fabric Dyeing    89

      *Batik*    90

      *Tie-Dye*    95

11    Fiber Techniques    103

      *Weaving on a Frame Loom*    103

      *Macramé*    114

      *Stitchery: Traditional and Contemporary*    125

12    Jewelry    147

13    Mosaics    163

14    Papermaking by Hand    171

15  Printing  189

*Woodcuts*  189

*Linocuts*  197

*Silk Screen on Paper*  203

*Silk Screen on Fabric*  214

16  Stained Glass  219

17  Ceramics  233


Part 3                            *Professional Portfolio*  255

18  Craftspeople at Work  257

Appendixes  295

*A Crafts Shops and Galleries*  295

*B Crafts Museums*  299

*C Suppliers*  301

Glossary  305

Index  311

# Preface

Based on more than twenty years of experience in teaching crafts to students at various levels, I have come to believe that there are two characteristics basic to human nature: (1) everyone possesses to some degree the potential for creative accomplishment, and (2) everyone needs the satisfaction of doing (making) something with one's hands. In our present educational system, however, the creative potential of many students is often not developed and in our age of "canned and instant everything," virtually every material need, including all forms of entertainment, is provided ready-made; therefore, the joys that come from working with one's hands and the subsequent pride in good craftsmanship are often difficult to attain. I believe that failure to satisfy these two basic needs might well contribute to frustration, uncertainty, and confusion as to one's creative potential.

In no way am I suggesting that a course in handicrafts is all that is necessary to solve the problems of society, but I do believe the study of arts and crafts will go a long way toward opening the windows of the mind and soul to a means of satisfying one's creative potential. Helping students at all levels to find meaningful outlets for their creativity through working in the crafts will aid significantly in giving them insight into their problems, in building new confidence through which to face life, and in instilling a high level of belief in their ability to function creatively.

It becomes, then, a major responsibility of the teacher in the visual arts to help students discover and develop their creative potential and to provide the special ambience necessary for creative individuals to flourish. Most investigators in the field of creativity agree with Dr. E. Paul Torrance that the creative individual is often guided by a different set of values and a constant search for uniqueness and new tasks to conquer.[1] Because of this divergency, the individual may feel in the minority among peers, teachers, and family. Efforts to cope with the resulting psychological estrangement, unless wisely guided, may lead the student to repress or even abandon altogether these creative tendencies. To get along with the group, a student may develop certain tricks for coping with conflicts either by camouflaging his or her abilities so they are less noticeable or by "bulldozing" through, sometimes becoming completely obnoxious in the process. In any case, the highly creative student may often be prone to such problems as faulty or uncertain self-concept, learning disabilities, behavioral problems, and various neuroses not experienced by less creative individuals.

For those of us who teach arts and crafts, Dr. Torrance outlines six roles that he believes are essential in helping creative students maintain their creativity and continue to grow.

1 Provide a "refuge" for the student from vicious attacks by the world. The educational system as it presently exists must often be somewhat coercive in approach and emphasize the establishment of behavioral norms that the highly creative student may find impossible to abide by. How many teachers have realized that the outstanding student who wants to "go the extra mile" is discouraged by peers because his or her enthusiasm makes the rest of the class look bad.

2 Be a sponsor or patron. The creative individual needs someone with prestige to offer protection from the reactions of peers who may be less than understanding long enough to give creative thinking the opportunity to develop. The student who, deep down, really wants to strike out in new directions needs the support of an older, wiser individual who will furnish reinforcement.

3 Help creative students understand their divergence. Creative individuals often do not understand their behavior and need assistance in coping with their artistic natures. Sometime the really creative student is made a pariah by peers and, sadly, by family as well. An understanding teacher who is willing to listen can make all the difference.

4 Allow the student to communicate thoughts and ideas. In many cases, the ideas of creative individuals are so far ahead of those of their classmates (and sometimes of their teachers as well!) that they feel they have no one who will even listen, let alone understand. In almost every instance in which students have come to me for help, all they needed was someone who would listen with a sympathetic ear and who would inspire them with courage to carry out their creative ideas.

5 See that creative talent is recognized. Tests that measure student potential in many areas are often designed to favor the convergent thinking, good-grade-getters who may have little creative ability. The recognition of superior divergent students is essential if a place is to be found for them in our educational system. In addition to the many tests given to students of all levels to measure all sorts of abilities and potentials, why not design a test to detect and measure creativity levels?

6 Help parents understand the creative student. The teacher can guide parents in handling the child's unusual questions and ideas and assist them in aiding the child to develop creativity. I think teachers in the field of art, more than in any other perhaps, have to reassure parents that their son's or daughter's divergency is not cause for distress, but rather reason for rejoicing.

Dr. Torrance further maintains that a highly creative person (teacher) is required to guide creative students, but the teacher should not be so absorbed in his or her own creativity so as not to allow the student to be creative as well. The teacher must be open-minded, able to listen to and *hear* what the student is saying, and keep all senses completely alive. Intuition must function fully, communicating warmth and safety. The teacher must fully understand the creative process and allow it to operate while maintaining contact with reality.

In recent years, recognition of developing creative potential in students of all ages has led to increased emphasis on arts and crafts education in our schools and colleges and to the need for creative, well-trained, and dedicated teachers in this area. Courses of study leading to degrees in art education and certification as teachers of art are offered by most liberal arts colleges. Standards for teacher preparation programs are specified by the various state boards of education. Those of the state of Virginia are typical.[2]

In searching for a suitable textbook for a course in basic crafts, I found numerous works available covering individual crafts such as weaving, jewelry, metalwork, enameling, and so forth, as well as a few how-to-do-it books geared to the elementary and secondary levels; however, no one text contained theoretical background information, comprehensive procedural coverage of a number of crafts, and orientation of crafts into a general art education program that could serve as a suitable text for students of crafts at various educational levels, as a guide for those teaching such courses, and as a self-help manual for those working without a teacher.

With the hope of providing such a text, I undertook the present work. It is based on my considerable experience as a practicing craftsperson and as a teacher of arts and crafts, fortified by years of reading, research, and discussions with students and other teachers in the arts. The information presented has been thoroughly tested in my classes in manuscript form with a high level of acceptance by students.

Procedural instructions, while as complete as possible, have been kept simple and direct. Although I have assumed that a competent instructor will be present to demonstrate each step and supply additional help where needed, the procedural chapters might be used by the amateur craftsperson working alone.

I felt that illustrations would be more meaningful to students if mostly student works were shown. Therefore, I have taken photographs in the procedural sections as well as those showing finished work under actual working conditions in the studio. Because it is also important for the student to become familiar with the work of successful craftspeople, a "professional portfolio" is included as well.

*Notes*
1  E. Paul Torrance, *Guiding Creative Talent* (Englewood Cliffs, N.J., Prentice-Hall, 1962), 7.
2  Virginia State Board of Education Division of Teacher Education and Certification, *Standards for Approval of Teacher Preparation Programs in Virginia* (State Department of Education, Richmond, Virginia 23216). For certification of teachers of art, the standards are a minimum of thirty-three semester hours, with a minimum of nine hours required in each of three areas: (1) two-dimensional media and concepts including design, drawing, painting, graphics; (2) three-dimensional media and concepts, including design, sculpture, ceramics, crafts; (3) history of art and related areas (dance, music, theatre, architecture, photography, communication arts). Although standards for teacher preparation are similar among the various states, potential teachers should write to the board of education in the state in which a job is to be sought for up-to-date requirements.

# Acknowledgments

In compiling and writing this work, I have incurred many debts and obligations. I wish to express my sincere and humble thanks to all those friends, colleagues, and students who have given me encouragement and help. I am especially grateful to:

- The many students I have been privileged to teach, particularly to those whose work is pictured in this book
- Professors Richard Pumphrey and Thelma Twery, my colleagues in the art department at Lynchburg College, for allowing me to photograph work done by students in their design and graphics classes
- Gallery owners Penny Bosworth, Frances Harris, Bob Lieby, and Andy Williams for allowing me to photograph selected works of the artists they exhibit, and to the artists themselves for their permission to publish these photographs in the "Professional Portfolio" section of this book
- Lucille Ferrell, secretary to the Art Department of Lynchburg College, for her patience and assistance in typing the manuscript
- The staff of the Lynchburg College Library, particularly to Deborah Beckel and Carol Pollock for their invaluable aid in locating sources
- The staffs of various organizations who shared their involvement in crafts with me, especially Elizabeth Ford and Kenny Fisher of the City of Lynchburg Recreation Department; Elinor Hopkins and Diane Smith of the Adult Care Center of Central Virginia; Kay Mantiply and Linda Blythe of the Adult Day Care Center of Virginia Baptist Hospital in Lynchburg; Beth Smith of the Y.W.C.A. Art Camp; Joan Lowery, Joan Wray, and Lowell Thomas of the Association for Retarded Citizens Workshop

For information and comments on art education in the public schools, I wish to thank Richard W. Layman, associate director for fine arts in public schools of the Commonwealth of Virginia, Christine Crist, art teacher in Altavista, Virginia, and Jackie Yeatman, art teacher in Lynchburg, Virginia. Dr. Al Wilson, director of the Belle Boone Beard Gerontology Center at Lynchburg College provided me with invaluable information on crafts programs for the elderly. Gertrude Shook, fiber craftswoman, Keysville, Virginia, gave me permission to describe her soft sculpture work. Terry D. Sumey, my dearest and most trusted friend, helped immeasurably with his advice, encouragement, and unfailing confidence in this work as he does in all my endeavors.

A special note of appreciation is extended to Professors Ralph A. Parente, Jr. (Anna Maria College), Neil Britton (Virginia Wesleyan College), Stephanie Santmyers (North Carolina A & T State University), Beverly J. Semmens (University of Cincinnati), Blair C. Archer (California State University, Long Beach), Alan C. MacTaggart (Lander College), Dana F. Johnson (University of Northern Colorado), Barbara H. Noel (Southeastern Massachusetts University), and Arthur Guagliumi (Southern Connecticut State University) for their very helpful reviews of the manuscript.

Virginia Irby Davis
Lynchburg, Virginia

# Part 1    *Theoretical Aspects*

# 1 Crafts and Society

**Working Definitions and Philosophy**

Intelligent study in any field of endeavor requires, first of all, that the student identify and formulate working definitions of essential terms. In the field of crafts this may present some difficulty. Such words as *craft, craftsman,* and *craftsmanship* have become imbued with great diversity of meaning. The word *craftsman* itself (and indeed any word ending in *man*), which has always been applied to both male and female workers in the crafts, has in recent years become cause for concern. Substitution of such designations as *craftsperson, craftspeople, artisan,* or sometimes *handcrafter,* while often awkward, has become the acceptable practice. When we further consider the age-old debate of "art versus craft," the waters become more muddied. Define we should, however, and assuming for the moment that the words craft, craftsmanship, and craftsman or suitable substitutions are valid, concrete terms capable of definition, we can formulate the following basic premises:

1  A producer working in a particular craft will fabricate an end product of some sort.
2  The design of this product will be based on a concept in the mind of the producer and will be motivated by a material need or be done to satisfy a creative urge of the producer.
3  This concept will be influenced by the producer's knowledge, training, experience, and attitudes and will presumably follow the principles of good design.
4  The concept will be translated into tangible form by the producer's hands.
5  The producer's facility with the hands will be governed by a degree of skill and dexterity, dependent on training and experience.
6  Suitable materials will go into the fabrication of the product. The producer will have adequate knowledge of the properties, limitations, and integrity of the materials and will fashion them with every refinement of technique and method.

7 Tools necessary to the fabrication of the product will be so skillfully manipulated that they will become extensions of the producer's hands, eyes, and mind.

8 The end product will function as a utilitarian and/or decorative object and be aesthetically pleasing in either case. It may or may not be a one-of-a-kind object, though there will inevitably be minor variations because of hand production if a number of similar objects are made.

9 The product will find an owner or user who will acquire it for its utilitarian or decorative value. The product will, in all likelihood, be more expensive than a mass-produced object.

An attempt to consolidate these premises into a workable definition might result in such a statement as: A producer (craftsperson) formulates a concept and, by exercising certain skills, uses the necessary tools to fashion from suitable materials an end product (crafted object) that will be meaningful to the user by fulfilling a need and/or evoking an aesthetic response.

To resolve the art versus craft debate, we can feasibly substitute the words *artist* for producer and *work of art* for product in the list of basic premises. Quite a similar definition for art would result: An artist formulates a concept and, by exercising skills, uses the necessary tools to fashion from suitable materials a work of art that will aesthetically communicate the artist's concept to a receiver.

Amid charges of "oversimplification" from colleagues who have expounded on these subjects in numerous chapters and volumes and being fully aware of the controversy such a statement might precipitate, I nevertheless maintain that for all practical purposes, art and craft are so closely related that a sharp line of demarcation is neither necessary nor desirable. The artist must be a good craftsperson and the good craftsperson an artist if both are to contribute to society the full scope of their creative abilities. The attitude that only the so-called "fine arts" (painting, sculpture, architecture, music, drama, and so forth) are capable of eliciting a deep aesthetic response from a user or viewer is narrow and outdated today, when the dedicated professional craftsperson is also an artist and the large body of exciting work being produced in all the crafts is worthy of classification with other fine works of art. One has only to consider the numerous museums of fine art, which include in their exhibition schedules annual crafts shows, to realize that at last in America, as has long been the case in other countries, we are rapidly developing awareness of fine crafts as the "backbone of the arts."

**Evolution of the Artist-Crafter**

The concept of the craftsperson as artist has evolved over a long period of time and has come to full realization as a part of our contemporary culture, in which the craftsperson is no longer regarded as simply a maker of useful things with the hands but also as a producer of objects having aesthetic appeal, or "art works," if you will.

It is beyond the scope of this work to go into a full scale treatment of the history of crafts, but a few major developments must be mentioned. The Paleolithic cave dweller, who first discovered that by chipping away at a chunk of flint an axe head or a skinning knife could be made, probably paid little conscious attention to designing their resulting tools to please their sight and touch. Interest lay only in functional utility. That so many of these objects are aesthetically pleasing must be because of an innate sense of design possessed by the cave dweller. In any case, this early human became the first of a long line of artisans producing handmade objects to make life more comfortable for their users. From that time on, the maker of things has been a necessary and valuable member of society, and the objects made through the centuries give us an interesting picture of what humans have found necessary as tools, utensils, and objects to adorn both person and habitat.

The excellence of the jewelry, coins, pottery, metalwork, and other handcrafted objects remaining from ancient Greek civilization indicate that the Greeks held handcrafts in high regard. Greek artisans produced their wares for members of the aristocracy and the state rather than for sale to the general public. This patronage, coming from a knowledgeable clientele with definite ideas about what they wanted, together with the Greek love for beauty tempered by moderation and desire for order, created the ideal climate for Greek artisans to make the works of their hands masterpieces of classical beauty and elegance, yet restrained and completely functional. In spite of this indispensability to daily life, however, the Greek artisan, whether citizen or slave, was never given the esteem accorded statesmen, soldiers, or philosophers. In *Politics* Aristotle advocated denial of citizenship to those who lived by the works of their hands.[1] Thus, in Greek society, we see a situation in which the end product was valued more than the person who made it.

During the very early Middle Ages, artisans began to band together to form workshops according to their specialties. The large monasteries also gathered groups of artisans to produce objects associated with religious worship: carvings in wood and ivory, tapestries, mosaics, gold and silver vessels, stained glass, crucifixes, rood screens, illuminated manuscripts, and the like. Traveling organizations of artisans arose during this era, thus contributing to the diffusion of styles from one area to another. Handicrafts could be easily transported by great trade caravans that spread these objects all over the civilized world.

The power and influence of craftsmen in medieval Europe was manifested by the rise of craft guilds about 1250 A.D. These guilds or "mysteries" were occupational associations comprising those artisans working in a particular craft, such as weavers, masons, and carpenters, as well as those engaged in the pursuit of music, painting, sculpture, and architecture. The guilds sought to protect their members from competitive artisans in neighboring cities. They set standards of workmanship and price scale, and worked toward gaining greater status for their members in society. Organization was based on division of members into masters, journeymen, and apprentices.

Guilds existed for the purpose of furthering the economic, social, and sometimes political welfare of their members. Guilds often became very powerful organizations that were able to exercise a great deal of control over town governments. Within the guild, the apprenticeship system had the positive effect of ensuring a continuing supply of artisans to carry on a particular craft, because members were trained and indoctrinated into traditional practices. Negatively, the exclusiveness of the system kept away many who might have made great contributions, and the jealous guarding of technical knowledge inhibited the flow of learning into the public domain. The guilds reached their peak of influence during the fourteenth and fifteenth centuries, declining rapidly thereafter, though some survivors such as the London Livery Companies exist to this day.[2]

Until the Renaissance, artists and artisans had been essentially on the same social level. Painting and sculpture were considered mechanical arts, and the artist was the equal of any craftsperson. With the development of Renaissance humanism, strongly influenced by the ideas of classical Greece and Rome, a definite separation of handicrafts and art came into being. The visual arts were raised to the status of fine arts, along with music, drama, and poetry, and the handicrafts became "minor" or decorative arts. The idea of the craftsperson as a manual worker, artisan, or technician and the artist as an intellectual genius on a much higher level was to persist for hundreds of years thereafter.

The technological and socioeconomic changes that occurred as a result of the Industrial Revolution in the late eighteenth century and well into the nineteenth—invention of new machines with resulting increase of volume, division of labor, and mass production—meant that craftspeople, who individually produced handcrafted articles, were replaced by machine operators who produced, together with other workers, thousands of identical objects to satisfy the demands of the new markets and the increased purchasing power of the masses. The mass-produced object was often poorly designed and devoid of any aesthetic appeal, but it was inexpensive and therefore available to practically anyone. When the majority of the public is willing to accept shoddy merchandise and mediocre craftsmanship, the good artisan working slowly and with great care to produce fine, unique objects of beauty is forced to give up the workbench and turn to industry for a livelihood.

In the late nineteenth century there began, particularly in England, a move toward a revival of the crafts. This move was sparked primarily by the energy and enthusiasm of William Morris and the Pre-Raphaelite group. Morris, appalled by the ugliness of industrial products and influenced by the art of the Middle Ages, established a workshop devoted to the production of paintings, carvings, and furniture in 1861. He later expanded his operations to include tapestries, fabrics, carpets, and stained glass. Morris advocated a revival of the working techniques and standards of the Middle Ages and hoped that the splendor of medieval decorative arts could flourish again during his time. His beliefs concerning the need for making beauty a part of everyday life, together with the freshness and originality of his work, exerted a tremendous influence on the taste of the Victorian era.[3]

Somewhat later, in 1919, Walter Gropius, a German artist and architect issued a pamphlet that said in part: "Architects, sculptors and painters, we must all return to the crafts. For art is not a profession. There is no essential difference between the artist and craftsman. . . . Let us create a new guild of craftsmen, without those class distinctions which raise an arrogant barrier between craftsmen and artists. Together let us conceive and create the new building of the future which will embrace architecture, sculpture and painting in unity and one day will rise to the skies, from the hands of millions of workers, as the crystal symbol of a new coming faith."[4] This pamphlet was the manifesto for the soon to be established Bauhaus in Weimar, Germany. Here, together with a faculty of such artists as Johannes Itten, Lyonel Feininger, Gerhard Marcks, Wassily Kandinsky, Paul Klee, Laszlo Moholy-Nagy, Josef Albers, and others, Gropius hoped to train students, on the basis of a craftsman's apprenticeship, to bring together in their work the best of the arts and crafts accompanied by academic art. All entering students were required to take a basic course taught by Itten, who set forth three aims:[5]

1  To free the creative powers and thereby the art talents of the students
2  To make the student's choice of career easier
3  To convey to the students the fundamental principles of design for their future careers

The basic course lasted one semester. Upon successful completion, students began three years of training and study of materials and tools, space, composition, color, construction, representation, and nature. After determining which materials were most appealing, the student concentrated on working in these under the direction of workshop masters (*Formmeister*). The final phase of training was carried out in the field, where the student worked under actual industrial conditions. Despite being plagued by internal friction among the Formmeister, financial difficulties, and troubles with the government, the Weimar years of the Bauhaus were reasonably successful. In 1925 the Bauhaus moved to Dessau and the work begun at Weimar was continued there, until the school was forced by political and economic pressures to close its doors in 1933. The principles put into practice at the Bauhaus have had a great and lasting effect on contemporary art education and on furthering the idea that artists and craftspersons are not two opposing camps but rather, if not one and the same, certainly so closely related that it is ridiculous to quibble over minor differences.

**Crafts in America**
The early settlers of America included many skilled craftspeople. As the country grew, the work of metalsmiths, furniture makers, weavers, potters, glass blowers, and others was in great demand and the craftsperson became an increasingly important member of the community. One has only to look at such items as silverware, pewterware, and furniture produced by these people to realize that their work has not often been surpassed in quality and beauty. By 1850, however, hand fabrication of such objects had given way to factory production, and the same general decline of crafts and craftspeople as had happened in Europe was the case in America as well.

Toward the end of the nineteenth century, there had occurred in other parts of Europe a reaction to the ugliness of machine-made products similar to that exemplified by Morris and his group in England. Work produced by the followers of Jugendstil in Germany, Modernismo in Spain, and the style developed in France, which came to be known as art nouveau, advocated a return to high standards of hand craftsmanship, even when objects were made with the aid of machines. Influenced by the French rococo style and Japanese decorative arts, art nouveau was characterized by curving lines, asymmetrical designs, exotic themes, sensitively drawn plant and insect forms, and highly idealistic portrayals of women.

The art nouveau movement made its way to America and greatly influenced Lewis Comfort Tiffany who, in 1893, opened a studio in Corona, New York, for the production of stained and blown glass. He became noted for his favrile glass work, producing lamps, vases, windows, and other decorative objects in the art nouveau style. Tiffany believed, as had William Morris, that beautiful objects should be a part of one's everyday surroundings; but unlike Morris, he was willing to use machines to produce the number of objects necessary to satisfy such a goal. Tiffany's work enjoyed a period of great popularity, fell into disfavor in the 1920s, and is now much in demand again by art collectors. Aside from the contribution of his own work, Tiffany's ideas and success did much to encourage the small number of studio craftspeople who were working during that era.

The crafts revival in the United States, which dates from the late 1920s, was nurtured by the efforts of those few dedicated workers in the crafts who attempted to maintain their own working studios at that time. Working in ceramics, glass, metal, weaving, and other crafts, having no established national crafts tradition as precedent, and being able to turn nowhere for instruction in most cases, these artisans taught themselves the necessary techniques, maintained high caliber production despite personal hardships, and most important, began passing their knowledge on to other workers.

In addition to the contributions of these individuals, there are several major developments that ushered in the revival of crafts as well as the present prestigious image of the artist-crafter in the United States:

1  In the late 1930s and early 1940s, a large number of artists and craftspeople, who had taught at, been trained at, or been influenced by the Bauhaus, migrated to America and exerted a tremendous influence on American arts and crafts. Many of these people were integrated into the faculties of American colleges while some established their own schools and workshops in various parts of the United States. Josef Albers became associated with Black Mountain College (North Carolina) in 1933, and in 1949 became chairman of the department of design at Yale University. Walter Gropius came to Harvard's Graduate School of Design in 1937. In that same year, Laszlo Moholy-Nagy founded the "New Bauhaus" in Chicago, which later became the influential Chicago Institute of Design.

2  Schools and colleges began to include in their curricula courses devoted to the teaching of various crafts, so for the first time it was possible for anyone to get classroom training in pottery, weaving, jewelry-making, and other crafts as well as in painting, drawing, and sculpture. An early effort in this direction had been made by Dr. William G. Frost who, after assuming the presidency of Berea College (Kentucky) in 1893, became interested in mountain crafts. During the years that followed, Dr. Frost established the first

school in the southern highlands "for providing careful instruction and preparing teachers in the arts."[6] Today, crafts courses are taught in practically all art schools, as well as in a great many liberal arts colleges. Alfred University, Cranbrook Academy, the Art Institute of Chicago, Pratt Institute, the Art Center School of Los Angeles, and the University of Georgia are only a few from a long list. Crafts schools, such as Penland School of Crafts, Penland, North Carolina, and Arrowmont School of Arts and Crafts, Gatlinburg, Tennessee, (and many others) offer training in all the crafts. Numerous summer workshops of short and long duration all over the United States offer concentrated crafts sessions under the direction of prestigious professional teachers.

3  The formation of regional crafts associations, guilds, and leagues has been instrumental in promoting the work of their members and in making the public conscious of well-crafted objects. Founded in 1929 and typical of many others in existence in various part of the United States is the Southern Highlands Handicraft Guild, comprising individual and group members from a nine-state area. The guild operates retail shops in various locations and sponsors several crafts fairs each year.[7]

4  Perhaps the one person who did more to further the American crafts revival than any other was Aileen Osborn Webb (Mrs. Vanderbilt Webb, 1892–1979). Webb, a patron of and worker in the crafts, founded in New York in the early 1940s a retail outlet called *America House*. As a means of disseminating information about the activities at America House, she periodically issued a mimeographed bulletin, which later became the magazine *Crafts Horizons* under professional editorship.[8] Now renamed *American Crafts,* the magazine is the official journal of the American Craftsmen's Council, an organization founded by Webb in 1943 for the purpose of establishing contact among craftspeople in the United States. With the organization of the World Craftsmen's Council in 1964, her interest in and guardianship of the crafts was established on an international level. Recognizing the need of craftspeople for a display place at museum level, Webb was instrumental in founding the Museum of Contemporary Crafts (now the *American Crafts Museum*) in New York City.[9] Her support of, enthusiasm for, and belief in the American

craftsperson until her death at the age of eighty-seven in 1979 did much toward ensuring the prestige of the dedicated, mature crafter in today's society.

5 Opportunities for the exposure of the work of craftspeople at all levels has resulted in an increased awareness and appreciation by the public of well-designed and beautifully crafted objects. Such opportunities are afforded by:

    a Regional and local crafts fairs open to all, amateur and professional alike, who want to rent a space to show and sell their wares.

    b Juried regional crafts exhibitions and fairs under the sponsorship of various organizations. Typical of these are the four regional fairs held at various times through the year and sponsored by American Crafts Enterprises, Inc., a subsidiary of the American Crafts Council. Locations for these fairs are Baltimore, Maryland; Dallas, Texas; West Springfield, Massachusetts; and San Francisco, California.

    c Periodic exhibitions of the work of craftspeople at established art museums throughout the United States.

    d Numerous retail outlets established by individuals or groups for the sale of fine professional crafts.

    e The increasing number of commercial galleries that sponsor handcrafted objects as well as paintings and sculpture.

    f Touring exhibitions such as *Objects: U.S.A.,* which opened at the Smithsonian Institution in the fall of 1969. This exhibition, sponsored by the S. C. Johnson Company of Racine, Wisconsin, contained the work of 250 artist-crafters selected by Lee Nordness, director of the Lee Nordness Galleries in New York.[10]

**Crafts Today**

From the cave to the museum has been a long and difficult journey for craftspeople. Today, perhaps for the first time since the Renaissance, the professional in the crafts is in a position to assume a rightful place as a full-fledged member of the fine arts community, commanding respect from the public and enjoying a well-earned position of prestige among fellow artists. It is even possible once more to make a decent living by producing fine craft work.

Crafts have become a part of our daily lives not only from the standpoint of collecting finely crafted objects for their utility and aesthetic appeal but also from the standpoint of furnishing an avocation for increasing numbers of people. Many amateurs are sincerely motivated, and with diligent study and practice are able to become quite competent crafters.

It is indeed encouraging to see this trend toward working with one's hands, which was so much a part of the lives of our forebears, who, coming from Europe or other countries with a crafts tradition, knew how to use their hands. Indeed, the early settlers of America *had* to be crafters in order to construct their homes, build furniture, and make all objects needed for daily living. Frustration at being unable to find meaning in life can bring about a state of being that Dr. Viktor Frankl calls the existential vacuum.[11] By the existential vacuum, Frankl means life devoid of worth, a sense of inner emptiness, a feeling of total and ultimate meaninglessness of life. The existential vacuum manifests itself mainly in a state of unrest, boredom, and depression. In advanced cases alcoholism, drug addiction, and even suicide may result. Dr. Frankl further believes that one's work usually represents the area in which the individual's uniqueness stands in relation to society, which is not so much a matter of what the work is but of how well the work is done. This brings us right back to craftsmanship!

Today, as never before, people have the time and affluence to pursue an avocation in addition to regular work. Looking at television or playing golf (both good hobbies) palls if one can make a pot, build a chair, or weave a rug. Unfortunately, because of the lack of training in technical procedures and principles of design and aesthetics, so many hobbyists work diligently to turn out little more than "busywork," valuable as a time-filling or therapeutic measure but usually not conducive to the production of well-crafted objects.

Through the continued combined efforts of dedicated professional crafts workers, teachers, crafts associations, museums, galleries, and a large body of sincere amateurs, I hope a national crafts tradition will continue to grow in America such as has existed for centuries and still does in Japan and many parts of Europe, particularly in the Scandinavian countries.

That schools, colleges, and arts and crafts centers will continue to offer courses in the crafts and staff their faculties with competent professionals capable of passing their knowledge on to their students is essential to the growth of the crafts movement all over the world.

*Notes*

1  Aristotle, *Politics* 3.5, trans. Jowett (New York: Viking Press, 1957).
2  For an account of these modern survivors of the medieval craft guilds, see the *Encyclopedia Britannica,* 1971 ed., vol. 14, 151–52.
3  William Morris set forth many of his beliefs concerning art, beauty, social welfare, and so forth in his written works. A delightful example is *News from Nowhere,* first published in 1891 (reprint, New York: Longman, Green, Co., 1917).
4  Walther Scheidig, *Crafts of the Weimar Bauhaus,* trans. Ruth Michaelis-Jena and Patrick Murray (New York: Reinhold Publishing Co., 1967). Original edition published by Edition Leipzig under the title *Bauhaus Weimar, Werkstattarbeiten.*
5  Johannes Itten, *Design and Form, the Basic Course at the Bauhaus,* trans. John Maas (New York: Reinhold Publishing Co., 1964). Originally published in Germany under the title *Mein Vorkurs am Bauhaus, Gestaltungs und Formenlehre.*
6  Allen H. Eaton, *Handicrafts of the Southern Highlands* (New York: Russell Sage Foundation, 1937).
7  For more detailed information concerning the Southern Highlands Handicraft Guild, refer to *Crafts Horizons,* 24, no. 3(June 1966); *Crafts in the Southern Highlands* published by the guild, 930 Tunnel Road, Asheville, NC 22805; and Eaton, *Handicrafts.*
8  *American Crafts,* (formerly *Crafts Horizon* magazine) published bimonthly by the American Craftsmen's Council, 401 Park Avenue South, New York, NY 10016.
9  The new and much expanded American Craft Museum on West 53rd Street in New York City opened in October 1986 with the premier exhibition *CRAFT TODAY: Poetry of the Physical,* sponsored by Philip Morris Companies. The official book of the opening exhibition, featuring work created since 1980 by 286 leading American craftsmen is available from American Craft Council Publications, 40 West 53rd Street, New York, NY 10019.
10  Lee Nordness, *Objects U.S.A.* (New York: Viking Press, 1970). This is an invaluable source for the crafts student and teacher, because it contains, in addition to an extremely well-written account of the author's views on crafts, biographical sketches and illustrations of the work of some 250 foremost craftspeople working in the United States in 1970.
11  Viktor E. Frankl, *Man's Search for Meaning: An Introduction to Logo-Therapy,* (Boston: Beacon Press, 1963).

*Suggested Readings*

Mattil, Edward L. *Meaning in Crafts.* 3rd ed. Englewood Cliffs, N.J.: Prentice-Hall, 1971.
Robertson, Seonaid Mairi. *Crafts and Contemporary Culture.* London: George G. Harrap and Co. and UNESCO, 1961.

# 2 Crafts and the Art Education Program

As we have seen, the crafts revival of the 1930s and 1940s was greatly facilitated by the increased availability of diverse craft courses offered by various learning centers. These courses range in intensity and scope from the weekly two-hour meetings of hobbyists at local activity centers, guided by amateur or semiprofessional instructors, to full-scale programs at accredited colleges taught by highly trained educators and culminating in a degree in fine arts. Master's programs in crafts are offered by some schools.

Courses in crafts are, therefore, firmly established as a part of the art education curriculum along with those offered in painting, drawing, sculpture, graphics, photography, and ceramics. In order to appreciate fully the scope of this achievement, it is necessary to realize that the whole field of art education itself has followed a long and torturous path to become accepted as a part of the general education program; a summary of this will help us to integrate crafts intelligently into the overall picture.

## Why Study Arts and Crafts?

Incredible as it might seem today, there are still some parents (and some educators as well) who distrust any educational program that puts too much emphasis on the fine arts. In a tight economy this distrust is reflected in the unfortunate fact that the fine arts program budget of an educational institution is usually the one cut first. By the same token, a fine arts facility is usually the last to be built on most college campuses. If a "liberal arts" education is based on those studies founded in lasting human values, it is difficult to understand why art (which has been around since Paleolithic times) should be thus relegated to a minor role in the educational system.

11

The question is often asked, "Why is it important to study art?" There are, of course, numerous approaches to answering this question but from a standpoint of the place of art study in the total educational picture, the most reasonable answer is that no person in a single lifetime can hope to do, be, or experience everything that comprises the history of humankind. However, one can, through the study of art, approach an understanding of this experience. The artist (creator of a work of art) can respond to some experience of life or to some inner vision through skill and imaginative creativity. He or she can shape some material (the medium) such as oils and canvas, clay, wood, stone, metal into a visible form that will communicate to other human beings the artist's response to the environment and his or her interpretation of experiences and environment. The study of many artist's works throughout the centuries thus becomes a means of absorbing the whole range of human experience. In his essay "Experience, Nature and Art," John Dewey elaborated on this idea: "If, however, not knowledge but art is the final flowering of experience, the crown and consummation of nature, and knowledge is only the means by which art, which includes all practice, is enabled to attain its richest development, then it is the artist who represents nature and life at their best."[1]

The history of art and the history of humankind have gone hand in hand, and the art of any era must necessarily reflect the cultural spirit and the events of the time in which it was produced. A typical example is Romanesque architecture of eleventh century Europe. The so-called Dark Ages were past, the long-dreaded millennium or end of the world that most believed would occur in the year 1000 had not arrived as expected, and the spirit of religious enthusiasm was growing. By way of thanksgiving, pilgrimages were being made to sacred sites, and the world was putting on a "white mantle of churches" decorated with works of art glorifying God and reflecting the religious awakening of the period. In studying the paintings, sculpture, architecture, and crafts of this era, therefore, we become acquainted with the people, their physical and psychological experiences, and their reactions to these experiences as well as to the sociological, economic, religious, and cultural customs of the times.

From the beginning of recorded time, there have been certain members of every society more adept than others at making significant expressions of their reactions to their environment, the visible form of which

has come to be known as *art*. Traditionally these gifted ones not only enrich their culture through their own talents, but attempt to train followers in the same disciplines and to impart to their fellow citizens an understanding and appreciation of their work.

There is evidence that prehistoric artists may have gone to school to learn their craft. In the early Stone Age caves at Limeuil in southwestern France, 137 stone "sketch-sheets" have been found, many of them poorly executed, with the details often corrected as if by a teacher's hand.[2] According to Pliny, drawing first appeared in Greek liberal education in the fourth century B.C., and somewhat later, the drawing teacher was a regular member of the teaching staff.[3] There are few major artists during all periods who did not teach several apprentices, and some, such as Rubens in Flanders and the Bellinis in Italy, established and maintained flourishing schools of art, having many students in all stages of development.

Because art activities have occupied a prominent place in the interest and attention of human beings from the earliest times, it would seem logical that the teaching and study of art would always have been a vital part of any organized school program. Although many educational leaders have recognized the importance of art in education, as stated earlier, the general attitude of those organizing and administering school programs has often been that art is unnecessary, or at best a leisure-time activity, a civilizational and educational luxury. As late as 1896, Herbert Spencer stated this position as such: "Accomplishments, the fine arts, belles-lettres, and all those things which, as we say, constitute the efflorescence of civilization, should be wholly subordinate to that knowledge and discipline in which civilization rests. As they occupy the leisure part of life, so should they occupy the leisure part of education."[4]

Periodic changes in the nature of art itself, as well as changes in philosophical and psychological trends of general education, have had major influences on the development of art education in our schools. It is beyond the scope of this work to make a complete review of such influences. Therefore, I have chosen to concentrate on the progressive change of attitude toward art from simply a servile copying or imitation of nature indulged in as a leisure-time activity or busywork to the realization that a work of art may exist for its own sake, purely as an expression of the artist's right to create freely in any way he or she chooses and to have this work assigned equal importance with other educational disciplines in a democratic ideal of civilization.

The concept of the artist as imitator appears early in literature in Plato's *Republic*. In book 10 he expounds the myth of the three beds: the ideal bed as created by God, the bed itself as made by a craftsman, and the third bed, one that appears as in a mirror. "And the painter too is, as I conceive, just such another—a creator of appearances, is he not? . . . No wonder then, that his work too is an indistinct expression of truth. . . . Then the imitator, I said, is a long way off the truth, and can do all things because he lightly touches on a small part of them, and that part an image. For example: A painter will paint a cobbler, carpenter, or any other artist, though he knows nothing of their arts; and if he is a good artist, he may deceive children or simple persons . . . and they will fancy they are looking at the real carpenter."[5]

The idea of artist as imitator was transmitted by Plato to Aristotle and interpreted anew by him in his *Poetics*. "Men, some through art and some through habit, imitate various objects by means of colour and figure. . . . To imitate is instinctive in man from his infancy . . . all men likewise, naturally receive pleasure from imitation. Imitation then, being natural to us, those persons in whom originally these propensities were strongest were naturally led to rude and extemporaneous attempts."[6]

Realize that the concept of art as set forth by Plato and Aristotle has been too often given a shallow or disparaging interpretation by educators. There is a great deal of material written by Herbert Read, Ronald Levison, Paul Friedlander, and S. H. Butcher that bears out Plato's and Aristotle's assumptions.[7] In fact the foundation of Read's whole book, *Education Through Art,* is the thesis expressed by Plato: that art should be the basis of education. Read says, "It is surely one of the curiosities of the history of philosophy that one of the most cherished notions of this great man has never been taken seriously. . . . Scholars have played with his thesis as with a toy: they have acknowledged its beauty, its logic, its completeness, but never for a moment have they considered its feasibility. They have treated Plato's most passionate ideal as an idle paradox, only to be understood in the context of a lost civilization."[8] In any case, the shallow interpretation

prevailed, and the idea of the production of art as a crude uncreative imitation of truth, or simply as a pastime or extra activity not to be classed with the intellectual disciplines necessary for an aristocrat's education, exerted a tremendous influence upon the status of the artist until the Renaissance. Throughout antiquity and the Middle Ages, the visual arts had been considered as mechanical arts rather than as liberal arts, with the artist being relegated to the status of worker-craftsman, skilled beyond ordinary means to be sure but still a worker.

About 1400 there occurred in Italy, and more specifically in Florence, a rebirth or rediscovery of the classical past, an emphasis on humanism and a conscious return to classical ideals of logic, order, beauty, and reason. The rebirth came to be known as the Renaissance. The movement eventually spread all over Europe and marked the transition from medieval to modern times. It was an age of discovery, on the one hand, discovery of the classical past with its humanism, and on the other, discovery by human beings of themselves as individuals with dignity, worth, and intelligence. The desire to explore the physical world, to probe and prove scientific phenomena, and to gain knowledge of the individual as a person were the primary motivating forces of the Renaissance. In such an atmosphere of intellectual awakening and of brilliant accomplishments in science, mathematics, medicine, literature, and all the arts, it was inevitable that artists should take advantage of the opportunity to promote their creative ability, gain recognition, take their rightful places in society as individuals of culture and learning. As H. W. Janson points out, "Thus, when the artist gained admission to this select group, the nature of his work had to be redefined: he was acknowledged as a man of ideas . . . and the work of art . . . the visible record of his creative mind. He often became, himself, a man of learning and literary culture . . . [either] the man of the world, self-controlled, polished, at ease in aristocratic society . . . [or] the solitary genius, secretive, idiosyncratic, subject to fits of melancholy and likely to be in conflict with his patrons."[9]

Students of the great masters of the Renaissance were thoroughly trained in such scientific disciplines as human anatomy and linear perspective; they traveled to Greece and Rome to study classical ruins firsthand. In painting, emphasis was on a strictly realistic presentation of an environment that looked "right"; that is, a painting should be a "window on the world," with the artist having little latitude for creative improvization. The painting was a faithful record rather than the artist's free interpretation. This situation was to prevail until the middle of the nineteenth century.

## Development of Art Education

Freedom as the guiding principle of education was first established by Jean-Jacques Rousseau (1712–1788) who, according to C. D. Gaitskell, believed that teaching should be related to childhood interests and that education should be concerned with the everyday life of the child. "Let children be children, Rousseau advocated, and let them learn through self initiated activities."[10] Rousseau's theories of naturalism in education are set forth in his pedagogical novel *Emile,* the underlying theory of which advocates that education should do nothing but give the child an opportunity to develop his or her natural gifts unhampered by the corrupting influences of civilization. All learning should be from an inner realization, and the ultimate goal of education should be to teach men to live. Gaitskell cites the following as a typical quote from *Emile:* "What must we think of the barbarous education which sacrifices the present to the uncertain future, which loads the child with chains of every sort, and begins by making him miserable, in order to prepare him, long in advance for some pretended happiness which it is probable he will never enjoy?"[11] True, many of Rousseau's theories are considered impractical and even laughable by today's educational standards, but they did lay the foundation for the themes of free expression in those arts that were to become prevalent in the nineteenth century.

Rousseau's theories greatly influenced later educators, particularly the German educator Friedrich Froebel, who established the first kindergarten in 1837, and the American philosopher and educator John Dewey. Froebel, like Rousseau, believed that children should be allowed to develop naturally without restriction by too many rules. He further developed the idea of using objects with basic geometric shapes in teaching, because cubes, rectangles, squares, and circles were "perfect" forms. By relating these geometric shapes to objects around them, children would gain a better understanding of their world. Similar theories were later used by the French artist Paul Cézanne, who sought to develop new ways of depicting natural objects from basic geometric forms. He explored shifting viewpoints and modeling forms through subtle variations in color values, and intensities. Cézanne's theories became the basis of much of modern art, particularly of cubism.

Froebel saw the classroom as a miniature society and each student as an active participant of that society. That he was vitally concerned with the fostering of creativity in children is seen from his writings: "Unless we would cripple our children's lives both now and for the future, we must educate them in accordance with the demands of their nature and with the present stage of human growth. Therefore, the present time makes upon the educator, and all those who have charge of children, an inescapable demand—they must grasp children's earliest activities and understand their impulse to make things and be freely and personally active; they must encourage their desire to instruct themselves as they create, observe and experiment."[12]

John Dewey (1859–1952) has, more than any other American educator, promoted the idea that art and art education are vital elements in a democratic society. One of the founders of the functional school of psychology, Dewey explored the relationship of the learner to his or her environment and to the society in which he or she lives. Dewey was concerned with the teaching of art, and his book *Art as Experience* is a classic work in the philosophy of aesthetics.[13] In this book, Dewey says that the ideal human community is dependent upon its aesthetic component. This is, indeed, a far cry from Spencer's idea of art as an efflorescence of civilization. In his essay "Individuality and Experience" Dewey uses the pendulum simile, saying that the study of art in schools "shows a swing of the pendulum between two extremes, though it must be admitted that the simile of the pendulum is not a good one, for the schools remain, most of them, most of the time, near one extreme, instead of swinging periodically and evenly between the two. Anyway, the two extremes are external imposition and dictation, and free expression."[14]

There is no better example of "external imposition and dictation" in the arts than the Academy of Painters and Sculptors founded in France in 1648 under the leadership of Charles LeBrun. The academy gained control of French art by establishing rules and regulations for the standardization of the arts. Regulations ensured that art was used for the glorification of the king and the state. The powerful academy, and its dogmatic insistence on rigid rules and regulations, set the standard in artistic endeavor for over two centuries. It was virtually impossible for any artist not following the dictates of the academy to have work accepted in the yearly salon exhibitions. In 1863 when the salon jury rejected over four thousand paintings because of favoritism and prejudice, Emperor Napoleon III decreed that a separate exhibition be held for the rejected works because such a furor ensued. This was the famous "Salon des Refusés," which in itself was not a great success, but it did accomplish two important things. It brought to light the defects of the academy system, (1) marking the beginning of its decline in power and, most important, (2) establishing the idea that the artist has the right to create and teach as he or she pleases rather than limiting his or her creative efforts to the narrow boundaries of arbitrary rules. This is, of course, the basic premise of the "art for art's sake" theory that was to become the cornerstone in the development of modern art and lead to such movements as impressionism, postimpressionism, fauvism, cubism, futurism, nonobjectivism, and many others, featuring the names of such creative geniuses as Manet, Monet, Cézanne, Van Gogh, Picasso, and Braque, to list only a few. Truly, Dewey's pendulum had swung to the other extreme, that of free expression. It would seem that with the introduction and eventual acceptance of the concept of "art for art's sake" and with the proliferation of the many movements mentioned, the field of art education might show the same growth. To some extent, certain changes did begin to occur around the middle of the nineteenth century in both Europe and America. The introduction of programs of "linear drawing," the appearance of drawing exercise books, such as those authored by Walter Smith, a Massachusetts educator, and the establishment of training courses for prospective art teachers were tentative first steps. Unfortunately, however, the major emphasis was on a rigidly dictated development of technical skills in the realistic rendition of objects and learning by rote of such principles as geometric perspective rather than on encouragement of creative expression. Gaitskell points out that even today, one may find in certain elementary classrooms "art" lessons based on linear drawing "in the belief that the hand and eye should be trained, disassociated from thought."[15]

## Changes in Art Education

Frank Cizek, who in 1901 became chief of the Department of Experimentation and Research at the Vienna (Austria) School of Applied Arts, was responsible for an important breakthrough in theories of art education for children. Cizek believed that children's art should be based on their emotional responses to the environment, events, and people around them. Thomas Munro, who visited Professor Cizek's classes in Vienna, wrote, "The small workroom, crowded with some fifty boys and girls from seven or eight to fifteen was a delight to watch. What could more completely justify a method of instruction . . . than the fact that it obviously gave children such a good time in the process? No one who has ever been present at an old-style school art lesson and seen or suffered himself, in the cramped, painful and smudgy task of copying, could have failed to enjoy the spectacle of animated industry."[16]

The new system of art teaching was gradually brought to England and America by Thomas Munro and A. W. Dow, among others. These influences, along with such innovative approaches to art training as those of the Bauhaus (see chapter 1) and other institutions dedicated to progressive education, together with the effects of the various movements being developed in Europe in the early twentieth century radically changed elementary and secondary school art programs. Unfortunately, many teachers, because of lack of training, were unable to handle these unfamiliar ideas of freedom of expression and often adopted a laissez-faire attitude in which freedom to grow according to natural laws meant that children should have license to do pretty much as they liked, without responsible and knowledgeable supervision. If stimulus and guidance from a well-trained and caring teacher is lacking, creative freedom can produce results just as deplorable as those from rigid supervision. No matter how much creative freedom is allowed, the classroom teacher must use acceptable teaching methods and strike a fine balance between too little and too much supervision.

## Objectives of Art Education in the Crafts

How best to nurture the creative process in children has been the object of much serious research by art educators and psychologists since 1950. Based on these researches, Gaitskell defines the general objective of art education today as a means of assisting in the intellectual, emotional, and social growth of the learner according to his or her needs and capacities: "Every teacher attempts to give his students a map with which they may orient themselves to the world. . . . The art teacher hopes that as a result of his instruction, children can be brought to view life in personally expressive and visual terms—moving at various times from observation to intuition, from feeling to memory, and from the creation of symbols to meaningful responses to the work of others. Art today is a field of study that can help develop worthy citizens, people who enjoy intellectual and emotional control, people with skill and initiative and people who are aware of their world."[17]

Every young child just beginning to notice the environment must come to grips with materials and objects, and the earliest lessons involve gaining an understanding of the qualities and behavior of these. The wood floor is hard, the shag rug upon it is soft, water is wet, sand is dry. Objects may be piled atop one another to build forts and castles; if they are not well constructed they will topple. Plastic materials, such as clay or dough, may be shaped by pushing or pulling; hard materials may be shaped or altered by treatment with a tool. The hands and fingers may be used to manipulate all sorts of materials; string or glue may be used to join several objects together; pencils and crayons will make marks on any available surface. In short, children learn to control and change their environment by using their hands and appropriate tools to translate their ideas into visible form. When this occurs, the child has made the first steps into the world of the crafts.

Parents must realize that providing children with a wide variety of materials and objects to explore and manipulate, together with constant encouragement to express their innate creativity, is essential to their early development. Almost every exceptionally creative student whom I have taught has had, from earliest childhood, all manner of educational toys, books, and materials with which to create things. These students have also been encouraged to ask questions, explore the environment, wonder about the universe. To accomplish this, children *must* be led past the coloring book and the television set if they are to begin to explore their full creative potential. Subsequent training through the elementary school years must continue to reinforce exposure to increasing numbers of experiences, with ample time to explore these experiences, space in which to work, and constructive evaluation of the results.

By the time students reach secondary school, they should be ready for more sophisticated techniques and materials with guidance. Through continued practice, they will develop skills in conjunction with their creative abilities, which will go with them throughout their lives.

If one major aim of education is to produce artists (makers of things, that is, craftspeople), then the importance of crafts training as a part of education from the earliest years through college cannot be overemphasized. Recognition by educators and educational administrators of the necessity for developing craftsmanship and creativity in our students is vital to the healthy growth of our entire educational system. This concept has been well summarized by Herbert Read: "Education may, therefore, be defined as the cultivation of modes of expression. . . . It is teaching children and adults how to make sounds, images, movements, tools and utensils. A man who can make such things well is a well educated man. . . . All faculties of thought, logic, memory, sensibility and intellect are involved in such processes . . . and they are all processes which involve art: for art is nothing but the good making of sounds, images, etc. The aim of education is therefore, the creation of artists . . . of people efficient in the various modes of expression."[18]

Periodic evaluations of standards in any educational discipline is both necessary and healthy. Nowhere is this more true than in the field of art education. The new directions and modes of artistic expression; the advent of new materials and technological developments; the changes in the character of art itself; the complex nature of our rapidly changing society; and the paradox of a world whose boundaries are constantly shrinking but whose horizons are at the same time expanding to outer space make it imperative that art and the teaching of art move forward and reach all people.

The artist, of all people, cannot exist in a social and/or intellectual vacuum. The old concept of the artist as the introverted "ivory tower" dweller who must retire from the world in order to create can no longer be accepted. It is not surprising, then, to find that there has been in the last decade a growing tendency among art critics, art historians, art educators, and practicing artists to question the traditional values of art education as presently taught in our schools and colleges, and to suggest that it may be high time that we reexamine and restructure the whole program. If, as I believe, all art is a form of communication and if our art students are not being taught to communicate, then, yes, the system needs overhauling.

Contemporary art education must employ the methods, approaches, and concepts that will enable the art student to be at home in the world and to be a viable, contributing, communicating member of a complex society—a communicator who examines the world and communicates what he or she observes and feels through visual statements, be they paintings, drawings, graphics, architectural renderings, photographs, crafts, or whatever. This is certainly not to say that all traditional methods in the teaching of art need to be discarded, although some critics advocate such drastic steps as doing away with the teaching of design principles, as rejecting any role that labels an artist as an aesthetician, or as obliterating the term *artist* to describe the producer of creative communications.

There are some things, however, that do not change, even in art education. The basic elements of art, the principles of organization, and the theories of aesthetics are the same today as they always have been. Students should learn them as a part of their art training, if only so they will know when and how to break the rules with intelligence and creativity! To teach art without including a study of design principles is like giving students a background in American history without mentioning George Washington, the Emancipation Proclamation, or World War II. No, the problem is not with the basic ideas and facts themselves, but with how we as art educators guide our students toward understanding the changes in our world, what these changes have caused, and how they, as artists, can use the basic principles to make creative, meaningful statements in the Space Age. This can only be accomplished by encouraging students to explore all forms of expression, both traditional and avant-garde; to question the validity of all that is called art, both past and present; to learn not only to use the traditional techniques and materials, but also to experiment with any and all new media; to make the most of their creative abilities; and most important of all, to keep open minds and think for themselves, which should be the ultimate goal of all education.

## Notes

1 John Dewey, "Experience, Nature and Art," in *Art and Education* (Merion, Pa.: Barnes Foundation Press, 1947), 23. The essay was adapted from Professor Dewey's book *Experience and Nature* (Chicago: Open Court Publishing Co., 1925).

2 Ronald Schiller, "Those Mysterious Cave Paintings," *Reader's Digest,* March 1971, 158. The article is condensed from the original, published in *Travel* magazine.

3 H. I. Marrou, *A History of Education in Antiquity* (New York: Sheed and Ward, 1956).

4 Herbert Spencer, *Education: Intellectual, Moral and Physical* (New York: D. Appleton and Co., 1896). Quoted in an essay by Francis T. Villemain, "Democracy, Education and Art," in *Readings in Art Education,* ed. E. W. Eisner and D. W. Ecker (Waltham, Mass.: Blaidsell Publishing Co., 1966), 409.

5 Plato, *The Republic,* trans. Jowett (New York: Random House, Modern Library, 1957), 360ff.

6 Aristotle, *Politics and Poetics,* trans. Jowett (New York: Viking Press, 1957), 223ff.

7 For the sake of brevity, I have refrained from citing specific quotes from those authors mentioned. Works referred to were: Herbert Read, *Education through Art* (London: Faber and Faber, 1943); Ronald B. Levinson, *In Defense of Plato* (Cambridge, Mass.: Harvard University Press, 1953); Paul Friedlander, *Plato, an Introduction,* trans. Hans Mayerhoff (New York: Pantheon Books, 1958); S. H. Butcher, *Aristotle's Theory of Poetry and Fine Arts* (New York: Dover Publications, 1951).

8 Read, *Education through Art,* 1.

9 H. W. Janson, *History of Art* (Abrams, N.Y.: Prentice-Hall, 1962), 305–6.

10 C. D. Gaitskell, *Children and Their Art,* 2d ed. (New York: Harcourt, Brace and World, 1970), 25.

11 *Ibid.*

12 Friedrich Froebel, *A Selection from His Writings,* ed. Irene M. Lilley (Cambridge: Cambridge University Press, 1967), 97.

13 John Dewey, *Art as Experience* (New York: Minton, Balch and Co., 1934).

14 John Dewey, "Individuality and Experience," in *Art and Education* (Merion, Pa.: Barnes Foundation Press, 1947), 32.

15 Gaitskell, *Children and Their Art,* 33.

16 Thomas Munro, *Art Education, Its Philosophy and Psychology* (New York: Liberal Arts Press, 1956), 237.

17 Gaitskell, *Children and Their Art,* 47ff.

18 Read, *Education through Art,* 11.

*Suggested Readings*

Barkan, Manuel. *A Foundation for Art Education.* New York: Ronald Press, 1955.

Bassett, Richard, ed. *The Open Eye in Learning: The Role of Art in General Education.* Cambridge, Mass.: MIT Press, 1969.

Battock, Gregory, ed. *New Ideas in Art Education.* New York: E. P. Dutton, 1973.

De Francesco, Italo L. *Art Education: Its Means and Ends.* New York: Harper, 1958.

Landis, Mildred. *Meaningful Art Education.* Peoria, Ill.: C. A. Bennett Co., 1951.

Lowenfeld, Viktor. *Creative and Mental Growth.* New York: Macmillan Co., 1970.

————. *The Lowenfeld Lectures: Viktor Lowenfeld on Art Education and Therapy.* University Park: Pennsylvania State University, 1982.

Madeja, Stanley S. et al. *The Artist in the School.* St. Louis: Cemvel, 1970.

McFee, June King. *Preparation for Art.* 2d ed. Belmont, Calif.: Wadsworth Publishing Co., 1970.

Pappas, George. *Concepts in Art and Education.* New York: Macmillan Co., 1970.

Rousseau, Jean-Jacques. *Emile.* London: J. M. Dent and Sons, 1911.

Sparks, Roy. *Teaching Art Basics.* New York: Watson-Guptill Publications, 1973.

Wickiser, Ralph L. *An Introduction to Art Education.* New York: World Book Co., 1957.

Ziegfield, Edwin, ed. *Education and Art: A Symposium.* Paris: UNESCO, 1953.

# 3  The Arts-Crafts Teacher

It has been said that education is the enculturation of each rising generation. It is a deliberate attempt on the part of the older members of a cultural unit (family, tribe, state, country) to instill into their children a sense of their cultural heritage and the traditions of the society in which they live; to furnish them with contacts to the persons, things, and events in their environment that will provide the experiences necessary to cope adequately and enable them to become productive members of that society. In an ideal system, each child is carefully and sequentially introduced to a wide body of knowledge in many fields. It is well known among educators that there is an ideal time in a child's development to introduce each new skill or segment of knowledge—reading, writing, history, language, driving, and so on. If the knowledge is introduced either before or after the child is ready, it will not be as easily absorbed as it could have been at the ideal time.

Most educational systems are organized into grades or classes in which groups of children of similar age and development are fed large doses of knowledge. I have no quarrel with fact feeding. Indeed, it is essential that students be introduced to important dates and events in history, rules of grammar, scientific data, mathematical skills, great philosophical ideas, religious history, language and literature, the visual and performing arts, and all else that goes into the training of a well-educated individual. But group fact feeding is only a part of the equation. Equally important, and perhaps even more so, is recognizing that each student is a unique individual whose creative potential must be developed to its fullest extent. Therefore, all children should have available to them the sort of individual training that will open their eyes to the world around them, point them in the direction of unlimited horizons toward which their minds can venture, make them aware of the creative power within themselves and show them how to use it, instill in them the desire to learn and search out facts for themselves, and, above all, give them an awareness of their own uniqueness and personal worth. The problem, then, becomes how best to accomplish the imparting of necessary knowledge and skills while maintaining the individuality of each student as much as possible.

## Qualifications of the Arts-Crafts Teacher

Accomplishment of the tremendous task of teaching requires large numbers of dedicated teachers who are highly trained in one or more disciplines, who are widely read in many, who are enthusiastic about the development of young minds, who are familiar with the psychology and behavior of students of all ages, who have observed and worked with children in many situations, who recognize that each child is a unique individual, and who will continue to broaden their own minds with in-service training and study throughout their careers.

Besides these basic qualifications necessary to all teachers, the arts-crafts teacher should, of course, have a thorough background in all facets of art—in its history, in contemporary developments and changes in the nature of art, in the principles of design and aesthetics, as well as in studio practice. Technical procedures for working in a variety of media both traditional and new should be understood, and the teacher should be, in his or her own right, an actively producing worker in one or more of these media. The teacher should be able to think creatively, as well as recognize and foster the creative potential of students, which will necessitate a clear understanding of the creative process (see chapter 4). Of major importance is the ability to approach all art with an open mind and to impress students with the necessity of evaluating art without prejudice before making up their minds as to its merit.

These qualifications, together with a sincere dedication to the study of art as a vital part of the total education of all children, will enable the art teacher to fulfill the role of introducing students to a diversity of art experiences. These experiences in art will aid students in developing their creative potential and in applying this potential, not only to the exploration of art forms but to the enhancement of all facets of their daily lives as well.

Art teachers who have concentrated their interest in the area of the crafts will probably have worked with their hands since childhood. They will have learned to use tools to cut, pound, saw, scrape, and gouge. They will have built things, taken things apart to see how they work, explored and manipulated all manner of materials. This interest in creating and exploring with the hands will have followed them through adolescence and into adulthood. Training in the arts will have enabled them to apply more sophisticated techniques to their interests; they will have developed a feeling for good design and formulated high standards of craftsmanship. Each teacher will bring his or her total knowledge to bear in inspiring students to make the most meaningful expression of which they are capable.

The crafts teacher will have had extensive training in one or more crafts and may have become a master potter, weaver, jeweler, or enamelist, as well as possess a working knowledge of a number of other crafts. The teacher will keep abreast of new methods and materials and incorporate these into the teaching program as needed. Membership in regional or national crafts organizations and participation in workshops, seminars, and craft shows will provide contact with craftspeople throughout the country who are a dynamic part of the contemporary crafts revival. "But all this will be largely worthless if it does not culminate in the personal discovery of art as giving form to the random, unorganized, sometime chaotic experience in the student's own life. For it is the function of art to make life bearable by giving form to the overwhelming chaos of experience, and to preserve and convey to others the delights of moments of illumination."[1]

## Teaching Art: Goals and Tasks of the Arts-Crafts Teacher

In the beginning of this chapter, some goals of education were outlined. Within the framework of these goals, the teacher of arts and crafts is faced with several specific tasks. Teacher must make students aware of their environment and attempt to evoke from them an aesthetic response to their surroundings. Students must be motivated with the desire to make a visual expression of their responses; they must be introduced to a variety of tools, materials, and techniques necessary to translate their thoughts into visual form; they must be trained in the principles of good design; and finally they must be convinced of the worth of their efforts and contributions to the total body of artistic expression by learning what others have done in the span of recorded art history.

### Environmental Awareness

We are all very much creatures of our environments and from the time children are first able to look around them, distinguish objects, see light and color, and hear sounds, they are acted upon by the environment. Contemporary research in how the child is influenced would seem to indicate that there can even be strong prenatal effects, depending on the mother's diet, activities, interests, and emotional attitudes. Being naturally inquisitive, young children reach out to touch and grasp, to see, to hear, and to react to what is present in their world. At first, the reaction is purely physical, but soon rapidly developing intellect and emotions begin to function, and thoughts and feelings begin to guide the physical reaction. As soon as children are able to handle a marking implement, they will begin to scribble visual interpretations of familiar objects and persons on whatever surface happens to be available. The environmental influences and experiences to which children are subjected form the basis of their knowledge of life at any given developmental stage. Response to these influences will determine the form of visual symbols children will make to express feelings about the environment. The problem for the teacher is to direct students through the "scribble" stage toward sharper, more meaningful experiences, toward increased perceptual awareness by opening their eyes to what is around them and motivating them to respond aesthetically to the myriad of commonplace sights in their daily existence. Unfortunately, the complexity and abundance of what we see every day tends to dull our sensitivity. For example, we see hundreds of trees but seldom stop to examine them for differences in their growth configuration, textural variations of their bark, size and shape of their leaves—in short the type of observation that makes the difference between *merely looking at* an object and *really seeing it*. By pointing out and discussing the many nuances of environmental influences, the teacher can greatly enrich each child's perceptual awareness of life.

## Aesthetic Response

Increased sensitivity to and sharper observation of the environment will usually motivate children to respond more deeply to their world. The very complexity and variety of daily experiences, however, can lead to trite, ordinary responses if some attempt is not made to direct the student's attention toward a more discriminating approach—toward seeing the unusual and beautiful in the commonplace, toward a response that goes beyond mere notation and cataloging, toward a sense of what is valuable and meaningful. Naturally, the older, more mature child will be capable of developing deeper aesthetic responses, but research has shown that

preschool children can be taught to understand the aesthetic nature of their environment. Young children can go beyond the earliest stages of simply recognizing and naming an object to an awareness of some characteristics of that object, how the various elements that constitute its makeup work together to give it more value, beauty, and worth than some similar object. Through the guidance of teachers, who themselves are sensitively attuned to the aesthetic nature of our environment, students at each level of development can be made more aware of the aesthetic dimension of experience.

## Expressional Motivation

The student may carefully observe a certain object and respond to it by becoming interested enough to want to say something about it, yet come to the classroom and not be able to make the desired expression because motivation is lacking. At this point, the teacher must act as the catalyst between observation and expression by providing the motivational spark that will aid the student in translating a response into visual form. Once the student's concept has been formed, it is the teacher's responsibility to provide stimulation so the idea is activated and executed. The amount and means of motivation necessary to accomplish this will vary with each individual. Some children are "self-activators" while others need a great deal of stimulation.

The teacher may stimulate motivation in many ways: verbal discussions, audiovisual aids, field trips, classroom models (plants, animals, rocks, for example), demonstrations, guest lecturers, special exhibits, reading assignments—all these and many other approaches are possibilities. Regardless of the means chosen, the teacher should try to make the stimulative experience as vivid as possible, yet not provide so much material at one time that the student is overwhelmed. By constant and careful appraisal, the sensitive teacher soon learns just how much initial activation each child needs. By regular evaluation of the child's progress, the teacher can determine when booster doses are necessary to bolster lagging interests, when additional technical information is necessary, and when to make suggestions for carrying the work to a successful conclusion. The teacher must be especially careful at this point, however, to allow students the freedom to "make their own mistakes" and to present a final statement that reflects a student's feelings, not those of the instructor.

## Tools, Materials, and Techniques

In order to translate ideas into visual form, the student will choose a medium, select the necessary tools and materials for working in that medium, and in most cases, follow a more or less standard method of procedure. The teacher must introduce these technical aspects to students according to their developmental level, ranging from simple crayons, tempera, and modeling clay of the elementary grades to such highly sophisticated media as welded sculpture and lithography in senior high school or college. The teacher should, of course, be thoroughly familiar with the media and techniques being used, demonstrate each step if possible, and perhaps have on hand examples or slides of completed work executed by professionals or, better still, by other students. With older students, a printed handout sheet listing tools, materials, and procedure is helpful, though these should not be so detailed that the student is left no room for experimentation. Students should be allowed sufficient time to become familiar with the intricacies of each new medium, to manipulate, to make several starts, to waste a certain amount of materials. Until students gain facility in handling a new medium, they will be very much concerned with technical considerations and cannot be expected to devote full attention to creating a meaningful form. For suggestions in teaching individual crafts, refer to chapter 6 and procedural instructions in part 2.

## Good Design

Along with training in the use of materials and the handling of procedures, students must also be given information about the principles of good design and composition. In many ways, this can become the most difficult task of all, not only because of the rules involved but also because a feeling for good design goes far beyond a mere learning of rules. It must include the development of sensitivity to such subtle and almost unexplainable considerations as beauty and good taste, as well as an instinct for how a design principle may be intelligently altered or broken to result in a more original and creative statement.

Because chapter 5 is devoted to design principles, little more need be said here, except to remind the teacher that the developmental level of the student must always be considered, and care taken that the concept being introduced is not too complicated or technical for the student to absorb. Fortunately, students at all levels can understand something about design. With careful planning on the teacher's part, they should experience little difficulty.

## Art History

No matter how skilled the student becomes in translating concepts into visual expressions, the result will have little meaning unless he or she relates it to the creative expressions of other artists. The importance of art and its relation to the history of humankind is discussed in chapter 2. Because the history of art is in effect a history of human response to the environment dating from prehistoric times, students must understand that their own efforts at making visual expression of responses to the environment thus become a part of art history, even though a particular contribution may never be recorded and handed down to subsequent generations.

Therefore, the study of art history must become a living, exciting thing for each student through discussions, films, slides, readings, and visits to museums. Naturally, the extent and depth of what is presented must depend on the readiness of the students to absorb the material and relate it to their own work. Art history survey courses as well as "art appreciation" courses taught in many colleges are open to serious criticism, and all too often consist of dull lecture/slide presentations, with endless numbers of slides shown in a darkened room in which the student is expected to stay alert and awake and to remember each work, each artist, dates, and other miscellaneous facts. Some specific criticisms about most art survey courses are:

- Attempt to cover too much material in too little time (no art history survey should be attempted in less than four semesters)
- Cover only western European art, with little or no mention of such topics as Oriental, Islamic, African, eastern European art, or art of the Americas
- Fail to integrate art with economic, social, political, military, and other historic events
- Put too much emphasis on works, names of artists, dates, and other factual material, rather than the concepts and ideas that have led to the production of great works and the development of various styles and movements
- Are so involved with fact feeding so much so that students are given little or no time to think about art, to understand art, and to form opinions as to the validity of art study in their own education
- Spend so much time on the study of ancient art that there is often little time left to cover modern and contemporary art

It would appear that art educators need to be aware of these problems and attempt to restructure their art survey courses to better meet the needs of arts and crafts students.

Because crafts in most art history and appreciation courses are usually neglected or at best relegated to a minor position, the teacher of crafts must place particular emphasis on the handicrafts of various eras and cultures. A collection of slides showing crafts ranging from the votive figures of prehistoric times to the works of contemporary professionals is an invaluable teaching aid. These should be supplemented by slides showing selected examples of student work. At every stage, the history of crafts should be related to the history of other art forms, such as drawing, painting, and sculpture. In part 2 of this work, each craft presented is introduced with a brief historical summary.

*Developmental Levels*
I have repeatedly emphasized the importance of taking into account the developmental level and individuality of each student when making lesson plans. Growth and development rates vary greatly among children. At each educational level, the teacher will find significant differences in the ability of students to absorb a given concept. Because the making of visual expressions involves a much greater personal involvement and response from the student than, say, the learning of historic facts and dates, the teaching of arts and crafts must be, of necessity, done on an almost individual basis. For this reason, so-called lesson plans must be particularly flexible in the arts.

A tremendous amount of research and study has been devoted to the subject of developmental levels, with a number of studies aimed at determining what art activities and expressions children are capable of at any given age and educational level. It is beyond the scope of this work to go into a detailed analysis of these levels. For further information on activities best done at a given age, refer to the writings of Howard Conant,[2] Kenneth Lansing,[3] Frank Wachowiak,[4] Manuel Barkan,[5] and Charles Gaitskell.[6]

In formulating a course of art study for any age level, the teacher must keep in mind five considerations:

1  The visual expression of any student will depend upon an accumulated knowledge of life—observations and experiences and responses to these—and will be a highly individual thing.

2  Students at any age level will vary in ability to create.

3  An individual trying a new medium or technique will go through a stage of manipulation at any level. This is true, whether we are talking about a preschool child or a mature professional artist.

4  Although general guidelines for any level of development may be laid down, any such scheme must be highly flexible to allow for individual differences and overlapping ability levels.

5  Considerable leeway must be given for experimentation, and students must be encouraged to make responses that are not necessarily similar to the responses of their peers.

Conant puts it very well when he says, "We should not attempt to classify, but rather encourage maximum individual growth through art, by consistent and progressive emphasis on creativity and the deepening of aesthetic sensitivity in every year of a person's education and adult life."

**Standards of Achievement for the Crafts Student**
What to expect from one's students in the way of artistic achievement is always a problem for the teacher. Results will depend, in addition to those factors already mentioned, on motivation, cultural backgrounds, ability of the teacher to instruct and inspire, available facilities, and available time. It is assumed that the teacher will have formulated a set of objectives for the educational level of the class being taught.

The major problem, then, becomes one of setting standards for the accomplishment of these objectives. Standards should not be so low that students can get by with mediocre effort, nor should they be so high that students will be discouraged from trying because they know in advance that the result will not measure up to the teacher's expectations. Mediocrity is, unfortunately, all too often the standard for much student work; however, students should be encouraged to put forth the very best effort of which they are capable, and their work should be evaluated accordingly.

In any group of students, the majority will probably produce work fairly comparable in quality. Remember that most groups will also include a few who are slower to learn than others, as well as some who are exceptionally bright, so standards for these students must be adjusted somewhat.

## Evaluation and Grading of Crafts Projects

When faced with evaluating student achievement, the mathematics or history teacher has a comparatively easy time. Either the student can or cannot work an equation; the student has or has not learned the date and results of an important battle. The art teacher, however, has no exact system of measurement on which to rely. How, for instance, does one assign a number or letter grade to aesthetic response or creativity; or what is the "right" way to draw a tree? The assignment of grades immediately sets up an atmosphere of competiton with other students. Because art is such an individual endeavor, there can be little or no relativity or basis of comparison among students in a given group.

Unfortunately, though, our educational system is such that some sort of evaluation must be made and grades reported in order to inform students and their parents of the student's progress. Most contemporary art educators agree that if grades in art classes must be assigned, they should be given on the basis of evaluation of the art work of each student, on the creative and aesthetic progress that the student has made, on the knowledge that he or she has gained, on the student's attitude toward what is being done, and on his or her technical facility in handling tools and materials.

The teacher should encourage each student to set standards of self-evaluation, to look critically at everything produced, to retain that which is good, and to modify or discard that which does not measure up. To see a student take the hammer to a poorly crafted pot, to unravel an unsatisfactory section of weaving, or to tear up an inept drawing is a healthy sign, for it means that discrimination in assessing one's own work is being developed. The "I made it, therefore I must keep it" theory should be discouraged at all costs. The teacher should, of course, help the student to formulate realistic objectives and standards of evaluation through patient, constructive criticism and encourage the student to seek ways for self-improvement.

Because some sort of grading system must be resorted to consider the evaluation sheet in Table 3.1, which takes into account individual achievement and results in a grade that can be shown on the student's record. The scheme is based on a system in which six characteristics are rated from 0 to 5 and the resulting point total translated into a letter grade.

## ART PROJECT EVALUATION SHEET (Table 3.1)

| Student's Name Student | John | Project Panel | | Stained Glass | | |
|---|---|---|---|---|---|---|
| | **0** | **1** | **2** | **3** | **4** | **5** |
| **A. Concept** | | | | X | | |
| **B. Execution** | | | X | | | |
| **C. Creativity** | | | X | | | |
| **D. Craftsmanship** | | | | X | | |
| **E. Design Elements** | | | X | | | |
| **F. Intangible Quality** | | | X | | | |

**Total points for project** 14    **Letter grade for project** C−

**Instructor's comment:**

A good initial concept has been carried out with less than average imagination. An abstract approach would have been more creative. Craftsmanship is acceptable but soldered joints are poorly done. Color choice is fairly good, but individual motifs are a bit large for the size of the piece and placement of the elements suggests color relationships have not been well planned.

**Explanation of grading system:**

Projects are evaluated for six characteristics, as indicated by A–F above. Each characteristic is rated from 0 to 5 as follows:

$0$ = No merit
$1$ = Poor
$2$ = Fair
$3$ = Average
$4$ = Good to excellent
$5$ = Outstanding

*Note:* 30 points would be the highest total by this system and equivalent to a grade of A.

---

Qualities rated on the evaluation sheet are:

A  Concept: What is the theme or original plan for the work? What is the student trying to depict or say about the chosen theme? How has the subject matter been seen and how has it been presented?

B  Execution: How well is the concept carried out? Has the student said what was intended? Has the student make a trite expression or a mature, well-thought out approach?

C  Creativity: How original has the student been? Is the approach obvious or ordinary, or is it fresh and novel?

D Craftsmanship: How well has the student understood and used materials and tools? Have technicalities of the procedure been mastered? Is the resulting work well constructed?

E Design elements: Have the elements of art and principles of composition been well used? Has integrity to materials been maintained? Is the piece well unified? Does it have sufficient variety to maintain interest?

F Intangible quality: This is a rather nebulous characteristic made up of such abstracts as aesthetic appeal, good taste, beauty, and so forth and is based primarily on how the completed piece comes across to the evaluator.

Point ratings are assigned to each characteristic as follows:

- 0 indicates no merit at all
- 1 indicates very poor effort, highly unsatisfactory
- 2 indicates moderate effort, much room for improvement
- 3 indicates generally average achievement, still considerable room for improvement
- 4 indicates good to excellent achievement, mostly satisfactory
- 5 indicates outstanding achievement, little if any improvement possible

I use this evaluation sheet in my classes and give it to students with point values, letter grade, and instructor's criticisms and suggestions. Total point values are translated to letter grades on the following basis:

- A      30 points
- A−     27–29 points
- B+     24–26 points
- B      21–23 points
- B−     18–20 points
- C      15–17 points
- C−     12–14 points
- D       9–11 points
- D−      7–8 points
- F      Below 7 points

Anything below a score of 15 is indicative of mediocre achievement.

When evaluating student work, the teacher must be careful to preserve the dignity and self-esteem of the student. It is not enough to say that a work is not good; the student must be given valid reasons why the work is or is not good and be encouraged to improve knowledge and technical skill. Under no circumstances should the teacher ever compare the work of one student with that of another. Whenever possible the critique should be made privately in a personal conference. Criticism tempered with encouragement and suggestions for improvement makes for a good evaluation.

*Notes*

1 Seonaid Mairi Robertson, *Craft and Contemporary Culture* (London: George G. Harrap and Co., 1961), 101.
2 Howard Conant and Arne Randall, *Art in Education* (Peoria, Ill.: Charles A. Bennett, 1963).
3 Kenneth M. Lansing, *Art, Artists and Art Education* (New York: McGraw-Hill Book Co., 1970).
4 Frank Wachowiak and Theodore Ramsay, *Emphasis: Art* (Scranton, Pa.: International Textbook Co., 1965).
5 Manuel Barkan, *Through Art to Creativity* (Boston: Allyn and Bacon, 1960).
6 Charles D. Gaitskell and Al Hurwitz, *Children and Their Art,* 2d ed. (New York: Harcourt, Brace and World, 1970).

*Suggested Readings*
Barkan, Manuel. *A Foundation for Art Education.* New York: Ronald Press, 1955.
Bassett, Richard. *The Open Eye in Learning.* Cambridge, Mass.: MIT Press, 1969.
Conant, Howard. *Art Education.* Washington, D.C.: Washington Center for Applied Research in Education, 1964.
Conrad, George. *The Process of Art Education in the Elementary School.* Englewood Cliffs, N.J.: Prentice-Hall, 1964.
Gaitskell, Charles D., and Margaret R. Gaitskell. *Art Education during Adolescence.* New York: Harcourt, Brace, 1964.
Greenberg, Pearl. *Art and Ideas for Young People.* New York: Van Nostrant, Reinhold, 1970.

Herberholz, Donald W., and Kay Alexander. *Developing Artistic and Perceptual Awareness*. 5th ed. Dubuque, Iowa: Wm. C. Brown Co., 1985.

Hubbard, Guy. *Art in the High School*. Belmont, Calif.: Wadsworth Publishing Co., 1967.

Jacobus, Lee A. *Aesthetics and the Arts*. New York: McGraw-Hill Book Co., 1969.

Knudsen, Estelle H. *Children's Art Education*. Peoria, Ill.: Knudsen and Christenson, 1957.

Langer, Susanne K. *Problems of Art*. New York: Charles Scribner's Sons, 1957.

Silberstein-Storfer, Muriel. *Doing Art Together*. New York: Simon and Schuster, 1982.

Wachowiak, Frank. *Art in Depth*. Scranton, Pa.: International Textbook Co., 1970.

Weitz, Morris. *Problems in Aesthetics*. New York: Macmillan Co., 1959.

# 4 Crafts and Creativity

**An Overview of Research in Creativity**

Ever since Lewis M. Terman carried out his classic studies on giftedness in children in 1925, there has been increasing interest among educators in the special problems encountered in the training of children who are considered "gifted."[1] Terman's original study was based on the results of group or individual intelligence tests given to one thousand children in California schools. The resulting I.Q. scores were evaluated and selected children in the top 3 percent were labeled as gifted. During the next thirty years or so, many other investigators worked within these same guidelines verifying and adding to Terman's original data, invariably using the I.Q. score as the primary basis of measurement. In most of these studies, the word *gifted* was applied and the term came to be almost synonymous with high I.Q.

This approach has two major limitations. First, because the typical I.Q. test primarily measures the ability of the subject to remember and reproduce previously learned information and to think convergently, it cannot take into account the subject's ability to think divergently, a trait that is so necessary to creative performance. The convergent thinker, in attempting to solve a particular problem, will consider all available information (known facts, previous experiences) and direct these along converging paths to come up with one "best" or "correct" solution to the problem. The divergent thinker, on the other hand, will direct similar information, facts, and experiences along many diverging paths, often arriving at several solutions to the same problem. In other words, the convergent problem solver thinks in one direction while the divergent problem solver thinks in many directions.

The second limitation is that the I.Q. score does not take into account the wide variance often noted between high I.Q. and creative ability. Later investigators have found that creative ability depends on a wide range of traits, and indeed, may have little relation to I.Q. scores, which would seem to indicate that the broader term *creative* might be preferred to the word *gifted*.

It has long been a recognized fact among researchers that all children possess the spark of creativity to some extent, but the spark is rarely cultivated, quite often stifled, and seldom developed to anywhere near its full potential. As our society becomes directed more and more toward mechanized and high-tech specialization with emphasis on quantity of production, humans become more and more robotlike, directing their efforts toward mass production of consumer goods. Thus, creative individuals who might contribute their divergency toward quality production become lost in the crowd, and their creative potential is never realized. At the same time, if this twentieth century Space Age is going to truly "take us to the stars," it is essential that creativity be recognized as one of our most valuable human assets. Development of creative potential must receive top priority from government, industry, and the educational system to ensure that each individual will have the opportunity to develop and contribute creative potential to the fullest extent.

A major problem for educators, then, is how best to nurture the creative spark: what approach, course of study, classroom climate, and teaching procedures will provide the optimum atmosphere for creativity? How can our schools encourage and develop in students at all levels, the open minds, the free imaginations, and the willingness to accept the challenge of finding fresh and unordinary solutions to new and existing problems? Before attempting to answer these questions, let us explore some theoretical aspects of creativity itself.

Among the ancients, it was common practice to ascribe divine origin, inspiration, or direction to the act of creativity. The creative person does draw from within the flash of insight that leads to a new concept and the air of mystery that surrounds this unique power of humans. It is not surprising, therefore, to find that most investigation concerning the nature of creativity has been carried out since 1950, when J. P. Guilford called attention to the need for such research in an address to the American Psychological Association.[2] He made three points that were to become the basis for most investigations in creativity from that time to the present:

1 High intelligence (I.Q.) is an inadequate explanation and largely responsible for lack of progress in the understanding of creative people.

2 Creativity represents patterns of primary abilities and also depends on other traits including interests, attitudes, and temperament.

3 Testing and research indicate the existence of certain factors influencing creativity, such as sensitivity to problems, ideational fluency, ideational novelty, flexibility of thinking, and abilities to synthesize, analyze, evaluate, and reorganize.

In an address to educators of Sacramento County, California, in 1959, Dr. Guilford extended and reinforced his 1950 predictions, reiterating the need for continued investigation in the nature of creativity, especially to determine what unique abilities exist in the area of creativity and what kinds of abilities these are.[3] He stated that educators can help prepare students to perform creatively by encouraging them to think divergently. He said that the intellectual atmosphere of our schools is such that "brawn is preferred over brain, there is a general drive toward mediocrity and teachers do not prefer the more creative students."

Following Dr. Guilford's lead there has been widespread interest among educators and psychologists in the investigation of creativity. An article prepared by Getzels and Madaus for the fourth edition of the *Encyclopedia of Educational Research* published in 1969 gives a general overview of creativity as a problem in education, with a survey of major work done through mid-1968.[4] It contains notes pertaining to definitions and major theories, and relates creativity to personality traits, intelligence, and school performance taken from the work of such researchers as Guilford, Torrance, Yamamoto, Getzels, Maslow, and others. For reference to more recent work and that being presently done, consult current issues of *Psychological Abstracts*.[5] It is encouraging to see more and more research being carried out on the subject of creativity with investigators attempting to answer such questions as: What is the nature of creativity? How can creativity be nurtured at all levels in the educational process? What is creative teaching and how can it best be carried out in the classroom? Is creativity something that can be taught? Can creativity be detected by tests and if so, what kinds of tests? Other recent investigations have been concerned with such topics as relationship of creative ability to brain hemispheres, extrasensory perception and creativity, women and creativity, creativity and dreams, and how the imagination works.

Of timely interest in our computer-oriented society are certain investigations aimed at exploring what effect computers might have in enhancing or limiting creativity, in what ways computers might be useful to artists as design tools, the need for computer literacy among art students, how computers might be used in making aesthetic decisions, computer graphics as a new subject for the art student, and how computers might be used creatively in teaching art. It is beyond the scope of this work to address such provocative and exciting questions in depth. The student can seek more information in the list of suggested readings at the end of this chapter.

**Characterizing Creativity and the Creative Individual**
There have been many attempts to define creativity. In the *Symposia,* Plato says the true artists are those who "bring into birth some new reality."[6] In our own time, Rollo May says, "Creativity is the encounter of the intensely conscious human with his world,"[7] while Carl Rogers defines creativity as "the emergence in action of a novel relational product, growing out of the uniqueness of the individual."[8] Whatever definition we accept, it seems clear that creativity is the ability to arrive at a novel, useful solution to a problem or need through subjective, inspired, divergent thinking; the solution may be in the form of an actual product or an original thought.

In attempting to characterize the creative individual, most investigators agree there is little or no correlation between intelligence (I.Q.) and creative ability. Erich Fromm says that the creative individual "has the willingness to be born every day": He sets forth four conditions for creativity: (1) the capacity to be puzzled, (2) the ability to concentrate, (3) the ability to feel a sense of self, and (4) the ability to accept conflict and tension resulting from polarity.[9] Guilford emphasized the importance of divergent thinking, characterized by four major attributes.

1  Flexibility of thinking: The ability to attempt new ways to reach a goal, to restate and redefine old methods and adapt them in a number of different ways.
2  Fluency of thinking: The ability to come up with a number of new ideas concerning the problem at hand in a relatively short time.
3  Originality of thinking: The ability to suggest new, novel, and unstereotyped ideas.
4  Elaboration: The ability to present ideas developed to a high degree of complexity.

The existence of these attributes has been tested and verified by a number of different investigators. In 1970 Dellas and Gaier reported their agreement with Guilford and further proposed that the creative individual shows a preference for the complex, the rich, the dynamic, and the asymmetric.[10] They also indicate the presence of "perceptual openness" in the creative individual—an awareness of and receptiveness to the outer world and inner self. Adjectives used by other investigators to describe the creative person are discerning, uninhibited, curious, open-minded, receptive, and industrious.

Creativity should not be confused with talent. Talent is an inherent potentiality within each of us, a given ability; for example, the ability to make music, bake a cake, draw, perform well in athletics. Talents are there whether we choose to use them or not. Creativity, on the other hand, can exist only as the act, the doing, the manifestation of a given talent. As Rollo May puts it, "Great talent plus great encounter equals great creativity."

The idea that only a chosen few can be creative is unacceptable. Each individual has a certain potential for creativity. Given the necessary stimuli and proper atmosphere, this potential can be enhanced to the extent one is willing to respond to the stimuli. Dr. E. Paul Torrance, chairman of the department of educational psychology at the University of Georgia, reports on an interesting survey he and his wife, J. Pansy Torrance, associate director of Georgia Studies of Creative Behavior, carried out summarizing the success of various methods used in attempting to teach children to think creatively. Dr. Torrance says: "It does seem possible to teach creative thinking. The most successful approaches seem to be those that involve both cognitive and emotional functioning, provide adequate structure and motivation and give opportunities for involvement practice and interaction with teachers and other students." Dr. Torrance warns however that "no teaching and no disciplined approach to creative problem solving will guarantee creativity. They only increase the probability that creativity will occur."[11] Also, creativity is not to be considered only in the context of artistic production. Although it is true that the visible products of creativity are often most evident in this realm, creativity can be exercised in all phases of life: by the scientist in the laboratory, the teacher in the classroom, the student in writing a term paper, or the homemaker in preparing a meal.

**Stages in the Creative Process**

Although there is some evidence that creative solutions to problems sometimes occur full blown in an "inspired moment," it is far more likely that creative action occurs over a period of time and in certain recognizable and verifiable stages. This creativity phase that occurs over a period of time has been investigated by a number of researchers and the stages identified by various names. Generally researchers agree that the stages are four in number:

1  Preparation: The creative individual becomes sensitive to a problem, perhaps a need for some change in an existing product or process or for some entirely new creation. Using acquired or inherent skills (talent, if you will) and knowledge gained from past experience or education, the problem is defined and several possible solutions mulled. If one of these seems particularly suitable, the individual may select it at this point and consider the problem solved. If none of the projected solutions seem right, the individual may decide to think about it for a while, even turning to unrelated problems or details.

2  Incubation: There is little or no conscious effort to actively solve the problem during this period. The subconscious mind is allowed to digest and have full play with the problem.

3  Illumination: After some time, a flash of insight will occur and the conscious mind will realize that here is the solution that may be "just right." This is the stage which some investigators term "AHA!"

4  Verification: The projected solution is applied to the problem and tested in all its aspects with minor revisions made as necessary to bring the solution to perfection.

**Testing for Creativity**

Investigations in the field of creativity include much work aimed at the development of tests suited to the measurement of creative abilities. See various issues of *The Mental Measurement Yearbook* for descriptions of such tests.[12] Other tests designed by various investigators concerning the aspects of creativity (creative attitudes, perception, potential, and so on) are listed in the publication *Tests in Print,* issued periodically by the University of Nebraska Press.[13]

One investigator who has been concerned with this phase of creativity is Dr. Torrance, formerly at the University of Minnesota, where he and his associates developed the Minnesota Tests of Creative Thinking.

These tests, designed to measure the factors of fluency, flexibility, originality, and elaboration, have been revised and renamed the Torrance Tests of Creative Thinking.[14] The tests consist of a series of verbal and figurative tasks, requiring thought processes analogous to those involved in recognized creative activities. The verbal test requires the tester to respond to questions about pictures, to suggest how an object might be improved, and to imagine outcomes of an improbable situation. The figurative tests require completion of open drawings, construction of new pictures, and elaboration of common shapes.

Such tests are most useful in helping educators assess creative potential in students of all age groups, but remember that creativity is an extremely complex attribute and may depend on a number of other factors that might not be picked up by a given test. Therefore, care must be exercised in the interpretation of results, which should be done only by evaluators who are trained to make such interpretations.

**Creativity and Crafts**

Because all art activity is, of necessity, creative activity, the importance of nurturing the creative spark in art and craft students at every level of development cannot be overemphasized. The extent to which the student is able to bring creative abilities to bear on the conception and execution of work in any medium will determine the aesthetic and practical value of the finished work. Therefore, the problem for the teacher becomes one of motivating students to *want* to use their creative abilities, supplying the necessary tools and materials and enough technical information about their use to enable students to handle them with some skill, then allowing them time and freedom to carry out their own ideas and make mistakes, until the students reach a point at which they need additional advice concerning design principles, aesthetic considerations, or perhaps more advanced technical information.

Thus, the teacher has to find a balance between giving instruction that is so completely defined and specific as to leave the student little room for creative expression, or adopt the laissez-faire approach—"Here are the tools and materials, create something!"—without supplying students with sufficient motivation or foundation on which to base their work.

A certain amount of group instruction can be given, but because levels of creative ability are different for each student, instruction soon becomes a very personal, individual exchange between student and teacher. The teacher must become acquainted with each student's potential for creative expression and adapt the amount of instruction and encouragement to the individual need of each person in the classroom. In this way, each student, whatever the level of ability, will be given the climate in which individual creativity can develop to the fullest possible extent.

**Current Trends in Creativity Research**

The value and scope of the contribution any individual makes to society depends largely on how well creative abilities have been developed and utilized. In our present educational system, the creative capacity that exists to some extent in all childen is all too often thwarted or stifled in the early grades. Subsequently the individual goes through life never realizing even a small part of his or her creative potential. Perhaps the greatest need in education today is the training of school personnel to understand the nature of the creative process, to appreciate its value, and to foster the creative development of their students by encouraging them to think divergently as well as convergently. This could be aided, possibly, by special courses in creative thinking, which need to be developed and included in school and college curricula. Early recognition of high creative potential could be facilitated by the use of special tests for creativity that should be given routinely in the schools. In this way, through the efforts of creativity-minded educators, the vast untapped creative potential of students at all levels could be recognized, developed, and utilized for the advancement and betterment of society.

*Notes*

1 Lewis M. Terman, et al, "Mental and Physical Traits of a Thousand Gifted Children," in *Genetic Studies of Genius,* vol. 1 (Stanford, Calif.: Stanford University Press, 1925).

2 J. P. Guilford, "Creativity," *American Psychologist* 5 (1950) 444–54. Address of Guilford, president of the American Psychological Association, given to Pennsylvania State College, 5 September 1950.

3 J. P. Guilford, "Creativity: Its Measurement and Development," in James Dyal, ed., *Readings in Psychology: Understanding Human Behavior* (New York: McGraw-Hill Book Co., 1967), 275–85. Adapted from an address presented to educators of Sacramento County, California, 20 January 1959.

4 J. Getzels and G. Madaus, "Creativity," in *Encyclopedia of Educational Research,* 4th ed. (New York: Macmillan Co., 1969).

5 *Psychological Abstracts* are published monthly by the American Psychological Association, Lancaster, Pennsylvania, and Washington, D.C., Harold P. Van Cott, executive editor.

6 Plato, *Symposia,* trans. Suzy Groden and ed. John A. Brentlinger (Amherst: University of Massachusetts Press, 1970).

7 Rollo May, "The Nature of Creativity," in *Creativity and Its Cultivation,* ed. Harold Anderson (New York: Harper, 1959), 55–58.

8 Carl R. Rogers, "Toward a Theory of Creativity," in *Creativity and Its Cultivation,* ed. Harold Anderson (New York: Harper, 1959), 69–82.

9 Erich Fromm, "The Creative Attitude," in *Creativity and Its Cultivation,* ed. Harold Anderson (New York: Harper, 1959), 44–54.

10 Marie Dellas and E. L. Gaier, "Identification of Creativity: The Individual," *Psychological Bulletin* 73, no. 1 (1970) 55–73.

11 E. Paul Torrance and J. Pansy Torrance, *Is Creativity Teachable?* (Bloomington, Ind.: Phi Delta Kappa Educational Foundation, 1973).

12 O. D. Buros, ed., *The Mental Measurement Yearbook,* 8th ed. (Highland Park, N.J.: Gryphon Press, 1978). All editions should be searched for specific tests. The Torrance test appeared first in the seventh edition published in 1971.

13 James V. Mitchell, Jr., ed. *Tests in Print,* vol. 3 (Lincoln: University of Nebraska Press, 1983).

14 E. Paul Torrance, *The Torrance Tests of Creative Thinking* (Lexington, Mass.: Personnel Press, 1966).

*Suggested Readings*

Beechhold, Henry F. *The Creative Classroom.* New York: Charles Scribner's Sons, 1971.

Brown, Devin. *Creative Programming for Young Minds.* Charleston, Ill.: Creative Programming, 1981.

Callahan, Carolyn M. *Developing Creativity in the Gifted and Talented.* Reston, Va.: Council for Exceptional Children, 1978.

Casey, Edward S. *Imagination: A Phenomenological Study.* Bloomington: Indiana University Press, 1976.

D'Amico, Victor. *Creative Teaching in Art.* Scranton, Pa.: International Textbook Co., 1955.

Dutton, Denis, and Michael Krauoz, eds. *The Concept of Creativity in Science and Art*. The Hague, Boston and London: Martinus Nijhoff, Publishers, 1981.

Gardner, Howard. *Art, Mind and Brain: A Cognitive Approach to Creativity*. New York: Basic Books, 1982.

Getzels, J. W., and P. W. Jackson. *Creativity and Intelligence*. New York: John Wiley and Sons, 1962.

Hahn, Robert O. *Creative Teachers: Who Wants Them?* New York: John Wiley and Sons, 1973.

Harrison, Elizabeth. *Self Expression through Art*. Toronto: W. J. Gage, 1960.

Lee, James L., and C. J. Pulvino. *Educating the Forgotten Half*. Dubuque, Iowa: Kendall/Hunt Publishing Co., 1978.

Lowenfeld, Viktor. *Creative and Mental Growth*. New York: Macmillan Co., 1970.

May, Rollo. *The Courage to Create*. New York: W. W. Norton & Co., 1975.

McFee, June K. *Preparation for Art*. 2d ed. Belmont, Calif.: Wadsworth Publishing Co., 1970.

Merritt, Helen. *Guiding Free Expression in Children's Art*. New York: Holt, Rinehart and Winston, 1964.

Perkins, D. N. *The Mind's Best Work*. Cambridge, Mass.: Harvard University Press, 1981.

Reichardt, Jasia, ed. *Cybernetics Art and Ideas*. Greenwich, Conn.: New York Graphic Society, 1971.

Rothenberg, Albert, and Carl R. Housman, eds. *The Creativity Question*. Durham, N.C.: Duke University Press, 1976.

Taylor, Irving A., and J. W. Getzels, eds. *Perspectives in Creativity*. Chicago: Aldine Publishing Co., 1975.

Torrance, E. Paul. *What Research Says to the Teacher*. (N.E.A. Creativity Bulletin, series 28).

Vernon, P. E. *Creativity: Selected Readings*. Baltimore: Penguin Publishers, 1970.

Warnock, Mary. *Imagination*. Berkeley: University of California Press, 1976.

Warren, Bernie, ed. *Using the Creative Arts in Therapy*. Cambridge, Mass.: Harvard University Press, 1984.

White

 High light

 Light

 Low light

 Medium

 High dark

 Dark

 Low dark

 Black

*(Colorplate 1) Nine-step value scale from white to black with a neutral gray in the center (equal mixture of black and white). From Otto Ocvirk, Robert Bone, Robert Stinson, and Philip Wigg,* Art Fundamentals: Theory and Practice, *5th ed. Wm. C. Brown Publishers, Dubuque, Iowa. Copyright © 1985 Otto Ocvirk, Robert Bone, Robert Stinson, and Philip Wigg. All Rights Reserved. Reprinted by permission.*

*(Colorplate 2) Dispersion of white light through a prism, forming a spectrum. From Richard Phipps and Richard Wink,* Invitation to the Gallery: An Introduction to Art. *Copyright © 1987 Wm. C. Brown Publishers, Dubuque, Iowa. All Rights Reserved. Reprinted by permission.*

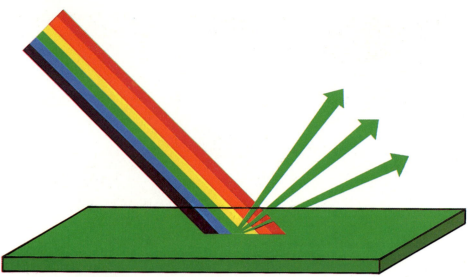

(Colorplate 3) Light ray strikes a green object and all wavelengths except those registering as green are absorbed. The green wavelengths are reflected into the eye and the object is perceived as green.

**Color Wheel**

(Colorplate 4) Color wheel showing three primary hues (red, blue, and yellow), three secondary hues (orange, green, and violet), and six tertiary hues (yellow-green, blue-green, blue-violet, red-violet, red-orange, and yellow-orange). From Richard Phipps and Richard Wink, Invitation to the Gallery: An Introduction to Art. Copyright © 1987 Wm. C. Brown Publishers, Dubuque, Iowa. All Rights Reserved. Reprinted by permission.

White

High light

Yellow

Yellow-orange

Light

Yellow-green

Orange

Low light

Green

Red-orange

Medium

Blue-green

Red

High dark

Blue

Red-violet

Dark

Blue-violet

Violet

Low dark

Black

(Colorplate 5) *Each hue (color) at its maximum intensity (brightness) has a normal value (lightness or darkness). The value of a hue may be raised (lightened) by adding varying amounts of white. The value may be lowered (darkened) by adding varying amounts of black. From Otto Ocvirk, Robert Bone, Robert Stinson,* and Philip Wigg, Art Fundamentals: Theory and Practice, *5th ed. Wm. C. Brown Publishers, Dubuque, Iowa. Copyright © 1985 Otto Ocvirk, Robert Bone, Robert Stinson, and Philip Wigg. All Rights Reserved. Reprinted by permission.*

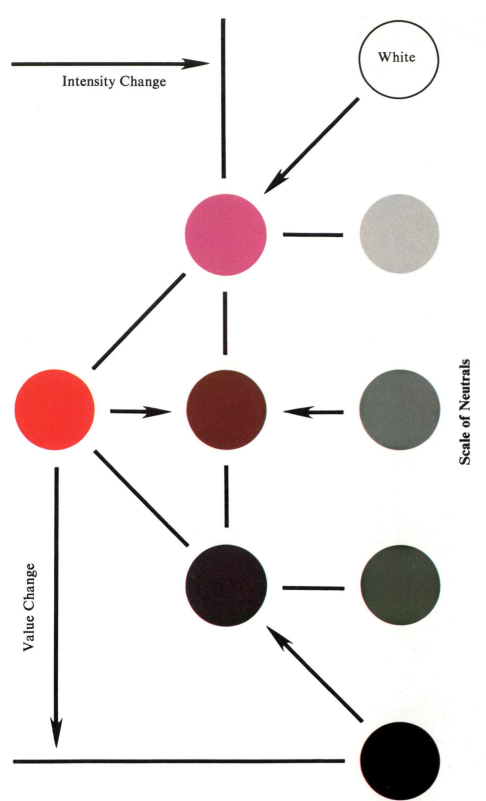

(Colorplate 6) The intensity (brightness) of a hue may be altered by any one of four ways: (a) by adding white (lightens value, raises intensity), (b) by adding black (darkens value, lowers intensity), (c) by adding a neutral gray (value remains the same, intensity is lowered), (d) by adding to the hue varying amounts of its complement (opposite on the color wheel). For example, adding a small amount of green to red produces a gray red; adding a small amount of red to green produces a gray green. Mixing equal amounts of red and green produces a neutral (gray). From Otto Ocvirk, Robert Bone, Robert Stinson, and Philip Wigg, Art Fundamentals: Theory and Practice, 5th ed. Wm. C. Brown Publishers, Dubuque, Iowa. Copyright © 1985 Otto Ocvirk, Robert Bone, Robert Stinson, and Philip Wigg. All Rights Reserved. Reprinted by permission.

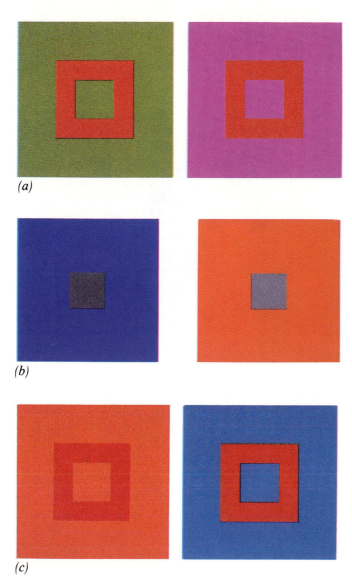

(a)

(b)

(c)

*(Colorplate 7) Illustrations of the law of simultaneous contrast. (a) Red-orange against yellow-green appears more intense than against red violet, since red orange and yellow green are farther apart in the wheel and therefore the differences are made greater. (b) A neutral gray appears to have an orange cast against blue and a blue cast against orange. (c) The same orange appears less intense against red-orange than against blue, which is its complement. From Johannes Itten,* The Elements of Color. *Copyright © 1970 Van Nostrand Reinhold Company. All rights reserved. Reprinted by permission of the publisher.*

# 5 Basic Design for Crafts Students

Whether we are aware of it or not, we are constantly involved with design. The selection of a tie or a scarf to compliment an outfit, the arrangement of furniture in a room, the placement of pictures on a wall, the planting of a shrub or bush to enhance a spot in the garden, the arrangement of food on a platter—all these and much more in our daily lives require active participation in the design process. We are surrounded by infinite numbers of design patterns in nature: leaves on a stem, bark on various trees, lines and markings on a seashell, cloud shapes, sand formations on a beach at low tide. Daily we see the results of how we utilize design in the structure of a building, the layout of a park, the environment of a shopping mall, the lines of an automobile body, our children's toys. If these things work well, if they fulfill their functions efficiently, and if they are pleasing to the sensibilities, in all probability they are well organized, and therefore can be called "good design."

A study of the basic principles of good design is essential for students of the crafts. Because of the wide diversity in materials and techniques employed in the various crafts and because of the relatively small size of most handcrafted pieces, special problems are likely to be encountered, requiring not only a thorough knowledge of design principles but also practice in adapting these principles to the smaller format.

Design is the one common characteristic of all good works of art. Whether we are considering a building, a painting, a sculpture, a piece of jewelry, a ceramic pot, a woven wall hanging, a serigraph, or a stained glass window, the work is indeed "well designed" if it is aesthetically pleasing, if all its elements blend into a harmonious form, and if there is sufficient variety present to draw our eyes back to it time after time. If these ingredients of good design were not held in common, there would be no basis of comparison between a fifth century B.C. Greek vase and a Jackson Pollock painting, for example, two quite different expressions possessing the same universal design principles.

Principles of design are universal and unchanging. An understanding of them is one of the most important tools of any student of the arts. At the same time, the principles are flexible and versatile enough that they can be applied to a wide variety of media and utilized to convey the unique expression of each individual artist.

Lectures, demonstrations, and assigned problems concerning design should be included in the teaching of crafts classes at all levels. Much has been written on the subject of artistic design and many excellent works are available to the serious student. Some of these are listed at the end of this chapter. The present treatment is not meant to be a complete course in design, but seeks only to offer basic precepts common to all works of art, to apply these to the specific needs of the crafts student, and to suggest approaches that will aid the student to arrive at original designs.

**Components of Art**

In looking at any work of art, we must consider three components: *subject matter* (what the work is about), *form* (how the work is organized), and *content* (what the work means or the message it conveys, if you will). These three components can be individually defined, but keep in mind that they are so interrelated as to be almost inseparable, especially if one attempts to delineate form from content.

*Subject matter* may be anything within the artist's experience or knowledge—an object, either human-made or existing in nature, the human figure in myriad poses and situations, a mood, an image of the mind, a natural phenomenon. In short, *anything* may serve as fair game for the artist's interpretation because that interpretation is the important consideration, not the object itself. The object or theme chosen as subject matter serves only as the starting point, the irritant, the excitant that stimulates a reaction in the consciousness of the artist, evoking a response that is translated into a visual expression of what is seen in and felt about the object. The interpretation, in its final form, usually follows one of three approaches. It may be a faithful reproduction of the subject (realistic interpretation); it may bear some resemblance to the object but be essentially a distillation or summary of the more characteristic elements of the object (abstract interpretation); or it may be a completely free expression inspired by but bearing no resemblance to the object (nonobjective interpretation). As noted in chapter 2, the artist's freedom to interpret subject

matter in any chosen way (art for art's sake) is the result of a long battle pioneered by such individualists as Delacroix, Courbet, and Manet, continued by the Impressionists, and brought to full manifestation by Cézanne, Picasso, and many other twentieth century artists.

The *form* of a work of art is concerned with how it is put together; the total organization of *all* elements in the work. If everything works well, good design is achieved and results from how the artist has used tools and materials, knowledge of the principles of organization (rhythm, repetition, balance, contrast, dominance), and the elements of art (line, value, color, texture, and shape) to give tangible expression to creative interpretation. Creative, intelligent use of the principles of organization and the elements of art will usually result in a well-ordered, unified expression of the artist's intent. Because media and technique are so important in three-dimensional work, the maker of handicrafts must be especially adept at integrating his or her chosen medium and method of working with the elements of formal organization.

Though subject matter may be well chosen and formal organization of its interpretation skillfully executed, the final work will be of little importance unless it has a significant *content*. If the artist has seen the subject with sensitivity and responded deeply to it, the resulting visual form will make a meaningful statement. It will say, "This is how I feel about what I see in my world." In his fine little book *The Shape of Content,* the late American artist Ben Shahn said some pertinent things about the inseparability of form and content.[1]

The creation will communicate the artist's meaning to those who see and use it, or better still, stimulate the viewer or user to find a new and different meaning in the work. It follows, therefore, that the deeper the meaning (content) the more significant the statement. Thus, the work of art stands as a communication between artist and observer, which may be illustrated schematically as in table 5.1.

Most courses in basic design (sometimes called art fundamentals) are devoted to a thorough study of the *elements of art* and the *principles of organization,* with specific problems assigned to give the students practice in their use. Courses of this nature are traditionally required of all students majoring in the arts and, therefore, become an important part of their training.

Often, however, students who enroll in a crafts class are not art majors, and usually have no training in arts or crafts. It is especially important that these students be given a thorough introduction to basic design principles and be assigned specific problems in applying these principles.

**Elements of Art**

The artist has access to five basic visual tools that can be used separately or in combination to express infinite meanings. Just as the writer of poetry and prose uses nouns, verbs, adjectives, and other parts of speech to record thoughts and interpretations, so the artist employs the elements of art—*line, value, texture, color,* and *shape* to make a visual statement.

Each element is discussed separately, but realize that several elements may exist together in most works so each influences and is influenced by the others. Along with the discussion of each element, several examples of student work that solve specific problems in the use of each element will be included.

**Table 5.1**
Schematic diagram of line of communication from artist to observer.

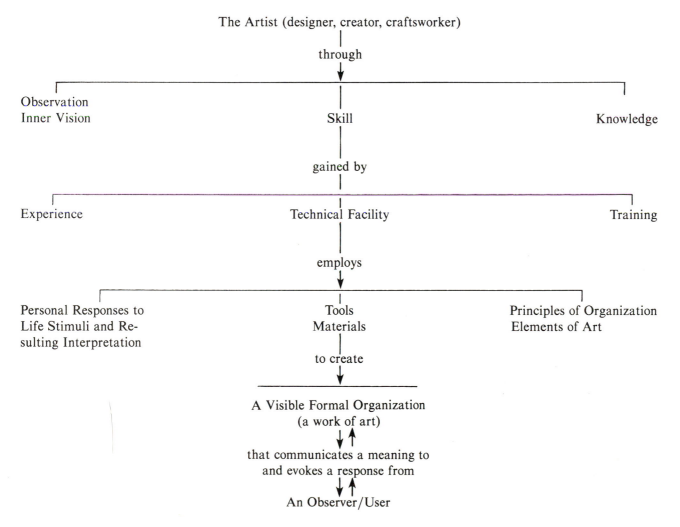

Note: *The two directional arrow between work of art and the observer/user denotes that the persons who see or use a work must respond to it or else the work of the artist will have little meaning for them.*

*Line*

If a pointed implement capable of leaving a visible mark moves across a surface capable of receiving that mark, the result is a line. Thus, a drawing consists of an infinite number of points moving in different directions, defining the appearance or action of the object being depicted. Paul Klee spoke of line thus: "An active line on a walk, moving freely, without goal. A walk for walk's sake. The mobility agent is a point, shifting its position forward."[2] Line as such does not exist in nature. When an artist draws a tree branch, for example, he or she uses a line to define what appears to be the edge of the branch. What the artist is really recording is a contour, and the line he or she draws serves to separate the area of the branch from the area of the sky behind it.

Lines may be characterized by their physical qualities as being thin or thick, long or short, straight or curved (see figure 5.1).

A line may move in any direction—vertically, horizontally, or tipped at an angle—and may change direction gradually or abruptly (see figure 5.2).

The position of a line in an area, will serve to divide that area into various parts (see figure 5.3).

The instrument used to draw the line, and in most cases, the surface on which it is drawn will affect the character of the line (see figure 5.4).

The student should experiment with many types of lines drawn with a variety of instruments to become familiar with the communicative possibilities of lines.

Lines may be used to express various moods, conditions or emotions. For example, vertical lines may express aspiration (reaching upward); horizontal lines may express quietness, stability, or dependability, while diagonal lines may express excitement, unrest, or agitation (see figure 5.5).

A line may be purely decorative or calligraphic, adding pleasing enhancement to the surface upon which it is placed as in figure 5.6. Figure 5.7 illustrates students' works in which lines are used to create the overall design.

*(Figure 5.1) Lines may vary widely in character. They may be long, short, thin, thick, straight, or curved.*

*(Figure 5.2) Lines may move in any direction— vertically, horizontally, or at an angle. They may change direction gradually or abruptly.*

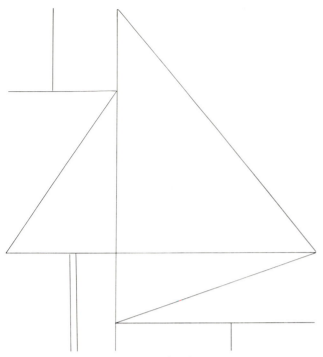

(Figure 5.3) Lines serve to divide an area into parts, depending on where they are placed.

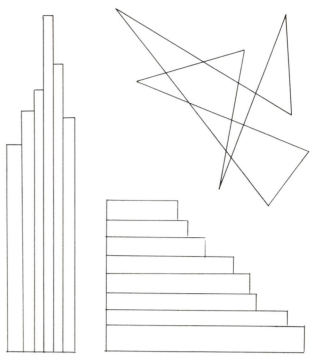

(Figure 5.5) Lines may express many moods, emotions, or conditions. The line drawings here might express aspiration, stability, and excitement.

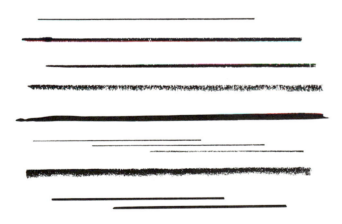

(Figure 5.4) Lines vary in character according to the instrument used to draw them. Lines shown were drawn with pencils, pens, pastel crayons, brush, goose quill pen, and wax pencil.

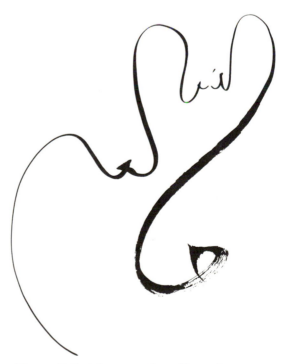

(Figure 5.6) A line may be calligraphic in nature and serve purely as a decorative element.

(a)

(c)

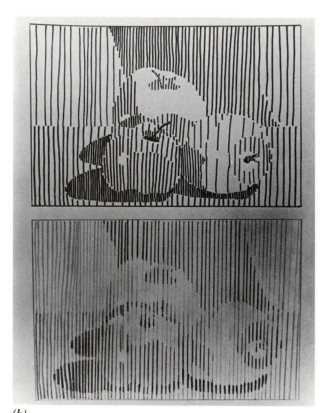

(b)

(Figure 5.7) Student work: design problems using line.

(d)

*Texture*

Texture appeals to our tactile (touch) sense, and occurs when variations are placed on the surface of any material whether they be actual ridges, bumps, or depressions (or lack of these) or only arrangements of light and dark patterns that give the appearance of surface variation. The former is *tactile* or *actual texture,* while the latter is *visual* or *simulated texture.* The difference may easily be seen by considering two pieces of fabric, one a ribbed corduroy and the other a printed material that appears textured although it is smooth to the touch (see figure 5.8).

Actually, tactile and visual responses are very closely related and when, for example, we look at textures in a painting, our minds employ both responses simultaneously.

Texture exists in all degrees of surface quality ranging from shiny smooth to extremely rough, as shown in figure 5.9. Texture abounds in natural forms as well as in arrangements created by human beings.

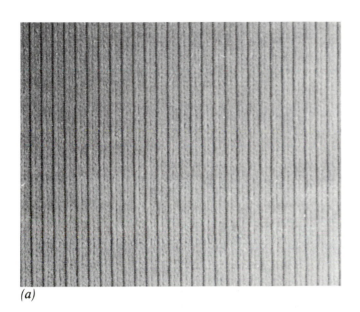

*(a)*

*(a)*

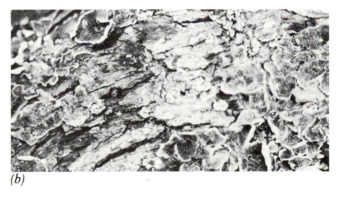

*(b)*

*(b)*

*(c)*

*(Figure 5.8) (a) Ribbed fabric having actual texture.*
*(b) Printed fabric having simulated (visual) texture.*

*(Figure 5.9) (a) Natural texture: evergreen tree branch.*
*(b) Lichens. (c) Bare tree branches.*

In both cases the contrast among textured surfaces adds variety and interest to what we look at (see figure 5.10). Our environment would be unbearably boring if all surfaces were alike in textural quality.

Exploration into the possibilities of actual textural surfaces have played an important part in the work of many twentieth century artists, notably the cubists and dadaists who put all manner of found objects and materials in their collages and papier-collés. Many diverse materials that would once have been discarded as trash are now acceptable for paintings, sculpture, and handicrafts in order to add textural interest to a work.

The emotional impact of texture is familiar to anyone who has delighted in stroking the soft fur of a cat or cringed upon contact with rough sandpaper. The very words used to describe surfaces—smooth, silky, rough, granular, spiny—are enough to evoke feelings of delight and displeasure, and the desire to touch environmental objects is inherent in human nature. From earliest infancy, we have to reach out and touch things, to feel with our hands and experience with our minds the wide variety of textures around us. Although I realize the practical necessity of museum signs that say Do Not Touch, I nevertheless feel that the viewer is deprived of a basic source of enjoying a piece of sculpture or pottery. For example, the hammered textures of the metal wall hanging depicted in figure 5.11 can be more appreciated if observers can touch it.

The crafts student must be especially well versed in the textural possibilities of various materials, not only from the standpoint of taking advantage of their inherent texture, but also from knowing how surfaces can be modified to add textural variety. Smooth metal, for example, can be hammered or tooled in a variety of ways for increased interest. Knowing which tool or technique to use to produce the desired textural effect is an important part of the crafts student's education (see figure 5.12).

(a)

(b)

(Figure 5.10) (a) Textures created by humans: redwood fence. (b) Ends of stacked railroad ties.

(Figure 5.11) Metal wall hanging with hammered textures (student work).

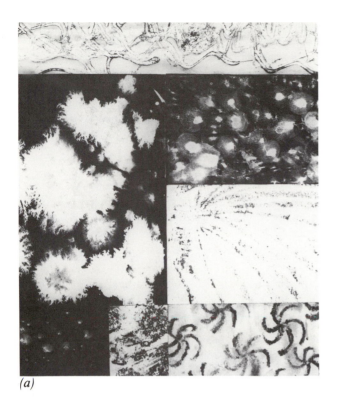

(a)

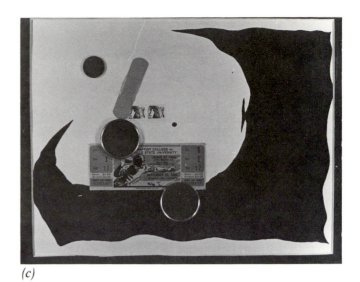

(c)

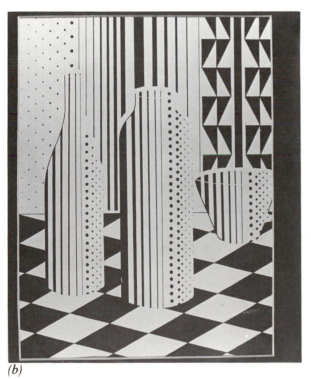

(b)

(d)

*(Figure 5.12) (a) Student work: design problem in texture. Experimental textures produced with various media. (b) Student work: simulated texture produced with line, shape, and value. (c) Student work: textures produced with actual materials (collage). (d) Student work: texture effects through use of line.*

*Value*

The element of value is concerned with the characteristic of lightness or darkness, that is, the quantity of light reflected to the eye from an object. Value is closely related to color and will be considered later in this chapter as a chromatic property. Achromatically, value may be thought of as the entire range of tonal quality from complete light to complete darkness. The *value pattern* in a work consists of the total relationship among all the lights and darks. The term *chiaroscuro* pertains to the manner in which lights and darks are used to model form in a painting. If the contrast is extreme, the term *tenebrism* is used.

The artist must translate this range by using white for greatest light, black for complete darkness, and various mixtures of the two to create gray tones in between. A value scale may be constructed by using white at one end, black at the other, equal mixtures of black and white for the midpoint or neutral gray tone, and various proportions of white and black to arrive at other shades of gray. Value scales may be composed of as many as nine tones or shades because this seems to be the range that the average person can easily distinguish (see colorplate 1).

A knowledge of value is important to the artist in creating patterns of light and dark for decorative effects or in giving the illusion of three dimensionality by light-dark modeling. One must also take into account the

*(a)*

*(Figure 5.13) (a) Student work: design problems in value.*

*(b)*

natural or *local value* of the material being used, which exists apart from the amount of light it receives (see figure 5.13).

## Shape

Shape in art may be defined as an area of measurable dimensions whose boundaries are sometimes delineated sharply by a definite continuous edge or are somewhat amorphous in character with soft or indistinct edges. Shape may be indicated by color, value, texture, or lines. Shape by its very nature is usually assumed to exist on a more or less two-dimensional or flat plane. It may, however, be three-dimensional, in which case the terms *mass* and/or *volume* are used to designate it. Three-dimensional shape exists in space and therefore has a definite relationship to the space that surrounds it.

Shape may be representational and look like specific objects, or may be purely decorative, creating a pleasing *pattern* or arrangement on a surface. Some shapes are sharply geometric—circles, squares, rectangles, triangles—and carefully constructed with ruler and compass or cut from some material. Others are free-form or *biomorphic* in character, resembling protoplasmic organisms such as amoebae (see figure 5.14).

Shape relationships in a work are greatly affected by size and placement, as well as by color, value, and texture of the various shaped areas. The student must be careful to consider the overall appearance of the final work, so the shapes used will contribute to an unified, harmonious statement.

*(a)*

*(b)*

*(Figure 5.14) Various shapes cut from construction paper. (a) Geometric shapes. (b) Biomorphic (free-form) shapes.*

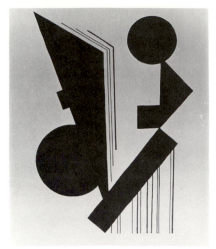

(a)

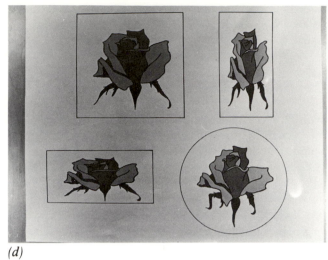

(d)

(b)

(e)

(c)

*(Figure 5.15) Student work: design problems in shape.*

The shapes themselves are usually the positive elements in the total design, but the spaces between the shapes (negative spaces) also enter into the work and must be carefully considered also (see figure 5.15).

## Color

Of all the art elements, color is perhaps the one that evokes the most interest from both the artist-crafter who employs it and the viewer of the finished work. At the same time, color is by far the most complex of the elements and its misuse can ruin an otherwise perfectly good design. Color has been the subject of a tremendous amount of investigation done by Albert Munsell, Josef Albers, Faber Birren, and many others, all of whom spent years in studying it. Fortunately, certain color principles can be briefly outlined, and upon these the student can base a personal investigation of color. Indeed, color *must* be experimented with and experienced firsthand if it is to be understood and appreciated.

Color is produced when white light (sunlight) is broken down (dispersed) into its component wavelengths or electromagnetic vibrations. This can be illustrated very simply by passing a beam of sunlight through a transparent, solid, triangular piece of optical glass called a *prism,* which disperses the ray of light into a visible *spectrum* composed of the spectral hues red, orange, yellow, green, blue, indigo, and violet, the wavelengths of which range from 32 millionths of an inch at the red end to 16 millionths of an inch at the violet end (colorplate 2).

The dispersion of light into the color spectrum was first demonstrated in 1666 by Sir Isaac Newton, the English physicist and mathematician. Although indigo was included in the Newtonian designations of spectral hues, it is not considered a separate hue by contemporary investigators. A natural manifestation of spectrum formation is the rainbow, seen when the sun shines after a shower. Moisture-laden air acts as a prism and the rays of light passing through are broken down into component hues, which in turn are seen reflected in the sky opposite the sun.

Numerous explanations of why we see color have been advanced. One of the most commonly accepted is based on the theory concerning the molecular structure of pigments, which give color to objects. When light strikes a pigment, it absorbs certain wavelengths and reflects others; therefore, the color the eye perceives depends on which wavelengths the pigment absorbs and which it reflects (colorplate 3).

Color media, whether they be oils, pastels, watercolors, or crayons, are made of pigments or dyes formulated on this principle. A red pigment contains materials that will absorb all wavelengths except those registering as red, and these will be reflected into the eye so we "see red."

*The Color Wheel.* The study of color theory may be approached in many ways, but the simplest is through the use of the color wheel, based on a system of primary, secondary, and tertiary hues (colorplate 4).

Red, yellow, and blue are basic or primary colors placed on the wheel at equal distances apart to correspond to the points of an equilateral triangle. By mixing equal quantities of two primaries, we make a secondary hue. For example, red + blue = violet; red + yellow = orange; yellow + blue = green. Each secondary hue so obtained is placed on the wheel midway between its two parent primaries. Again, by mixing equal quantities of each primary hue and the secondary hue adjacent to it, we arrive at six tertiary hues—red-orange, yellow-orange, yellow-green, blue-green, blue-violet, and red-violet, each of which is placed on the wheel midway between its parent hues. It is, of course, possible to mix many more hues by carrying the process further, but twelve hues are usually standard for a wheel of this type. Once the color wheel has been established, it serves as a useful means for understanding other basic principles of color use.

If a line is drawn directly across the wheel between the pairs red, red-violet and yellow, yellow-green, the wheel will have been divided into warm hues (reds, oranges, yellows) and cool hues (blues, greens, violets). Artists know that warm colors used in a painting tend to come forward, while cool colors tend to recede. By using this knowledge, Cézanne formulated his *color modulation theory* that led to a whole new way of painting: form is modeled by warm and cool colors rather than by the traditional value change of color.

Any two hues directly across from each other on the color wheel are said to be *complements*. A mixture of any two complements will result in a neutral or gray. Note also, that a mixture of the three primary hues will have the same result.

Various color relationships or *color schemes* may be worked out. The most common of these are:

- Monochromatic: Various values and intensities of a single hue are used together. A monochromatic color scheme can become somewhat monotonous, and it is well to include an accent of the complementary hue for interest.
- Complementary: A scheme is based upon any two complements. Because of the maximum contrast of complements, they should not be used in equal proportions within the scheme.
- Triadic: A scheme is composed of any three hues equally distant apart on the wheel. Again, proportions should be varied for interest, with one hue chosen as the dominant color and the other two used as accents.
- Analogous: Any three or four colors adjacent on the color wheel are used together in a scheme; for example, red-orange, orange, yellow-orange, and yellow may be schemed together.
- Split complement: Any hue schemed with the hues on either side of its complement; for example, yellow may be schemed with blue-violet, and red-violet.

*Major Properties of Color.* Three major properties of color are *hue, value,* and *intensity.*

*Hue* is simply the name of the color, or more properly the position that the color occupies within the spectrum. In this state, the hue is said to exist in *spectrum intensity.*

*Value,* as we have seen, refers to the quantity of light that an object reflects. In the absence of color, value is represented by black, white, and various mixtures of the two (grays). Therefore, when black or white is added to any hue at its spectrum intensity, that hue will be darkened or lightened, and various shades (by the addition of black) and tints (by the addition of white) will be obtained (colorplate 5).

*Intensity* is the brightness or dullness of a color, or the *quality* of light that it reflects. There are several ways of modifying intensity. Simplest and most often done, is to add to the hue enough of its complement to arrive at the intensity desired (colorplate 6).

The appearance of any hue is directly affected by other hues placed around or near it. This is the basis for the *law of simultaneous contrast,* which states that when a hue (or modification thereof) is placed next to another hue, the differences between them will be intensified and this will be in the direction of the complement (colorplate 7).

As is the case with all the other art elements, color may also be used to express mood, feeling, or ideas. In fact, color may have a more direct and universal emotional impact on humans than any of the other elements. Our language is full of such terms as "a true blue friend," "a yellow coward," and "a white flower of innocence" and such symbols as red for danger and black for despair or death. Religious art through the centuries has fully employed symbolic color: blue for truth, fidelity, and representation of the Virgin Mary, green for hope and fertility, purple for sorrow and penitence, red for passion and blood. Psychologists studying the effects of wall colors in factories, offices, and institutions have found that walls painted in warm cheerful colors will stimulate workers to increase output, while the walls of hospitals painted in cool colors are conducive to a relaxed, restful atmosphere for patients.

The student learns intelligent use of color only through experimentation and application. Although the preparation of a color wheel, value and intensity scales, and various color schemes is considered by some to be outmoded, tedious exercises, they can provide invaluable experience in the use of color if executed creatively.

**Principles of Organization**
Although the elements of art have been treated as separate entities, they are very closely related. The artist must combine them creatively and with full knowledge of their properties to design the visual form that will express his or her desired meaning most clearly. Control of the art elements can only be accomplished through knowledge and skillful use of the principles of organization, some of which are balance, rhythm, movement, proportion, economy, and dominance. Because of the diverse ways in which the principles can be used, the explanation will be kept fairly simple for the sake of brevity.

*Balance*
The principle of balance is concerned with the visual distribution of the various elements in a work of art in such a way that the viewer feels a sense of equilibrium or stability. If the work is divided with an imaginary vertical or horizontal axis, the elements on either side of the axis should appear to have the same weight. If the elements are precisely the same on either side of the axis, *symmetrical* or *formal* balance has been obtained. If the elements are not exactly the same but appear to be balanced or give the "feeling" of being balanced, then the balance is *asymmetrical* or *occult*. Asymmetrical balance is usually more dynamic and visually interesting than symmetrical balance. A *radial* distribution of elements occurs when one or more shapes appear to revolve around a central point.

*Rhythm*
A good design is based on some sort of rhythm—the elements therein flow in an ordered fashion. There is a definite pattern that ties the work together into an harmonious whole. Certain elements may be given dominance or emphasis as a point of interest, but these must bear a logical relationship or chaos will result. Rhythm is usually accomplished by repetition of certain elements either by simple duplication or by a more complex and varied similarity.

*Movement*
Closely associated with rhythm is the principle of movement. The directional force of the various elements must be accomplished in such a way as to move the eye in an orderly fashion from one part of the work to another. Usually the composition will draw the eye to the starting point from which it begins the cycle of viewing all over again.

*Proportion*
Each part of the composition must bear a definite size and placement relationship to every other part. One extremely large shape or area of color will appear out of place if it is not balanced by proportionate shapes or colors in other parts of the composition.

*Economy*
A major fault of most student work is that too many elements are included, thus resulting in a confused jumble. Usually the more simple and direct a composition is, the more effective it will be. Nothing should be included that does not contribute to the total expression of the artist's intent.

*Dominance*
A good design will have one major or dominant motif and all others will be subordinate. The dominant motif is sometimes referred to as the center of interest.

In addition to the elements of art and the principles of organization, two other considerations must be taken into account by the successful designer of crafts: (1) the function to be served by an object will largely dictate its form and (2) the final appearance of the work will be governed to a great extent by the properties and limitations of the material being used.

The student must remember that it is quite possible, however, to employ the principles of organization and arrange the elements of art in such a way that the completed work has perfect unity, yet the composition is dull and uninteresting. When this occurs, usually the artist has not paid sufficient attention to the necessary ingredient of *variety*. There must be a certain amount of contrast among the elements—subtle differences in the sizes and intensities of repeated shapes and colors, variations in textural quality, changes in directional forces, introduction of countermotifs—all of which serve to add variety to a work.

**Design in Crafts**
Thus, good design is an ordering of the formal elements of art by using the principles of organization to arrive at a unified expression with sufficient variety to make the visual form perpetually interesting. The evolution of a well-designed form usually involves several steps; the artist's eyes must be open to the world that surrounds us, to really *see* rather than to just look at; careful thought must be given to what is seen, and when the

response is deep enough there will follow (1) organization of observations, thoughts, and responses into a (2) concept, idea, or theme. This in turn will lead to (3) execution of the idea, involving selection of media and techniques, and close attention to craftsmanship and design principles.

Realize, however, that the slavish following of any set of rules will not guarantee a work of art because the elements of art and principles of organization seldom exist as separate entities. They must be used together with thought and care to arrive at the best possible

statement of the artist's intention. The artist must add a unique personal touch through imagination and original interpretation (creativity) to arrive at a new and exciting concept, and learn to think beyond the ordinary, the trite. So many art students are content to execute the first idea that comes to mind. It is fairly safe to say that this first idea is perhaps so obvious that it has probably occurred to many others as well. The artist must constantly ask, "Why am I doing this? What has moved or inspired me? What am I trying to say? How can I say it creatively?" Halfhearted effort must be replaced with intensy of purpose that will spur the artist to do the best job possible. It is then, and only

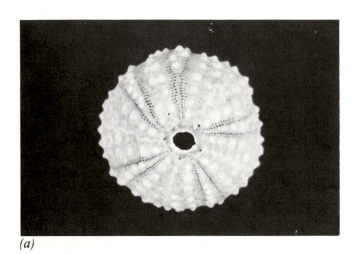

(a)

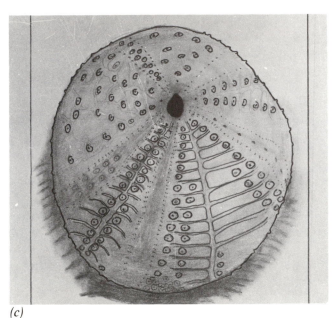

(c)

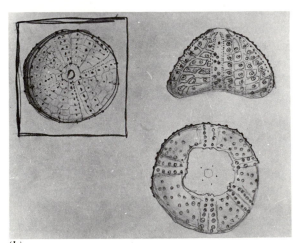

(b)

(Figure 5.16) (a) Sea urchin shell used as inspiration for jewelry design. (b) Preliminary pencil sketches of various aspects of the shell. (c) Large drawing of the shell requiring careful study and attention to detail. (d) Abstract drawing of the sea urchin (1). (e) Abstract drawing of the sea urchin (2). (f) Abstract drawing of the sea urchin (3). (g) Pendant based on abstract drawing of the sea urchin.

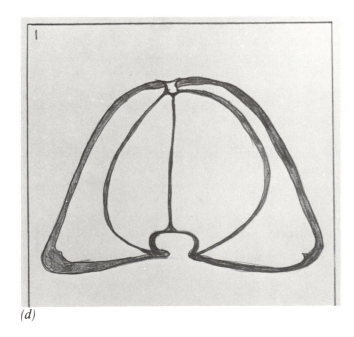

(d)

then, that the envisioned and executed form will have meaningful content and be a worthwhile example of the artist's effort.

**An Approach to Original Design**

Students in crafts classes (and other art classes as well) are often at a loss for suitable designs for their work. A common complaint is: "But I don't have any ideas, I don't know what to do." When this happens, suggest that the student turn to nature for inspiration. Trees, leaves, flowers, fruit, seed pods, rocks, shells, insects, birds, fish, and animals all furnish abundant inspiration for designs.

Once an object of interest is selected, have students make rough sketches of various aspects of the object (see figure 5.16). Follow that with a large, rather objective (realistic) drawing of the object. The next step for students is to make several drawings, modifications, and abstractions, thinking of various ways in which the object might be depicted, perhaps emphasizing one feature, enlarging another, or trying a cubistic or surrealistic approach with one. From these sketches, something will evolve to serve as inspiration for designing a finished work, in the case of figure 5.16, a piece of jewelry.

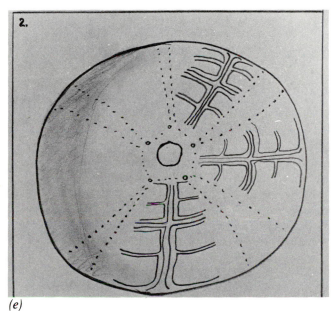
(e)

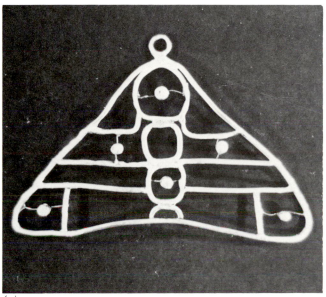
(g)

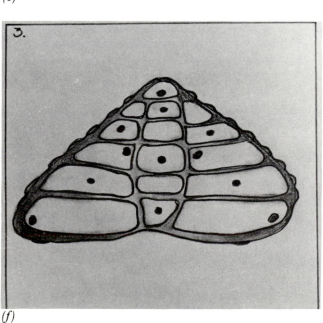
(f)

In addition to objects from nature, the human figure and countless everyday objects can be subjected to the same sort of analysis to arrive at design ideas. Along these lines, refer to the section dealing with an original approach in *Encounter with Art* by Hastie and Schmidt. The authors show many different ways in which an artist has interpreted an ordinary apple.[3]

Each craft medium presents its own particular design problems and these are discussed more fully in part 2. A good design can often be modified for execution in several media. The student should be encouraged to make quick sketches and doodles of what he or she observes, with an eye to using them as designs for crafts projects.

Much excellent, high-quality work in all the crafts is being currently executed by professionals in this country and abroad. The student can study the numerous examples on the various crafts pictured in part 2, as well as in books of a more general nature that present surveys of works being produced in all the crafts (see list of suggested readings at the end of this chapter). The periodical *American Crafts,* referred to in chapter 1, is an invaluable source of information and gives illustrations of the works of contemporary craftspeople.

One of the best ways to study professionally produced crafts is to attend local and regional crafts exhibitions and fairs, and to visit shops that specialize in the sale of fine craft work.

### Notes

1  Ben Shahn, *The Shape of Content* (Cambridge, Mass.: Harvard University Press, 1957).
2  Paul Klee, *Pedagogical Sketchbook* (New York: Frederick Praeger, 1953).
3  Reid Hastie and Christian Schmidt, *Encounter with Art* (New York: McGraw-Hill Book Co., 1969), 126–39.

*Suggested Readings*

Bates, Kenneth F. *Basic Design.* Cleveland: World Publishing Co., 1970.

Bevlin, Marjorie Elliott. *Design through Discovery.* New York: Holt, Rinehart and Winston, 1970.

Dayan, Ruth and Wilburt Feinberg. *Crafts of Israel.* New York: Macmillan Co., 1974.

De Sausmarez, Maurice. *Basic Design: The Dynamics of Visual Form.* New York: Reinhold, 1964.

Evans, Helen Marie. *Man the Designer.* New York: Macmillan Co., 1973.

Hanks, Kurt, Larry Belliston, and Dave Edwards. *Design Yourself.* Los Altos, Calif.: Wm. Kaufmann, 1977.

Itten, Johannes. *Design and Form.* New York: Reinhold, 1964.

Lacey, Jeannette F. *Young Art: Nature and Seeing.* New York: Van Nostrand, Reinhold, 1973.

Martin, Grace O. *Approaching Design through Nature: The Quiet Joy.* New York: Viking Press, 1977.

O'Brien, James F. *Design by Accident.* New York: Dover Publications, 1968.

Ocvirk, Otto G. et al. *Art Fundamentals: Theory and Practice.* 4th ed. Dubuque, Iowa: Wm. C. Brown Co., 1981.

Pearson, Katherine. *American Crafts: A Source Book for the Home.* New York: Stewart, Tabori and Chang, 1983.

Scrase, Pat. *Let's Start Designing.* New York: Reinhold, 1966.

Sidelinger, Stephen J. *The Color Manual.* Englewood Cliffs, N.J.: Prentice-Hall, 1985.

Sieber, Roy. *African Textile and Decorative Arts.* New York: Museum of Modern Art, 1972.

Taylor, John F. A. *Design and Expression in the Visual Arts.* New York: Dover Publications, 1964.

Young, Frank M. *Visual Studies: A Foundation for Artists and Designers.* Englewood Cliffs, N.J.: Prentice-Hall, 1985.

# 6 Organizing a Crafts Program

**General Considerations**

Because of the wide diversity in types of craft programs, it is difficult to offer suggestions that will fit all cases. When a specific program is being planned, those organizing it must consider such factors as:

- What is the primary purpose of the program? Is it educational, and if so at what level? Will certain standards have to be met as, for example, those specified by the various states for teacher training or for the public school curriculum? Is it a recreational program designed to serve a particular community, and if so is there sufficient community interest and backing for the program? Is the purpose primarily therapeutic or rehabilitative, and can it meet the recommended standards for such programs?

- What is the nature, location, and image of the sponsoring group? Once the commitment is made to a program, will dependable support be available?

- To whom is the program directed? Is it designed to reach children, young adults, the elderly, the handicapped, the underprivileged, the affluent, or some combination of these?

- What facilities will be needed for the program? Can these be designed and built to specification, or must already existing space be utilized? How can this be done?

- What personnel will be needed to staff and administer the program? Will they be salaried or serve on a volunteer basis?

- What is the scope of the program? What crafts will be offered and at what level? What hours will be maintained and at what times of year?

- What sort of funding will be needed? What amount of money will be needed and who will provide it? Will those participating in the program be expected to bear a portion or all of the cost?

From these few general considerations, it is evident that the planning of a crafts program of any sort is no small undertaking. Add to these the specific needs of such programs that are described in chapter 7, and it is obvious that a good crafts program requires careful planning to organize and a dedicated individual or group to keep it running smoothly.

Further discussion of specific programs is beyond the scope of this text; however, an important consideration common to all programs is the utilization of efficient space, equipment, and materials.

*Page from student notebook showing design and color plans for silk-screen print.*

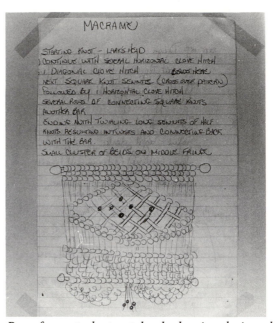

*Page from student notebook showing design plans for macrame.*

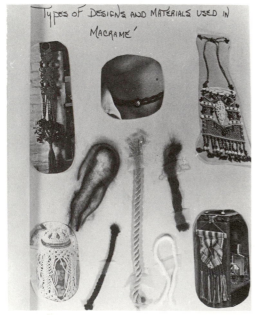

*Page from student notebook showing materials and thinking for macrame designs.*

*Page from student notebook showing samples made during experiments with papermaking.*

**The Crafts Room or Workshop**

When organizing a program in which a number of crafts are to be taught in one room, careful use of available space is essential. Unlimited space and funds to set up a program is the ideal but is seldom the case. All too often, when a new program is being instituted, it is hampered by cramped quarters and limited budget. The instructor must organize the space well and use care when purchasing equipment and supplies to ensure the availability of the basic tools and materials needed. Supplemental purchases may then be made as funds become available.

It is rarely possible that the crafts room can be designed and built to desired specifications, so existing space must be organized to accommodate all the work to be done there. A specific area of the room should be designated for each craft, and all tools and materials for that craft kept convenient to that location. Perhaps the only way to minimize the possible or inevitable chaos

when twelve to fifteen students are working on a number of different crafts in the same room is to provide a definite space for all tools, equipment, and materials. Assign a certain number of students to work in a given space at one time (see table 6.1). Insist that everything used be put back in place and the work area cleaned up when the class is over. In an area designed for metalwork, for example, tools are hung with hooks on pegboard. Welding equipment, vise, and buffer-grinder motor are conveniently placed within this area. A portion of the workbench top is protected with insulating brick for welding and soldering operations. Metals and other materials are kept in boxes and on shelves underneath the workbench. Shelves above provide space for work in progress and additional supplies. When tools must be shared among related crafts, these may be located in adjacent areas so equipment may be easily reached and shared.

*Work area and tool board for metalwork and/or jewelry.*

**Sign-up sheet for crafts projects.** (Table 6.1)

| | PROJECT 1 Date Due _____ | PROJECT 2 Date Due _____ | PROJECT 3 Date Due _____ | PROJECT 4 Date Due _____ |
|---|---|---|---|---|
| *Coiling (3 students)* | | | | |
| *Enamel on Metal (2 students)* | | | | |
| *Fabric Dyeing (2 students)* | | | | |
| *Fiber Techniques (3 students) Weaving* | | | | |
| *Jewelry (2 students)* | | | | |
| *Macramé (3 students)* | | | | |
| *Mosaics (3 students)* | | | | |
| *Papermaking (2 students)* | | | | |
| *Relief Prints (3 students) Woodblock and Linoleum* | | | | |
| *Silkscreen (3 students) Paper Fabric* | | | | |
| *Stained Glass (2 students)* | | | | |
| *Stitchery (3 students)* | | | | |

*Note:* Number of students in parentheses are maximum to work in any one craft at a time.

Each craft requires its own particular methods of storage for tools and supplies, and the instructor must carefully devise a system that will work most efficiently in a particular situation. The best system is one that will keep the materials and tools within convenient reach of those who will use them, without their having to waste time searching for a particular hammer or a pair of pliers.

Efficient organization of the crafts room must also provide for certain mechanical and logistical needs.

*Lighting*
An abundant amount of light, whether artificial or natural, is essential. Artificial sources include overhead fluorescent tubes or large incandescent bulbs. Some instructors prefer a mixture of the two, feeling that this more closely approximates the quality of natural light. Each work station should be equipped with a small high-intensity light that the worker can direct as needed. Windows should be equipped with blinds or shades so the room can be darkened for showing slides and films.

*Water Supply*
Second only to lighting in importance is an abundant and convenient source of water. Ideally, there should be several large sinks, preferably made of stainless steel, placed in convenient locations and supplying both hot and cold running water.

*Electrical Outlets*
Provision for plugging in such equipment as enameling kilns, buffing and grinding motors, soldering guns, hot plates, power tools, and the like should be provided where needed throughout the room. A minimum of one double outlet should be at each work station. Some equipment, such as larger kilns, require special plugs and voltage. Installations should be done by a professional electrician where needed.

*Safety Equipment*
Such items as welding goggles, plastic eye shields, and respiratory filters should be kept near the equipment requiring their use. Make a hard and fast rule that necessary protective gear be worn when such operations as grinding, sawing, buffing, filing, and breaking glass are carried out because all may be a source of danger.

A first aid kit should be kept nearby and immediate attention given to any sort of injury no matter how minor. Any piece of equipment producing heat, such as kiln, wax pot, or hot plate, should be insulated from the tabletop by a heavy asbestos mat. Several fire extinguishers should be placed at convenient locations.

*Cleaning Equipment*
The availability of bench brushes, dustpans, brooms, and trash receptacles will encourage students to clean up their work areas when they have finished working. The instructor should insist on this, even when custodial service is provided. Waste materials, such as solvents and plaster, should be disposed of in suitable containers and should *never* be poured down the sink. An exhaust fan should carry away harmful fumes.

*Teaching Aids*
A large blackboard, a bulletin board, and a projection screen should be standard equipment in the crafts room. Filmstrips, slides, and reference books are always helpful and these should be convenient for students to reach and use.

*Storage Space*
When so many diverse operations are being carried out in one area, storage of working materials, work in progress, and special equipment can become a real problem. A corollary of "Murphy's law" states that there is always just a bit less space available than is actually needed. As many items as possible should be kept at or near the spot where they will be used, but additional storage areas are always necessary. These must be utilized wherever and whenever possible. Periodic cleaning out and reorganization of such areas is essential to prevent clutter.

**Tools and Equipment**
When tools and equipment are being ordered, consider purchasing the best quality available. Students are notoriously hard on equipment, and the few extra dollars spent on good quality tools will be worth it many times over. Make periodic checks on all tools and equipment, and repair or replace them whenever necessary. Instruction manuals that come with most equipment should be carefully filed because these often contain valuable information for trouble shooting and maintaining the tool. The instructor should be familiar

with the workings of each piece of equipment so minor adjustments and repairs may be quickly and easily made without having to wait for someone to service the equipment. A supply of spare kiln elements, soldering tips, saw blades, and other items requiring frequent replacement should be kept on hand as well as a maintenance tool kit containing pliers, hammers, screwdrivers, and the like.

## Materials and Supplies

When ordering working materials such as wools, glass, enamels, woodblocks, and all the other myriad supplies necessary for a crafts program, anticipate what will be needed for at least a semester or season, not only to ensure that supplies will not run out but also to take advantage of bulk discounts and freight rates. A file of catalogs from suppliers should be kept up to date and these should be compared for differences in pricing and special discounts. A number of larger suppliers have branch warehouses in various parts of the country for quicker service and freight benefits. A list of suppliers for various crafts is given in appendix C.

Local mills, shops, and salvage yards should be scrounged for sources of secondhand and scrap materials, which may be had at greatly reduced prices or sometimes just for the asking. Often enthusiastic students are good at searching out such sources and, with very little encouragement, will bring into the studio all manner of usable "junk."

Few hard and fast rules will fit all situations in any craft program. Space availability, fund allocations, program needs, and many other factors enter into a program's development, and each instructor must devise one that will best meet the needs of those who will use it.

Remember that the amount of space, quality of tools and equipment, and abundance of materials on hand will never of themselves ensure a good crafts program, which can only evolve through the careful planning and dedicated efforts of a highly trained and diligent teacher who has the ability and enthusiasm to inspire students to put forth their best efforts in utilizing their creative abilities. As pointed out in the beginning of this work, the production of highly creative and beautifully crafted objects should be the major goal of any crafts program. Without this goal, the program will foster only "busywork" and make little or no contribution to the creative development of the participants.

# 7  Crafts Today

In the early days of our country, necessity dictated that the settlers be proficient in many diverse crafts in order to provide furniture, clothing, utensils, and other household items for their homes. Both men and women, and often the older children as well, were skilled in such crafts as spinning, weaving, metalworking, woodcraft, pottery, candlemaking, and the like, each producing objects within his or her expertise for family use or for trade with neighbors for other goods. As time went on, certain people began to specialize in one or more of the crafts, eventually setting up small workshops in their homes or in separate buildings, producing their wares as silversmiths, candlemakers, weavers, quilters, cordwainers (shoemakers), or whatever their specialty happened to be.

Today, replicas of these shops can often be seen in such restorations as Williamsburg (Virginia) and Old Sturbridge Village (Massachusetts), with present day craftspeople producing crafts much as our ancestors did, often using original tools. During the summer, colonial crafts celebrations are frequently held at historic sites, such as the annual Fourth of July Colonial Crafts Weekend at Ashlawn, President James Monroe's home near Charlottesville, Virginia. Many craftspeople engage in blacksmithing, spoonmaking, quilting, lacemaking, basketry, candlemaking, caning and rushing, as well as in several other crafts (see figure 7.1).

Although the necessity to be proficient in such skills no longer exists, crafts have assumed important and vital roles in our contemporary society.

Beginning with the crafts revival of the late 1920s (see chapter 1) increasing numbers of people have become involved in crafts in one way or another. Courses in many crafts are available at every level, from those taught as a hobby at neighborhood centers to full-fledged degree programs in colleges and universities.

(a)

(b)

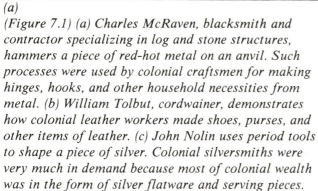

(Figure 7.1) (a) Charles McRaven, blacksmith and contractor specializing in log and stone structures, hammers a piece of red-hot metal on an anvil. Such processes were used by colonial craftsmen for making hinges, hooks, and other household necessities from metal. (b) William Tolbut, cordwainer, demonstrates how colonial leather workers made shoes, purses, and other items of leather. (c) John Nolin uses period tools to shape a piece of silver. Colonial silversmiths were very much in demand because most of colonial wealth was in the form of silver flatware and serving pieces.

(c)

Many professional craftspeople are in the business of producing well-designed and beautifully crafted pieces with many media in their own studios. Their art objects may be seen and purchased by discriminating collectors at crafts fairs, in crafts shops, and in museum shops.

The hands-on experience of participating in crafts activities has received increased recognition by twentieth century society because of the tremendous recreational value it offers, serving as a primary outlet for human self-expression, providing a means of social communication, and satisfying the inherent creative urge that exists in every human. This recognition has led to the institution of crafts programs in schools at all levels, in camps, on playgrounds, and in community centers all over the country. Such programs serve large segments of the population in all age groups and have much to offer those who participate in them.

The growing realization of the therapeutic value of crafts activities has led to their inclusion in numerous institutional programs to provide both diagnostic and remedial treatment under the supervision of trained art therapists. Such programs are designed for improvement of emotional and mental health, for rehabilitation of physical and emotional handicaps and for development and/or improvement of functional motor skills in affected people of all ages.

Thus, the older idea of crafts as just a means of "making things" must, in view of the maturing of the crafts field and the importance of crafts in today's society, be greatly revised. Crafts and the people who engage in them are fulfilling a vital role in making life better for millions of people. Let us look at some representative craft programs across the country that *are* successful working models.

**Crafts in the Educational System**
The place of crafts in art education at the college level is dealt with in other chapters of this work. A survey of current college catalogs indicates that many colleges and universities offer courses in crafts at beginning, intermediate, and advanced levels. Some offer only a few courses, such as printmaking and jewelry, while others have a wider range of choice. Some with large art departments offer bachelor's and master's degrees with concentration in crafts.[1]

Several schools, such as Haystack Mountain School of Crafts (Deer Isle, Maine), Appalachian Center for the Crafts (Gatlinburg, Tennessee), and the Penland School (Penland, North Carolina), are devoted primarily to the teaching of crafts and offer both degree and nondegree programs.

The crafts rooms of colleges, as well as secondary and elementary schools are usually filled wth students engaged in learning procedures for a number of crafts (see figure 7.2).

*(Figure 7.2) Lynchburg College crafts students work on papermaking, stained glass, coiling, and macramé.*

Departments of education in the various states issue periodic guidelines for programs of instruction in the public school system.[2] In addition to these state publications, each regional school system, whether city or county administered, issues its own set of guidelines that are applicable to particular needs and conditions in its locality. Based on conversations with teachers and supervisory personnel in a number of localities, I have discovered that because of available classroom hours, budgetary considerations, and special needs of students in a particular area, it is difficult for educators to always offer a structured art program in grades kindergarten through fifth. However, materials are made available and classroom teachers are encouraged to include art-related activities in their lesson plans. They are aimed at the development of attitudes, understanding, and appreciation of the arts as they relate to our society; at an introduction to the various arts and crafts media; and at the experience of creating objects with the hands.

It is also evident that art programs may vary somewhat from place to place within any state, because the development and delivery of a local school's art curricula is usually a local responsibility. Local programs may also be influenced by educational priorities of the community as well as by resources available to fund various educational programs. Under ideal conditions, schools should introduce students to creative endeavor in kindergarten, although it is usually in the middle school environment (grades sixth through eighth) that children are first introduced to structured classes in art. These courses revolve around "exploratory art," with the objective of presenting the elements of art, and experience in the use of various two- and three-dimensional media. Beyond eighth grade, participation in the arts is often on an elective basis, and those with a particular affinity for the crafts begin to develop their potential at this stage in their education.

In gathering material for this text, I visited a number of schools in which crafts classes were in progress. One particular school system presented art for the first time to students in the seventh grade. The course was exploratory in nature and students could elect to continue basic art in the eighth grade. Ninth grade students were introduced to principles of design and composition and thereafter could continue their art training for the remaining three grades, studying painting, drawing, lettering, and such crafts as batik, stitchery, printing and weaving, as well as basic three-dimensional approaches. The art teacher feels that crafts are all too often taught separate from art, as if "now we are going to do crafts, have fun, and not worry about good design and quality." She believes that crafts in the classroom are vital to any art program as long as the elements of art and principles of composition are a part of it, too. Students enjoy and need the experience of working with their hands to produce objects and to know that art is not just painting and drawing (see figure 7.3).

(Figure 7.3) Student works on cardboard loom to make woven wall hanging. Note dried plant materials that will be incorporated into the work.

Because of the necessity of working within a small budget, teachers in public schools are limited in the variety of crafts they can offer and must choose those that do not require a large initial outlay for equipment and supplies. Sometimes, however, extra funding for equipment may be justified as a capital investment. Considering the tremendous obstacles faced by most local school boards in trying to reconcile the need for balanced public education in all areas of learning against available time, money, specific needs of students, and community priorities, it is perhaps understandable that art programs are often the first to be curtailed. At the same time, there are many who believe that a background in art is basic to a well-rounded life and that art programs in schools should not be sacrificd in favor of other disciplines.

Paul D. Houston, superintendent of the Tucson Unified Schools, Tucson, Arizona, writes: "At a time when the nation at large seems more oriented toward the arts than ever before, the plight of Arts Education in the schools is perhaps at an all time ebb." He points out the value of the arts as being an integral part of good education, not only as a means of strengthening small motor skills, perception, and skills relating to other parts of the curriculum but also as a means of developing the flexible thinkers and creative problem solvers so necessary to contemporary society. "The arts are a whole way of knowing about the world, of understanding it, of tasting it and touching it that gives insight and value to things in ways that no other discipline can."[3]

Perhaps the ultimate answer is early and periodic testing of children for levels of creative ability and aptitude in the arts, then placing these students (after the completion of a basic elementary and middle school education) into special high schools devoted to training in the visual and performing arts.

## Crafts as Recreation

As our society becomes more civilized, mechanized, and technically oriented, work operations in the office, factory, and home are generally made less time-consuming and arduous. Human beings are thus freed from the necessity of working long hours, which together with improvements in wage scales and standards of living, offers many people "leisure in society." A decision must therefore be made concerning how best to fill this leisure time with constructive recreational activities. Michael and Holly Chubb, who divided recreation activities into sixteen categories based on percentage of participation among adult Americans, rated arts and crafts as fifth.[4] Because the first four categories are held by such passive pasttimes as watching television, listening to the radio, social visits, and reading, it would seem fair to say that arts and crafts activities could be rated first on the basis of active participation by adult Americans. The authors place sports and exercise as seventh on the list.

Richard Kraus estimated that two out of every five Americans took part regularly in some form of arts and crafts activity and said, "Millions of Americans have found new forms of self renewal in their leisure activities. . . . Increasingly we have come to realize that recreation benefits our nation greatly, both by strengthening and improving community life and by contributing to physical and mental health."[5] Sponsorship of recreational activities has been asumed not only by clubs, social organizations, and community groups but also by governmental, business, and educational organizations as they come to realize that recreational programs make for happier, better adjusted citizens because people of all ages need to play in order to keep mentally and physically fit.

Although sports activities are highly beneficial to the physical well-being of those who participate in them, recreational leaders generally agree that crafts activities, more than any other, provide opportunities for all individuals to produce objects with their hands from raw materials about which they can say, "I made this, it is an expression of something within me, of my latent creativity and here it is for all to see." This act of making something, which is usually of far more value to the individual involved than the object itself, fulfills two basic human needs: to explore one's creative potential and to communicate with others through the results of one's creative effort.

For children, the opportunity to engage in manipulative crafts experiences will develop latent talents and abilities, will challenge their mental processes through the solving of such problems as how to prepare various materials and use them, will help cultivate manual dexterity, will encourage interaction with others, and will foster pride of accomplishment. In short, creating with the hands will contribute greatly to the mental and emotional development of the whole child.

With so much emphasis now being placed on early retirement, with the average age of the population increasing, and with older people being healthier and living longer, recreational leaders must pay increasing attention to developing programs especially suited to senior members of our society. A great many older people are often already skilled in one or more crafts, and can revive their interest in these as well as learn new skills that will give them confidence in their abilities to still "do things" and fulfill their need to interact socially with others, which is perhaps more important at this age than at any other.

The city of Lynchburg, Virginia (population approximately 68,000), sponsors an excellent all-around recreational program administered by its Department of Recreational Services. This program is typical of thousands of programs being administered all over the United States. The total program, described as a highly workable model, includes athletics, children's theatre, children's ballet, ranger/naturalist programs, seven senior centers, twenty play centers, a number of parks and play lots, a community cablevision program called "All the Arts," gymnasia, and a full schedule of arts and crafts activities.

The arts and crafts program administered by the department consists of some fifty classes a year for children and adults in a wide variety of activities. For example, the 1985–86 program included classes in ceramics, drawing, painting, calligraphy, photography, stenciling, stained glass, soft sculpture, basketry, and several of the needlecrafts (quilting, crewel embroidery, needlepoint, knitting, and crochet). Classes are taught either by members of the staff or by other qualified teachers hired on a per class basis. Classes are held at the Recreation Service Center, which is a converted elementary school building. The six- to eight-week classes meet once a week for two to three hours. Nominal fees are charged and class size is limited to 12 or 15 persons. Most classes are taught at the beginners level, though if demand is sufficient, more advanced classes may be offered occasionally. Participation varies according to the time of year and will range from 150 to 300 students per quarter.

The building itself is ideally suited for the arts and crafts program, providing office space for administrative staff as well as space for the various activities themselves. Former classrooms have been equipped with chairs and long tables for work; one room has a wall-sized mirror and barre for ballet classes; another is equipped with easels for the painters. The rooms are light, clean, and spacious, providing an ideal place to create under the supervision of enthusiastic leaders. In the basement level, there is a large ceramics room where one can learn to cast in molds, throw on one of several potter's wheels, or hand-build pots from clay.

The senior centers in Lynchburg offer a variety of activities for those over sixty, including recreational and educational programs, crafts, field trips, exercise groups, and special interest clubs. A similar program for senior citizens in Clearwater, Florida, called Senior Citizens Services, Inc., provides a number of services such as adult education, employment, health services, housing, legal aid, recreation and social activities, and an active arts and crafts program. As an outlet for the sales of crafts produced by participants in the program, the Crafts Center Gift Shop was established in 1964. Yearly gross sales are now in excess of $150,000 of which 80 percent goes back to those whose work is sold.

Summer programs in Lynchburg, in addition to classes at the service center, offer activities at twenty outdoor play centers throughout the city. Programs include crafts, films, traveling arts and crafts, swimming, games, and athletic programs. Such basic supplies as paper, glue, paints, crayons, pencils, brushes, and scissors are always available for daily use. Supplies for planned crafts are brought in as needed, and three times during the summer, each center is visited by a traveling crafts teaching team that offers concentrated sessions in special activities, including such projects as the making of plaster masks, basic needlepoint, felt applique, basketry, sand painting, puppets, and batik. Ceramic programs are available at some centers. Completed works from all programs are displayed during the annual Christmas open house and the annual children's summer art show.

Obviously such a far reaching and diverse program requires a great deal of planning and scheduling (as much as a year in advance) and careful attention to the ordering of supplies, as well as constant supervision to ensure that all runs smoothly. It also requires enthusiastic, dedicated and well-trained personnel, a high degree of community interest and participation, and a city government that recognizes the value of such programs and is willing to allocate adequate funds to keep it in operation.

## Crafts as Therapy and Rehabilitation

In its broadest medical sense, "therapy" refers to the treatment of mental and physical disorders in patients of all ages through structured programs designed to contribute to the care of the patient, to promote recovery, to rehabilitate, to occupy time, to train in the learning (or relearning) of motor skills, and to improve the overall well-being of those under treatment. Therapy programs are administered by trained specialists under a doctor's direction and consist of planned activities of all sorts, depending on the patient's needs and condition. Programs may cater to children, adults, or the elderly in all stages of physical or emotional illness, with such handicaps as lost limbs, blindness, or deafness. Delinquent and gifted individuals are included also.

In recent years, the value of creative experiences in the arts and crafts generally has come to be recognized as a means of dealing with the problems of communication, socialization, self-expression, and manipulation of the environment. It is also a vehicle for fostering increased self-awareness, confidence, and esteem in those who may be isolated, fearful, confused, and often angry because of their difficulty in coping with the world around them. Arts and crafts programs designed to help patients meet these goals are usually included in the structure of most hospitals, rehabilitation centers, veteran's facilities, nursing homes, and other institutions devoted to helping people find a more useful and happy life.

A survey of the literature dealing with art therapy as a new discipline within the field of mental health emphasizes the growth of interest in such therapy during the last twenty years.[6] Edith Kramer sees art as a "basic function of human society" and as the "creating of configurations which serve as equivalents for life processes"; therefore when used as therapy, art may contribute greatly to both the diagnosis and healing of emotional problems. She writes: "Art is a method of widening the range of human experiences by creating equivalents for such experiences. It is an area where experiences may be chosen, varied and replaced at will. It is an artificial world but it has the power to invoke genuine emotions." Thus through the act of creating, undesirable instinctual urges and impulses that may cause conflicts within the individual and with those around him or her may be refined or sublimated into more constructive and therefore more socially acceptable directions. Kramer continues: "The art therapist's main field of action remains the process of sublimation wherein the material (aggressive energy) undergoes that final transformation by which it is formed into tangible visual images and the peculiar fusion between reality and fantasy, between the unconscious and the conscious which we call *art* is reached."[7]

Institutional or clinical therapeutic art programs designed to help patients cope with conflicts that arise between the fantasy within the inner self and the reality of the world are staffed by art therapists who have been trained not only in the arts but also in recreation, education, and psychology at both the undergraduate and graduate levels. Art therapists work with psychiatrists, psychologists, special education experts, and other members of the institutional staff. Training in art therapy is a fairly decent development, but more and more schools are offering opportunities to acquire the necessary background.

Lynchburg College, for example, offers a joint art-psychology major designed to provide basic undergraduate training for those students interested in a career in the field of art therapy. During their senior year, students enroll in courses that give practical field training in art therapy and gain experience, under supervision, in clinical and educational settings. Training often includes working with handicapped and/or emotionally disturbed persons. Graduate programs leading to a master's degree in art therapy are offered by a number of schools.[8] Guidelines for training in art therapy are set forth by the American Art Therapy Association and may be obtained from them.[9]

The Education of all Handicapped Children Act, passed in 1975, established the right of all exceptional children to an education in a setting as near to the regular classroom as possible. Donald Uhlin and Edith DeChiara say: "The importance and value of art in the lives of exceptional children has been more fully realized. Responsibility for developing, facilitating and adapting art programming and activities for exceptional children has been extended to regular classroom teachers, art teachers, and special education teachers as well as art therapists." Nevertheless, Mr. Uhlin and Ms. DeChiara feel that there is a distinction between art education therapy and art therapy in that "art education therapy uses art for remedial purposes in (cases of) handicap and dysfunction to improve the quality of the child's learning process (and) takes place in a school setting. Art therapy, on the other hand uses art for diagnostic purposes and assists the patient/client to meet emotional and psychological problems or disorders . . . [and] usually takes place in clinical or institutional settings in a one to one relationship."[10]

Helen Landgarten has presented numerous case studies dealing with the clinical use of art as therapy for persons of all ages in individual, family, and/or group treatment.[11]

**Crafts for the Elderly and Handicapped**
In addition to the general areas we have discussed in this chapter, crafts activities are a part of many other programs that meet a wide variety of human needs.

*Adult Day-Care Centers*
Today, about 50 percent of persons sixty-five years old and over are older than seventy-five. This statistic together with the fact that more and more women are working outside the home means that there is often no one at home during the day to provide necessary care and attention for the elderly. In order to provide supervised care for those not quite active enough to enjoy a regular senior center, yet still able to get about and want the stimulation that social interaction with others provides, adult day-care centers are springing up all over the country. These are modeled after the concept of child day-care centers as places for supervised care during the day by trained personnel with structured programs that provide diverse activities.

Two such centers were opened in Lynchburg in 1984, and while they are basically similar in concept, purpose, and program, one is a medical model and the other a social model. Both offer social, creative, and recreational activities although the abilities of those at the medically oriented Day-Care Center may be more limited due to their medical disabilities.

*Vocational Rehabilitation Centers*
Centers for vocational rehabilitation usually serve mentally retarded and physically handicapped citizens eighteen years of age and older. Although they provide training and learning experiences in many areas of self-help, one of the most important training programs is designed to develop specific work skills in handicapped individuals through the production of crafts items. Clients work under supervision in a shop environment making many types of crafts items, including doll

houses, wooden figures, plaques, aprons, quilts, jewelry, ceramics, and macramé plant hangers. Items produced are often sold in a small shop or at an annual bazaar. Such experiences give the clients prevocational training, gradually enabling them to be eligible for placement in a more advanced sheltered workshop environment.

*Crafts in Camps*
Crafts activities have always been a standard part of the programs of summer camps, both those that are privately owned as well as those sponsored by organizations such as the Boy Scouts and Girl Scouts. College teachers are deluged each year with letters from camp directors seeking students to take summer jobs as arts and crafts instructors, recreational leaders, and counselors. Indeed, this is an excellent way for students to gain experience, particularly if they plan to go into the teaching profession. In recent years in addition to camps offering a full general program, specialty camps that concentrate on offering training in a particular interest, such as in crafts, have been developed. Children learn design principles, study examples from art history, and work in several media to complete a number of projects.[12]

From this brief survey of various crafts programs, it seems evident that crafts activities enhance the lives of many millions of people, either through direct participation or through the enjoyment of products that craftspeople create. There are few people in our society who are not touched in some way by crafts and the people who produce them. In America, we began as a people who were crafts oriented by necessity; we went through a period when handmade crafts were at a low ebb because of our dependence on machine-made objects; we experienced a rekindling of interest in the crafts in the second decade of the twentieth century; this gradually turned into a true renaissance for the crafts. Now in the 1980s, crafts activities are very much a vital part of our lives.

Roslyn Siegel writes: "In the last twenty years, the entire field of crafts has exploded with energy, virtuosity, and creativity." She refers to the distinction between art and craft that has been of such concern to craftspeople and says, "Perhaps the most exciting change in crafts of the past 20 years is the blurring of that artificial distinction. Practically every notable craftsperson to emerge in recent years possesses several academic degrees, has studied both the history of art and the mechanics of technique, and combines intense practical experience with formal theoretical knowledge."[13]

## Notes

1 It is beyond the scope of this text to list specific schools and courses. This information may be found in the *College Catalog Collection* on microfiche, published by Career Guidance Foundation, 8090 Engineer Road, San Diego, California 92111.

2 The following publications issued by the Commonwealth of Virginia, Department of Education, Richmond, Virginia 23216, are typical of such guidelines: *Standards for Accrediting Schools in Virginia* adopted July 1983; *Standards of Learning Objectives for Virginia Public Schools (Art); The Child and Art: An Elementary Art Curriculum Guide for Virginia* published July 1974; *Guide, Art Education for the Secondary Schools* published in August 1971.

3 Paul D. Houston, "Why Johnny Can't Draw," *Art Education* (May/June 1988). 43–45.

4 Michael Chubb and Holly R. Chubb, *One Third of Our Time: An Introduction to Recreation Behavior and Resources* (New York: John Wiley and Sons, 1981).

5 Richard G. Kraus, *Social Recreation: A Group Dynamic Approach* (St. Louis: C. V. Mosby Co., 1979).

6 See list of suggested readings and recent issues of the *American Journal of Art Therapy* (formerly *Bulletin of Art Therapy*), Elinor Ulman, editor, published by Norwich University, Northfield, Vermont.

7 Edith Kramer, *Art Therapy in a Children's Community,* 2d ed. (Springfield, Ill.: Charles C. Thomas, Publisher, 1973), 8, 23.

8 For information about schools offering both undergraduate and graduate work in the field of art therapy see: Andrea Lehman, ed., 14th ed. *Peterson's Annual Guide to Undergraduate Study,* (Princeton, N.J.: Peterson's Guides, 1984); Amy J. Goldstein, ed., *Peterson's Annual Guide to Graduate and Professional Training,* (Princeton, N.J.: Peterson's Guides, 1986); *GRE/CGS Directory of Graduate Programs,* (Princeton, N.J.: Educational Testing Service, 1986).

9 American Art Therapy Association, P.O. Box 11604, Pittsburgh, Pennsylvania 15228.

10 Donald M. Uhlin and Edith DeChiara, *Art for Exceptional Children,* 3rd ed. (Dubuque, Iowa: William C. Brown Publishers, 1984).

11 Helen B. Landgarten, *Clinical Art Therapy,* (New York: Brunner/Mazel Publishers, 1981).

12 For a complete listing of camps of all varieties, refer to *Peterson's Summer Opportunities for Kids and Teen-Agers,* 3rd ed. (Princeton, N.J.: Peterson's Guides, 1986).

13 Roslyn Siegel, "Women in Crafts," *Women Artists News* (Winter 1985): 4–5.

## Suggested Readings

Alkema, Chester J. *Art for the Exceptional.* Boulder, Colo.: Pruett Publishing Co., 1971.

Benson, Kenneth R., and Carl E. Frankson. *Arts and Crafts for Home, School and Community.* St. Louis: C. V. Mosby Co., 1975.

Farrell, Patricia, and Herberta Lundegren. *The Process of Recreation Programming: Theory and Technique.* 2d ed. New York: John Wiley and Sons, 1983.

Fedea, Elaine, and Bernard Fedea. *The Expressive Arts Theories.* Englewood Cliffs, N.J.: Prentice-Hall, 1981.

Fleshman, Bob, and Jerry L. Fryrear. *The Arts in Therapy.* Chicago: Nelson-Hall, 1981.

Graham, Peter J., and Lawrence R. Klar, Jr. *Planning and Delivering Leisure Services.* Dubuque, Iowa: William C. Brown Publishers, 1979.

James, Philip. *Teaching Art to Special Students.* Portland, Maine: J. Weston Walch, publisher, 1983.

Kramer, Edith. *Art Therapy with Children.* New York: Schocken Books, 1972.

Kramer, Edith, and Laurie Wilson. *Childhood and Art Therapy.* New York: Schocken Books, 1979.

Kraus, Richard. *Recreation and Leisure in Modern Society.* 3rd ed. Glenview, Ill.: Scott, Foresman Co., 1984.

———. *Recreation Leadership Today.* Glenview, Ill.: Scott, Foresman Co., 1985.

———. *Recreation Program Planning Today.* Glenview, Ill.: Scott, Foresman Co., 1985.

Kraus, Richard, and J. E. Curtis. *Creative Administration in Recreation and Parks.* St. Louis: C. V. Mosby Co., 1973.

Russell, Ruth V. *Planning Programs in Recreation.* St. Louis: C. V. Mosby Co., 1982.

Tillman, Albert, and Ruth Tillman. *The Program Book for Recreation Professionals.* Palo Alto, Calif.: National Press Book, 1973.

Ulman, Elinor, and Penny Dachinger, eds. *Art Therapy in Theory and Practice.* New York: Schocken Books, 1977.

Warren, Bernie, ed. *Using the Creative Arts in Therapy.* Cambridge, Mass.: Brookline Books, 1984.

Williams, Geraldine H., and Mary H. Wood. *Developmental Art Therapy.* Baltimore: University Park Press, 1977.

# Part 2  *Procedural Instructions for Specific Crafts*

*Crafts presented in part 2 are those found to be most feasible for inclusion in a general crafts course in which space and budget considerations are important. The designs show that students receive a well-rounded education in those crafts most popular in our society. Specialized offerings, such as bookbinding and leatherwork, are beyond the scope of a general crafts course. A wide variety of crafts have been presented, including more advanced ideas that will encourage students to go forward and explore several crafts in greater depth.*

*Unless otherwise noted, all photographs are taken by the author. Step-by-step procedural photographs were made of students working in the classroom. Examples of finished works in the procedural sections are by students.*

## Introduction

The directions and procedures for the various crafts in part 2 are intended to furnish basic instruction to students in a classroom situation, where gaining a general knowledge of a variety of crafts is the goal. At the same time, the instructions are given in sufficient depth that students can progress to more advanced work. The suggested readings will furnish more detailed information than is possible to cover in this text.

Before beginning a craft, the student might browse through several of these titles and read what is pertinent to the craft he or she wishes to create. Successful craft work depends on several factors:

1   Developing an understanding of the possibilities of the craft being attempted
2   Learning the basic techniques necessary to manipulate and control the tools and materials involved
3   Developing the techniques so learned to the point that they can be used to express personal creative abilities and potential
4   Developing a sense of good design by studying basic design principles and by looking at the work of professionals in the crafts
5   Developing careful work habits and procedures that will contribute to good craftsmanship

Many good designs have been spoiled during execution by failure to pay attention to good craftsmanship. Twentieth century crafts workers in all media have been noted for their active exploration of new concepts, materials, and approaches. Reaching out in new directions has resulted in work that is highly creative and exciting. Boundaries are crossed and many diverse materials are combined, often resulting in works that are no longer "pure" weaving, mosaic, or stitchery, for example. These works are categorized by the term *mixed media,* applied to any art work that combines several different approaches and materials. Examples of work of this nature are included in part 3, "Professional Portfolio."

At the same time, the student must be aware that he or she must first become knowledgeable about and proficient in traditional approaches and historic evolution of a particular craft in order to exploit the potential of that craft. The most successful creators in the crafts are those who strike a healthy balance between the traditional approaches and the greatly expanded concepts of contemporary directions.

# 8   Coiled Basketry

The craft of coiling (sometimes called wrapping) is related to certain forms of basketry as well as to weaving. It is accomplished by building a structure with a flexible ropelike material (the *core* or *coil*), by spiraling the core into the desired form, and at the same time, by wrapping the core with yarn, thread, raffia, or some other fibrous material that binds the whole thing together with evenly spaced lashing stitches. The wrapping may be partial (some of the core shows) or complete (none of the core shows). Throughout history, craftspeople have realized that the coil method of construction results in very strong forms, and the technique has been used traditionally in the making of both pottery and baskets.

Archeological evidence indicates that almost all cultures from Neolithic times on have employed the techniques of basketry, not only to make functional containers for domestic use but also to construct shelters, home furnishings, clothing, protective armor, snares for animals and fish, funerary receptacles, and even boats and other vehicles of transport. Because there are few areas in the world where the raw materials for making baskets do not exist, it is reasonable to assume that basketry is the one "universal craft." Probably it was done long before the knowledge of pottery was developed. Indeed, woven basket molds possibly served as foundations for early pottery makers. Techniques of basketry, such as twining, plaiting, weaving, and particularly coiling, have remained practically unchanged since before 3000 B.C.

With the revival of interest in the fiber arts, it is only natural that the ancient techniques of basketry should be reexplored and adapted to contemporary creative expression. Thus, today craftspeople are using coiling techniques not only to make functional receptacles but also to construct a wide variety of forms of a sculptural nature.

**Procedures for Basket Coiling**

The only tools necessary for making coiled constructions are a pair of scissors and a needle with a large eye, such as a raffia needle. (see figure 11.37 in chapter 11).

The most commonly used foundation material is a soft ropelike core made from twisted paper and covered with a fiber mesh as shown in figure 8.1. This may be obtained in various sizes; those most commonly used are fiber cores with quarter- and half-inch diameters. Other foundations such as sisal rope, cotton clothesline, and sea grass are often used. The sea grass is especially suitable when certain parts of the core are to be left exposed. The wrapping material may be any of a wide variety of yarns, wools, and cords described in chapter 11. These may be light or heavy, depending on the size of the piece being made.

The technique of coiling may be compared to weaving, by equating the foundation core to the warp and the wrapping material to the weft. The form is built by winding the wrapped foundation coils in a spiral around itself and attaching the wrapped coils to each other by stitches that are sewn through the preceding coil. A coiled form such as a basket is most often begun from the center bottom as illustrated in figure 8.2. The base may be round or oval as desired.

It is essential that the coiling operation be begun properly. The wrapping material (weft) must be wound firmly onto the core (warp) with the threads very close to each other. A loosely wound coil will result in a flimsy piece. Steps shown in the sequential photographs and accompanying instructions indicate the basic procedures for making a coiled pot or basket form. The student should make a small practice piece to gain proficiency. Once the basic steps are mastered, the same procedure may be used to arrive at more creative results including sculptural forms.

To begin the construction, cut a length of core about two yards long and trim one end so it tapers. Cut a length of wrapping material (weft) about three or four feet long and thread it into a needle with a large eye (see figure 8.3).

*(Figure 8.1) Materials for coiling. Shown are two sizes of fiber core, sea grass, cotton rope, clothesline, and various weft materials.*

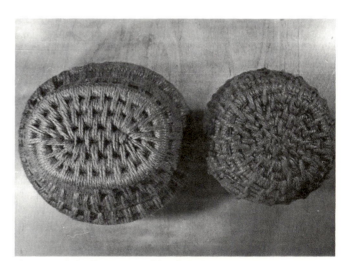

*(Figure 8.2) Bottoms of basket forms may be round or oval as shown.*

Begin wrapping the core with the weft thread about two inches back from the beginning of the taper and wind firmly to about a half inch from the tapered end of the core (see figure 8.4).

Bend the tapered end of the wrapped section back toward the main body of the core to form a loop and secure by sewing through the core with the needle (see figure 8.5).

Continue wrapping the core, covering the tapered end and bring the needle back up through the center of the loop. To hold the wrapped core in place, you may use either the *lazy squaw stitch* or the *figure eight stitch.* The lazy squaw stitch is visible and spans two or more coils, while the figure eight stitch is hidden and made between two adjacent coils. Being somewhat stronger than the lazy squaw stitch, the figure eight is recommended for larger pieces (see figure 8.6).

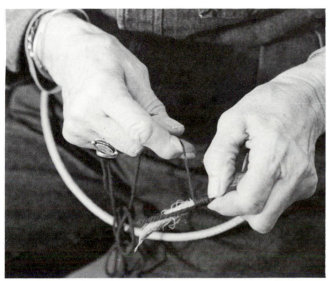

*(Figure 8.3) Beginning the construction. A two-yard length of core is convenient to work with. If length of core and weft are too long, they will be awkward to work with.*

*(Figure 8.5) Loop formed and needle being passed through center.*

*(Figure 8.4) Initial loop around which all subsequent coils will be wound.*

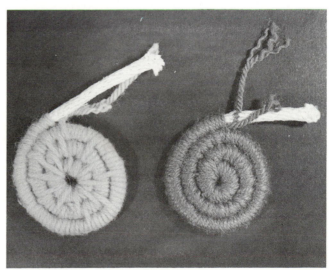

*(Figure 8.6) Left: lazy squaw stitch. Right: figure eight stitch.*

Continue the construction by wrapping a certain number of turns, placing a holding stitch, wrapping a certain number of turns, placing a holding stitch, and so on. New weft is added by laying the new end of thread along the core, covering it for about an inch with the original weft and continuing as before. New core is added by cutting a new length of core, tapering the end of both the new piece and the original core (see figure 8.7a). Lay the two tapers together and secure with a small piece of masking tape. This is then covered with the weft thread as before and the construction continued (see figure 8.7b).

When the bottom of the piece is large enough, the formation of the basket is continued by beginning to raise the core so that it rests upon rather than beside the coil next to it. Construction is continued, and the shape of the form is governed by where the adjoining coils are placed.

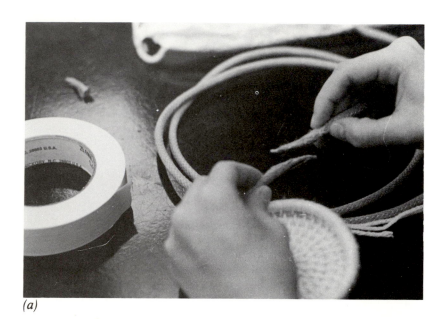

(a)

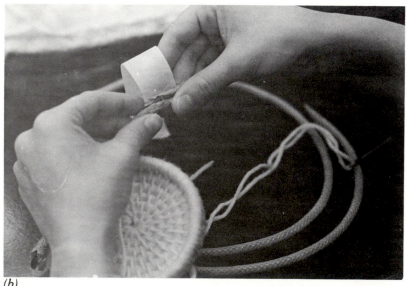

(b)

*(Figure 8.7) (a) Method of tapering ends of core in preparation for adding new length of core. (b) Tapered ends are placed next to each other and wrapped with masking tape.*

A number of variations may be introduced into coiled construction. The *lace stitch* is one such variation and results in an open or lacy appearance. Lacing is accomplished by wrapping the lazy squaw holding stitch with several turns of weft before proceeding with wrapping the core. Beads may be inserted between coils, by threading the needle through the head before making the lazy squaw or figure eight stitch. Beads may

also be attached so that they hang on the outside of the work as shown in figure 8.8.

The work is finished by trimming the end of the core into a *very gradual* taper, laying it flat against the next lower coil and stitching over both coils. The end of the thread is brought back under the wrapped portion and clipped off (see figure 8.9).

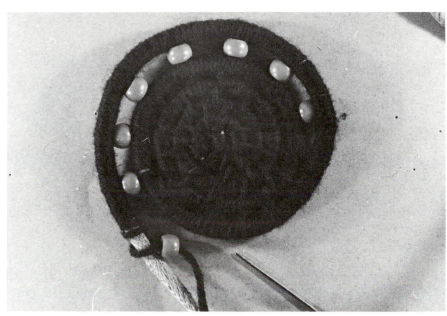

*(Figure 8.8) Method of working lace stitch and inserting beads.*

*(Figure 8.9) Method of finishing off piece.*

Coiling should not be thought of simply as a means of producing basket or pot forms. Contemporary craftspeople are using the technique to arrive at all sorts of sculptural forms and jewelry, as well as at numerous variations of the traditional basket shapes. For examples of such work, study the sections on coiling in the various references given. Coiling is also being incorporated with other techniques into contemporary fiber art of all types.

Examples of student work are shown in figure 8.10.

Suggested Readings*
Brown, Margery. *The Complete Book of Rush and Basketry Techniques.* New York: Larousse, 1983.
Chamberlain, Marcia, and Candance Crochett. *Beyond Weaving.* New York: Watson-Guptill Publications, 1974.
Fellman, Barbara C. *Fun with Baskets.* New York: Charles Scribner's Sons, 1975.
Glasshousser, Suellen, and Carol Westfield. *Plaiting Step by Step.* New York: Watson-Guptill Publications, 1976.

(a)

(b)

*(Figure 8.10) (a) Large multicolor coiled form with lid.*
*(b) Large tray form with design.*

Harvey, Virginia. *The Techniques of Basketry.* Seattle, University of Washington Press, 1986.

Kissell, Mary Lois. *Basketry of the Papago and Pima Indians.* Glorietta, N.M.: Rio Grande Press, 1972.

Meilach, Dona Z. *A Modern Approach to Basketry.* New York: Crown Publishers, 1974.

Meilach, Dona Z., and Dee Menagh. *Basketry Today with Materials from Nature.* New York: Crown Publishers, 1979.

Raycroft, Don, and Carol Raycroft. *Country Baskets.* Des Moines, Iowa: Wallace-Homestead Book Co., 1976.

Stephenson, Sue H. *Basketry of the Appalachian Mountains.* New York: Van Nostrand, Reinhold, 1977.

Thompson, Frances. *Antique Baskets and Basketry.* Cranbury, N.J.: A. S. Barnes, 1977.

Wright, Dorothy. *The Complete Book of Baskets and Basketry.* N. Pomfret, Vt.: David and Charles, 1983.

*Few if any works have been written specifically on the subject of coiling. The works listed, however, all have sections on coiling techniques or show examples of coiled basketry.

# 9 Enamels on Metal

Enameling is the art of bonding finely ground vitreous materials to metal surfaces by heating the metal to a sufficiently high temperature to melt the enamel, thereby forming a glasslike coating on the metal. Because enamels are composed primarily of pulverized glass, the art of enameling is apparently an outgrowth of glass manufacturing. It seems reasonable to assume that those ancient civilizations having a knowledge of glass would also very shortly discover how to bond melted glass to metals and clay. (Enamels are closely related to ceramic glazes, because both are composed essentially of the same chemical substances as glass.) Enamels are practically indestructible, being unaffected by time, natural elements, chemical action, and virtually everything else short of a direct blow with a heavy implement.

Some authorities classify certain decorations on the walls of the palace of the Egyptian pharaoh Rameses III at Telel Yehudia (circa 1190 B.C.) or those on palace walls and gates in Babylon (sixth century B.C.) as enamels, but these are more properly labeled ceramic glazes because they are applied to a clay base rather than to metal. The Greeks of the sixth and fifth centuries B.C. fused ground glass onto metal as decorative elements for their sculptural representations of gods and goddesses, and also used enameled pieces as jewelry. The Greeks are also credited with the development of an early form of *cloisonné*.

The Romans continued such developments, but it remained for the artists of the Byzantine era to bring enameling to its first high state of perfection, particularly in such ecclesiastical objects as altar crosses, chalices, book covers, and the like. Enamels were often combined with precious gems and gold for brilliant, jewellike effects. Byzantine enamels reached their greatest perfection during the ninth and tenth centuries. Enameling as an art form also reached high states of proficiency and sophistication in early China, Japan, and India and remains so until this day.

Any history of enameling in Europe, however brief, must mention the origin of the Limoges technique in France (circa 1450), the work of the great Renaissance artist Benvenuto Cellini (1500–1571), and the magnificent creations of the Russian court jeweler, Peter Carl Fabergé (1846–1920). For photographs of fine examples of European enamels, the student should study the beautiful little book by Isa Belli Barsali listed in the suggested readings.

Beginning in the 1930s, American crafts workers became interested in enameling and have produced some very fine work during the last fifty years. Time-honored techniques are being explored and integrated into the more contemporary approaches as the enamelist searches for new ways of creative self-expression. Although enamels have been used traditionally for the production of small jewellike objects, contemporary enamelists are thinking in terms of such works as large enameled murals covering great wall areas, and are learning to handle enamels with the same freedom and creativity that has marked other twentieth century art media.

**Procedures for Enamel Crafting**
The different types of tools, equipment, and materials needed for enameling are shown in figure 9.1.

*Firing Equipment*
The *kiln* is an insulated, steel-jacketed oven with front-loading door that either pulls down or opens sideways. It is powered by electricity and should be wired into its own fuse box to minimize uneven heating and temperature fluctuations. The kiln should be equipped with a pyrometer for accurate temperature

*(Figure 9.1) Materials and small tools used for enameling.*

measurement. Kilns are available in a variety of sizes, with the 8-by-12-by 5-inch firing chamber being adequate for average size pieces, and the 17-by-17-by-8-inch size being reserved for larger work. Firing elements are made of nichrome wire, and a spare set of elements should be on hand for quick replacement in case of burnout.

*Firing forks* are used to transfer the trivet holding the work to and from the kiln. *Asbestos or insulated gloves* should be worn to protect the hands when working at the kiln. *Trivets or firing racks* are made of heavy duty nichrome mesh and are used to support the stilted work for firing. The 6-by-6-inch and 12-by-12-inch sizes are those most often used. They should be prepared for use by going in about a half inch from two opposite edges of the trivet and bending the edges down at a right angle. This raises the trivet sufficiently to get the firing fork under it easily. Steel *star stilts* and ceramic *plate pins* are used to support the work on the firing rack during application of enamels and subsequent firing.

*Preparation and Application Equipment*
*Abrasive cleaners,* such as Comet or Ajax, and Amaco metal cleaner made up according to manufacturers instructions are used to prepare a metal. It is convenient to keep this cleaner made up in a glass container with lid so small pieces can be put into it for cleaning. Use *copper tongs* for inserting and removing work from the cleaner. Very fine *steel wool* is used for polishing bare copper, and a flat *carborundum stone* is used for wet finishing edges of trays or bowls after enameling. An *atomizer or pump spray bottle* is used for spraying gum solution onto metal surfaces for better enamel adhesion. One part *Amaco gum solution* is diluted with three parts water.

Brass mesh screen *sifters* are used for sifting enamels onto metal surfaces. Various small tools such as *spatulas, wire angles, scribers, and brushes* are used to manipulate the enamels. Various *drawing implements,* such as pencils, compasses, and rulers, will aid in drawing and sketching designs. *Tweezers* are useful in removing wet stencils from work.

*Materials—the Enamels and the Metals*
Materials include the enamels and the metals. Expressed in the simplest terms, enamels are finely ground glass. More technically, enamels are composed of various chemicals that will melt and form glass when mixed together and heated. These chemicals are silica (the glass former), borax or lead oxide (fluxes), and potash or soda for stability. When fired, this mixture results in a colorless, transparent enamel. Various metallic oxides are added to the formulation to produce color; for example, cobalt oxide yields blues and cooper oxide yields greens. The addition of an opacifier such as tin or zinc will result in an opaque or opalescent enamel.

In the manufacture of enamels, the raw materials are mixed together, heated in a furnace until they melt, then cooled and broken into chunks. This process, known as *fritting,* serves the double purpose of fusing the materials into an homogeneous state as well as rendering the lead content nontoxic. For use, enamels are ground to various sizes from 60 to 200 mesh, with 80 mesh being the size most commonly used. Commercial enamels require no further preparation before use, except that some workers prefer to wash the transparent enamels by mixing them with water, allowing them to settle, and pouring off the very fine particles that remain in suspension, thus rendering the transparents somewhat more clear and brilliant.

Enamels are available in a wide range of colors and may be transparent, opaque, or opalescent. The student should develop an awareness and appreciation of how the various enamels may be used to take full advantage of their colors as well as the interplay between the various types available. Ideally, each student should carry out tests on all enamels available to determine their appearance under various conditions of application and firing, but this is time-consuming and often not feasible in a classroom situation. The instructor, however, should certainly prepare test panels showing results when each transparent enamel is fired over copper, over foils, and over a white opaque background. Tests should also be made of the opaque enamels over a copper background. Test panels should be mounted near the workbench for easy reference by students.

In addition to the regular 80 mesh enamels already described, there should be on hand transparent liquid flux, crackle enamels in various colors, a can of separation enamel, various lusters, fine line black, a set of painting enamels such as Amaco Versa-Colors, silver foil, asphaltum varnish, and a supply of enamel lumps and threads. Uses for these special materials will be described subsequently in this chapter.

Almost any metal may be used as a foundation for enamels, however, special conditions apply to all but gold, silver, and copper. Of these, the expense involved rules out all but copper for classroom use. Some enamelists cut and hammer the desired shape from 16- or 18-gauge copper. This is a time-consuming procedure requiring a great deal of skill; so for student use, purchase commercially available spun copper forms, such as small bowls, trays, and tiles. Small stamped shapes for making jewelry items are also available. Small pieces of scrap copper are used for learning the various techniques before more ambitious work is undertaken.

*Applying Enamel to Metal*
Before applying enamels to any metal, the surface of the metal must be thoroughly cleaned to remove grease, finger marks, oxidation, and other grime. The classic method is to heat the copper to a dull red color then pickle it with nitric acid. But for classroom practice, a vigorous scouring with an abrasive cleaner such as

Comet usually suffices. The piece is clean when a film of water will remain on the surface without beading as figure 9.2 illustrates.

For particularly stubborn cases, the piece may be immersed in a commercial solution such as Amaco metal cleaner. Use tongs for this operation and rinse the cleaned metal in running water. Allow the cleaned piece to drain dry, being careful not to touch the clean surface with the fingers.

Enamels are applied to the metal in a number of different ways, all of which will be covered in the section describing the techniques. When enamel application is complete, by whatever means, the piece, supported by a stilt, is placed on a firing rack. The entire setup is lifted by means of a firing fork, and placed in the kiln, which has been heated to 1500 degrees farenheit (see figure 9.3). This temperature will mature most enamels.

*(Figure 9.2) The metal is clean when water sheets across its surface.*

*(Figure 9.3) Test pieces onto which enamel has been sifted are lifted with the firing fork and placed in the hot kiln.*

There are a few "soft-firing" enamels that mature about 50 degrees lower and some "hard-firing" ones that require about 50 degrees higher. The student will learn by observation how to judge when the enamel surface is properly fired. The piece is watched carefully during firing, either through the peephole in the kiln door or by opening the door briefly. When the melted enamel surface has reached an "orange-peel" appearance, the entire setup is removed from the kiln with the firing fork and placed on a fireproof surface to cool.

Kiln temperature should be maintained as close as possible to 1500°F. At cooler temperatures the enamels will not melt properly; at very high temperatures the enamels will be overfired and tend to burn out, particularly around the edges. Flat pieces should be weighted with a piece of heavy metal (an old flatiron is excellent) while cooling, to prevent warping. The orange-peel appearance is the result of deliberate underfiring, and all subsequent firings on the same piece should be carried to the same stage, with only the final firing being carried to the point where the surface is completely smooth and very shiny. This procedure prevents excessive burn-out of the enamel on the edges of the piece, which occurs if all firings are carried to complete maturity. After the first firing is complete, the reverse side of the piece will be covered with fire scale as a result of oxidation of the copper. Loose fire scale may be brushed away with a stiff brush; if complete removal is desired the surface is again polished as described previously. Sometimes the fire scale itself has such a beautiful appearance that it may be covered with a transparent enamel and fired, either to remain as is or to serve as a background for further decorative treatment. A number of these decorative techniques are covered in the following section.

*Basic Techniques of Enameling*
The techniques are arranged in order of difficulty from basic through intermediate to more advanced. The simpler techniques should be thoroughly mastered before proceeding to more difficult ones. *Sifting,* sometimes called *dusting,* is by far the simplest method of application and is always the first learned. It is accomplished by placing a spoonful of the enamel into a small basket made of a fine-mesh brass wire screen, which is held over the piece to be enameled. When the edge of the basket is gently tapped, the enamel sifts through the screen onto the surface of the copper (see figure 9.4). Several enamel colors may be sifted on the piece at the same time for a multicolor effect.

Enamels may be sifted directly onto flat surfaces, but if the piece being enameled is a bowl or other form with sloping sides, a coat of gum solution must first be applied with a brush or atomizer and the enamel applied to the wet surface. Enough enamel should be applied so the color of the copper is no longer visible through the unfired enamel. If one desires to build up thick coats of enamel, it is better to apply several normal coats, firing between each addition.

*(Figure 9.4) Enamel powder is being sifted onto the surface of small copper shapes. Note that the sifter is held in one hand and is tapped gently with the forefinger of the other hand.*

*Counterenameling:* All flat pieces must be counterenameled; that is, enamel is applied to the back of the piece as well as the front. The purpose of this is to equalize tension on both sides of the piece so the fired enamel will not later crack and chip off. Any enamel may be used, though most manufacturers supply a counterenamel mixture that usually fires to a neutral tweed effect. Excess enamels that accumulate on the work surface during the sifting process may be gathered up, sifted, and added to the counterenamel jar. The surface to be counter enameled is always done first then fired before the reverse side is begun.

*Stenciled enamels:* Designs may be applied over previously fired solid background colors by utilizing stencils made from paper towels or coffee filters. Definite shapes may be cut, or the straight edges of the paper used to form sharply defined areas. For use, the paper stencil is dampened and placed on the surface to be enameled, then dry enamel is sifted over it. The stencil is carefully removed with tweezers so as not to disturb the design. Excess enamel sticks to the damp paper for easy removal. Figure 9.5 illustrates the entire process.

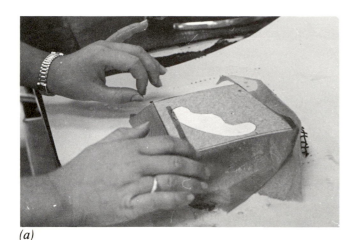

*(a)*

*(c)*

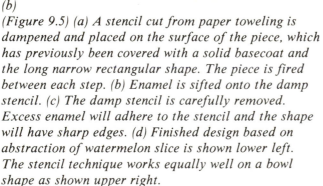

*(b)*

*(d)*

*(Figure 9.5) (a) A stencil cut from paper toweling is dampened and placed on the surface of the piece, which has previously been covered with a solid basecoat and the long narrow rectangular shape. The piece is fired between each step. (b) Enamel is sifted onto the damp stencil. (c) The damp stencil is carefully removed. Excess enamel will adhere to the stencil and the shape will have sharp edges. (d) Finished design based on abstraction of watermelon slice is shown lower left. The stencil technique works equally well on a bowl shape as shown upper right.*

Stencils may be cut from stiffer paper and used to obtain soft, hazy edges by holding the stencil somewhat above the piece while sifting the enamel. Any fairly flat object placed on the surface of the copper will act as a stencil—leaves, twigs, grasses, weeds, shells, netting. The possibilities are endless and when used creatively in combination with other techniques leads to some fascinating results. (see figure 9.5d).

*Spatula techniques (also called "charging" or "inlay"):* Various small spoon-shaped spatulas, angled wire tools, scribers, and brushes are used for placing enamels in precise designs, especially when several colors are to be aligned next to each other. Enamels may be used wet (wet-charging) or dry (dry-charging).

*Sgraffito techniques:* Designs may be sgraffitoed (scratched) through a layer of unfired enamel that has been sifted over a previously fired base coat. The fired base coat is first sprayed lightly with gum solution, then the top layer is sifted over and allowed to dry before the design is scratched in. Any pointed tool such as a scriber or pencil point is used for scratching in a design. After sgraffitoing is complete, tip the piece to allow loose enamel to fall away from the design. For variety, thick and thin lines may be combined, and in some areas, the top layer of enamel scratched away completely.

*Designing with foils:* Paillons (pronounced pie-yons), which are shapes cut from very thin sheets of gold or silver foil, may be adhered to a base coat of previously fired enamel, then covered with various *transparent* enamel and refired. The shiny foil reflects light through the transparent enamels for shimmering effects. Foils come in small packets of several very thin sheets. For use, a sheet of foil is placed between two layers of tracing paper and cut with scissors to the desired shapes. Avoid handling the bare foils with the fingers. The foil paillon is pricked all over with a steel sewing needle to allow gases to escape during firing. Spray the fired base coat lightly with gum solution, pick up the tiny paillons with a gum-moistened brush, and place them in position on the surface. Allow the piece to dry thoroughly, place it in the kiln for a few seconds until base coat begins to soften, remove the piece from kiln, and rub the paillons with a spatula or burnishing tool to adhere them to the enamel. Return the piece to the kiln for complete fusion. After cooling, apply transparent enamels by sifting or charging, and refire.

*Painting with enamels:* Prefired enameled surfaces may be used as backgrounds for painted designs. For delicate designs (similar to traditional china painting) commercially prepared colors, such as Amaco Versa-Color, may be used. Using brushes to apply the color, build up the design gradually with successive coats of color to achieve shading and details and fire the piece between layers of color. Final accents may be added with fine-line black, which is an intense black overglaze paint, suspended in an oil base. It is applied with fine brushes or pens, allowed to dry throughly, and fired. For bolder designs, grind regular 80 mesh enamel with a mortar and pestle until it is very fine, then suspend it in a small amount of liquid flux. The mixture is brushed freely onto a prefired enameled surface, allowed to dry, then fired. This technique works especially well with bold abstractions and nonobjective designs. In addition to brushing, the enamel-flux mixture may be applied by spattering, flowing, swirling, slinging, and so forth.

*Metallic lusters:* Gold, platinum, and copper lusters are usually used to apply final accents to work done by various techniques. The lusters are applied to fired enameled surfaces and refired when dry. The medium in which the luster is suspended must be driven off slowly. By inserting the dried piece into the hot kiln briefly then withdrawing it, you can accomplish this. The process is repeated several times, then firing is carried to completion.

*Threads and lumps:* Enamel threads are varying lengths of opaque enamel having the approximate diameter of heavy sewing thread. When placed on a prefired enameled base coat, they fuse to the surface during firing, resulting in a linear pattern. Threads are best used as accents; they should be carefully placed and color relationships should be considered.

Enamel lumps are small chunks of either transparent or opaque enamels, which when placed on a prefired base coat and refired will melt and give small areas of brilliant color. The degree of melting will depend on firing temperature and length of time in the kiln. With less firing, the chunks will remain slightly raised; with more firing, they will melt and sink into the base coat.

Lumps and threads are also used in the technique known as *scrolling*. Scrolling involves special tools consisting of angled metal with pointed tips inserted in long wooden handles. They come in pairs and are used to swirl or scroll lumps and threads *in the kiln* as one draws the tip of the tool through the molten surface.

Low firing transparent lumps work best; these are placed as desired on a prefired base coat and placed in the kiln. When they begin to melt, the kiln door is opened. The tip of one tool is placed on the work to steady it, the tip of the other tool is pushed and pulled around through the melted enamels. The work must be done quickly, and the hands *must* be protected with insulated gloves. The process requires a great deal of practice and should be preplanned so the molten lumps are not simply mixed around at random.

*Advanced Techniques of Enameling*
The techniques covered thus far are more or less basic to the craft of enameling and are those that should be mastered by students before going on to the more complicated ones we review next.

*Cloisonné* (pronounced cloy-sahn-ay) is perhaps the oldest known method of enameling and is so named because the design is made by constructing small cells or "cloisons" to contain the enamels on the surface of the metal. Strips of a special, flat "ribbon" wire are bent into the desired shapes and placed on edge on a prefired base coat (see figure 9.6a). When all cloisons are in place and the design complete, the entire surface is dusted with a light coat of clear flux and fired, thereby fusing the cloisons to the surface of the piece (see figure 9.6b). The cells are then wet-charged with enamels, the piece is dried and refired. The enamel should be even with the top of the cell. Often, not enough enamel is packed into the cells, therefore, it will sink too much. If this occurs, add more enamel and refire (see figure 9.6c). Because of the time-consuming nature of the technique, professional enamelists usually work with gold and silver. In the classroom, however, perfectly acceptable work may be done with copper wire. Cloisonné is especially effective when combined with foils. During firing, fire scale will have formed on the uppermost edges of the cloisons and may be removed by stoning (see figure 9.6d).

*Champlevé* (pronounced cham-play-vay) consists of making depressed areas in the surface of bare metal, either by gouging with chisels or chasing tools or by etching with acid, which is the simplest method for classroom use. The resulting depressions are inlaid with enamels. Designs for champlevé must take into account that some metal will be left free of enamel and will become an integral part of the overall design. (Review positive and negative space in design covered in chapter 5.)

The metal blank is cleaned on both sides and the design scratched on one surface with a scriber. The entire piece including edges and back, *except* the areas to be etched, are painted with a coat of asphaltum varnish or melted wax. When dry, the piece is placed in an acid bath made by one part of nitric acid to three parts water. Add the acid slowly to the water, *never* add the water to the acid. Allow the acid to eat into the unvarnished areas until the desired depth is obtained. Use a glass container, such as a small Pyrex dish, to hold the acid and handle the work with tongs. The acid will react rather quickly and must be watched closely, so it will not eat too deeply.

When etching is complete, remove the piece from the acid bath, rinse it thoroughly with water and dry. Remove the asphaltum with turpentine. Counterenamel the piece and fill the depressions with enamels by wet-charging. Dry thoroughly and fire. When cool, polish the bare copper and cover with a coat of clear lacquer for protection. The lacquer may be omitted and, instead, the surface dusted with a light coat of clear flux and refired.

An alternate method is to cover the *entire* piece with asphaltum. When the piece is almost dry, scratch through the surface with sharp tools down to the bare metal. Proceed with etching and finishing as described previously.

*Grisaille* (pronounced gree-si) is a French term that refers to a painting done in tones of gray (*gris*). It is a painstaking and delicate technique, requiring much practice. Once mastered, however, it produces some elegant effects, particularly when used for portraiture. The work is done on a panel that has been counterenameled then covered with a base coat of hard opaque black and refired. Painting is done with a commercial white enamel, or a painting mixture may be prepared with a quantity of white opaque enamel that has been ground in a mortar until it is very fine.

Draw off the excess water and add several drops of an oil medium, such as oil of lavender to the fine enamel. The mixture should resemble thick tempera paint and be very smooth. Sketch the design in thin white and fire. The picture is then built up by applying successive thin coats of white, which will gradually achieve the value range desired. The piece is refired between each application. Be careful to underfire each time or burn-out will occur during the many necessary firings. A

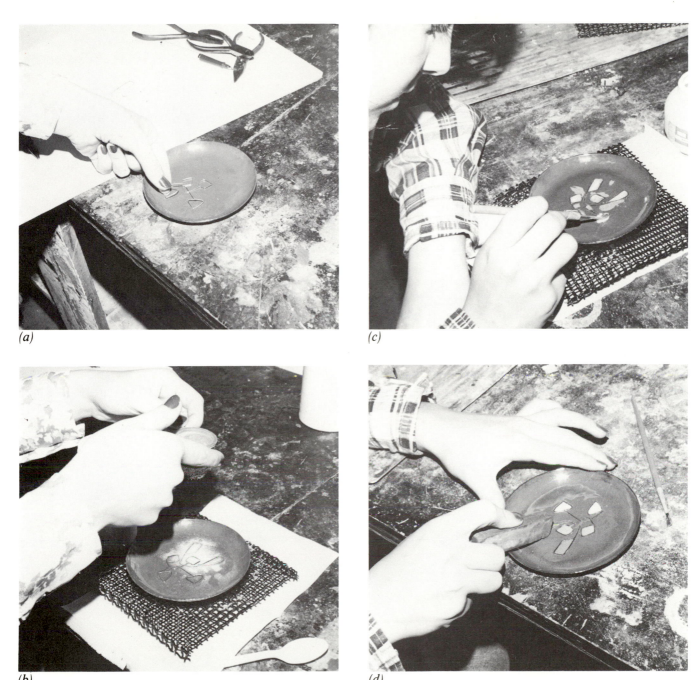

*(a)*

*(b)*

*(c)*

*(d)*

*(Figure 9.6) (a) With jewelry pliers, various shapes are bent from flat cloisonne wire and placed on the surface of a shallow saucer that has previously had a base coat of enamel fired onto it. Be sure wire shapes fit onto the surface. (b) Coat of clear flux is sifted over wire shapes and fired. This will adhere the wire to the surface of the piece. (c) Cells or cloisons are filled with various colors of enamels by wet-charging. This step must be carefully done and excess enamels removed with a small brush and angle tool. (d) Fire scale is removed from top edges of cloisons by stoning with a wet hand stone. Be careful not to scratch the enamel.*

professional enamelist friend of mine who does incredible grisaille says she often fires a piece as many as thirty-five to fifty times to achieve the results she wants. Perhaps this is why we see so little grisaille.

*Miscellaneous Techniques of Enameling*
*Crackle enamels* are specially formulated liquid mixtures that, when applied over a prefired base coat and refired, produce a random pattern of crackles over the entire surface. Crackle enamels work best on shaped pieces such as bowls and trays with some depth, and less well on small or flat pieces. They will not work on bare copper. A wide color range is available. The enamels are applied by dipping, spraying, or brushing, although the latter method often leaves unsightly brush strokes. Perhaps the best method to achieve a smooth coating is to pour the well-mixed liquid enamel into the piece, swirl to cover the surface, and pour off the excess. The piece must be completely dry before firing. Results will depend on several variable—thickness of crackle coat,

thickness and type of base coat, firing time—thus the method lends itself well to experimentation. Do not allow crackle enamels to dry out in the bottle or they will be ruined.

*Separation enamel* is a black, oil-based liquid that breaks up or separates the undercoats into interesting patterns when applied either solidly or in a design over fired base coats. The separation enamel should be applied thinly, allowed to dry, and fired to a somewhat higher temperature than usual.

Because of the many variables involved in enameling (thickness of enamels, types of enamels, variations in firing times, temperatures, additives, combinations of techniques), the possibilities for experimentation are almost limitless. Once basic techniques are mastered, students should begin to explore the craft as a means of expressing creative ideas and freedom of expression at their highest levels (see figure 9.7).

*(a)*

*(b)*

*(Figure 9.7) (a) Student work: two pieces with stencil work, sgraffito and utilization of fire scale. (b) Student work: fire scale patterns and swirled lumps. (c) Student work: example of cloissone technique.*

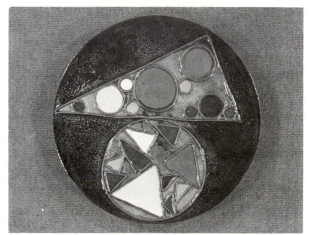

*(c)*

*Suggested Readings*

Amaco. *Metal Enameling.* Indianapolis: American Clay Co., 1968.

Bainbridge, Henry C. *Peter Carl Fabergé, His Life and Work.* London: Hamlyn Publishing Group, 1966.

Barsali, Isa Belli. *European Enamels.* London: Paul Hamlyn, 1969.

Bates, Kenneth F. *Enameling Principles and Practice.* Cleveland and New York: World Publishing Co., 1951.

————. *The Enamelist.* Cleveland and New York: World Publishing Co., 1967.

Conway, Valerie. *Introducing Enameling.* New York: Watson-Guptill Publications, 1970.

Farber, L. G., ed. *Ceramics Monthly Handbook on Copper Enameling.* Columbus, Ohio: Professional Publications, 1956.

Rothenberg, Polly. *Metal Enameling.* New York: Crown Publishers, 1969.

Seeler, Margaret. *The Art of Enameling.* New York: Van Nostrand, Reinhold, 1969.

Thompson, Thomas E. *Enameling on Copper and Other Metals.* Highland Park, Ill.: Thomas E. Thompson Co., 1950.

Untracht, Oppi. *Enameling on Metals.* Philadelphia and New York: Chilton Books, 1962.

Winter, Edward. *Enameling for Beginners.* New York: Watson-Guptill Publications, 1962.

Zechlin, Katherine. *Creative Enameling and Jewelry Making.* Translated by Paul Kuttner. New York: Sterling Publishing Co., 1965.

# 10   Fabric Dyeing

The art of coloring fabrics through the use of dyes is an ancient one, having been known in the Eastern countries long before the birth of Christ. The desire to make one's environment as aesthetically pleasing as possible is an inherent characteristic of human beings. Therefore it is only natural that clothing, wall coverings, upholstery, and other textile-oriented parts of our surroundings should be embellished with pattern and color. We know that printed fabrics were being produced in Mesopotamia five thousand years ago. Egyptian paintings dating from 2500 B.C. show textiles decorated with geometric designs in bright colors, and this tendency has been continued throughout history down to our own time.

Color is imparted to fabric through the use of various pigments known as dyes. Dyes are compounds that react chemically with textile fibers, imparting color and becoming a part of the fibers themselves. Until the mid-nineteenth century, dyes were obtained from natural sources—for example, alizarin crimson, indigo blue, and logwood brown from plants; cochineal scarlet and kermes red from insects; Tyrian purple from a species of snail; and yellow ochre and Prussian blue from minerals. Tyrian purple was greatly valued by the rulers and nobility of the Roman Empire, and was so costly that it could only be afforded by the extremely wealthy, thus giving rise to such expressions as "royal purple" and "born to the purple."

In 1856 the British chemist Sir William Henry Perkin developed the first synthetic dye, alizarin purple or mauve, from aniline (aminobenzene), which is a product of the destructive distillation of coal. Since that time, numerous other synthetic dyes have been developed and have largely displaced natural dyes for commercial use.

Dyes, both synthetic and natural, are used extensively by craftspeople in various processes such as batik, tie-dye work, fabric printing, and the production of hand-painted fabrics. Certain contemporary weavers and other crafts workers have become interested in producing their own dyes from natural materials such as walnut hulls, onion skins, grasses, berries, and the like. Two methods (batik and tie-dyeing) for the decoration of fabrics by dyeing will be described.

## Batik

Batik (from a Javanese word meaning "wax painting") is a process by which cloth absorbs dye only in the areas untreated with wax or a starch paste. The cloth is dyed either by dipping the fabric into a dye bath or by painting the dye on with a brush. Batik is, therefore, a *resist* process, because the wax or other block-out substance repels or resists the dye. Subsequent waxings and dyeings are made until the desired effect is achieved, whereupon the waxed surface of the fabric is "crackled," dipped into a final dye bath, and allowed to dry. Then, the wax is removed by scraping or boiling. During the final dyeing, the dye seeps into the cracked areas of the wax, giving the final product an overall network of tiny lines called crackles or veining, typical of true batik.

Although exact origin of the batik process is not clear, it may have originated in the ancient Asian kingdom of Sumer, spreading from there to other parts of the world, particularly to the Malay archipelago (Indonesia). The process reached a high state of perfection in Java and from there was introduced into Europe by Dutch traders during the seventeenth century. With government encouragement and assistance, production of batiks, following traditional methods, is today a major industry in Indonesia. An institute devoted to batik research has been established in Djokjakarta.

Because traditional methods of batik production are quite complicated, time-consuming, and require large vats of dyes and other materials, many contemporary Western craftspeople have developed modification of the process, which have resulted in many innovative and creative efforts. Two basic modifications of the traditional method are presented in this chapter, these being ones that I have found to be most practical in the classroom where limited available time, space, and materials are primary considerations.

### Batik Using Procion® Fiber Reactive Dyes

The basic tools and materials necessary for the process are shown in figure 10.1. *Wood stretcher strips* such as those used by painters for stretching canvas make excellent frames on which fabric to be batiked may be stretched. A range of lengths such as 12, 16, 20, 24, 30, 36, and 40 inches will permit work in a wide variety of formats and sizes. *Thumb tacks* are used to attach the fabric to the frame. To stretch the cloth, cut a piece about 2 inches larger all around than the finished work is to be. Assemble the frame, lay fabric on top, and push a tack through the fabric into one side of the frame. Go to the opposite side of the frame, stretch the fabric taut, and insert a tack. Repeat on each of the remaining two sides. Continue the process, working first on one side and then the other; place tacks about one inch apart until the fabric is stretched tightly on the frame.

*Pencils* are used to sketch designs directly on the fabric. Soft black pencils work best, and the lines will usually not show after the fabric is waxed and dyed.

*(Figure 10.1) Tools and materials for batik.*

*Waxes* used for batik are usually mixtures of beeswax and paraffin. A 50:50 mixture gives good adherance and flexibility and cracks well without flaking off. Blocks of especially formulated batik wax are available at nominal cost. *A hot plate* with variable temperature controls is used for heating the wax. *A double boiler* is essential for melting wax. Wax is a potential fire hazard and should never be melted directly over heat. The double boiler provides a safe method because the temperature of the boiling water in the bottom pan is sufficient to melt and heat the wax to the proper temperature. If the wax is not hot enough, it will not penetrate the fabric property.

*Brushes* are used both to wax the fabric and to apply the dyes. Use inexpensive ones in a variety of sizes, and keep wax brushes separate from dye brushes.

*Tjantings* of various sizes are the traditional tools used by the Javanese for drawing lines with melted wax onto the fabric. They consist of a wooden handle to which a small metal reservoir having a hollow tip is attached. When the reservoir is placed in the hot melted wax, it fills and then may be carried to the fabric for use. To minimize dripping, hold a folded paper towel under the tip until you place it on the fabric. Width of lines may be controlled by the speed at which you move the tool. Students should practice the technique on scrap fabric until they gain dexterity. Periodically return the tool to the hot wax so proper temperature will be maintained.

*Procion® dyes* are fiber-reactive, cold-water dyes developed in England in 1956 by Imperial Chemical Industries. When these dyes are used on fabrics, the dye molecules react with the fiber molecules and form a bond (thus the term *fiber reactive*), affording great durability and light fastness. The dyes are extremely concentrated, come in a dry powder form, and may be used for dip dyeing or painted directly on the fabric in selected areas. A good range of colors is available, and they may be mixed to form other hues. It is useful to make a color chart of test swatches showing various colors and mixtures. Useful data sheets are available from distributors as well as from ICI America.[1]

To prepare Procion® dyes for use, make two solutions.

1 Stock solution: To one teaspoon dry dye powder (measure very accurately) in a jar with screw cap, add one cup salt solution made as directed in the following list. Cap jar, label, and store. Stock solutions may be made and kept on hand until needed.
2 Working solution: Into a small plastic, cup measure two tablespoons stock solution. Add one-half teaspoon soda solution made as directed in the following list. Mix well and use within *one hour* for painting on stretched fabric.

*Fabrics* for use with Procion® dyes must be made of natural fibers such as cotton, linen, silk, or viscose rayon. These dyes will not work on synthetic fabrics, because the dye molecules must have natural fiber molecules with which to react. New fabrics contain sizing and must be washed before use. Light- or medium-weight fabrics are best because the wax and dyes will penetrate them more easily.

*An electric iron* is used to iron the wax out of finished work. *Large plastic buckets or basins* are used for dip dyeing. *Plastic or rubber gloves* will protect the hands from the dyes. Solutions of salt (sodium chloride) and washing soda (sodium carbonate or sal soda) are made as follows:

1 Salt solution: Mix four tablespoons of common salt with one quart of water.
2 Soda solution: Mix one cup of washing soda with one quart of water.

Newspapers and clean white paper, such as newsprint, are used to absorb the wax from the fabric after the work is completed. Commercial fabric dyes in dark colors (black, brown, navy, deep purple) are used for the final dipping of the fabric. Rit, Tintex, and Putnams are all good. Mix the contents of one dye packet into about a quart of very hot water, stirring until all the powder is dissolved. Fill the bucket or basin about two-thirds full of cold water, and mix well. Standard measuring cups and spoons are used for measuring the required quantities of dyes and other materials. Small plastic beverage cups are useful for mixing working solutions of dyes.

*Procedure*
Stretch washed, dry fabric on stretcher strips using tacks (see figure 10.2).

Sketch design on fabric with soft pencil or charcoal. Cover any areas that are to remain the original fabric color with melted wax, using brush or tjanting as shown in figure 10.3. Paint on prepared working solutions of dyes as desired (see figure 10.4).

When all colors have been applied, allow work to air dry overnight. Brush melted wax over all areas not previously waxed. The wax is applied by scrubbing the melted wax vigorously into the cloth over a small area at a time. The brush will cool quickly and must be redipped into the hot wax constantly. The melted wax *must* penetrate the fabric or it will chip off during later steps (see figure 10.5).

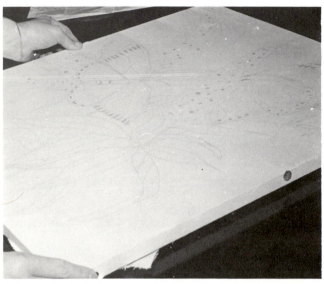

(Figure 10.2) Fabric stretched on wood frame with design sketched on.

(Figure 10.4) Dye solutions applied to fabric by brushing.

(Figure 10.3) Wax being applied to fabric with tjanting. This blocks out certain portions of the fabric so it will remain original color.

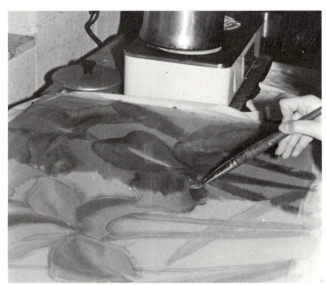

(Figure 10.5) Hot melted wax is applied to entire surface of dyed fabric.

Remove waxed fabric from the frame. Crumple slightly to induce cracking of the wax. It is a matter of choice whether to induce a great deal of cracking or not quite so much. This step will prepare the work to receive the dye, which will penetrate the cracks and produce the fine network of lines that characterize batik. (see figure 10.6).

Prepare the dipping bath as directed previously. Immerse the crumpled fabric into the dye bath and leave it for at least ten minutes. Stir occasionally with a smooth wooden stick and be sure the entire work remains completely immersed as indicated in figure 10.7.

Remove dyed piece from dye bath. Plastic or rubber gloves at this point will prevent staining of the hands. Spread the dyed work out on a layer of newspaper, roll up the fabric inside the papers, and apply pressure to remove excess moisture (see figure 10.8). Unroll and hang fabric to dry.

Wax is removed by placing the work between layers of newspaper and ironing with a hot iron until all wax is melted and transferred to the paper (see figure 10.9). It is a good idea to place sheets of plain newsprint on either side of the fabric to prevent transfer of print from regular newspaper. A small residue of wax will remain in the cloth, which does not matter if the work is to be

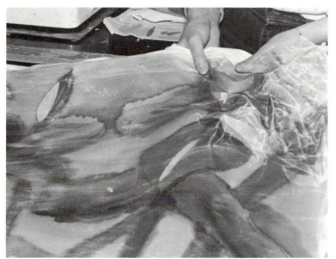

*(Figure 10.6) Waxed fabric is removed from frame and "crackled" by hand.*

*(Figure 10.8) Fabric is rolled in newspapers.*

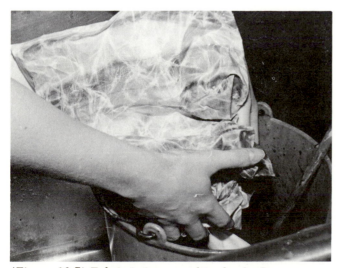

*(Figure 10.7) Fabric is immersed in dye bath.*

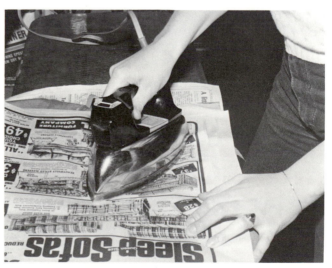

*(Figure 10.9) Wax is removed from fabric by ironing between sheets of newspaper.*

framed and used as a wall hanging. If desired, this residue can be removed by washing the piece in dry cleaner's solvent.

Examples of finished student work are shown in figure 10.9.

*Crayon Batik*
A procedure that appeals especially to younger students is the so-called crayon batik method. For this method stretch fabric on a frame and sketch design as previously outlined. Prepare colors by melting bits and pieces of wax crayons with paraffin wax in about a 1:2 ratio. Muffin tins are useful for this because they will

hold a good range of colors, and the whole tin can be placed in a large flat pan containing water for melting the wax over the hot plate. Paint melted colors onto the fabric in the desired pattern, making sure that the wax penetrates the fabric.

When painting is complete, remove the work from the frame and proceed with the remaining steps as in the regular method. An advantage of the crayon method is that color and wax are applied at the same time. It does not lend itself to quite as much control as the regular method, however, and not as much detail can be obtained.

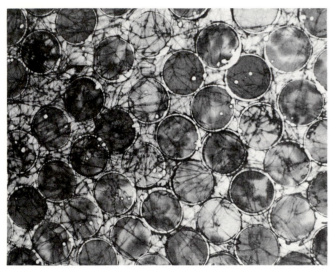

(a)
*(Figure 10.10) Student work: batik.*

(b)

(c)

*General Notes*

Because successful batik depends so much on color relationships, the student should review the principles of color theory as outlined in chapter 5. Designs for batik should consist of fairly simple patterns. Avoid "picky" details because these would be more or less obscured by the final network of crackled lines. Liquid dyes applied to fabric will bleed or run into each other. Sometimes this does not matter, and actually may be utilized to accomplish free, loose effects and to shade one color with another. If running of one color into another is undesirable, a thin line of melted wax may be drawn around all motifs before dyes are applied to the fabric.

**Tie-Dye**

The craft of tie and dye, commonly called "tie-dye" is, like batik, a *resist* process, depending for its appearance on the dye not penetrating certain portions of a fabric bound together with cord or clamps or sewn with stitches. When the fabric is dipped into a dye bath, the dye will not penetrate the tightly bound areas, and patterns will result from how the fabric was folded and bound before dyeing. The origins of tie and dye are somewhat obscure, but we are certain that the craft was known in various Middle Eastern countries as early as the sixth and seventh centuries A.D., and perhaps earlier.

In the Malay-Indonesia area the craft was called *plangi*, meaning many colored, while in India similar work was called *Bandhana*, from band, meaning to bind. The Japanese called the craft *shibori* meaning tied or knotted. Similar work was known in such far-flung areas as North Africa, Peru, Mexico, and in some middle European countries. Tie-dye is still widely practiced in the states of West Africa, and contemporary American craftspeople have adopted the techniques for their own work.

Although, with practice, a great deal of control can be exercised and rather precise designs produced, the techniques are simple enough to appeal to those who cannot draw or who have received little training in the arts. It is, therefore, an ideal craft for younger children, the elderly, and the handicapped. Because minimal equipment is needed, as shown in figure 10.11, the craft is especially suitable for programs in which budgetary considerations are important.

*Materials and Equipment*

*Fabrics:* Almost any type of fabric may be used, although natural fibers, such as cotton, linen, silk, and wool, usually accept dyes more easily than synthetics, and the results are more permanent. If synthetic fabrics are employed, dyes made especially for these fibers should be used. Cotton sheeting is an inexpensive and readily obtainable material and accepts the various dyes well. New fabrics should always be washed thoroughly to remove sizing, and ironed to eliminate wrinkles prior to use. Lighter colors are preferable to the darker shades because these provide more contrast with the dyes.

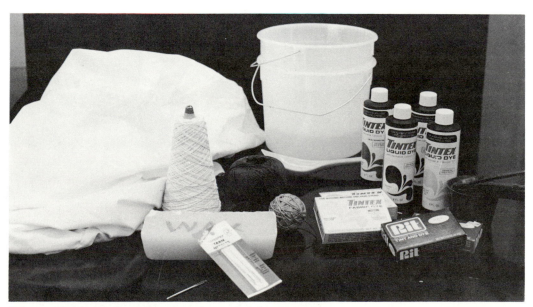

*(Figure 10.11) Tools and materials needed for tie and dye technique.*

*Binding materials:* While linen twines of various weights are most desirable for use as binding cords, other materials such as yarn, cotton threads, raffia, rope, plastic cords, wire, rubber bands, and the like may be used. Clothespins, clamps, and clips of various kinds may also be utilized. Cords and threads are often coated with wax or flour paste after binding to afford greater resistance to the dye. Binding cords should be tied *very* tightly for maximum dye resistance.

*Dyes:* For classroom use, household dyes are a good choice, because they are readily obtainable in both powder and liquid form and come in a wide variety of colors. The deeper colors are usually more satisfactory for dyeing and provide greater contrast. Dyes should be mixed according to directions. Intensity of colors will depend on concentration of the dye bath, temperature of the water, and length of time fabrics are left to soak. Experimentation will show which procedures work best under particular conditions. The fiber-reactive Procion ® dyes, described in the batik section, may also

be used, though they may be considerably more expensive than household dyes when mixed in the necessary quantities for dipping large pieces of fabric.

*Dye vessels:* Buckets and other containers should be of sufficient size to accommodate the fabric without crowding. Containers may be of plastic or glass for cold dyeing, and of stainless steel or enamel for hot dyeing. Avoid iron or aluminum utensils because these may react unfavorably with the dyes.

*General Procedure*
A variety of needles, scissors, stirring sticks or spoons, old newspapers, plastic or rubber gloves to protect the hands, jars for storing dyes, and a large sink for rinsing dyed fabrics will be needed to tie-dye a fabric. The procedure used takes eleven steps.

1. Prepare fabric by washing with detegent, rinsing well, and hanging to dry. Iron fabric to remove wrinkles.

*(a)*

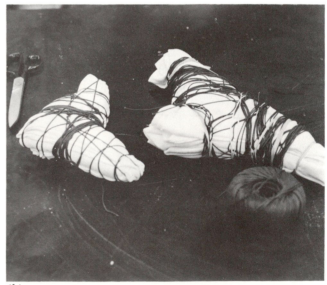

*(b)*

*(Figure 10.12) (a) Fabric being bound at intervals after having been gathered up from a center point. This will result in concentric circle pattern. (b) Fabric bundles tied into triangular form.*

2. If a definite pattern is to be followed, mark fabric lightly with a pencil to indicate location of bindings or folds.
3. Prepare fabric for dyeing by binding, twisting, folding, sewing, or knotting as illustrated in figure 10.12.
4. Prepare dye baths according to directions.
5. Dye prepared fabrics by total or partial immersion (see figure 10.13).
6. Rinse until water runs clear.
7. Partially dry fabric.
8. Remove bindings.
9. Rebind and redye if additional colors and patterns are desired.
10. Redry fabric.
11. Iron completed work.

*Preparation Methods*
Numerous techniques for preparing the fabric for tie-dye may be followed, but these can be generally grouped into three categories: binding, folding, and sewing. There are, however, so many variations and combinations within the general divisions that an almost endless variety of effects may be obtained. For example, objects such as pebbles, marbles, blocks of wood, glass blobs, beads, shells, seeds, nuts, and grains of rice may be bound into the fabric resulting in a dot or spot pattern. Fabrics may be folded or pleated in a wide variety of ways, each of which will give a different result. Running or whipping stitches may be sewn into the fabric in various shapes and pulled to draw the fabric up into puckers and folds (this is known as *trikit*), which will resist the dye and result in patterns.

Some of the more basic approaches and results are presented here. Once these are learned, the student should exercise his or her own ingenuity to explore many other possibilities. Because of wide variations in binding techniques and individual differences in approach, it is difficult to give specific instructions for tie-dye. Indeed, one of the attractive features of the process is the very diversity and virtual impossibility to duplicate results exactly.

*(Figure 10.13) Fabric being dyed by total immersion.*

Basic methods of fabric preparation for dyeing and the effects after dyeing are shown in figures 10.14, 10.15, 10.16, and 10.17.

A   Fabric is folded and clamped between strips of wood. Edges only are dipped into dye (see figure 10.14).
B   Small glass blobs are bound into fabric at random intervals using rubber bands.
C   Fabric is folded lengthwise, then back upon itself and bound into a compact bundle.
D   Fabric is gathered lengthwise and knots tied into it at intervals (see figure 10.15).
E   A square of fabric is picked up in the center, allowing the folds to fall as they will. Binding is done at intervals down the length of the bundle. This is the method to achieve concentric circles.
F   One end of fabric is bound and other end sewn with running stitches in diamond shapes and pulled to pucker the fabric. This is a combination of binding and stitching.

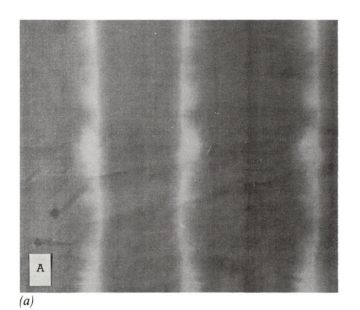

(a)

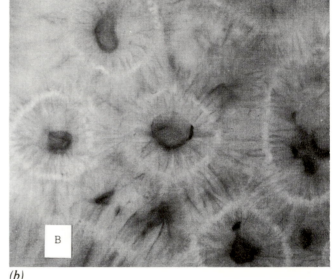

(b)

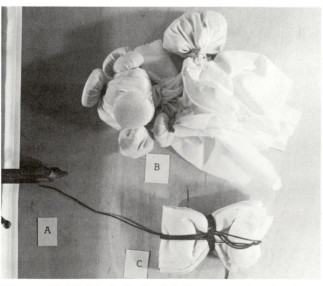

(Figure 10.14) Methods for fabric preparation for tie-dye.

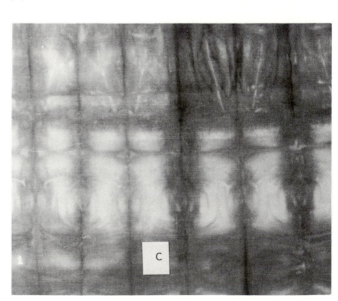

(c)

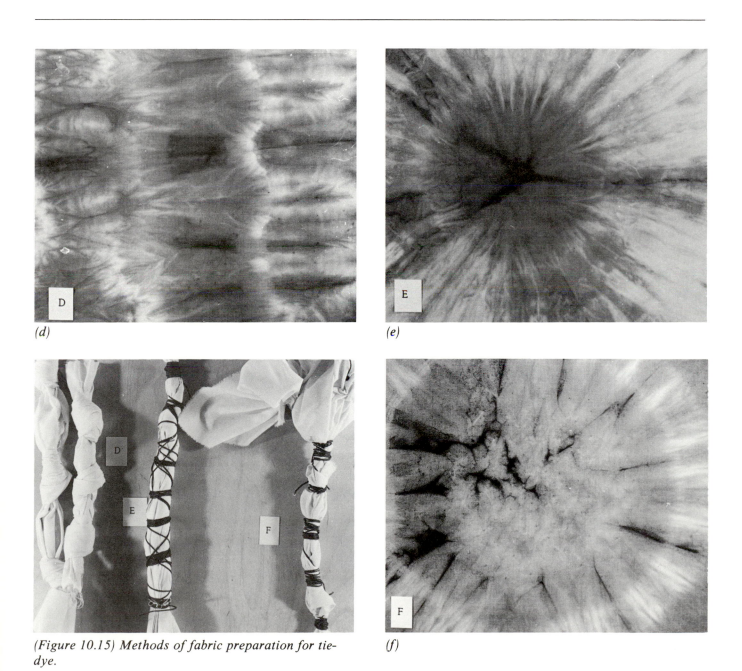

*(d)*

*(e)*

*(Figure 10.15) Methods of fabric preparation for tie-dye.*

*(f)*

G Figure 10.16 is similar to figure 10.15F except that stitching is done in center of fabric and outer portions are bound.

H Fabric is folded lengthwise, clamped with clothespins, and partially dipped.

I Large square of fabric is folded into triangle shapes by bringing corner to corner until bundle is as small as desired, and binding is as shown.

J Fabric is crumpled into a ball and bound very tightly into a compact ball (see figure 10.17). This technique is known as *marbling*.

K Fabric is folded edge to edge then rolled into a long tube. The ends are bound and the whole thing twisted into as tight a coil as possible. Bind the coil very tightly at intervals.

L A square of fabric is folded edge to edge; this repeated until a small bundle is obtained. This is bound as shown.

Figure 10.18 shows detail of student work on length of fabric dyed by various methods.

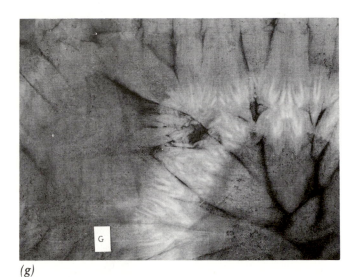
(g)

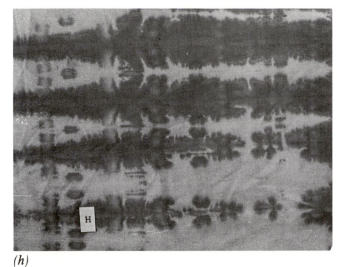
(h)

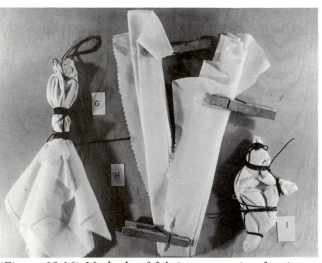
(Figure 10.16) Methods of fabric preparation for tie-dye.

(i)

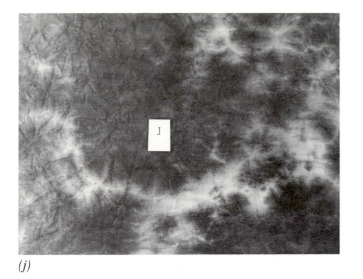

(j)

(k)

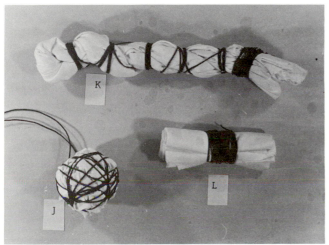

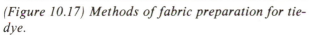

(Figure 10.17) Methods of fabric preparation for tie-dye.

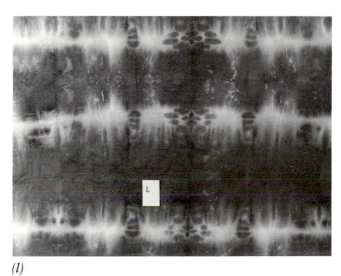

(l)

(Figure 10.18) Student work: length of fabric dyed by various methods.

**Note**
1 ICI America, Inc., 151 South Street, Stamford, Connecticut 06904.

*Suggested Readings*

Adrosko, Rita J. *Natural Dyes and Home Dyeing.* New York: Dover Publications, 1971.

Ash, Beryl, and Anthony Dyson. *Introducing Dyeing and Printing.* New York: Watson-Guptill Publications, 1970.

Belfer, Nancy. *Designing in Batik and Tie Dye.* Worcester, Mass.: Davis Publications, 1972.

Dryden, Deborah M. *Fabric Painting and Dyeing for the Theatre.* New York: Drama Book Specialists, 1981.

Johnson, Meda P., and Glen Kaufman. *Design on Fabrics.* New York: Van Nostrand, Reinhold, 1967.

Krevitsky, Nik. *Batik: Art and Craft.* New York: Reinhold Publishing Co., 1964.

Larsen, Jack Lenor. *The Dyer's Art: Ikat, Batik, Plangi.* New York: Van Nostrand, Reinhold, 1976.

Lesch, Alma. *Vegetable Dyeing.* New York: Watson-Guptill Publications, 1971.

Maile, Anne. *Tie and Dye as a Present Day Craft.* New York: Taplinger Publishing Co., 1963.

Meilach, Dona Z. *Contemporary Batik and Tie-Dye.* New York: Crown Publishers, 1973.

Proctor, Richard M., and Jennifer F. Leu. *Surface Design for Fabric.* Seattle: University of Washington Press, 1984.

Proud, Nora. *Textile Printing and Dyeing.* New York: Reinhold Publishing Co., 1965.

Samuel, Evelyn. *Introducing Batik.* London: B. T. Batsford, 1968.

Thomas, Anne Wall. *Colors From the Earth.* New York: Van Nostrand, Reinhold, 1980.

Warming, Wanda, and Michael Gaworski. *The World of Indonesian Textiles.* Tokyo, New York, and San Francisco: Kodanchs International, 1981.

# 11    Fiber Techniques

Of all the arts and crafts practiced since the beginning of time, the fiber arts (weaving, stitchery, textiles, and macramé) are probably among the oldest; yet they are the most difficult to trace historically, not only because of the relatively fragile nature of fibers themselves but also because of the utilitarian nature of the early objects made from natural fibers. Through constant use for clothing, household furnishings, and occupational purposes, the fibers simply wore out. In spite of this, however, certain ancient specimens do exist, and we know, for example, that a variety of woven cloth was produced during the New Stone Age (circa 8000–2000 B.C.) because fragments of fishing nets and clothing made from flax have been excavated from Neolithic remains of dwellings in Switzerland.

**Weaving on a Frame Loom**
Traditionally, weaving is the process of entwining two sets of threads or yarns together at right angles in such a way that a solid, flat piece of fabric is formed. One set of parallel vertical threads (the *warp*) is held under tension by some means; and other threads (the *weft*, also called *woof* or *filling*) are passed horizontally over and under the warp threads to form the solid web of cloth.

Looms and other devices for holding the warp threads in tension seem to have developed at about the same time in many early cultures. The Egyptians, for example, had looms as early as 3500 B.C. and used them in the manufacture of cloth from flax and other natural fibers. Such was the case in Chinese and Middle Eastern civilizations as well.

Natural fibers for weaving are derived from either animal or plant sources. Fibers from the flax plant are among the oldest known fibers, and linen cloth woven from flax was highly prized by the ancient Egyptians. Wool fibers obtained from the fleece of sheep were used for weaving in many ancient cultures, and numerous references to both linen and wool are to be found in the Old Testament. The Romans are credited with developing an improved breed of sheep, which became in turn the ancestors of the famous Merino sheep of Spain, source of the finest wool in the world. Cotton, the most abundant of all textile fibers, was being woven into cloth in India long before the time of Christ, and was probably known as early as Neolithic times. It was introduced into Greece in the fourth century B.C., and spread into other parts of Europe by about the first century. Silk, derived from the silkworm cocoon, was being produced in China about 2600 B.C. Silk fabrics were highly valued for clothing in other parts of the world, particularly by the Persians, Greeks, and Romans; but the manner of silk production was not known outside the Orient until two monks, under orders from the Roman emperor Justinian, traveled to China in the sixth century to steal and smuggle silkworm eggs back into Byzantium.

The natural fibers mentioned as well as some less widely used ones, such as mohair, camel hair, sisal, hemp, and raffia, were the major raw materials for weaving until the late nineteenth century. In 1884 a French scientist, Hilaire de Chardonet, developed a method for synthesizing artificial silk from cellulose. Since that time, the production of many more synthetic fibers, such as nylon, orlon, dacron, dynel, and other polyesters, has proliferated. The abundance, durability, and ease of maintenance of the synthetics has led to their widespread adoption not only for clothing but for many other household and industrial uses as well.

During the weaving process, some means of maintaining even tension on the warp threads is necessary so that the weft threads can be conveniently inserted. Through the centuries, weavers have invented many such devices, ranging from the primitive method of tying warps to a horizontal tree branch and weighting the threads with stones or another branch to modern power looms, later models of which are completely automated and controlled electronically. Somewhere in between lies the approach sought by many contemporary craftspeople— to produce a wide variety of woven objects by hand without the aid of the traditional floor or table harness loom. Such an approach is often referred to as "off-loom weaving" or frame weaving. It is to frame weaving that this section relates, because most schools and colleges offering general crafts courses have neither the space nor the budget to accommodate sophisticated mechanical weaving equipment.

## Basic Weaves

The beginning weaver can easily learn the various ways of interlocking warp and weft threads by constructing a simple cardboard loom as pictured in figure 11.1 and by making a sampler incorporating the various weaves as illustrated in figure 11.2.

Cut a piece of heavy cardboard (scraps of mat board work well) to a convenient size, say 5-by-7 inches, 7-by-9 inches, or even larger if desired. With the aid of a ruler, make pencil dots across each narrow end, making the dots one-quarter inch apart and one-half inch from the end. With a sharp blade, cut from each dot to the edge of the board, making slits all along each end. Into these slits, thread cord until the entire loom is warped. Thread the eye of a weaving needle with yarn and practice making the various weaves as outlined and pictured later in this section. To aid in threading the needle, cut a small slip of paper, fold it in half crosswise, encase the end of the yarn in the paper, and slip the whole thing easily into the eye of the needle. Instead of being slipped through the needle, weft thread is often wound on a *bobbin,* especially for larger works. Another method is to form a *butterfly* with the yarn (see figure 11.3).

The needle, however, suffices for smaller pieces and for samplers. Figures 11.4 through 11.17 show various basic weaves. In order to more clearly demonstrate the procedures, I have used a small cardboard loom on which the sizes of the warp and weft threads have been greatly exaggerated. The beginning off-loom weaver should practice the various weaves until he or she can accomplish them with ease.

*The tabby or plain weave* is the most common and probably the most used of all the weaves and is accomplished by simply lacing the weft thread alternately over and under every other warp thread, (under one and over one). Figure 11.4 shows a loom with several rows of tabby completed and the needle inserted for the next row.

Tension on the weft thread should be kept fairly constant and rather loose. By incorporating a bit more yarn than is actually needed into each row, you can attain constant tension. This step is known as *bubbling* or *arcing,* and will prevent the edges of the weaving from becoming distorted. After several rows of weft have been woven, these are pushed into place or *beaten* by means of a wooden weaving beater, or by a comb or fork.

(Figure 11.1) Cardboard loom and various materials for practicing basic weaves.

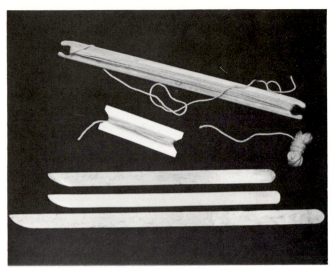

(Figure 11.3) Yarn wound on a wooden bobbin, on a cardboard bobbin, and made into a butterfly. Notice the shed sticks.

(Figure 11.2) Student work: completed sampler of various weaves.

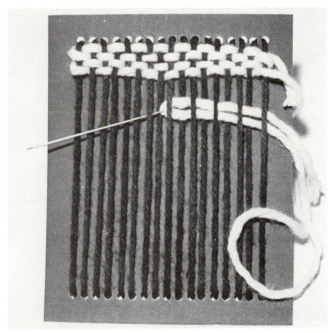

(Figure 11.4) Plain or tabby weave (over one, under one).

When a length of weft thread runs out, add new thread by weaving in the new length just below the previous one for a space of one or two inches or so, then continue the weaving. The joint will not be noticeable when the weft is beaten up. Loose ends of weft threads are allowed to remain at the back of the work to be later woven in, tied together, or clipped off.

The process of plain weaving is time-consuming and may become tedious. It may be speeded up somewhat with a *shed stick,* a long narrow piece of thin wood or cardboard inserted in the warp in such a way that its edge will lift alternate warp threads when it is turned on, thus forming a *shed* so the needle can be quickly passed through. Weave the next row by flattening the shed stick and working the weft thread through as usual (see figure 11.5).

When weaving larger panels it is well to incorporate several rows of tabby weave at each end (the *heading*) to give more stability to the finished piece (see figure 11.6). Many variations of the tabby weave are possible:

for example, over two, under two; over one under two; over three under one. Each will result in a slightly different texture as shown in the figures.

*Color changes* may be affected in several ways. When weaving rows of tabby the width of the piece, introduce the new color just as previously described for adding new lengths of the same color (see figure 11.7).

The *interlocking* method is useful when two areas of color join each other. Weft threads of one color are looped through weft threads of the other color, the joint occurring between the two weft threads as shown in figure 11.8.

The *dovetail* method is similar to interlocking, except that where two colors join they share a warp thread but are not actually looped together as figure 11.9 shows.

A third method is the *slit* technique in which the two colors do not actually join or even touch, and an opening or negative space is left between two warp threads (see figure 11.10).

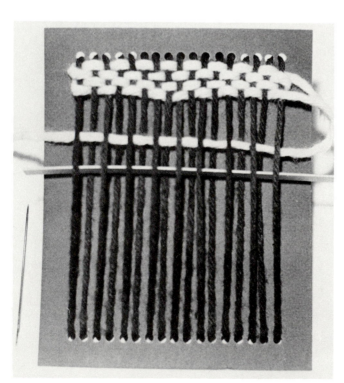

*(Figure 11.5) Shed stick used to raise alternate warp threads.*

*(Figure 11.6) Variations of tabby weave.*

*(Figure 11.7) Method of adding second color of yarn.*

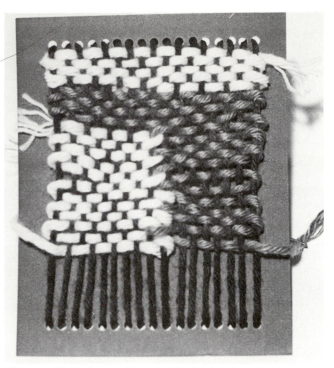

*(Figure 11.9) Dovetail method of joining areas. Compare with interlocking method.*

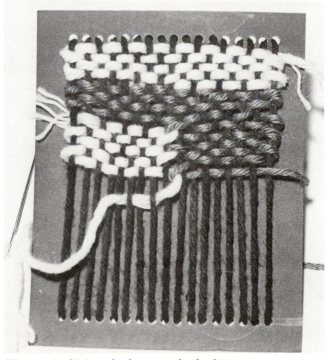

*(Figure 11.8) Interlocking method of joining two areas.*

*(Figure 11.10) Slit technique.*

The weaver is not bound to straight edge color changes, but may combine them with diagonals to achieve practically any shape desired (see figure 11.11)

*Additional Weaves*
In addition to the basic weaves already described, there are numerous other ways to introduce textural variety and interest into a woven piece.

With the *soumak* knot, the weft thread circles each warp thread by passing over the warp, then looping behind it and back over itself in front as figure 11.12 illustrates. The *Egyptian* knot is the exact opposite of the soumak, the weft thread being passed under the warp then looped over the front and crossing itself in back (see figure 11.13). In figures 11.12 and 11.13, note the difference in the textures of the rows of soumak and Egyptian weave. The rows are separated by rows of

tabby. Both the soumak and the Egyptian knot may be varied by changing the pattern of warps used, for example, over four and back under two, and so forth.

Another method of adding interest is to wrap the warp threads with weft yarn. Single, double, or even triple warps may be wrapped, resulting in long open areas or negative spaces as figure 11.14 shows.

Both cut and looped pile may be incorporated into weaving. Cut pile is achieved by use of the *ghiordes* knot, which is made with cut lengths of yarn. Each length is placed over two warp threads, the ends brought behind the warps, then pulled through to the front (see figure 11.15). For maximum durability, rows of ghiordes knots should be held in place with alternating rows of tabby. A variation of the ghiordes knot may be obtained by looping the cut length around only one warp thread as shown in figure 11.16.

*(Figure 11.11) Diagonal color areas.*

*(Figure 11.12) Method of doing the soumak knot.*

*(Figure 11.13) Method for Egyptian knot.*

*(Figure 11.15) Method for the ghiordes knot.*

*(Figure 11.14) Methods of wrapping warp threads.*

*(Figure 11.16) Variation of the ghiordes knot.*

Looped pile is achieved through use of the *rya* knot, which is similar to the ghiordes knot but makes use of a continuous warp thread rather than cut lengths. The loops are woven around a flat stick or piece of cardboard that helps control the length of the pile. Again, for strength, rows of rya should be held in place by rows of tabby (see figure 11.17).

Many other weaves are possible, and instructions for these may be found in weaving manuals. Those listed here are the most commonly used but imaginative use will provide the weaver with many variations and interesting effects.

*Frames and Foundations*
Weaving frames serve to hold the warp threads under tension, so weft materials may be easily incorporated. They may be as simple as a frame made from four artist's canvas stretcher strips fastened firmly together, with rows of small nails spaced evenly across the two ends. On the other hand, frames may be as complex as a large floor-model multiple harness mechanical loom designed to weave lengths of fabric up to 60 inches wide. For the crafts classroom, it is practical to have the shop construct several frame looms similar to that shown in figure 11.18.

*(a)*

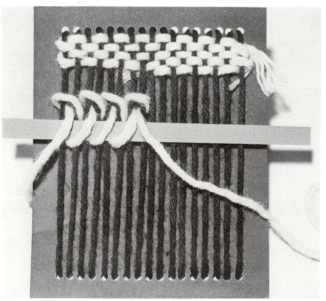

*(Figure 11.17) Method of forming the rya knot.*

*(b)*

*(Figure 11.18) (a) Weaving frame. Note two metal rods to aid in keeping edges of weaving straight. (b) Close-up of notched end of weaving frame. Note center brace that provides strength.*

The frame is made from strips of hardwood (maple in this case though oak or other wood may be used) measuring 1 ½ inches wide, ¾ inch thick, and 20-by-40 inches square, which is a convenient size for wall hangings. The frame is put together with brass screws and is protected with several coats of clear varnish. The assembly is braced with a sturdy center bar. Forty-seven notches placed ⅜ inches apart are cut into the end strips, and a slender metal rod is inserted lengthwise into holes on either side of the frame to aid in keeping the edges of the weave from bowing in because of too much tension on the weft yarn. Commercial frames may be ordered from crafts supply houses and come in a variety of sizes.

The simple cardboard loom described earlier may be adapted by substituting a thin piece of composition board, such as masonite, for the cardboard. Evenly spaced notches are cut or filed in the ends to hold the warp threads. Strips of ½-inch wood are glued across the top surface of the board about ½ inch from each end to furnish additional strength and to keep the weaving raised from the surface of the board. These foundation boards may be made in any convenient size and shape other than rectangular: squares, circles, ovals or even free form shapes are good.

Metal and rattan rings and hoops in various sizes (such as those used for macramé) are available from crafts supply houses; these may be warped and used as weaving frames. In this case, the frame usually becomes a part of the finished weaving (see figure 11.19).

Some weavers search out odd-shaped small tree branches and fashion looms from them. Again, these are usually incorporated into the final design. Odd-shaped pieces of driftwood make interesting weaving foundations.

Warping the frame loom should be carefully done and is more easily carried out if two persons work together, one stretching the warp and the other maintaining proper tension. Warp threads should be stretched fairly tightly to minimize stretching and loosening while the work is in progress (see figure 11.20).

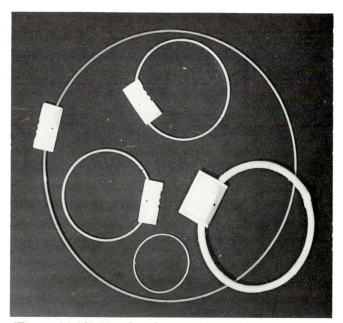

(Figure 11.19) Metal and rattan rings that may be used as weaving frames.

(Figure 11.20) Method of warping the frame loom.

*Weft Materials*

Contemporary weavers make use of a wide variety of fibers, both natural and synthetic. A visit to a yarn supply shop is an exciting experience, and the range of yarns almost overwhelming. Threads may be thick, thin, or a combination of both and range in color through the entire spectrum. Add to this array of yarns such materials as raffia, wire, plastic cords, leather thongs, dried grasses, sisal, jute, and the like, and it is evident that the weaver has available an infinite number of possibilities for materials to use in designing exciting and creative expressions (see figure 11.21).

Many supply houses furnish sample cards of the fibers they carry, and these provide an easy way to become familiar with various materials (see figure 11.22).

The weaving student should pay careful attention to color combinations and employ a scheme that will be pleasing to the eye. A good approach for the beginner is to assemble on the work table all yarns to be used in a piece to determine their compatibility. A monochromatic scheme using various intensities and values of the same color family is simple to work with,

and a combination of earth tones is almost always pleasing. A review of color principles as outlined in chapter 5 is recommended.

A characteristic of contemporary weavings is that they often not only have several varieties of fibers but also such objects as dried plant parts, beads, pine cones, seed pods, shells, bells, or bits of driftwood as well as numerous other objects incorporated into the design. Certainly this is a far cry from the traditional concept of weaving, but as in most crafts of our time, exploration of new materials, methods, and approaches has become a major motivating force. Weaving can no longer be placed in the narrow confines of utilitarian concept of fabrics for clothing and draperies, or even for decorative tapestries to hang on the wall.

Although much frame weaving is *single weave* consisting of the utilization of warp threads existing in a single plane, it is also possible to warp both sides of the weaving frame so that two layers of fabric result, which is termed *double weave*. The two layers may be kept separate or may be interconnected as desired. A great deal of negative space is often left in the top layer,

*(Figure 11.21) Various weft materials including knitting and rug yarns, novelty yarns, jute, raffia, and so forth.*

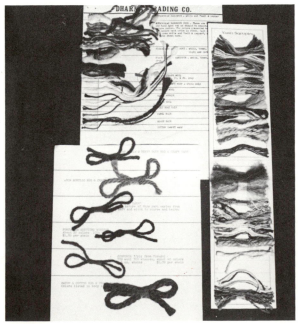

*(Figure 11.22) Sample cards from various yarn suppliers.*

allowing the bottom layer to show through. Double woven pieces are sometimes joined at both sides, thus forming a piece of *tubular weaving* that may be further modified by stuffing to make a three-dimensional form.

## Finishing

When a weaving is completed, regardless of the method of execution, some means of final finishing is usually necessary. If made on a loom, the work must be carefully removed from the loom by freeing the warp threads from the holding notches. As each loop formed by two warp threads is removed, it may be twisted and the resulting loop slipped over a small dowel rod. A strip of facing, made from linen or other sturdy fabric, may be sewn on the back of the work at top and bottom. If these strips are left open at the ends, metal or wooden rods may be slipped into the openings, thus providing both a means for hanging and a weight for the bottom. Long ends of warp cords at the bottom of the piece may be needle woven back into the work, or may be tied together at intervals to make a fringed edge. Additional cords may be tied in if heavier fringe is desired. Tassels are easily constructed to finish the bottom of the work. The method of tassel construction is shown in figure 11.23.

*(Figure 11.23) Method of tassel construction.*

## Other Weaving Approaches

Though the scope of this section is limited to off-loom or frame loom weaving, a brief description of some other approaches is given. References listed in the suggested readings will be helpful in further exploration.

*The multiple harness loom* are mechanical looms usually characterized by the number of *harnesses* or sets of *heddles* they employ. A harness is a device that raises or lowers a set of warp threads. Simple looms are usually two-harness looms, which means that the warps are divided into two sets of threads. During weaving, the harness lifts one set consisting of every other warp thread, thus forming the shed for the shuttle holding the weft to be passed through. This set of warps is then lowered and the other set raised so the weft can be passed through in the opposite direction. This is continued over and over until a length of fabric is developed. More complicated looms may have four or eight or twelve harnesses, enabling the weaver to manipulate more sets of threads and thus create intricate patterns and special weaves.

The *Inkle loom* is a two-harness loom designed especially for the weaving of long narrow bands of material to be used for such items as belts and straps for guitars and cameras. Bands may be joined together to achieve more width if desired.

The *backstrap loom* is a loom in which the weaver's weight pressing against a band around his or her waist (the backstrap) produces the necessary tension to keep the warp threads taut. Looms of this type originated in several primitive Asian and South American cultures, and even today are still used in Mexico and Guatemala. Backstrap looms have become particularly popular among young weavers, because they are easy to make, may be rolled up and carried around, and are fun to use.

A *card* or *tablet loom* is a cousin of the backstrap loom, and was developed in European and Asian cultures perhaps as long ago as the Bronze Age. Sets of cards (usually square but sometimes other shapes as well) numbering from ten to fifty are punched with holes near each corner of a card. Warp threads are strung through the holes, the ends tied together, and each end fastened to a hook or some other object to produce tension.

During the weaving, the cards are held in the hands and turned progressively so sheds are created through which the weft may be passed. Card weaving usually follows a predetermined, often quite intricate pattern.

*Sculptural weaving* has been created by weavers and other fiber artists who are, in recent years, no longer satisfied with producing flat woven panels and like objects. By turning toward three-dimensional expressions, these artists have woven fibers into more and more sculptural forms. A three-dimensional fiber form occupies space and is just as valid as a piece of sculpture as a stone or wood carving. Museums are beginning to hang fiber forms along with more traditional sculptural works. Fiber sculptures are often quite large and heavy, so their creators must not only solve problems of design and execution but also must consider such technical problems as hanging methods, weight distribution, and proper display (see student's works in figure 11.24).

**Macramé**
The tieing of knots is one of the oldest and most useful of human skills, which quite possibly has been a part of the knowledge of every culture since the beginning of time. Indeed, one wonders if the tieing of knots might not be one of those instinctive human traits that does not have to be learned. In any case, ropes and cords of various materials tied together with knots have been used for centuries to make such utilitarian objects as fishing nets, hammocks, bags, and pouches.

Prehistoric peoples made use of knotted animal sinews, vines, and grasses to tie arrowheads to shafts, stone axe heads to handles, and hooks to fish lines. Timbers were tied together to form the framework for crude dwellings and to make rafts. Peruvian Indians developed a sophisticated system of counting, using knots to record dates and business transactions (the quipa or knot-record) as well as to send messages. Sailors of such

*(a)*
*(Figure 11.24) (a) Student work: large round metal ring was bent into oval shape and made a part of the weaving. (b) Student work: panel woven on frame loom. Note method of attaching to dowel rods for hanging. Mostly tabby weave and variations with a textured area for variety. (c) Student work: panel woven on frame loom. Note loose treatment with negative spaces and insertion of various weeds and grasses.*

early seafaring cultures as Egypt, Phoenicia, and Greece used knotted ropes to rig sails, to lift cargoes, and to moor vessels.

Literature is full of references to the use of knots as a part of religious ceremonies and magical rites. The knot is also the basis of many supersitions; for example, in many primitive cultures, a pregnant woman is not supposed to wear a knot of any kind on her person, lest she experience a difficult delivery. Cowboys in many countries have traditionally learned the art of "sennit braiding" for making chin straps, whips, bridles, and other harness parts.

Ornamental knot work or macramé probably originated with early medieval Middle Eastern weavers, who tied the warp ends of woven rugs into a fringe of decorative patterns. The word macramé itself is of Arabic origin, coming from *mikrame* (towel or napkin) and *migramah*

(veil or protective covering). During the sixteenth century, the French were doing a form of decorative knotting called *filet de carásiere* and the Italians were making a knotted lace called *punto a groppo*. Both are quite similar in technique to what we now call macramé.

As already noted, practical knot work (marlinespike seamanship) was, of necessity, learned by seafaring men of all nations. Many sailors turned their knowledge of knotting into a pastime during long voyages to make many intricately patterned objects such as mats, lanyards, picture frames, purses, belts, and decorative coverings of all kinds for sea chests, bells, and other shipboard fittings. Such items, sometimes called "Macramara's lace," were also popular as gifts for family members or used for barter ashore.

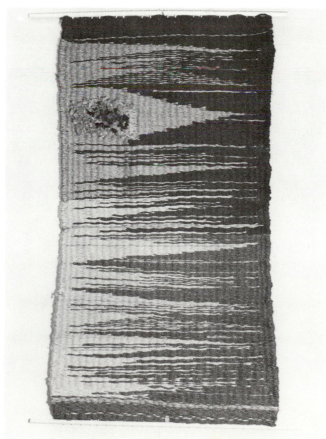

*(b)*

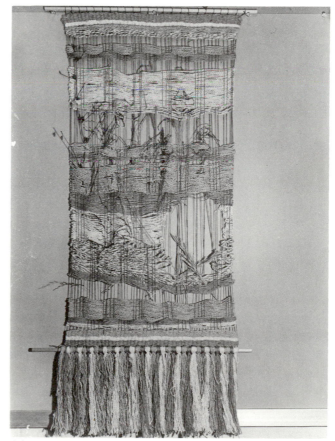

*(c)*

The revival of interest in all the crafts in the 1960s led to great popularity of macramé, in particular for the making of wearing apparel, bags, belts, and objects for the home, such as large wall hangings. Macramé is often combined with other fiber media as noted in the section on stitchery.

*Materials*
Because the basis of macramé is the tieing of knots with the fingers, little else other than the cords and twines used to make the knots is necessary. A few "T" pins, a foundation board, scissors, and some rubber bands will be useful while working (see figure 11.25).

Many types of strings and cords may be used for macramé, as long as they are reasonably firm, have a minimum of "stretch," and will hold up under the use the finished article will receive. Size and purpose of the finished work will have a great deal of bearing on the

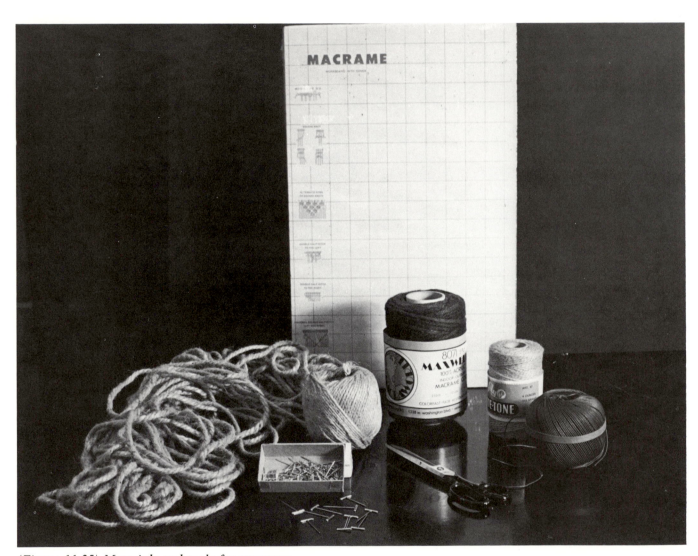

*(Figure 11.25) Materials and tools for macrame.*

cords selected. For the beginner, perhaps the best choice is a fairly heavy, natural color of jute twine, sometimes called macramé cord and sold in most crafts shops.

While work is in progress, twine may be kept uniform by working on a knotting board. This is a piece of thick rigid material, such as Celotex® cork or heavy cardboard, to which the foundation cord may be attached with pins or clips and the work pinned while it

is in progress. It is helpful to cover the board with a piece of heavy paper that has been ruled into one-inch squares; this will aid in keeping rows of knots and edges even as figure 11.26 depicts.

The foundation cord, which must be kept taut while working, may also be stretched between two "C" clamps attached to the work table or stretched between two nails placed on opposite sides of a door facing (see

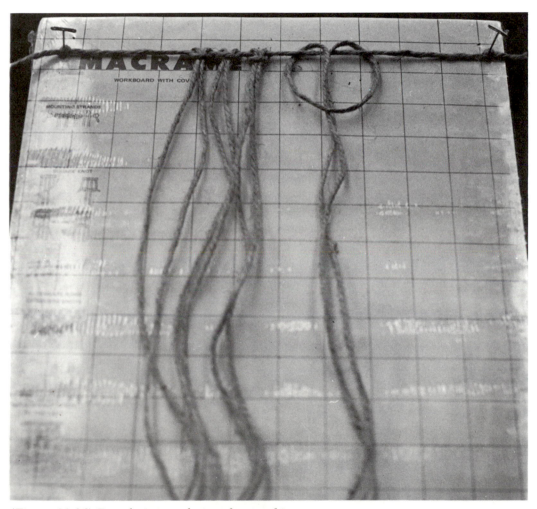

*(Figure 11.26) Foundation cord pinned to working board. Four working cords cast on with lark's head knot.*

figure 11.27). Very large pieces of work may be conveniently supported by a special "A" frame made of pieces of 2-by-4-inch lumber and commercial sawhorse clamps as illustrated in figure 11.28.

Successful macramé depends on the practicing of the various knots until they can be tied with ease. Once they are mastered, it is helpful to make a sampler, such as the one shown in figure 11.29, that will not only give additional practice in making the knots but will also serve as a permanent reference chart. Though a finished piece of macramé often appears to be quite complicated, most macramé is based on two easy-to-learn knots. There are, of course, many variations of the basic knots, but once the standard knots (the square knot and the double half hitch knot) are learned results

*(Figure 11.27) Foundation cord stretched between "C" clamps. Note working cords cast on it.*

*(Figure 11.28) "A" frame designed to hold large and heavy works.*

are limited only by the students' creativity and ambition. Students should analyze the demonstration photographs, follow each step carefully, and practice tieing the knots until they are mastered.

### The Basic Knots

The cords that are used to make the knots are called *working cords* and must be held in place on a horizontal *foundation cord* stretched by one of the methods previously described. The foundation may also be a wood or metal dowel rod, a ring, a small tree branch, or a piece of driftwood.

Attaching the working cords to the foundation is called *casting on* or *mounting* and may be accomplished in one of two ways, either with the *lark's head knot* or the *reverse lark's head* knot. To tie the lark's head, cut a length of cord and fold in half to make a loop. Place loop under the foundation with the loop pointing *down*.

*(Figure 11.29) Student "sampler" made entirely from the knots described in this chapter.*

Bring ends of cord over the foundation, pull ends through the loop, and tighten. Continue until the desired number of cords are mounted (see figure 11.30a). To make the reverse lark's head, place loop under the foundation with the loop pointing *up,* and bring ends of cord through the loop as before. The principal difference in the two methods is that with the larks head a horizontal ridge is formed along the bottom of the foundation.

The square knot is one of the two essential macramé knots and is tied with four cords as shown in figure 11.30b The two center cords are the anchor cords and the two outer cords are the knotting or working cords and are tied around the anchor cords as shown to make the finished knot. The square knot is sometimes called a flat knot, a reef knot, or a Solomon's knot. It is helpful to the beginner when practicing to use two different colored cords in order to see how the cords move from one side to the other.

The double half hitch (also called the clove hitch) is the second essential knot and is versatile in that it can be tied horizontally, diagonally, or vertically to form numerous pattern variations. Figure 11.31a shows the basic double half hitch tied from left to right. The left cord becomes the anchor cord and is pinned to the work board horizontally. Each other strand is then tied

individually around the anchor cord, resulting in a horizontal ridge of knots. When the left to right row is completed, the direction of the anchor cord is reversed and pinned horizontally from right to left, and again, each individual cord is tied around it as shown in figure 11.31b.

Diagonal hitching is accomplished by pinning the two outer cords at the desired angle and using the same hitching knot as before; tie individual cords onto the diagonal anchors as shown in figure 11.31c. The double half hitch may also be tied vertically as shown in figure 11.31d. This differs from horizontal and diagonal hitching in that the cord formerly used as the anchor becomes the knotting cord, being tied around each individual vertical strand.

Once variations of the clove hitch are learned, they can be worked into all sorts of attractive variations as illustrated in the sampler in figure 11.29.

*Additional Knots*
While a great deal of work can be done using only the two basic knots, the student will want to eventually learn more knots to add variety to macramé. Two such knots are described and numerous others may be found in various books in the suggested readings list.

*(a)*

*(b)*

*(Figure 11.30) (a) Method of mounting working cords on a dowel using the lark's head knot. (b) Method of tieing the square knot. Left, knot after tieing and moving to the top. Right, cords in position to be tied. It is helpful to use cords of two colors in learning this knot.*

*(a)*

*(c)*

*(b)*

*(d)*

(Figure 11.31) (a) Method of tieing the double half hitch knot. (clove hitch). Note that the anchor cord is pinned so that it stretches horizontally across the workboard and that the working cord is tied around it. (b) Reversing direction of the anchor cord and beginning to tie row of half hitches from right to left. (c) Arrangement of anchor cords for making rows of diagonal half hitches. (d) Method of tieing the double half hitch vertically.

The *overhand* knot is a very simple knot that may be used by itself to form patterns or alternated with the basic knots for design variations within the work. The overhand knot may be tied with either a single cord or with double cords as shown in figure 11.32. This knot is often used when a rather open or lacy appearance is desired. Overhand knots are also used to tie beads and other added materials in place.

The *Josephine* knot (also called the Garrick's bend) is a very decorative knot that may be tied singly (two cords) or doubly (four cords) as shown in figure 11.33.

Rows of vertically tied knots of the same type result in a *sennit* (see figure 11.34). Square knots tied successively will result in a flat sennit, while a twisted sennit will result if *half knots* are tied successively. The half knot is simply one half of a square knot.

*Working Methods*
When beginning a macramé work, a wall hanging, for example, the number of cords to be mounted depends on the width the finished piece is to be and the thickness of the cord being used, both of which are easy to determine. The length of the cords to be mounted is not

*(Figure 11.32) Method of tieing single and double overhand knot.*

*(a)*
*(Figure 11.33) (a) Method of tieing the single Josephine knot. (b) Method of tieing the double Josephine knot.*

*(b)*

always so easy to estimate, depending on the thickness of the cords, the type of knotting, the density of the piece, and so on. A general estimate is to cut cords four to six times the length the finished piece is to be, which means that when the cords are cut, doubled, and mounted, each working *strand* will be two or three times the length of the work. Underestimating length is not a tragedy, however, because additional lengths of cord may be added fairly easily as the work progresses.

Handling the many long cords required for a piece of macramé can lead to confusion unless a logical procedural organization is followed. Once the cord length is estimated, each cord should be cut and immediately cast onto the foundation dowel until the required number of cords are in place. Most of the length of each individual cord should be formed into a bundle (called a *butterfly*) and secured with a rubber band. As knotting proceeds, cord is released from these butterflies as needed.

When it is necessary to add additional lengths of cord, a simple method is to attach the two ends with a special fabric glue. Slightly fray the two ends, splice together by twisting, and apply the glue. Ends may also be sewed together with a needle and thread or even knotted, provided the knot can be hidden or worked into the pattern.

Such materials as beads, shells, metal tubing, wooden shapes, feathers, seed pods, and numerous other objects may be added to create interest in a macramé work. These must, of course, be chosen carefully to harmonize with the design, color, and mood of the work. The objects are usually tied to the work, or, in the case of beads, strung onto working cords. In any event, added objects should be firmly attached to the piece.

Macramé pieces may be finished or ended in various ways. Cord ends may be left hanging as they are, may be partially unraveled, or may be combed to further

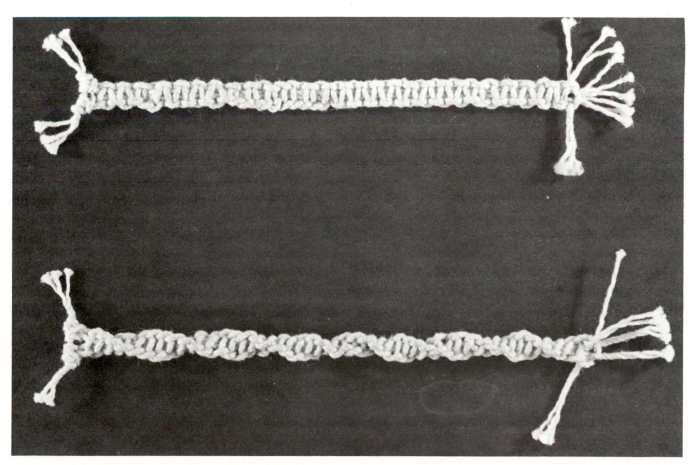

*(Figure 11.34) Top, a sennit of square knots that lies flat. Bottom, a sennit of half knots that twists around itself.*

release the individual filaments. Several cords may be gathered together and wrapped with an adjoining cord or another of a contrasting color. Several cords may be tied together with randomly placed overhand knots or knotted individually. Overhand knots may be combined with beads and various types of tassels may always be added. Again, the ending chosen should enhance rather than detract from the piece.

Today, while often making utilitarian knotted objects, craftspeople are exploring the creative possibilities of macramé more and more to construct unusual wall hangings, decorative screens, lampshades, and all sorts of wearing apparel and jewelry. Macramé techniques are also being used to construct sculptural forms. Combined with other fiber techniques, such as stitchery and weaving, new creative expressions are developed. Examples of student work are shown in figure 11.35.

*(Figure 11.35) (a) Note that cords are cast onto a small tree branch.*

*(b)*

## Stitchery: Traditional and Contemporary

The hand needlecrafts in general are those that are accomplished with needles carrying threads or yarns. This broad definition includes such crafts as knitting, crocheting, lace making, needlepoint, bargello, applique, and embroidery. Technically it might also include the tapestry arts, although these are most often considered a form of weaving rather than stitchery.

The needle itself is one of the most ancient of hand implements and probably evolved from primitive awls that were made from pieces of sharpened bone or horn and used by early peoples to puncture holes in hides or skins through which thongs could be threaded to make clothing. Early needles consisted of long thin pieces of iron, one end of which had been sharpened and the other end rounded with a groove to hold the thread in place. The needle reached Europe by way of China. By the late fourteenth century, the manufacture of needles was flourishing in Germany, later becoming an important industry in both Germany and England. Gradually the needle with the eye was developed and in 1885 the machine process for the manufacture of needles was perfected.

Ornamental needlework or embroidery is the art of applying designs to already woven fabrics using needles and various threads and yarns made of linen, wool, silk, and other materials. Embroidery was known in Egypt as early as 1500 B.C. and numerous references to needlework are to be found in the Bible. Intricately worked patterns have, for centuries been used to enhance wearing apparel and create textiles for the home. In many societies, learning to do needlework has long been considered an essential part of a young girl's training, and we have today, for example, many charming examples of "samplers" made by girls in Colonial America as a means of displaying the various stitches they had learned.

Perhaps the best known historic example of the needleworkers' art is the famous Bayeux tapestry, which is really not a tapestry at all but rather an embroidery measuring some 230 feet long and 20 inches wide, made in France in the eleventh century. It depicts the invasion and conquest of England by the Norman king, William I, in A.D. 1066. It is worked in eight colors of woolen thread on linen canvas and shows thousands of human figures combined with all sorts of foliage and animals in hunting and battle scenes. The work, while not of a religious nature, was originally commissioned by Bishop Odo and hung in the cathedral at Bayeux. It is now in the Bayeux Museum.[1]

Thus, we see that needlework has traditionally consisted of working decorative designs with various threads on a backing or ground of fabric using standard stitches. Such objects as hangings, table linens, chair covers, and the like are produced. Although this is a perfectly valid craft form and source of much enjoyment to many people, a problem arises because the skill exercised in carrying out the technique often becomes more important to the person doing the work than conceptual or aesthetic considerations, thereby leading to pedestrian results. The student choosing to follow this approach must make every effort to be as creative as possible and to produce a work that will be aesthetically pleasing as well as serve the purpose for which it is designed. The fact that many contemporary craftspeople are producing much excellent utilitarian work such as quilts, household linens, and banners is proof that traditional stitchery handled with imagination can be a viable craft.

The best grounds (backings) for embroidery are closely woven fabrics such as linens, silks, velvets, and the like. A small frame or *embroidery hoop* is usually used to hold the work firmly. All sorts of threads or *flosses* are commercially available in a wide variety of colors; these few materials, together with needles and a good pair of scissors are about all the embroiderer needs to get started.

Numerous ornamental stitches have been developed over the years and some of these have become more or less standard. A few of the more common ones are shown on the chart in figure 11.36. These should be practiced on a piece of scrap fabric until proficiency is attained. Better still, the student might design a small sampler that could be retained for future reference.

Stitchery as a contemporary craft uses traditional needlework concepts simply as a point of departure, and as a basis for making a strong creative statement not limited to standardized stitches or ordinary approaches. Thus, contemporary stitchery goes far beyond the concept of traditional needlework even though the same sorts of materials may be used. In discussing this basic difference, Arline K. Morrison writes, "Needlework is an end in itself, that end being a correct, perfectly formed stitch. Stitchery, on the other hand, is only a means to an end, that end being an idea, a concept or a statement worked in fiber with the stitches manipulated in any way one can conceive to achieve the desired result."[2] In fact, it may be well to play down the term *stitchery* and simply refer to what we are doing as *fiber art*.

It is with creative stitchery or fiber art, rather than traditional needlework, that this section is primarily concerned. The student must realize that the concept of the planned piece and the act of doing it is just as important as the end result; the finished work may utilize many variations and unorthodox combinations of stitches and materials. It may incorporate a variety of techniques—macramé, coiling, braiding, twining, crochet, quilting, weaving, and knitting in addition to or in lieu of the more usual stitchery with a needle. Such diverse materials as shells, twigs, beads, grasses, raffia, bits of metal, and feathers may be included, resulting in contemporary fiber art that is rather sculptural in character.

One hallmark of contemporary crafts is the tendency toward crossing traditional boundaries of classification. This trend is particularly evident in the fiber arts. Although I have recognized the value of learning traditional techniques in all the crafts in this book, I have at the same time repeatedly urged students to exercise the greatest freedom in deviating from established patterns when such deviation will contribute to a stronger, more creative statement. Nowhere is this approach more important than in creative stitchery. It is vital to think in terms of what one is doing to express one's ideas and to utilize fully the capabilities of the materials rather than concentrate on a specific result; to become involved in the process rather than in the aim to "make something"; to free the mind of confining rules in order to allow one's innate creativity to have full play.

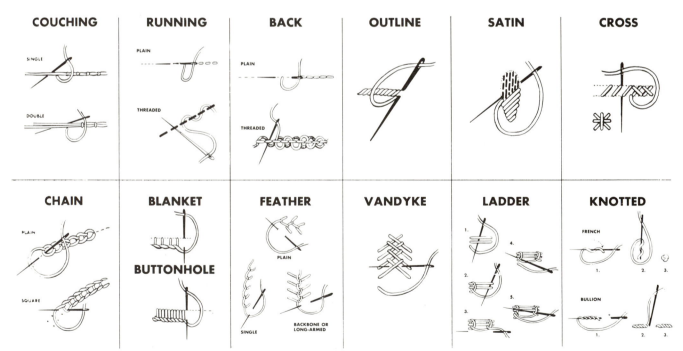

*(Figure 11.36) Basic stitches for creative stitchery.*
Note: *Stitchery diagrams reproduced through the courtesy of Lily Mills, Educational Division, Shelby, North Carolina.*

## Tools and Materials

The very fact that creative stitchery is such a "free-wheeling" craft also means that a long and specific listing of tools and materials is neither necessary nor desirable.

A selection of needles is, of course, essential. Various types of needles are shown in figure 11.37.

A Regular sewing needles, sometimes called "sharps." These are normally used in sewing operations and have small slender eyes suitable for carrying sewing threads.

B Embroidery or crewel needles; these have long eyes and are used with embroidery flosses, pearl cotton, and crewel wools.

C Raffia or chenille needles with large eyes, designed to carry heavy threads and yarns.

D Tapestry needles with blunt points and long eyes, used with a variety of yarns. These are often used in working on mesh canvas for needlepoint and bargello.

E Special needles, such as carpet needles, curved upholsterer's needles, and weaving needles, will probably be useful from time to time.

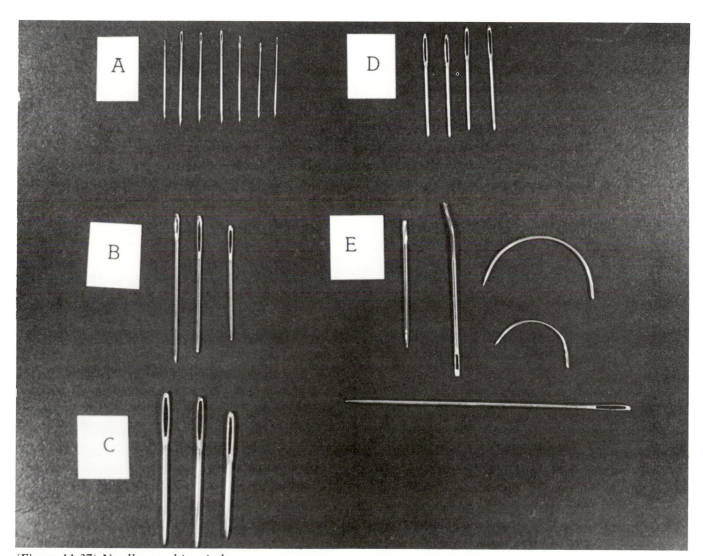

*(Figure 11.37) Needles used in stitchery.*

Fiber craftspeople are in universal agreement that the most important tool is by far a good pair of scissors (see figure 11.38). I recommend two pairs, a small one with a three-inch blade for detail work and trimming and a larger general purpose shear with a five- or six-inch blade. Both should be of the finest quality affordable and professionally sharpened periodically. Beyond this, one might want to invest in a small pair of surgical or manicure scissors and a pair of pinking shears.

Embroidery hoops consisting of two rings, one fitting inside the other with the outer ring having an adjustable screw, are useful for keeping fabric taut when doing embroidery techniques. For larger work, wooden frames especially designed for stitchery are useful (see figure 11.39).

Pins, both the straight or dressmakers variety and "T" pins, often called macramé pins, are useful for holding parts of the work in place until they can be permanently anchored.

There are probably no materials that cannot be used in some way for stitchery, and this being the case, it would be an endless task to try to compile a listing. The stitchery student is urged to examine all sorts of fabrics from delicate organdy to heavy burlap; all manner of cords, ropes, twines, yarns, and threads made from cotton, linen, wool, jute, and synthetics; all accessory items such as wire, lace, ball fringe, buttons, plastics, shells, beads, and found objects. In short, look at any and every material encountered as a possibility for creative use in stitchery. If there is a weaving or knitting mill nearby, numerous discarded fibers may often be had for the asking.

The diversity of materials can sometimes lead to their being used indiscriminately. This can be avoided, or at least minimized, if the stitchery student will take time to consider the potentialities and limitations of each available material. When planning a work, the student must carefully think out such factors as size and shape, design elements to be utilized, theme or mood to be conveyed, color scheme, and place in which the work is to be hung. Once this is done, the student is then in a position to choose those materials that will work together to make the final work the best possible statement of his or her vision and creativity.

*Methods and Techniques*
Many crafts require specific instructions for certain operations: preparing metals for enameling, cutting glass, warping a loom, and the like. In stitchery, there is really no "right or wrong" way. As long as it works and gives the desired effect, then it is *right*. Also, as already pointed out, creative stitchery combines many related techniques, which would certainly be beyond the scope of this chapter to discuss in detail. Information and

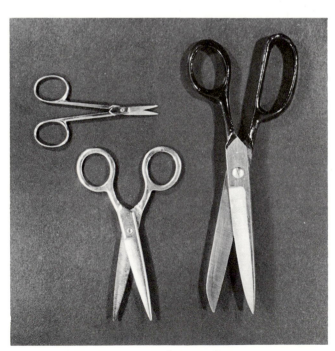

*(Figure 11.38) Scissors used in stitchery.*

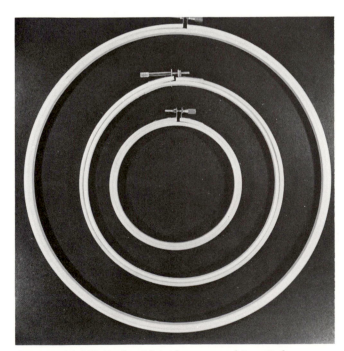

*(Figure 11.39) Embroidery hoops used in stitchery.*

instruction for crochet, needlepoint, bargello, knitting, appliqué, and quilting are readily available in numerous books (see suggested reading list). It is in order, however, to reveiw certain techniques briefly.

*Appliqué* is a variation of embroidery, in which shapes are cut from one type or color of fabric and attached to a backing of a different fabric. The edges are then usually finished with ornamental stitches (see figure 11.40). Although a wide variety of fabrics may be combined for the design elements, the background material should be relatively firm and closely woven for greater stability of the finished work. Designs may be representational or abstract. It is a good idea to cut preliminary shapes from paper and shift them around on the backing until a pleasing arrangement is obtained. The paper shapes may then be used as patterns to cut fabric pieces that are, in turn, pinned or basted to the fabric backing. Edges of the shapes may be left raw if desired. For a more finished method of attachment, turn under the edges of each piece about one-quarter inch and baste or pin down; the pieces are then fastened with a small running stitch just inside the turned under edge. An alternate method is to use one of the commercial bonding webs such as Stitch Witchery® to heat seal the pieces to the backing. Ornamental stitches may be overlaid on the patches as desired. Appliqué patches may also be padded or "stuffed" with polyester fiberfill

before being stitched down for a three-dimensional look. This is a variation of the technique known as *trapunto*.

*Canvas embroidery:* Stitchery that is done on a backing of mesh canvas and covers the entire surface of the canvas is called *needlepoint* (see figure 11.41). Needlepoint canvas is graded by how many holes there are to the inch. Canvas with five or seven holes to the inch is called quick point or gros point; ten to fourteen holes to the inch is needlepoint and 16 or more holes to the inch is petit point. Canvas is obtainable in the regular *leno* type, which is most often used for general work, or in a plastic type, which is much stiffer and therefore suitable for three-dimensional forms. Needlepoint designs are usually fairly structured with vertical and horizontal stitches predominating, although the technique can be freely adapted to result in designs more compatible with the concepts of creative stitchery. Small pieces of needlepoint may also be incorporated into other works.

Wools and yarns are selected according to the mesh size of the canvas being used. Rug yarns are suitable for the larger mesh or gros point work, while tapestry and Persian wools are best for regular needlepoint. These yarns may be separated into smaller strands for petit point work.

*(Figure 11.40) Folded edge applique by Marylin Sween. Photo courtesy of Kathy Farmer, The Quilt Shop, Lynchburg, Virginia.*

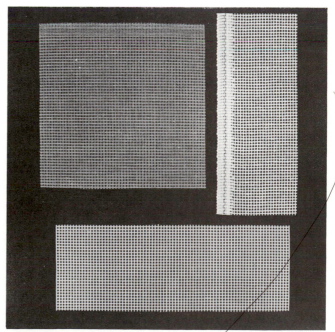

*(Figure 11.41) Canvases used in needlepoint and bargello. Top left, double weave leno; top right, single weave leno; bottom, plastic canvas.*

Needlepoint is worked with a blunt tapestry needle that carries thread or wool in and out of the holes in the canvas as desired. Because of the geometric nature of the canvas itself, designs for canvas work are usually made of horizontal and vertical elements, although curved forms are possible as well. A wide variety of stitches may be used in needlepoint, some of which are shown in figure 11.42. Others may be found in books devoted to needlepoint.

A variation of needlepoint that is also worked on canvas mesh is called *bargello* or *Florentine work*. Bargello is also somewhat structured in that it traditionally follows mathematical designs in which the pattern is built up by stitching over a certain set number of holes, with one straight stitch and stepped stitches forming the design. (see figure 11.43). Florentine stitch variations are shown in figure 11.44. Bargello is relatively easy to do, because once the first pattern motif is established on the canvas, it serves as a guide for the remainder of the motifs.

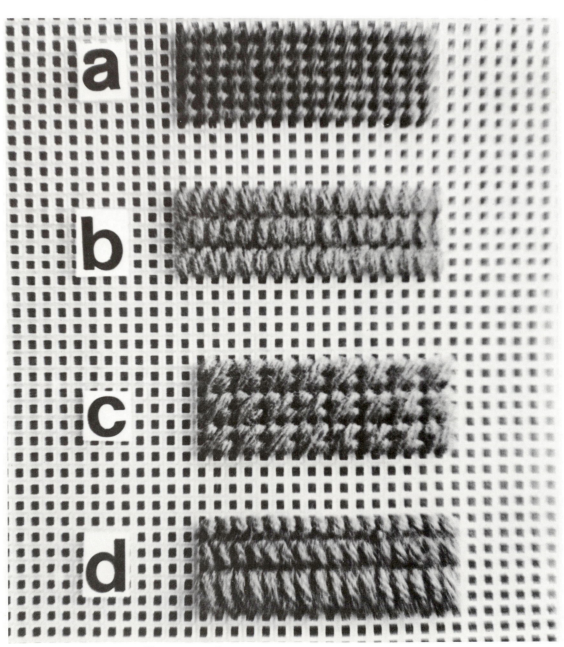

*(Figure 11.42) Basic needlepoint stitches.*

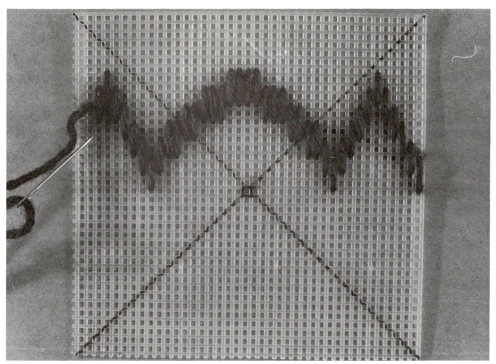

*(Figure 11.43) Method of beginning a bargello design.
Once the first row is set up, it is quite easy to work the
rest of the rows in the same manner as the guide row.
If it is important to center the design, the center of the
canvas should be located as shown.*

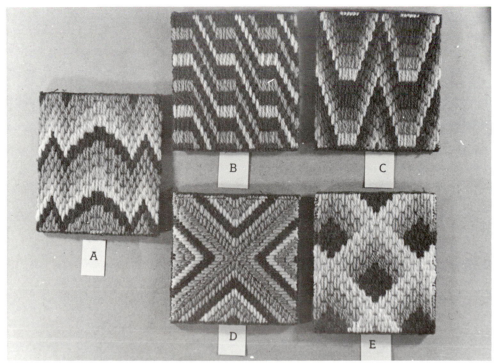

*(Figure 11.44) Typical bargello designs. Courtesy of
Terry D. Sumey.*

Free-form versions of bargello are being created by contemporary stitchers who wish to depart from the structured (and sometimes monotonous) nature of traditional bargello. This approach adds exciting new dimensions of flexibility and experimentation to this very old craft. The same wool types and needles as described for needlepoint are used for bargello.

*Crochet* is a method of making interlocking loops from wool using a special hook to form the desired pattern. Whenever the word *crochet* is mentioned, one immediately thinks of the bedspreads, afghans, potholders, purses, and baby apparel seen at church bazaars and county fairs. It is true that much crochet work consists of such utilitarian objects but is certainly not limited to these, for contemporary craftspeople are discovering that crochet can be a versatile medium in itself or combined with other techniques in stitchery or in the making of sculptural forms.

In doing crochet work, the hook is held in one hand as if it were a pencil, though any way that feels comfortable works just as well. The yarn is controlled by letting it pass through the other hand with tension kept uniform by the index finger. Crochet stitches may be made loose or tight. Each person usually finds the best way of handling the yarn to arrive at the effect desired. The size of the yarn and hook used will also play a part in the appearance of the work. The important thing is to keep the tension uniform whether it is loose or tight.

Tools and materials for crochet are quite simple, because all that is needed is an assortment of crochet hooks, some yarn, and a pair of scissors. Crochet hooks are of two types: (1) the steel variety used with finer threads for more delicate work, ranging in size from 00 (the largest) to 14 (the smallest) and (2) the aluminum or plastic variety for larger hooks designed to carry heavier yarns. The sizes of the larger hooks are designated by letters, from C (the smallest) to K (the largest). There are also very large hooks lettered, P, Q, R, and S for very heavy yarns (see figure 11.45). Although it is convenient to have the complete range on hand, in actual practice one becomes accustomed to a few hooks of the sizes most often used and these are usually sufficient.

Wools and threads for crochet are many and varied. The student should visit a well-stocked needlecraft shop and examine the various types available: very fine linen or cotton threads; wools and yarns such as worsted, rug yarns, "fisherman" yarn, and cashmere; synthetics such as cordé and chenille; and the novelty cords such as boucle and the metallics. The work being executed will of course determine the type of yarn used. Often in a free-form contemporary piece, several types may be combined. Basic instructions for crocheting are given in the accompanying chart in figure 11.46

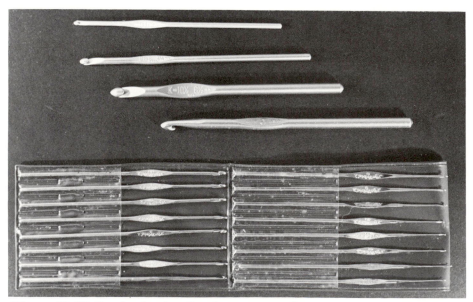

*(Figure 11.45) Crochet hooks of various types and sizes.*

## Foundation Chain

**1**

Make a slip knot on hook, held in the right hand. Thread yarn over left ring finger, under middle, and over index finger, holding short end between the thumb and middle finger.

**2**

Pass hook under and over yarn and draw it through loop on hook. Repeat for as many stitches as the directions specify.

## Single Crochet

**3**

Insert hook into second stitch from hook, under the two upper strands.

**4**

Pass hook under and over yarn and draw it through the stitch.

**5**

Pass hook under and over yarn again and draw it through the two loops on hook.

## Half Double Crochet

**6**

Pass hook under and over yarn, insert hook into third stitch from hook, and under the two upper strands.

**7**

Pass hook under and over yarn and draw it through the stitch. Pass hook under and over yarn again and draw it through the three loops on hook.

## Double Crochet

**8**

Pass hook under and over yarn, insert hook into the fourth stitch from hook, under the two upper strands.

**9**

Pass hook under and over yarn and draw it through the stitch, then pass hook under and over yarn again. Draw yarn through the first two loops on hook. Pass hook under and over yarn again and draw it through remaining two loops on hook.

## Treble Crochet

**10**

Pass hook under and over yarn twice, insert hook into the fifth stitch from hook, under the two upper strands.

**11**

Pass hook under and over yarn and draw it through the stitch. * Pass hook under and over yarn and draw through two loops, repeat from * twice more.

## Afghan Crochet

**12**

Using an afghan hook, make a chain the desired length. Insert hook in second stitch from hook, draw up a loop.

**13**

Keeping all loops on hook, draw up a loop in each chain stitch.

**14**

To work off loops, pass yarn under and over hook and draw through first loop.

**15**

* Pass yarn under and over hook, draw through two loops, repeat from * across.

**16**

One loop remains, to count as first stitch of next row.

**17**

* Insert hook under next vertical bar and draw up a loop, repeat from * across. Work off loops same as before.

*(Figure 11.46) Instructions for basic crochet stitches. Reproduced through the courtesy of Caron International, Rochelle, Illinois.*

*Knitting,* like crochet, consists of the formation of a fabric into continous loops of yarn or thread with needles. Basic differences are that knitting requires at least two needles, which do not have hooked ends as in crochet. Said to have been invented in Scotland, knitting was introduced into Europe in the fifteenth century. Hand knitters have traditionally produced caps, sweaters, and many other types of wearing apparel. Knitted elements are often combined with other fibers in contemporary stitchery. Standard (single-point) knitting needles may be made of either aluminum or plastic. They come in pairs, usually 10 to 14 inches long and are rated in millimeters according to diameter. For example, aluminum needles are numbered from 0 to 15 (2.1 to 10.2 millimeters). The larger the needle, the more loosely structured the finished product will be. Double-point needles are used in sets of four to knit seamless items such as socks and mittens. Circular needles are used to produce tubular seamless forms or large flat pieces when straight needles are not long enough (see figure 11.47).

Usually, the same yarns and cords as are used in crochet work will be suitable for knitting and choice will depend on the intended purpose of the knitted piece. Basic instructions for knitting are given in the accompanying chart in figure 11.48.

Basic *quilting* consists of making a "sandwich" of three layers of fabric that are then anchored together by a series of running stitches, usually done in a decorative pattern. The pattern itself may be the focal point of the work, or the stitches may be used to enhance other design elements such as appliqué or patchwork.

Traditionally, the quilting process has been and is used to produce warm clothing and bed coverings, but it is also a valuable adjunct to the creative stitcher's vocabulary for adding interest to fiber designs. Often, additional padding or stuffing of polyester fiberfill material or cotton batting is used to highlight certain areas. Sometimes individual "puffs" are made by cutting a circle of fabric, basting a loose running stitch around the edges, placing stuffing in the center, and pulling the thread ends to draw the form up into a puff.

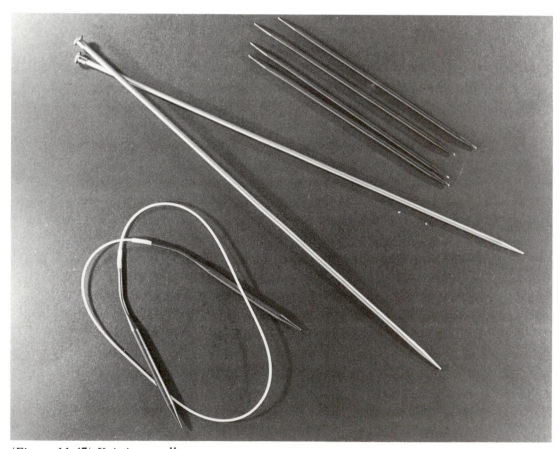

*(Figure 11.47) Knitting needles.*

## CASTING ON

### • the first step in knitting

This means putting the first row of stitches on the knitting needle. The loop of the slip knot you start with counts as a first stitch. Cast on loosely.

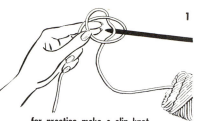

**1**

for practice make a slip knot 12" from end of yarn

**2**

hold needle in right hand — notice how yarn from skein is held

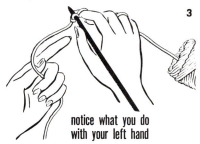

**3**

notice what you do with your left hand

**4**

loop left-hand yarn around thumb

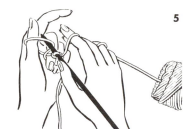

**5**

insert needle into loop on thumb

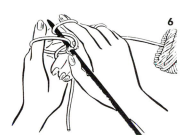

**6**

loop right-hand yarn around point of needle

*(a)*

**7**

draw yarn through loop on thumb

**8**

pull yarn in left hand to tighten stitch, easing loop off thumb — make 8 more stitches

## how to KNIT and PURL

### • the basis of all knitting

The movements in knitting are the same as in casting on. Push stitches on left needle up toward the point as you work. At end of row the needles change hands: full needle to the left hand, empty needle to the right.

**KNIT STITCH**
abbr.-k

**1**

hold needle with cast-on stitches in left hand, empty needle and yarn in right hand

**2**

slip point of needle into front of first stitch

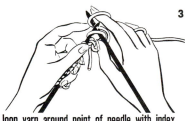

**3**

loop yarn around point of needle with index finger as you did for casting on

**4**

draw loop through stitch

**5**

right needle holds new stitch, old stitch is slipped off needle — work all knit stitches in same way

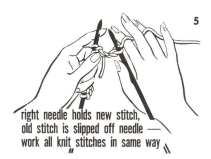

**PURL STITCH**
abbr.-p

**6**

hold needles same as for knit stitch but with yarn in front — slip point of needle in from back of stitch

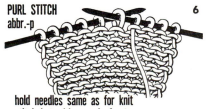

**7**

loop yarn around point of needle

**8**

draw yarn through stitch; slip old stitch off left needle — work all purl stitches in same way

*(b)*

*(Figure 11.48) Instructions for basic knitting. Reproduced courtesy of Coats and Clark, Inc., Consumer and Educational Affairs Department, New York, New York 10122. (Continued on next page.)*

## DECREASING and INCREASING
## • for shaping a garment

There are two ways of decreasing—you must learn both. The knitting instructions tell you which to use.

**one way of DECREASING,** abbr.- k 2 tog    1

knit two stitches together

**or, abbr.- p 2 tog**    2

or purl two stitches together

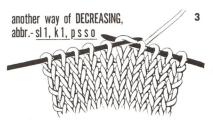

**another way of DECREASING,** abbr.- sl 1, k 1, p s s o    3

slip one stitch from left to right needle without knitting, abbr.- sl 1 ...

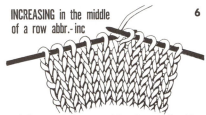

4

... knit one stitch, abbr.- k 1 ...

5

...with help of left needle, pass the slipped stitch over the knitted stitch, abbr.- p s s o

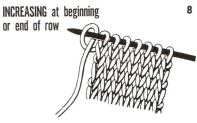

**INCREASING in the middle** of a row abbr.- inc    6

knit one stitch as usual but do not slip old stitch off left needle ...

7

...now knit a second stitch into the back of the same stitch - slip old stitch off

**INCREASING at beginning** or end of row    8

loop yarn around point of needle, as shown

*(c)*

## BASIC STITCHES and BINDING OFF
## • bind off loosely

To bind off ribbing, knit the k stitches, purl the p stitches.

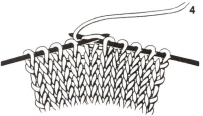

**STOCKINETTE** right side    1

knit one row ...

**STOCKINETTE** wrong side    2

... purl one row

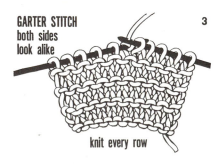

**GARTER STITCH** both sides look alike    3

knit every row

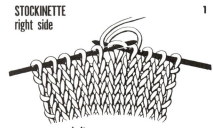

**RIBBING — k1, p1** both sides look alike    4

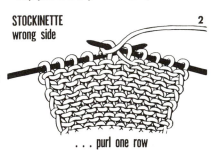

**RIBBING — k2, p2** both sides look alike    5

RIBBING draws the knitting together, making it elastic ... there are two basic types: knit one stitch (k1), bring yarn to front, purl one stitch (p1), take yarn back; repeat to end of row ... or, knit two (k2) and purl two (p2) ... if row ends with purl start next row with knit.

**BINDING or CASTING OFF**    6

knit two stitches loosely ... pass first over second stitch and off right needle ...

7

... one stitch remains on right needle; knit next stitch loosely and repeat ...

8

bind off all stitches but one; break yarn and draw end through stitch

*(d)*

*(Figure 11.48—continued)*

These may be used as accents for fiber works. An example of a quilted work is shown in figure 11.49.

*Three-Dimensional Fiber Art (Soft Sculpture)*
When craftspeople began to consider stitchery as a serious art form, it was inevitable that numerous innovations would appear to revolutionize traditional thinking in the fiber arts. This was especially so in the development of what came to be called "soft sculpture," meaning three-dimensional forms made primarily from fibrous materials. The pop artist Claes Oldenburg had, in the early sixties, created such oversized forms as drum sets, food items, typewriters, and bathroom objects from fabrics and vinyl plastics stuffed with filling of various kinds. Traditionally, because sculpture is thought of as being made from such hard and durable materials as wood, stone, and metal, the concept of creating three-dimensional forms from soft materials was a source of inspiration for fiber artists. Although early works exploring this concept were often thought somewhat radical, they are now accepted as valid fiber statements. The swing toward three-dimensional fiber works was described by Mimi Shorr of the American Crafts Council who, writing in *Saturday Review,* said: "The desire to create three-dimensional forms, to alter space or to surround the viewer has been the greatest motivation behind the recent burst of activity in fiber art. . . . Artists have found ingenious solutions by

*(Figure 11.49) Example of patchwork and quilting by Rosemary Lawson. Photo courtesy of Kathy Farmer, The Quilt Shop, Lynchburg, Virginia.*

building up texture into mass, by juxtaposing one plane against another and by constructing undulating wall sized surfaces which are themselves textured, layered or shaped. . . . Anyone viewing these works is always conscious of materials and methods."[3]

The Museum of Contemporary Crafts in New York City, conscious of the growing trend, exhibited early in 1972 the works of twelve well-known fiber artists, which created a great deal of interest in three-dimensional fiber art.[4] There are only a few museums today that have not at one time or another in the recent past included examples of fiber arts in their exhibitions.

The possibilities for three-dimensional fiber forms are, of course, almost limitless and include such approaches as shaped knitting and crocheting, all manner of knotted and coiled forms, stuffed and sewn shapes, and the like, giving the fiber artist a wide range of choice with which to exercise creativity. The student is referred to the many works in the suggested readings list for ideas.

A most interesting variation on the soft sculpture idea is found in the work of craftswoman Gertrude Shook of Keysville, Virginia, who creates whimsical character dolls that she calls "basket cases" (see figure 11.50). Materials include discarded panty hose, cardboard cores, such as those on which paper towels are rolled, polyester fiberfill for stuffing, scraps of yarn and cord for hair, remnants of fabric for clothing, scissors, a needle, and some heavy thread (see figure 11.51).

To make the doll's head, cut a five-inch length from the leg section of old panty hose. Gather one end and secure by tieing with thread. Stuff polyester filler material into the form until it is firm and roughly oval in shape. Secure loose end with thread and punch head form into desired shape (see figure 11.52).

(Figure 11.50) Three examples of soft sculpture dolls by fiber artist Gertrude Shook.

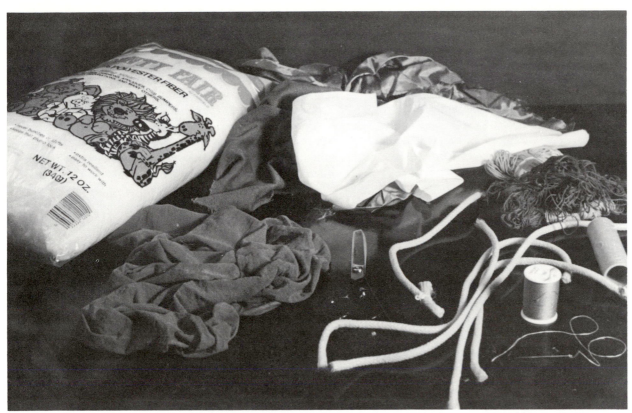

*(Figure 11.51) Materials for soft sculpture dolls.*

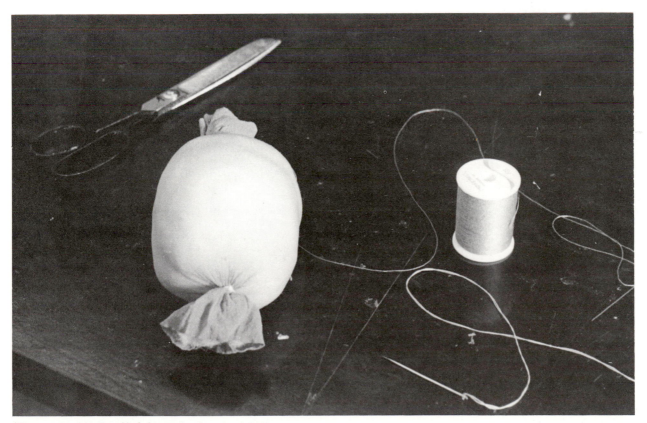

*(Figure 11.52) Stuffed form for head of doll.*

Features are formed by gathering the material and filling, and sewing at proper intervals; begin with the eyebrows, then make the eyes, nose, mouth, and ears (see figure 11.53).

Spacing of the features may be according to their position on a human face, but because these are imaginative creatures, much leeway may be allowed. Often, the more exaggerated the features are, the more interesting the result will be. Finish off features and add hair, beards, and accessories as desired.

The finished head is sewn to one end of the cardboard core that will form the body as figure 11.54 illustrates.

Prepare the cardboard "body" by punching six or eight small holes around the circumference of one end of the tube to which the head will be attached. Slightly below these holes, punch two holes opposite each other and about one-quarter inch in diameter to receive the "arms." Punch two similar holes at the other end of the tube to receive the "legs."

Arms and legs are formed from lengths of one-quarter-inch flexible fiber core or rope clothesline, and are inserted into the cardboard body as shown in figure 11.55. The loop joints serve as "elbows" and "knees" and provide a great deal of flexibility in positioning the finished doll.

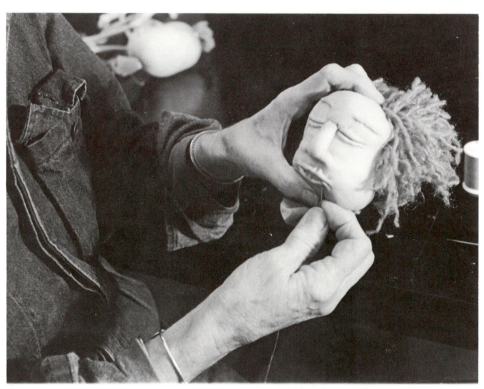

*(Figure 11.53) Finishing the features. Note hair made from scraps of yarn sewn to the top of the form.*

When head is attached and arms and legs are in place, dolls may be costumed as desired. The easiest approach is to make simple trouser-blouse outfits, but the student should allow full play to the creative possibilities of costuming these fun creatures by designing elaborate outfits, adding beads, fur, sequins, and other embellishments such as rings, bracelets, sunglasses, and the like. Hands are made from pieces of stocking, stuffed and sewn to simulate fingers. Feet are covered with "shoes" made from scraps of vinyl plastic or thin leather. The dolls may be made any size; no set rules need to be followed.

*Finishing:* How a fiber piece is finished depends to a great extent on the form of the piece itself and how it is to be used. Essentially "flat" work, such as banners and wall hangings, will probably require a backing of some fairly heavy fabric like corduroy or burlap. The edges of such pieces may be hemmed or perhaps edged with a contrasting decorative border. Commercial binding tapes are a possibility as well. Work may be mounted on masonite or plywood for use as screens or dividers. Be sure to plan extra fabric when the work is being designed to allow for finishing or mounting. If this has not been done, the work may be appliquéd or glued to a larger piece of fabric to provide the extra material needed.

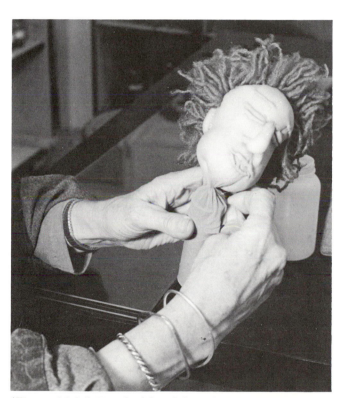

*(Figure 11.54) Finished head form being attached to one end of cardboard core.*

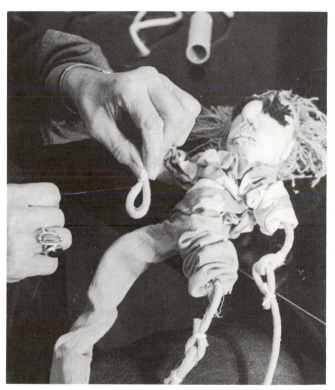

*(Figure 11.55) Partially completed doll, showing method of arm and leg construction with loops. Note simple shirt and trouser outfit.*

Some method of hanging must be provided. Loops or a hemmed channel through which a metal or wooden rod may be inserted is probably the simplest method. The hanging method chosen should not put any sort of strain on the work, nor should it damage the piece in any way. If the work is to hang in an area where there is a great deal of traffic, it should be treated with a soil-resistant material such as Scotchgard®. Large works that are to hang in public areas may need to be fireproofed. Works should not be hung in direct sunlight or extremely brightly lighted areas for long periods of time, because most fibers will eventually fade under these conditions.

The student should keep in mind that how a work is finished and hung is most important to the total appearance of the piece, and should be planned as carefully as the work itself. Examples of stitchery are shown in figure 11.56.

*(a)*
*(Figure 11.56) (a) Stitchery comprising loops of various lengths and parallel stitches of wool on burlap ground. (b) Abstract bird shapes worked on canvas with needlepoint and bargello stitches.*

Notes

1  An excellent description and account of the history of the tapestry may be found in Charles Gibbs-Smith, *The Bayeux Tapestry,* (London: Phaidon Press, 1973).

2  Arline K. Morrison, *Experimental Stitchery and Other Fiber Techniques* (Englewood Cliffs, N.J.: Prentice-Hall, 1977).

3  Mimi Shorr, "Fiber Sculpture," *Saturday Review* (20 May 1960).

4  Rose Slivka, "Hard String," *Craft Horizons* (April 1972).

*Suggested Readings*
*Weaving*

Alexander, Marthann. *Weaving on Cardboard: Simple Looms to Make and Use.* New York: Taplinger Publishing Co., 1971.

Blumenau, Lili. *The Art and Craft of Hand Weaving.* New York: Crown Publishers, 1955.

Breis, Helene. *The Weaving Book: Patterns and Ideas.* New York: Charles Scribner's Sons, 1981.

Chamberlain, Marcia, and Candace Crockett. *Beyond Weaving.* New York: Watson-Guptill Publications, 1974.

Creager, Clara. *Weaving: A Creative Approach for Beginners.* Garden City, N.Y.: Doubleday, 1974.

Held, Shirley E. *Weaving: A Handbook for Fiber Craftsmen.* New York: Holt, Rinehart and Winston, 1973.

Holland, Nina. *Inkle Loom Weaving.* New York: Watson-Guptill Publications, 1973.

————. *Weaving Primer.* Radnor, Pa.: Chilton Book Co., 1978.

Justema, William. *Weaving and Needlecraft Color Course.* New York: Van Nostrand, Reinhold, 1971.

Marein Shirley. *Off the Loom: Creating with Fibre.* New York: Viking Press, 1972.

Meilach, Dona Z., and Lee Erlin Snow. *Weaving Off-Loom.* Chicago: Henry Regnery Co., 1973.

Morrison, Phylis. *Spider's Games: A Book for Beginning Weavers.* Seattle: University of Washington Press, 1979.

Nauman, Rose, and Raymond Hull. *The Off-Loom Weaving Book.* New York: Charles Scribner's Sons, 1973.

Rainey, Sarita. *Weaving without a Loom.* Worcester, Mass: Davis Publications, 1966.

Regensteiner, Else. *Weaver's Study Course: Ideas and Techniques.* New York: Van Nostrand, Reinhold, 1975.

Specht, Sally, and Sandra Rawlings. *Creating with Card Weaving.* New York: Crown Publishers, 1973.

Sutton, Ann, and Pat Holton. *Tablet Weaving.* Newton Centre, Mass.: Charles T. Branford Co., 1975.

Taber, Barbara, and Marilyn Anderson. *Backstrap Weaving.* New York: Watson-Guptill Publications, 1975.

Weigle, Palmy. *Double Weave.* New York: Watson-Guptill Publications, 1978.

Wilcox, Donald J. *New Design in Weaving.* New York: Van Nostrand, Reinhold, 1970.

Wilson, Jean V. *Weaving Is Creative.* New York: Van Nostrand, Reinhold, 1972.

————. *Weaving Is for Anyone.* New York: Van Nostrand, Reinhold, 1967.

————. *Weaving Is Fun.* New York: Van Nostrand, Reinhold, 1971.

————. *Joinings, Edges and Trims.* New York: Van Nostrand, Reinhold, 1983.

*Macramé*

Andes, Eugene. *Far beyond the Fringe.* New York: Van Nostrand, Reinhold 1973.

Bress, Helene. *The Macramé Book.* New York: Charles Scribner's Sons, 1972.

Depar, Spencer. *Macramé, Weaving and Tapestry, Art in Fiber.* New York: Macmillan, 1973.

Harvey, Virginia I. *Color and Design in Macramé.* New York: Van Nostrand, Reinhold, 1971.

————. *Macramé: The Art of Creative Knotting.* New York: Van Nostrand, Reinhold, 1967.

la Croix, Grethe. *Beads and Macramé.* Translated by Eric Greweldinger. New York: Sterling Publishing, Co., 1971.

Meilach, Dona Z., *Macramé Accessories, Patterns and Ideas for Knotting.* New York: Crown Publishers, 1972.

————. *Macramé: Creative Design in Knotting.* New York: Crown Publishers, 1971.

————. *Macramé Gnomes and Puppets.* New York: Crown Publishers, 1980.

Paque, Joan Michaels. *Visual Instructional Macramé.* Milwaukee: Joan and Henry Paque, 1971.

Short, Eirian. *Introducing Macramé.* New York: Watson-Guptill Publications, 1970.

Smith, Harvey Garrett. *The Marlinspike Sailor.* Tuckahoe, N.Y.: John de Graff, 1971.

Stiles, Suzanne. *Creating with Macramé.* Texas: Design R. Crafts, 1972.

*Stitchery*

Brown, Elsa. *Creative Quilting*. New York: Watson-
    Guptill Publications, 1975.
Christensen, Jo Ippolito. *The Needlepoint Book*.
    Englewood Cliffs, N.J.: Prentice-Hall, 1976.
deDenne, Lynette. *Creative Needlecraft*. London:
    Octopus Books, 1979.
de Dillmont, Th. *The Complete Encylopedia of
    Needlework*. Philadelphia: Running Press, 1972.
Dendel, Esther Warner. *Needleweaving*. Philadelphia:
    Countryside Press, 1972.
Frew, Hannah. *Three-Dimensional Embroidery*. New
    York: Van Nortrand, Reinhold 1975.
Guild, Vera P. *Creative Use of Stitches*. Worcester,
    Mass.; Davis Publications, 1964.
Heard, Audrey, and Beverly Pryor. *Complete Guide to
    Quilting*. Des Moines, Iowa: Meredith Corporation,
    1974.
John, Edith. *Experimental Embroidery*. Newton
    Centre, Mass.: Charles T. Branford Co., 1976.
Kinser, Charleet. *Sewing Sculpture*. New York: M.
    Evans and Co., 1977.
Krevitsky, N. K. *Stitching: Art and Craft*. New York:
    Reinhold Publishing Co., 1969.
Laliberte, Norman, and Sterling McIlhany. *Banners
    and Hangings*. New York: Van Nostrand, Reinhold,
    1966.
Laury, Jean Ray. *Appliqué Stitchery*. New York:
    Reinhold Publishing Co., 1966.
Meilach, Dona Z. *Creating Art from Fibers and
    Fabrics*. Chicago: Henry Regnery Co., 1972.
Morrison, Arline K. *Experimental Stitchery and Other
    Fiber Techniques*. Englewood Cliffs, N.J.: Prentice-
    Hall, 1977.

Newman, Thelma R. *Quilting, Patchwork Appliqué
    and Trapunto*. New York: Crown Publishers, 1974.
Petersen, Grete. *Handbook of Stitches*. New York: Van
    Nostrand, Reinhold, 1970.
Phillips, Mary Walker. *Creative Knitting*. New York:
    Van Nostrand, Reinhold, 1971.
Rainey, Sarita R. *Wall Hangings: Designing with
    Fabric and Thread*. Worcester, Mass.: Davis
    Publications, 1971.
Reader's Digest. *Complete Guide to Needlework*.
    Pleasantville, N.Y.: Reader's Digest Association,
    1979.
Scobey, Joan. *Needlepoint from Start to Finish*. New
    York: Lancer Books, 1972.
Scrase, Pat. *Let's Start Designing*. New York: Reinhold
    Publishing Co., 1966.
Sommer, Elyse, and Mike Sommer. *A New Look at
    Crochet*. New York: Crown Publishers, 1975.
Stevens, Gigs. *Free Form Bargello*. New York: Chas.
    Scribner's Sons, 1977.
Waller, Irene. *Design Sources for the Fiber Artist*.
    Worcester, Mass.: Davis Publications, 1975.
————. *Designing with Threads*. New York: Viking
    Press, 1973.
Wilcox, Donald J. *New Design in Stitchery*. New York:
    Van Nostrand, Reinhold, 1970.
Williams, Elsa S. *Bargello: Florentine Canvas Work*.
    New York: Van Nostrand, Reinhold, 1967.
Wilson, Erica. *Crewel Embroidery*. New York: Charles
    Scribner's Sons, 1962.

# 12 Jewelry

Since prehistoric times, human beings have adorned themselves with ornaments, emblems, and badges of all sorts. Sometimes worn purely as decoration, they often served also to signify some official rank, such as chief, high priest, or medicineman; to ward off evil; or simply, for practical purposes, to hold articles of clothing together. Through the ages such ornaments, called jewelry, have been made of all manner of materials—wood, bone, shells, feathers, clay, and most particularly metals. They have often been inlaid with precious stones such as diamonds, emeralds, and rubies and lesser stones such as turquoise, amethysts, and opals.

Long a symbol of wealth and prestige, jewelry has always been and is still today prized for its beauty and intrinsic worth and is ranked among one's most valuable possessions. Since ancient times, jewelry has been given by one person to another to signify high regard, affection, and respect; it has been used as a medium of exchange; and it was very often placed in tombs of royalty and nobility to indicate the status and prestige of the deceased. Fine examples of ancient jewelry have been found in tombs in the Tigris-Euphrates valley and in Egypt, in excavations in Mycenae and Crete, and in many other locations indicating that most ancient civilizations practiced the art of jewelry making. They were familiar with such techniques as engraving, embossing, chasing, soldering, inlaying of precious stones into precious metals, and even in some cases casting with the lost wax process.

Collections of such wearables as earrings, finger rings, pendants, necklaces, brooches, anklets, and collars and such small personal objects as jeweled rosaries, boxes, reliquaries, and book covers are to be found in museums all over the world.

The Romans were extremely fond of jewelry, and it was not uncommon for wealthy citizens to wear rings on all ten fingers. Fibulae (buckles or clasps for fastening garments) in the form of portraits and mythical

147

creatures were also highly prized. Fine examples of these have been found wherever the Roman Empire spread. Cameos (relief engraved stones such as sardonyx, agate, or onyx) reached a high state of perfection in ancient Rome as did the art of enameled jewelry. Too, the Romans are said to be the first to give engagement and wedding rings.

During the Byzantine period, jewelry for personal adornment continued to be important, particularly in court circles; but the finest work was produced in the monastic workshops and reserved for ecclesiastical jewelry to be worn by the clergy and votive jewelry to adorn statues of the Virgin or the saints. Such usage continued through the Gothic period (twelfth to fifteenth centuries). Personal jewelry became an important form of investment for royalty and wealthy citizens during this period also.

During the Renaissance, however, jewelry reached new heights of popularity, and paintings made during this era show us kings, queens, gentlemen, and ladies dressed in costumes heavily encrusted with gold, silver, precious gems, and pearls attesting to the wealth and prestige of the wearers. The goldsmith occupied a particularly high place in Renaissance society, and many artists in other media produced notable works in jewelry as well. Benvenuto Cellini (1500–1571), for example, had as his patrons such illustrious names as Francis I of France, Cosimo de Medici of Florence, and several of the popes. Cellini also wrote a well-known work on the art of the goldsmith. During subsequent periods, especially with the onset of mass production, the art of the jeweler declined somewhat. In recent years, there has been a revival of interest in and a demand for fine one-of-a-kind pieces of handcrafted jewlery.

Contemporary jewelry artists, while understanding and rspecting traditional approaches and techniques, are, like craftspeople in most other media, more interested in exploring variations in processes, capabilities of materials, and innovative approaches to jewelry design than in adhering closely to traditional concepts.

## Materials

In the classroom, students can learn basic techniques for contructed metal jewelry by working with copper and brass in both wire and sheet form. It is with this approach that this section is concerned. Once basic techniques are learned, it is a simple matter to "graduate" to more expensive silver or even gold, because the working properties of the precious metals are quite similar to those of copper and brass and most of the physical operations are precisely the same.

An interesting and relatively inexpensive copper-brass alloy called "NuGold" is available in both wire and sheet form; it has the color of 14 karat gold and is easily worked, making it most practical for use in the classroom. Pewter is also used in the construction of jewelry as well as for casting.

Nonferrous (not containing iron) wire and sheet metal thicknesses are designated by Brown and Sharp (B. & S.) gauge numbers in the United States and by Imperial Standard Wire gauge numbers in Great Britain. Gauge numbers range from 0 to 30, the smaller the gauge number the thicker the wire or sheet. Table 12.1 shows B. & S. gauge numbers and thicknesses of metals most commonly used in jewelry making.

**Table 12.1**
**B & S. Gauge Numbers and Metal Thicknesses**

| B. & S. Gauge Number | Thickness (inches) | Uses |
|---|---|---|
| 8 | .1285 | Very heavy pieces |
| 12 | .0808 | Heavy rings and bracelets |
| 16 | .0508 | Average weight pieces |
| 18 | .0403 | Lighter rings, bracelets, pendants |
| 20 | .0320 } | Lightweight earrings, |
| 22 | .0253 } | bezels, laminations |

*Note:* 18 gauge sheet and wire is perhaps the most common weight for general use in student work.

The construction of metal jewelry involves a number of basic processes such as cutting, sawing, bending, stretching, hammering, soldering, piercing, stone setting, and polishing, each of which requires its own special tools. Because most tools used in jewelry construction are small hand tools and because the work itself is seldom very large, the jewelry workbench requires only a small space in the classroom. A bench pin, a small vise, and a motorized flexible shaft machine are essential and should be attached firmly to the workbench within easy reach. (see figure 12.1).

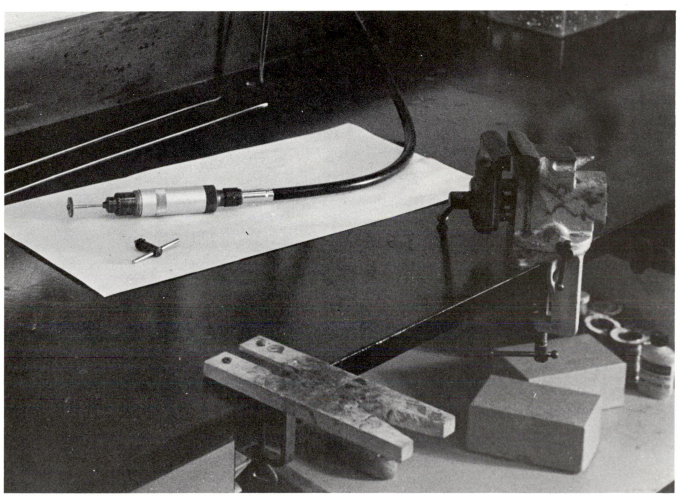

*(Figure 12.1) Bench pin, vise, and chuck of flexible shaft tool.*

Tools necessary for the basic processes of jewelry making are shown in figure 12.2.

Figure 12.2a shows several types of pliers used for bending, stretching, and manipulating wire (read illustration from top, left to right, then bottom, left to right).

- General purpose pliers (top)
- End cutter for cutting into close places
- Diagonal cutter for general cutting of wire
- Parallel plier, with flat jaws that open parallel to each other
- Flat nose shaping plier
- Round nose plier, with round tapered jaws (bottom, left)
- Needle nose or chain plier (bottom, right)

Figure 12.2b shows tools used for cutting, drilling, and filing operations (read left to right, top to bottom).

- Adjustable saw frame
- Saw blades, available in various grades from fine (8/0 to 0) to coarse (1 to 12); numbers 1/0, 1, or 2 most useful for sawing
- Drill bits of various sizes
- Assorted accessories such as buffs, burs, sanders, and emery wheels to fit the flexible shaft machine
- Aviation snips for cutting heavy metals
- Plate shears for cutting light metals
- Various files for smoothing cut edges (may be fitted into wood handles)

Figure 12.2c shows tools used for various shaping operations.

- Ring clamp for holding rings while filing
- Ball peen hammer, one end flat, one end round
- Rawhide mallet for flattening sheet metal
- Ring mandrel for sizing, shaping and stretching finger rings
- Burnishers (flat and curved), for smoothing metal in hard to reach spots and for bending bezels in stone setting
- Set of rings for accurately measuring finger sizes
- Double end scriber for marking metal
- Center punch, to be struck with a hammer for indenting metal

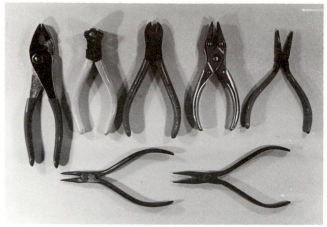

*(a)*

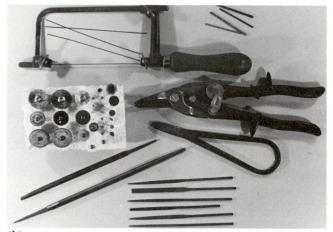

*(b)*

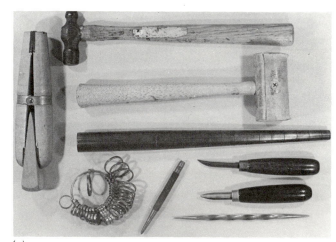

*(c)*

*(Figure 12.2) (a) Various types of pliers used in jewelry making. (b) Tools for sawing, cutting, scoring, and drilling. (c) Tools used in shaping and marking operations. (d) Section of workbench set up for soldering operations. (e) Tools for various operations.*

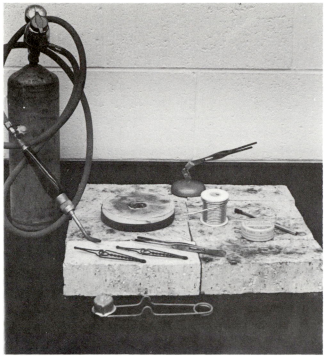

*(d)*

Figure 12.2d shows set up for soldering.

- Firebrick to protect table top
- Mounted sidelock tweezer (provides an "extra hand")
- Soldering unit, consisting of acetylene gas tank, pressure regulator, hose, handle and stem; number 2 stem best for general work
- Coiled asbestos in tin pan (Pins may be pushed into asbestos to hold object being soldered.)
- Solder, 50:50 or 60:40 alloy of lead and tin (A special nonlead solder for jewelry is also available and should be used for rings, bracelets, and other articles that will touch the skin.)
- Flux and flux brush (Flux is used to prevent oxidation of the metal while being heated and to assist the solder in flowing properly. A commercial flux may be used or a special flux may be made by mixing 1 ounce zinc chloride into 1 pint of water.)
- Various tweezers and clamps
- Spark lights

Figure 12.2e shows a variety of tools useful to the jeweler in various operations.

- Dapping block, used with dapping punches or round end hammers for doming metal circles
- Carbon mandrel, for soldering rings, pieces of tubing, and so forth
- Buffing compounds—emery, coarse and fine rouge, tripoli, and so forth—for use on cloth buffing wheels
- Bracelet bender, for making open end bracelets from metal strips
- Bending jigs, for making intricate bends in wire or metal strips
- Plate anvil, used as a surface for hammering metal
- Felt polishing sticks
- Wire brush for cleaning files

*(e)*

Students should spend several hours working with the basic tools and practicing the various processes. A good place to begin is by learning how to manipulate wire into various shapes.

*Basic Manipulations with Wire*
Because of the nature of the material, most jewelry made with wire will have a linear quality, and this characteristic should be taken into account when designing wire pieces. Sixteen or 18 gauge NuGold wire was used throughout the process illustrated.

Before wire can be used, it must be straightened as figure 12.3 shows. This can be easily accomplished if you place one end of a length of cut wire into the vise. Tighten the vise to hold wire firmly, grasp the other end of wire with pliers, and pull until you feel the wire stretch. Once the wire is stretched, it should be handled carefully to avoid further kinks.

Wire may be manipulated into various shapes as shown in figure 12.4.

A  Make loops of various sizes with round nose pliers by placing the end of a length of wire into the pliers and rotating the pliers back toward the wire until a loop is formed. The size of the loop formed will depend on where the wire is placed on the tapered ends of the pliers. The individual rings were made at the largest diameter of the pliers. These may be used as jump rings or a number might be joined together to form a chain or bracelet.

B  Sections of wire with loops at each end may be joined to form a chain as shown. Be careful that loops are made so they are in alignment and that links are the same length.

C  Decorative chain links are made with round nose pliers. To form link, make a loop in each end of a short length of wire. Place the center of the wire at the widest point of the round nose pliers. Push ends of wire down with fingers until loops meet back to back. The end of the central loop is then grasped horizontally with pliers and bent into a slight curve to ensure that the links will lie flat when joined, as shown.

D  Variations of chain links are made with round nose and flat pliers.

E  Coiled forms are made with round and flat pliers. Cut and straighten a length of wire. Make a tiny loop in one end with the smallest diameter of the round nose pliers. Begin winding wire around this

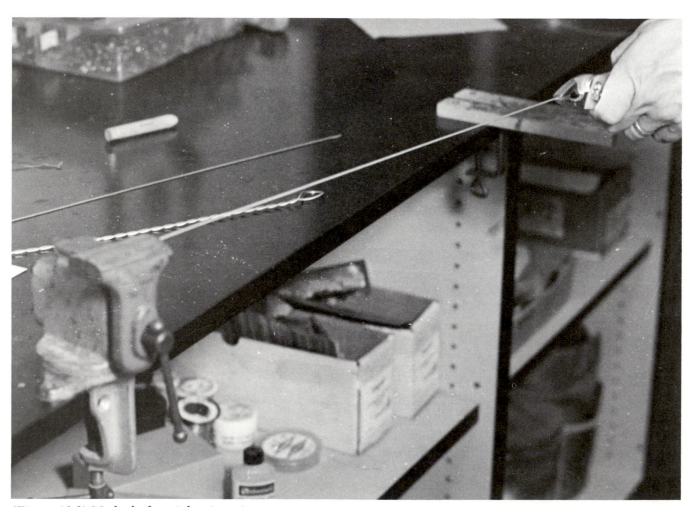

*(Figure 12.3) Method of straightening wire.*

loop in such a way that a flat coil is formed. When several winds have been made, grasp the flat coil horizontally in the flat nose pliers and continue winding until desired diameter is obtained. These forms can be made into pins, used as parts of a necklace, or soldered to flat surfaces for a decorative effect.

F Spiral coils may be made by winding wire around a wooden dowel rod of the desired diameter. These coils may be used as parts of other pieces or may be cut apart to form rings of larger diameter than is possible with the round nose pliers.

G The flat pliers are used to bend angles into wire as shown.

H Two or more strands of wire may be twisted together prior to forming into jewelry. Cut a length of wire somewhat more than twice as long as the twist desired. Straighten the length and bend it back on itself so each arm of the wire is of equal length. Place the two cut ends in a vise and tighten.

Into the loop at the the other end insert a large nail or short metal rod and, while pulling on the wire, twist it as tightly as desired. Wire may also be twisted with a hand drill, into the chuck of which has been inserted a cup hook. The wire may then be easily twisted if you crank the drill. Twists may be made with two and four strands of wire as shown.

I Interesting patterns are made when twisted wires are hammered flat.

J Other hammered forms are shown.

When metal is hammered, it becomes "work hardened," which means it becomes brittle and loses its malleability or pliability. Malleability may be restored by heating the metal in a flame to a dull red glow. This process is called annealing. When metals are heated, oxides form on the surface; they may be removed by dropping the hot metal into a pickling solution, such as Sparex, immediately after annealing. The solution may be made and kept in a covered Pyrex dish so it is always ready

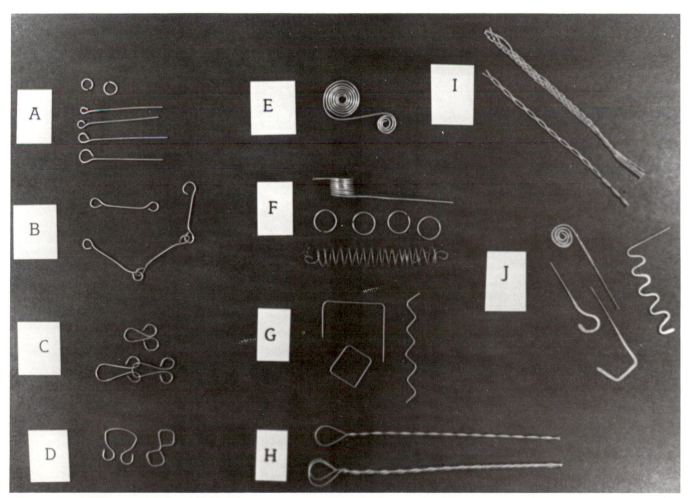

*(Figure 12.4) Wire manipulated in various ways.*

for use. Hammering is usually done with the flat end of a ball peen hammer on a bench anvil. The surface of the anvil should be kept smooth and polished, because any dents or scratches will be picked up by the metal being hammered and will be difficult to polish out. Once the basic techniques of manipulating wire are learned, the student should plan and execute several pieces utilizing these techniques.

*Basic Manipulations with Sheet Metal*
Whereas jewelry constructed from wire is linear in quality, jewelry made from sheet metal must take into account the flat, planar quality of the material. Processes such as sawing, bending, drilling, piercing, and filing are basic to this approach. The bench pin and jeweler's vise previously referred to will be used extensively. The bench pin or peg is made of a flat piece of hardwood about 8-by-3-by-1½ into one narrow end from which is cut a V shape about 1½ inches wide and 1½ inches deep. The other end is fitted with a special clamp that attaches firmly to the edge of the workbench. The bench pin serves as a support for metal which is being sawed, drilled, or pierced.

The vise should be equipped with smooth, flat, parallel jaws and is used for holding metal in place for operations such as filing or bending. The jeweler's saw is composed of an adjustable metal frame designed to hold a replaceable fine blade. The teeth of the blade should always point toward the handle of the saw because the down stroke does most of the work in sawing. Some practice is usually necessary to learn proper sawing technique, and the student can expect to break several blades in the process. When a blade breaks, remove it from the saw by loosening the front and back clamps. Insert one end of the new blade in front, clamp, and tighten. Place front end of saw into the V of the bench pin and press forward with the body while placing the other end of the blade in the back clamp. Tighten this clamp and release pressure, which will put the blade in tension. A properly inserted blade should make a "pinging" sound when thumped with a finger. To saw a piece of metal, first mark a cut line in the surface of the metal with the scriber, as figure 12.5 shows (16 or 18 gauge NuGold sheets are used in illustrations).

Place the piece in the bench pin so that the line to be cut is over the V. Begin the cut by moving the saw up and down with short strokes to make an indentation (see figure 12.6). Then by holding the saw in position, make long even strokes up and down. Try to keep the saw as close to the vertical as possible and do not exert force or rush the operation, either of which could cause blade breakage. Rubbing the blade occasionally with beeswax will help it to move more easily through the metal.

*(Figure 12.5) Using scriber to mark cutting line on metal.*

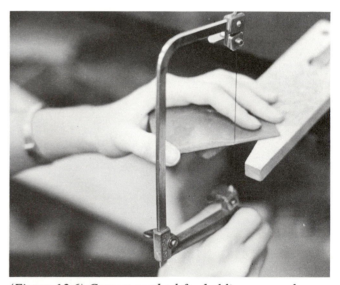

*(Figure 12.6) Correct method for holding saw and beginning the cut.*

To cut pierced designs or inside shapes from metal, first drill a small hole just inside the cutting line, then thread one end of the saw blade through the hole, reattach it to the frame, and proceed with the sawing.

Although drilling may be done satisfactorily with a hand drill, the flexible shaft machine is far more efficient. Assortments of drill bits of various sizes

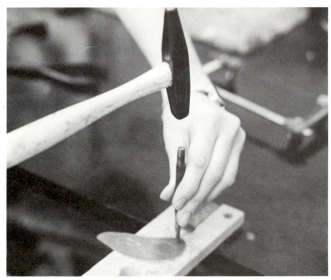

*(Figure 12.7) Using center punch to make indentation in metal.*

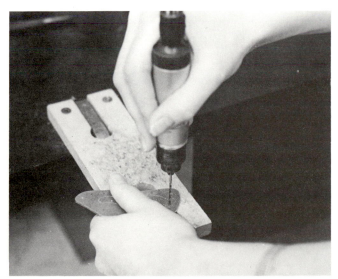

*(Figure 12.8) Correct method of using drill to make hole in metal.*

ranging from 3/0 to 8 will provide the capability needed for jewelry work. To drill a hole, place metal to be drilled on a firm support, place the point of the center punch on the spot where the hole is desired and tap it sharply with a hammer (see figure 12.7). This will make an indentation in which the point of the drill can be placed to keep it from sliding over the surface of the metal.

Choose a drill bit of the proper size, insert it into the chuck of the flexible shaft machine, (see figure 12.8). Support work to be drilled with the bench pin, place the top of the drill into the previously made indentation, and turn on motor. Apply moderate pressure, and be careful to keep drill vertical. Continue until hole is through metal. After continued use, drill bits will become dull and must be replaced with new sharp ones.

*Soldering*

Often, in the construction of jewelry, it is necessary to permanently bond two or more pieces of metal together. The easiest way to accomplish this is by *soldering,* which is the technique of fusing metals by using a second metal of a lower melting point.

Solders consist of special alloys and are compounded to melt at various temperatures, depending on which metals are being joined. For joining brass, copper, and their alloys, "soft" solder made of a mixture of lead and tin is generally used; 50:50 soft solder, for example, is one-half lead and one-half tin and melts at approximately 400° F.

Silver and karat gold solders, on the other hand, are compounded to melt at much higher temperatures and are called "hard" solders. Silver solder is an alloy of silver, copper, and zinc and may be obtained in three grades: (1) *easy,* which melts at 1325°F; (2) *medium,* which melts at 1390° F; and (3) *hard,* which has a melting point of 1450° F. All temperatures are considerably below the melting point of sterling silver, which is 1640° F. A hard solder flux containing borax is used with these solders.

Successful soldering depends on several conditions, regardless of whether one is using soft or hard solders.

• All surfaces to be soldered must be thoroughly cleaned by scouring with a commercial cleanser such as Comet or Ajax.

- Parts to be joined must fit together snugly with no gaps and be held together by some means during the soldering process.
- Parts to be soldered must be evenly heated. If one part is hotter than another, the solder will flow toward the hottest part. Always try to apply heat to the metal rather than to the solder.
- Just enough solder must be used to effect a good joint, but not so much that there will be an excess

to be removed through tedious filing. Knowing the right amount to use comes through practice and experience.

Figure 12.9 shows two general types of soldering: *butt joint* soldering and *sweat* soldering. Students should practice each until they are proficient. Figure 12.9a shows set up for butt joint soldering. The two pieces of clean metal are placed so the joints fit closely and are held in place by pins stuck into the firebrick. Flux has

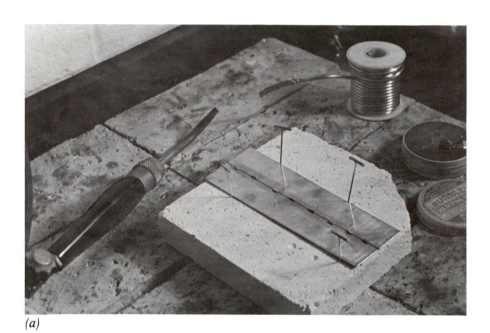

*(a)*

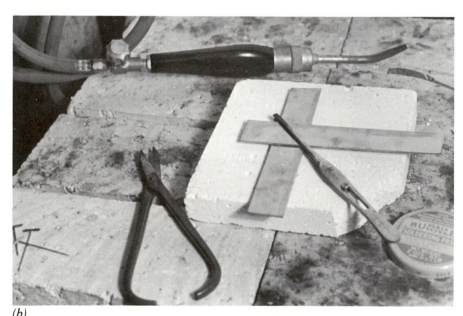

*(b)*

*(Figure 12.9) (a) Setup for butt joint soldering.*
*(b) Setup for sweat joint soldering.*

been brushed along the joint and tiny snippets of soft solder have been placed along the joint. Apply heat by beginning at the nearest end and progressing toward the other end until the solder melts and flows into the joint. An alternate but more difficult method would be to start heating the metal; as it becomes hot enough to melt the solder, hold the end of the solder still on the roll to the hot metal. One must work very rapidly and surely to avoid building up too much solder.

Figure 12.9b shows set up for sweat or layered soldering. The pieces of metal to be joined are cleaned and flux applied to the surfaces that will be bonded. Flatten solder with a hammer and cut tiny snippets with the plate shears. Place several of these on the lower surface and clamp the two pieces together with slidelock tweezers so a sandwich is formed. Apply heat with the torch until the solder melts and the top piece drops into place. Pieces soldered by either method are allowed to cool slightly until the solder is set, then are dropped into the pickling jar to remove fire scale. All soldering operations should be completed before any attempt is made to polish the work.

Sometimes it is necessary to carry out additional soldering operations on a piece that has already been soldered. In this case, the previously soldered joint must be protected in some way or it will become hot and loosen in the process. The previous joint may be clamped, or if this is not feasible, the joint can be painted with a paste made by mixing yellow ochre with water. Another method is to wrap the previously soldered joint with strips of wet asbestos paper.

*Finishing*
Good craftsmanship demands that jewelry pieces be finished as carefully as possible. This involves filing to smooth cut edges and polishing surfaces to a soft sheen. Files are available in various cuts from coarse to fine and shaped to fit every possible need—round, half round, flat, square, triangular, and so forth. Files used for jewelry should be reserved for this purpose only and should be kept clean by periodic brushing with the special file card having fine wire bristles.

The proper method of hand filing is shown in figure 12.10. The piece being filed is clamped into the vise and the file passed diagonally in one direction only over it, *away* from the user. *Do not* saw the file back and forth across the edge being filed. Begin with a fairly coarse file, then go to the finer grades. Final finish of an edge

may be made with fine emery paper or crocus cloth. Needle files of various shapes are useful for getting into small inside cuts.

Surface polishing is usually the very last operation carried out and is done to impart a sheen or luster to the surface of the work. If the piece is not particularly dirty, a simple hand polishing with a soft cloth and a compound such as Brasso will suffice. For heavier jobs, the flexible shaft tool equipped with a small muslin buff impregnated with a polishing compound will greatly facilitate the operation. Compounds are manufactured in cake or bar form and applied to the buffing wheel by allowing it to rotate on the surface of the cake until a quantity is picked up. Separate buffs should be kept for the various compounds.

If the metal has been scratched, remove scratches by buffing with tripoli compound (severe scratches may require use of emery compound). After scratches are removed, begin polishing with red rouge, and finally polish with jewelers rouge for a mirror finish. When using the buffing wheels, keep them in constant motion to avoid doing too much work in one spot, which might indeed introduce additional problems of grooves and scratches.

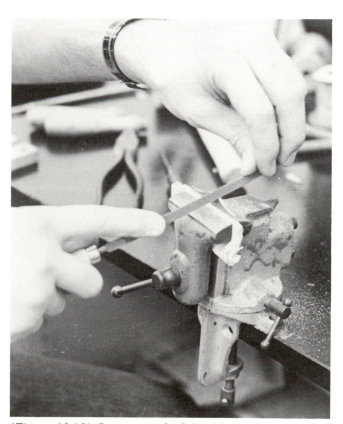

*(Figure 12.10) Correct method for filing metal.*

*Findings:* Findings are those small essential items such as pin backs, cuff link backs, ear clips and wires, catches, and joints, all of which can be made, if desired, but are so much better purchased because they are relatively inexpensive and certainly save considerable time and effort, especially in a classroom. It is also desirable to purchase ready-made chain unless something that is not available is needed.

*Texturing:* It is often desirable to texture the surface of a piece of metal, either completely or partially. More advanced methods of forming jewelry such as repoussé, engraving, chasing, granulation, and the like are texturing methods in themselves and are usually beyond the scope of a general crafts class in basic jewelry making. Certain textured effects can be arrived at rather easily, however. One of the simplest means of introducing texture is to place the flat pieces of metal on a block of soft wood and hit it with repeated blows with the rounded end of the ball peen hammer. This will produce indentations on one side and raised marks on the other.

*Stones:* Jewelry made by crafts students may be enhanced by the inclusion of a stone of some sort. The precious stones, such as diamonds, emeralds, and sapphires, require mountings of gold or platinum, of course, but there is no reason that such stones as tiger eye, bloodstone, obsidian, amethyst, agate, and other varieties cannot be used by students in their jewelry creations. These stones may be obtained from jewelers supply houses in either tumbled form (irregular polished chunks) or in cabochon form (one surface rounded, and the bottom polished flat) and are relatively inexpensive.

Stones of this type are sometimes attached to the piece with epoxy resin glue, but it is far better craftsmanship to mount the stone with a prong or claw setting. This entails preparing a thin metal base having a sufficient number of prongs to hold the stone in place.

The procedure for prong setting a tumbled stone is as follows. The stone is a tumbled piece of agate, of roughly triangular shape, to be set on a two-inch square of copper for a necklace medallion.

1  Trace the shape of stone, on a piece of paper. Prongs must be placed so that the stone will be held firmly. For this stone, three prongs will be sufficient. Others might require four or more prongs. Sketch prongs in position.
2  Cut out paper pattern and use it to scribe the shape on a piece of thin copper, brass, or NuGold.
3  Rough cut this shape from the metal with the plate shears. Prongs must be long enough to bend up over the stone and hold it in place. They are made longer than needed to begin with and the excess trimmed off later.

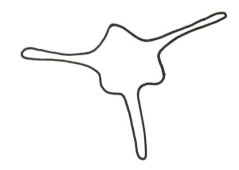

4 Refine the shape by filing so that the center portion is the exact size and shape of the bottom of the stone. Make the prongs as thin and delicate as possible.

5 Bend the prongs up slightly and sweat solder the base of the setting into place on the medallion.

6 Determine how long the prongs need to be to hold the stone, cut them to this length, file and round the ends.

7 Set the stone into place by bending the prongs up over the edges of it and pressing them into place with the end of the burnisher. Stone setting is usually the last step to be done on a piece, after all cleaning, polishing, filing, and so forth are finished.

*Jewelry Design*

Because jewelry becomes such a personal and individual possession and is usually much smaller in scale than work produced in other crafts, certain special design factors must be considered. The basic design principles as outlined in chapter 5 must, of course, be kept in mind. In addition, the jewelry student will find the following suggestions helpful.

- A piece of jewelry should fit the personality and characteristics of the person who is to wear it. For example, a small-boned woman with delicate features cannot usually wear a large, bold necklace.

- Some jewelry is utilitarian—cuff links, tie tacks, hair clips, pins, certain brooches and belt buckles, for example. Other jewelry is almost wholly decorative or aesthetic in nature—necklaces, earrings, most finger rings, anklets, bracelets, and the like. Other pieces such as crosses, stars of David, wedding bands, and fraternal emblems have a symbolic significance. Some few pieces might fulfill all three functions.

- There are definite shape, size, and weight limitations that the jeweler must observe. An earring, for example must not be so heavy that it will put excessive strain on the ear lobe. A pin back attached in the wrong place will cause a brooch to fall forward.

- The design of a piece of jewelry must be compatible to the purpose for which it is intended. A ring must not be too bulky or have projections that will cause discomfort to the hand of the wearer. A necklace must be designed to lie flat and fit the neck. All jewelry surfaces must be completely smooth so as not to scratch the skin or catch in the clothing.

- The style preferences and tastes of the wearer must be followed. Styles and tastes in jewelry have varied greatly through the ages as books describing the history of jewelry illustrate. Customs and tastes of various cultures have also influenced jewelry design as evidenced by such things as toe rings in some Asian countries, multiple bracelets and neck rings worn by some African tribes, and nose jewels in India.

The *wearability* of his or her work should be the primary concern of the jeweler. No matter how well crafted a piece is or how aesthetically pleasing, if it cannot be worn comfortably, it falls short of good jewelry design.

Although this section has dealt primarily with constructed metal jewelry, remember that an infinite variety of other materials might be used in and of themselves or combined with metals. As has so often been pointed out in this book, contemporary craftspeople consider any and all materials as possibilities for a particular craft. With jewelry, they are making use of such unusual materials as leather, animal bones and teeth, wood (both natural and petrified), plastics, glass, and even feathers. These certainly add a new and interesting dimension to the vocabulary of the jeweler and should by all means be explored.

Examples of student work are shown in figure 12.11.

*(a)*

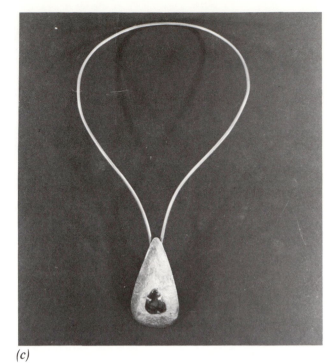

*(c)*

*(b)*

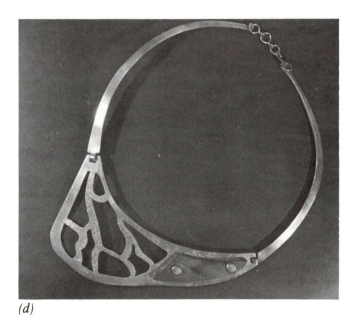

*(d)*

*(Figure 12.11) (a) Necklace of twisted wire. Drops of various lengths are formed by melting the end of straight sections of wire until a ball of metal forms. Center medallion is hammered and has soldered coil decoration. (b) Three pairs of earrings made of twisted wire. (c) Necklace of heavy-shaped wire. Pendant made of hammered shape slightly domed; prong set stone. (d) Necklace of hammered and sawed shapes; pierced design; piece of teakwood attached with rivets.*

*Suggested Readings*

Becker, Vivienne. *Antique and Twentieth Century Jewellery.* New York: Van Nostrand, Reinhold, 1982.

Brynner, Irena. *Modern Jewelry: Design and Techniques.* New York: Reinhold Publishing Co., 1968.

Chatt, Orville K. *Design Is Where You Find It.* Ames: Iowa State University Press, 1972.

Coyne, John, ed. *The Penland School of Crafts Book of Jewelry Making.* Indianapolis: Bobbs-Merrill, 1975.

Crawford, John. *Introducing Jewelry Making.* New York: Watson-Guptill Publications, 1969.

Evans, Chuck, *Jewelry: Contemporary Design and Technique.* Worcester, Mass.: Davis Publications, 1983.

Goldemberg, Rose L. *All about Jewelry.* New York: Arbor House Publishing Co., 1983.

Kallenberg, Lawrence. *Modeling in Wax for Jewelry and Sculpture.* Radnor, Pa.: Chilton Book Co., 1981.

Lewes, Klares. *Jewelry Making for the Amateur.* New York: Reinhold Publishing Co., 1965.

Morton, Philip. *Contemporary Jewelry.* New York: Holt, Rinehart and Winston. 1970.

Pelissier, Jaime. *The Jeweler's Craft.* New York: Van Nostrand, Reinhold, 1981.

Rose, Augustus F., and Antonio Curino. *Jewelry Making and Design.* New York: Dover Publications, 1967.

Sanford, William R. *Jewelry: Queen of Crafts.* New York: Bruce Publishing Co., 1970.

Sarett, Morton R. *The Jewelry in Your Life.* Chicago: Nelson-Hall, 1979.

Solberg, Ramona. *Inventive Jewelry Making.* New York: Van Nostrand, Reinhold, 1972.

Sprintzen, Alice. *Jewelry: Basic Techniques and Design.* Radnor, Pa.: Chilton Book Co., 1980.

von Newmann, Robert. *The Design and Creation of Jewelry.* rev. ed. Radnor, Pa.: Chilton Book Co., 1972.

Wade, Takashi. *The Art of Making Jewelry.* New York: Van Nostrand, Reinhold, 1975.

Warwick, James. *Beginning Jewelry.* New York: Charles Scribner's Sons, 1979.

# 13  Mosaics

The craft of mosaics entails forming a design or picture by adhering numerous small pieces of a hard, durable material (glass, fired clay, stone, pebbles) onto a supporting surface (wall, floor, panel, column). The bits and pieces may be adhered to the support surface with an adhesive and the interstices filled with a grouting material (plaster or mortar); or the individual pieces may be set directly into a cement or mastic that hardens, holds them into place, and is self-grouting.

Traditionally, mosaics have been made with either ceramic or glass cubes (tesserae), but contemporary mosaicists have expanded the work to such an extent that now we see mosaics made from practically any material that will fragment and adhere to a surface.

Mosaics were known in ancient Egypt and Mesopotamia, where they were employed as decorative elements in jewelry, or furniture, and on buildings as architectural embellishments. The Greeks as early as the fifth century B.C. used clay, marble, and glass tesserae as well as small pebbles to make floor mosaics. This practice was continued and perfected by the Romans. Numerous fine examples of wall, floor, and ceiling mosaics have been excavated in Italy and, indeed, everywhere that the Romans established colonies. Designs were composed of geometric patterns, scrolls, figures of heroes and the gods, and all manner of plant, animal, and marine life. Often the mosaics would be of a pictorial nature, commemorating some great battle or a mythological legend. Mosaics as religious art began as surface decorations for walls and other parts of the great basilicas that were built after the Emperor Constantine made Christianity the official religion of the Roman Empire in A.D. 323. Depictions of Christ, the apostles, the Virgin Mary, saints of the church, and numerous symbolic designs covered much of the interior surface of such basilicas as Sant' Apollinare in Classe (Ravenna), which H. W. Janson describes as "a shimmering realm of light and color where precious marble surfaces and the brilliant glitter of mosaics evoke the spiritual splendor of the Kingdom of God."[1]

Mosaics served the same purpose in these early churches that stained glass windows did in later Gothic churches—to illustrate biblical figures and events in such a way that the largely illiterate worshipers could understand them.

The art of the religious mosaic reached its greatest perfection during the Byzantine era in such architectural settings as the churches of Hagia Sophia in Constantinople, San Vitale in Ravenna, and later, Saint Mark's in Venice. Byzantine mosaics were noted for their extensive use of gold tesserae, which made the interiors of Byzantine churches even more brilliant than the early Christian ones.

Mosaics as an art form declined during the Renaissance, but enjoyed a brief surge of popularity during the "revival" in the nineteenth century, particularly in England. In the twentieth century, the mosaic mural has been used widely as architectural embellishment, the most spectacular examples being those by the Mexican artist Juan O'Gorman on the exterior walls of the library of the National University of Mexico (Mexico City). Contemporary mosaic artists, like those working in so many other crafts, are exploring the uses of new materials such as plastics, synthetic resins, and fused glass. They are making mosaics out of nails, bits of metal, chips of wood, found objects, shells, seeds, and multicolored pebbles as well as the more traditional clay and glass tesserae, to give new and exciting directions to the art of fragmented design.

Because basic procedures for making mosaics are fairly constant regardless of which fragmented materials are being used, instructions will be given for a small panel composed of ceramic tiles. Necessary modifications will be included to enable the student to progress to other materials and formats as desired.

### Materials and Tools

Tools and materials for creating mosaics are shown in figure 13.1. A *backing material* provides the base of support. For small panels designed to be used as wall hangings, pieces of masonite or plywood are satisfactory. These may be any desired size and shape.

*(Figure 13.1) Tools and materials for mosaics.*

For outdoor use, marine plywood is recommended. Any surface that is to be exposed to weather should be sealed with shellac, epoxy resin paint, or some other waterproofing compound. Very large panels must have some sort of bracing applied to the back for strength and rigidity. Mosaics may be applied to almost any surface, including walls, furniture, glass, metal, and preshaped forms, provided the base material has the required rigidity and strength to support the weight of the mosaic elements.

The word *tessera* (plural, tesserae) derives from the Latin word for "cube" or "four" and was originally applied to small glass or clay tiles used as *mosaic elements*. In contemporary usage, tesserae are used to designate fragments of any materials used for mosaicked surfaces.

Ceramic tiles may be purchased from supply houses or tile shops. They are usually three-quarter inch square, may be glazed or unglazed, and come in a wide range of colors. They are easily cut or broken into smaller geometric or random shapes.

Shards of colored glass may be cut or broken into small pieces for mosaic use. In the crafts classroom, this is an excellent way to utilize scraps of glass leftover from stained glass work. The scraps can be cut into definite shapes with a glass cutter, or may be placed between two thick layers of newspaper and broken into random bits with a hammer. Other sources of scrap glass are broken bottles, mirrors, and automobile taillights.

Additional sources of mosaic elements are such materials as scraps of wood, shells, pebbles, gravel, marble chips, seeds, whole spices, dried beans, eggshells, cork, plastics, linoleum, discarded costume jewelry, scraps of metal, glass marbles, and all manner of found objects. The possibilities are endless, but care must be taken to consider the practicality of the elements chosen and their suitability for the work being planned.

The choice of *adhesive* depends on several factors: the size of the project, where and how it will be used (indoors, outdoors), the material being adhered, and the supporting foundation. For small panels on masonite or plywood, Duco cement or one of the white casein or polyvinyl acetate-based glues (Elmer's Wilhold) will be adequate. For larger panels, epoxy resins should be chosen because they are extremely durable, have excellent bonding properties, and will stand up under any weather conditions. These adhesives are sold in

packages containing two separate components, the resin and a catalyst, that must be mixed together in equal quantities just before use. The mixture hardens rather quickly but maximum strength develops only on aging; therefore, epoxied work must be allowed to set undisturbed overnight for optimum bonding.

Commercial tile mastic may be used, especially when large surfaces such as walls are to be mosaicked, because it can be spread over large areas and the tesserae set directly into it. Mortars, cements, stucco, and concrete are often used for large architectural mosaics and should be mixed and used according to manufacturer's directions. *Grouting materials* fill in the small spaces left between the fragments after tesserae are bonded onto backing materials. Whether these spaces are grouted depends on the function of the work and the artist's personal preference. Some mosaicists feel that to leave the spaces ungrouted adds to the design qualities of the work; others think the work should be grouted regardless. All functional surfaces should be grouted but purely decorative surfaces may be grouted or not as desired.

Grout is a form of cement that is mixed with water until its consistency is smooth and creamy, somewhat like mayonnaise or whipped cream. Commercial grout, as purchased, is usually white but may be tinted with a powdered pigment, such as dry tempera, lampblack, yellow ochre, or a dry mix especially formulated to color grout.

Architectural mosaics set into a bed of cement are usually applied in such a way that some of the wet cement works its way up through the interstices, so additional grouting is not necessary. Grouted mosaics should have a final coat of clear commercial waterproofing compound or liquid wax, if they are going to be exposed to weather or receive hard use. Waterproofing should be repeated periodically as needed.

*Cutting or fracturing tools* for cutting ceramic tiles into definite shapes are tile cutters or nippers. Two types are available, either the "side-bite" varieties or those that allow the jaws of the cutter to be placed across the surface of the tile. For cutting tesserae from glass, regular glass cutters are used. (See chapter 16 on stained glass for directions on how to use cutters.) When random fragments of either glass or ceramic tiles are needed, they may be broken by placing the piece between thick layers of newspaper and striking it with sharp blows of a hammer. Wear plastic goggles to protect the eyes when cutting or breaking mosaic elements.

*Spreading and grouting tools* aid when you apply adhesives either directly to the support material or to the back of each tessera. Such tools as palette knives, trowels, and spatulas, are used. Select the tool that will best accomplish the job at hand. Rubber dish-scraper–type spatulas are useful for working grout into crevices. Plastic bowls and containers of various sizes are used for mixing grout.

*Cleaning and finishing tools* remove excess grout and finish the surface of the completed work. A supply of sponges, rags, paper towels, and brushes of several kinds should be on hand for this purpose. Excess grout should *never* be washed down the sink, because it will eventually clog the plumbing. Scrape grout from the bowl into the trash can, and wipe bowls and other implements clean with paper towels.

## Procedure

Procedure for a small panel from ceramic tile to tesserae includes six steps. First, a support surface must be prepared. *Masonite* usually requires no preparation because the surface is smooth and nonporous. For larger panels, some bracing may be necessary. If transparent glass is the mosaic material, the surface of the masonite should be sprayed or brushed with several coats of flat white paint, which will allow the light to reflect back through the glass and produce a much more brilliant appearance. A *plywood* surface is porous and should be sealed with a coat or two of acrylic plastic paint before mosaic elements are applied. For outdoor use or in any situation where dampness is a factor, marine plywood is recommended.

The second step involves designing the work (review general design principles in chapter 5). Designs for mosaics may range from a pattern of a few simple, well-integrated shapes to a full-scale pictorial representation. For beginners and especially for those less skilled in drawing, the simpler designs will be more successful. Extremely detailed designs are usually not suitable for mosaic work. The design may be sketched directly onto the support surface with pencil or charcoal (see figure 13.2).

*(Figure 13.2) Design is sketched on surface of masonite panel.*

Color relationships are important. You may work them out by making small preliminary sketches and coloring them with crayons or colored pencils. Because mosaics are made of very small fragments, the *total* design must be planned so that it will "carry" when viewed from a distance. An area that appears just right when viewed close-up during execution may be totally lost when viewed from a distance.

Preparation of tesserae is the third step in creating a mosaic. The three-quarter inch square ceramic tiles are usually cut into smaller shapes and sizes for use. By using the tile nippers as shown in figure 13.3, one may cut tile into smaller squares, rectangles, triangles, or irregular shapes. A great deal has been written about elaborate systems developed for cutting and placing tiles, and those who plan to do professional commissions might study these systems. In the classroom, however, a

good general rule is to utilize tesserae in sizes and shapes that will best carry out the directional nature and area patterns of the design. A good mosaic design "flows"; therefore, if tesserae shapes compete with this rhythm, the result will be chaotic.

The fourth step encompasses application of tesserae. One of two general approaches may be followed: (1) the adhering substance may be spread on an area of the design and the individual tessera pressed into it or (2) the back of each tessera may be "buttered" with the adhesive and pressed into place (see figure 13.4). When all tesserae have been adhered, allow work to dry overnight. Check dried work carefully for loose fragments and reglue as needed. Remedy mistakes by prying up badly set areas with the tip of a heavy screwdriver and doing those areas over.

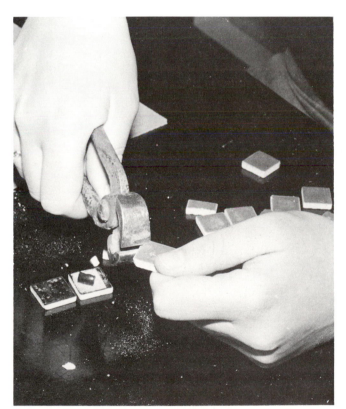

*(Figure 13.3) Nippers are used to cut ceramic tiles into small bits.*

*(Figure 13.4) Cement is applied to bits of tile that are then pressed into place on the panel.*

Grouting is the fifth step in creating a mosaic. Into a plastic bowl, pour enough dry grout to complete panel. Tint grout, if desired, with dry coloring material. Moisten the grout by adding small amounts of water and stirring until a smooth, creamy mixture is obtained (see figure 13.5). The consistency should be such that the grout may be easily spread, but not so thin that it is runny. Apply grout with putty knife or rubber spatula, forcing it down into the gaps between the tesserae as figure 13.6 illustrates. When entire panel is grouted, let it rest a few minutes, then begin to remove excess grout from surface of the panel by carefully scraping it with the flat edge of the putty knife or spatula. If any tesserae are dislodged, they must be replaced as the work begins to dry. As the grout begins to set, the remainder of the excess may be removed with dampened paper towels. Allow panel to dry completely, at least overnight.

*(Figure 13.5) Powdered tempera ia added to dry grout and mixed in. Water will be added slowly to the mixture until desired consistency is reached.*

*(Figure 13.7) Final cleaning of dry panel is done with stiff brush.*

*(Figure 13.6) "Buttery" grout mixture is forced into crevices between tesserae.*

Cleaning and finishing is the sixth and last step in the procedure. Final cleaning may be done by removing any bits of dried grout from textured areas with a stiff brush (see figure 13.7). Some mosaicists clean the panel with a solution of commercial muriatic acid, followed by a rinse with a solution of baking soda in water. The panel is finally rinsed thoroughly with water. If acid is used, protect hands, skin, and eyes to prevent acid burns. When the panel is dry, it may be waxed or treated with a waterproofing compound. It is then framed or mounted as desired.

The procedure given is for the *direct* method, meaning that the tesserae are set faceup, directly into the adhering material. This is a definite advantage, because one can see exactly how the design is progressing. The direct method *must* be used when the mosaic is of diverse materials with varying thicknesses. (See figure 13.8 for student work.)

*(a)*

*(b)*

*(Figure 13.8) (a) Student work: glass tesserae titled "Sunburst." (b) Student work: ceramic tesserae titled "Maltese."*

The *indirect* method is almost always used when a completely flat-surfaced mosaic is required, such as a table, counter top, or tray. In the indirect approach, the design is traced *in reverse* on a sheet of paper. The tesserae are then pasted *facedown* onto the paper with a water-soluble glue such as library paste. When all the tesserae have been applied and the work is dry, cover it with a piece of heavy cardboard and flip the whole assembly over. The paper containing the tesserae is then slid carefully onto the backing surface that has previously been coated with commercial mastic. When the mastic is dry, the facing paper is thoroughly wet with warm water on a sponge; when soft, it is stripped away from the tesserae. Grouting and finishing are done as described in the direct method. The indirect method is the traditional one used by mosaicists for centuries. Those specializing in large architectural commissions still use this method today.

*Note*

1. H. W. Janson, *History of Art,* 2d ed. (Englewood Cliffs, N.J.: Prentice-Hall, 1977), 197–99.

*Suggested Readings*

Aller, Doris, and Diane L. Aller. *Mosaics.* Menlo Park, Calif.: Lane Magazine and Book Co., 1959.

Fischer, Peter. *Mosaic History and Technique.* New York: McGraw-Hill Book Co., 1971.

Lovoos, Janice, and Felice Paramore. *Modern Mosaic Techniques.* New York: Watson-Guptill Publications, 1967.

Stribling, Mary Lou. *Mosaic Techniques.* New York: Crown Publishers, 1966.

Timmons, Virginia G. *Designing and Making Mosaics.* Worcester, Mass.: Davis Publications, 1971.

Unger, Hans. *Practical Mosaics.* New York: Viking Press, 1965.

Young, Joseph L. *Mosaics, Principles and Practice.* New York: Reinhold Publishing Co., 1963.

# 14  Papermaking by Hand

Paper—so commonplace, so plentiful, so much a part of our daily lives—was virtually unknown before the second century A.D., many centuries later than textiles, some of which are made from the same sorts of materials as paper. Both linen and cotton are derived from plant fibers as is paper. From the stalk of the papyrus plant, the ancient Egyptians made a material resembling paper, which was in use as a writing material as early as 2200 B.C. This was, however, not true paper but laminated thin sections of the plant stalk. True paper must be made by pulping plant materials with water and a caustic material until they are broken down into individual filaments, which are then gathered together on a screen to form sheets of true paper.

Although there is evidence that paper may have existed in China as early as 12 B.C., Ts'ai Lun, an official of the Chinese emperor Ho-Ti, is usually credited with the invention of paper in A.D. 105. In searching for a substitute for costly silk as a writing material, Ts'ai Lun devised a method for making paper from the macerated bark of mulberry trees, hemp plants, and old rags. He probably formed the first sheets on a primitive mould made from bamboo strips.

Kept secret in China for many centuries, the art of papermaking became known in Japan around A.D. 600 and spread from there to other parts of Asia. Papermaking was introduced into Egypt about A.D. 900. The Moors carried the knowledge of the process into Spain about 1150, whence it spread to all parts of Europe. Mills established in Fabriano, Italy, in the thirteenth century made a particularly fine grade of paper and are still producing paper today. The first paper mill in America was established about 1690 in Germantown, Pennsylvania, by William Rittenhouse and his sons.

The basic process of making paper by hand has changed little since its beginnings in China. Shredded plant materials (grasses, ferns, plant stalks, leaves) are boiled in a mixture of caustic lye and water to break down the vegetable fibers (cellulose) and separate them through washing from organic matter (lignin) and nonfibrous foreign matter, such as dirt. The crude pulp, known as "half-stuff," is further broken down by subjecting it to a beating process until the pulp is broken down into individual filaments, after which it is ready to be used in making paper. The pulp is placed in a large tub or vat and mixed with great quantities of water to form a slurry.

The papermaker's principal tool for making sheets is the *mould and deckle.* The mould with deckle in place is introduced vertically into the vat containing the slurry then brought up horizontally through the mixture, thereby capturing a thin layer of fibers from which the excess water is allowed to drain. The deckle is removed and the matted sheet retained on the mould is *couched* onto a piece of dampened felt.

Another piece of felt is placed on top the newly formed sheet and the whole process repeated until a stack of sheets and felts, called a *post,* has been accumulated. The post is then subjected to pressure to remove excess water and to further compress the paper fibers of the sheets until they are strong enough to be removed from the felts. The compressed sheets are allowed to air dry, after which they are ready for use. Sometimes the sheets are sized in a solution of gelatin to make the surface more suitable for accepting ink and watercolor.

In commercial papermaking, much the same procedure is followed, the various steps being carried out on large-scale automated production lines yielding many thousands of tons of paper a day. Paper made commerciallly is mostly from wood pulp, and ranges in type from newsprint to fine stationery. The uses for paper in our society are so numerous and varied that it would be difficult if not impossible to get along without it.

Artists have always been interested in fine handmade papers as a ground for drawings, watercolors, and especially graphics. A study of the works of such artists as Dürer, Rembrandt, Goya, Whistler, and others, a great part of whose work was done on paper, reveals the fine quality and durability of the handmade papers that they used.

As we have seen, paper was originally a handmade product. Through the years, in Europe and in Japan especially, limited quantities of paper are still produced by hand.[1] With the invention of the chemical pulp process for the production of paper from wood about 1850 and with the development of mechanized and automated paper machines, interest in making paper by hand declined sharply.

Early in the twentieth century in America, largely through the efforts of Dard Hunter (1883–1966), craftspeople's interest in papermaking by hand was revived. Professor Hunter spent many years researching the history and traditions of papermaking; he wrote several books that have become classics. In 1939 he established the Dard Hunter Paper Museum, presently located in Appleton, Wisconsin, and encouraged others to begin producing paper by hand.[2] Led by the veteran papermaker Douglas Howell, a small group of producers of handmade papers came into prominence in the early 1970s. Small workshops are producing beautiful handmade papers in limited quantities for artists.[3]

In the last decade, many artists have begun to experiment with making their own paper, not only as a support for their works in various media but also as a medium in its own right. They have discovered that by investing in a minimum of equipment and by following simple procedures, not only can they make sheets of fine paper but also they can shape the wet pulp into sculptural forms, cast it into molds, laminate various materials into it, and manipulate it into all manner of exciting works.

Before paper can be made, the raw materials must be broken down (macerated) into tiny threads of fibrils that will later interlace themselves on the surface of the mould to form a sheet of paper. In the studio, paper may be made "from scratch" by utilizing various types of vegetable matter; paper may be made by recycling various types of waste paper; and paper may also be made from old cotton or linen rags if a mechanical beater is available for breaking down the rags. Commercially available *cotton linters* may also be used to make paper pulp.

**Equipment**
Equipment needed for making paper by hand include:

- An electric blender with several speeds for breaking down raw materials to the pulp state.
- A kitchen food and meat grinder with assorted blades for chopping vegetable matter before boiling.

- A hot plate.
- A large enamel pot with lid for boiling vegetable matter with caustic and water. Do not use metal because it will corrode and impart undesirable impurities to the pulp.
- A large flat plastic tray to hold sizing solution.
- Felts for couching sheets of paper. These are commercially available or may be made from old blankets. The individual felts should be cut a few inches larger than the largest sheets of paper to be couched. A considerable number of felts should be available.
- Various cutting tools, such as heavy scissors, knives, and clippers.
- Assorted spatulas, spoons, and stirrers.
- Plastic buckets for soaking scrap paper and linter, and plastic containers with lids for holding prepared pulp. Empty margarine and cottage cheese tubs in one- and two-pound sizes are convenient.
- Two sheets of plywood, one-half inch thick, cut the same size as the felts. These are for improvising a press for the couched sheets.

The mould and deckle is the device used for forming sheets of paper (see figure 14.1). It consists of a wooden frame, the top of which is covered with a fine mesh screen of brass or fiberglass. This is the mould. Over the mould is placed a separate wooden frame (the deckle) that fits down around the edges of the mould, the purpose of which is to confine the pulp to the top of the mould and to form the feathered or deckled edge characteristic of handmade paper.

Moulds and deckles may be ordered from commercial suppliers or may be constructed in the shop without too much difficulty. Because moulds and deckles are perhaps the most important tools of the hand papermaker, they should be carefully constructed to last a long time.[4] For classroom use where budget is a factor, an inexpensive and acceptable mould may be made by attaching fiberglass screening to artists wood stretcher strips. The mould will be stronger if the corners are glued with waterproof glue; the wood may also be varnished if desired.

*(Figure 14.1) Mould and deckle assembled for use.*

Excellent moulds for round sheets may be made from commercial plastic embroidery hoops. Cut a piece of fiberglass screening somewhat larger in diameter than the hoops and secure it between the two sections of the hoop.

**Materials**
Materials for making paper by hand include:

- Vegetable and plant materials. Any natural material such as leaves, grasses, plant stalks, mosses, artichoke leaves, straw, cattails, soft vines and twigs and bark may be used as a source of cellulose.
- Waste paper. Paper towels, bags, construction paper, spoiled sheets from art classes, blotters, tissue paper, junk mail, egg cartons and so on may be recycled into paper pulp. Various types should be separated according to variety and color.
- Lint from the clothes drier makes an interesting addition to the paper pulp.
- Cotton linters are a by product of the cotton milling industry. These are available by the bale from various suppliers. Linters are a convenient source of rag pulp when no beater is available, or may be added to other papers being recycled to make a more durable product.

- Dyes for adding color to paper pulp. The Procion® dyes referred to in the fabric dyeing section (chapter 10) work very well. Commercial fabric dyes and inks may also be used.
- Chemicals used in the preparation of the paper: lye, alum, gelatin, cornstarch, and household bleach.

**Methods for Making Paper**
Two basic methods for preparation of the pulp (half-stuff) will be described, followed by procedures for making sheets and other forms of paper in the studio.

Plant and vegetable matter consists of cellulose and lignin, which form the framework of the plants and the pulp from which paper is made. Gather a considerable amount of raw plant materials. These may be a mixture of different kinds or all one variety. The less woody plants will be easier to handle in a classroom situation (see figure 14.2).

Cut materials into very small pieces with scissors or clippers. Grind with the food chopper, starting with the coarse blade and regrinding several times, then use successively finer blades as figure 14.3 shows. The resulting pulpy mass is placed in the enameled pot until it is two-thirds full.

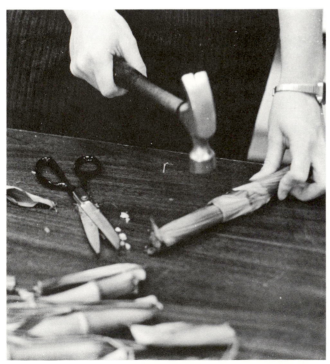

*(Figure 14.2) Young bamboo shoots being broken down with the aid of a hammer and shears.*

*(Figure 14.3) Grinding the cut up bamboo in a food grinder.*

Cover material with cold water and add 3 to 4 tablespoons of lye (see figure 14.4). *Note that lye is a highly corrosive substance and must be handled very carefully. Wear rubber gloves and eye shield for protection.* Simmer the mixture for two to three hours, stirring occasionally, after which the plant fibers should be pretty well broken down. Allow the mixture to cool and transfer the pot and contents to the sink. Run cool water into the pot allowing it to overflow for about fifteen minutes (see figure 14.5). This step removes all foreign materials and leaves the fibrous framework of the plants (cellulose).

If plant materials do not appear to be sufficiently decomposed after washing, they may be reboiled with additional lye for thirty to forty minutes and rewashed. Store pulp in a covered container and label its source. Further decomposition may occur, producing an unpleasant odor; this may be eliminated by adding a small amount of household bleach to the pulp. Just before use, run the pulp through the blender, which will "beat" it to the consistency necessary for making paper.

*(Figure 14.4) Ground plant material is placed in enamel pot and caustic lye is added. Water is added to cover mixture.*

*(Figure 14.5) Boiled pulp is washed with running water for fifteen to twenty minutes.*

Pulp can also be made from scrap paper and/or cotton linters. Collect waste paper and tear or cut it into very small pieces (see figure 14.6). Paper may be all one type or mixed. Remember that heavily printed and/or colored papers will add color to the pulp.

Soak the paper in water for at least two hours and preferably overnight. For strength, about 30 percent cotton linters may be added to the paper mixture. The soaked paper is reduced to pulp by running it in small batches through the blender (see figure 14.7). Keep ratio of pulp to water low so as not to strain the motor of the blender. Use short bursts of speed rather than prolonged beating. As each batch of paper is beaten, strain off most of the water and pour the pulp into a storage container as figure 14.8 illustrates.

*(Figure 14.6) Scrap paper is torn into small bits and soaked in water.*

*(Figure 14.8) Pulp is poured through strainer to separate it from water.*

*(Figure 14.7) Mixture is "beaten" with short bursts of speed until a smooth pulp results.*

Pure rag pulp may also be made by using only cotton linters. Proceed as directed for making pulp from scrap paper. Making pulp from newspapers is not recommended because this will result in a weak paper. Old cotton and linen rags may also be used to make pulp, provided a heavy-duty beater is available to break down the rags. There is a bit of verse by some anonymous eighteenth-century writer, which tradition says must be included in any work dealing with papermaking. It goes:

*RAGS make paper*

*PAPER makes money*

*MONEY makes banks*

*BANKS make loans*

*LOANS make beggars*

*BEGGARS made RAGS*

Whether this is true or not, paper made by hand with 100 percent rag content has always been the most desirable paper for fine books and works of art.

Making rag pulp from cotton and linen rags was accomplished in the early days of papermaking by first decomposing the rags by fermentation, followed by laborious beating with heavy wooden mallets. This endless task was made considerably easier by the invention of the stamping machine in the fifteenth century. In the seventeenth century, a cylinder beater containing a revolving roll to which sharp knives were attached was invented in Holland. This "Hollander" beater, with few modifications, is used in modern paper mills to prepare pulp from rags as well as in smaller manufacturing setups. Few schools will want to go to the expense of purchasing a beater, and for most purposes, pulp made from cotton linters is a very acceptable substitute. Regardless of source, once the pulp is prepared it is ready for a variety of uses.

To make sheets of paper, two people should work together. Fill the vat about two-thirds full of warm water. Add, with vigorous stirring, small amounts of prepared pulp. The percentage of pulp in the resulting slurry will determine the thickness of the sheets that will be formed. This must be determined by experience and governed by how the finished sheets are going to be used. It is important to keep the slurry well mixed during the process of making sheets. Figure 14.9 illustrates the process. Slightly dampen a number of felts and place one of these on a piece of plywood. Color may be added to the slurry at this point if desired.

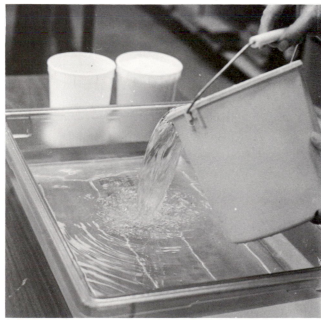

(a)

(b)

*(Figure 14.9) (a) Vat is filled with warm water, (b) Pulp is thoroughly mixed into water with aid of hand beater.*

Put the deckle in place on the mould and lower the whole assembly into the vat at an angle. Keep the assembly of mould and deckle horizontal and, with a scooping motion, bring it up through the slurry, capturing a thin layer of pulp on the screen (see figure 14.10). Allow the excess water to drain, and give the mould a brief shake backward and forward and side to side as figure 14.11 shows. This is necessary to mat and interlock the fibers of the sheet into a more cohesive mass.

---

(a)

(Figure 14.11) Mould is shaken from side to side and from front to back to interlock fibers. This is called "tossing off the wave."

(b)

(Figure 14.10) (a) Mould and deckle assembly is introduced into vat. (b) Mould is brought up through the slurry, capturing a layer of pulp on the screen.

After the mould has drained for a few seconds, remove the deckle and turn the mould upside down on the dampened felt so the newly formed sheet is in contact with the felt (see figure 14.12). This step is called couching (pronounced cooch-ing) and is shown in figure 14.13. Press down firmly and remove the mould, depositing the sheet onto the felt (see figure 14.14). Place another felt on top the sheet and repeat the process until a stack (post) of sheets and felts is obtained. End with a felt.

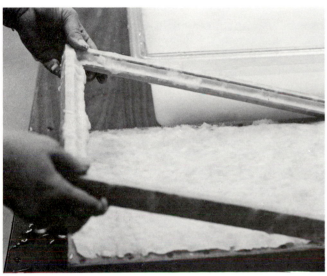

(a)

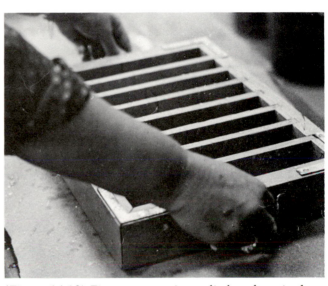

(Figure 14.13) Firm pressure is applied to deposit sheet onto felt. This is called couching.

(b)

(Figure 14.12) (a) Deckle is removed from mould. Notice typical "deckled" edge, characteristic of handmade paper. (b) Mould with sheet attached is turned face down onto a damp felt.

(Figure 14.14) Mould is lifted up leaving newly formed sheet on the felt.

179

Place the second piece of plywood on top the post and apply pressure to remove excess water and to further compress the sheets. If a press of some sort is available (such as a book press), the whole assembly may be placed therein. Adequate pressure may be obtained by placing several cinder blocks on top the post, or simply by one or more persons standing on the post, which is illustrated in figure 14.15. The pressed sheets are removed one by one from the post and allowed to air dry. They may be dried outside on a sunny day, may be hung on a line, or placed on a drying rack if available.

The finished sheets, called *waterleaf,* are ready for desired use. If they are to be used for pen and ink drawings, watercolors, or other fluid media, the sheets should be *sized* to fill the spaces between the fibers and to make a smoother, less absorbent surface. Various materials, such as rice flour, starch, gypsum, gelatin, and glue, may be used as sizing. These may be added directly to the blender when making pulp (internal or stock sizing) or may be applied to the dried sheets (external or surface sizing).

A useful sizing mixture may be made by soaking one package of unflavored gelatin in one-quarter cup cold water until water is absorbed. Then add one-half cup boiling water and stir well until all gelatin is dissolved. Mix two tablespoons cornstarch with one-quarter cup cold water and add gelatin mixture. Add an additional cup of water, stir until mixed, and cook the mixture until it thickens. Store mixture in a jar with a lid.

For internal sizing, one tablespoon of the mixture is added to each blender when pulp is being made. For external sizing, add one tablespoon of the mixture to one quart of warm water. The diluted mixture may be

*(Figure 14.15) Pressure is applied to the post to remove excess water.*

brushed onto the paper or placed in a shallow tray for the sheets to soak it in. The stock mixture will, of course, solidify because of the gelatin in it, but it may be reliquified by heating.

Handmade paper as a creative medium in its own right has, in the last few years, been explored by numerous artists who have produced many exciting and unusual expressions. Works made of paper are being displayed in many museums, papermaking workshops are being held, classes are being offered in schools, colleges, and universities, and books on the subject are beginning to appear.

Some approaches to the craft of papermaking are described. Others will doubtless occur to students involved in the process, for I know of few media that lend themselves to the flexibility of expression as does papermaking. Literally "anything goes" once the

student stops thinking in traditional patterns and frees the creative spirit of the mind and the technical facility of the hands to try new approaches. It should be remembered, however, that novel approach is not enough; worthwhile results will be had only when the student combines creativity with good design principles and aesthetic quality.

**Procedures for Using Handmade Paper**
*Hand-Formed Sheets with Embedded Objects*
Prepare a quantity of paper pulp. Place a sheet of heavy mat board on the work table and cover this with a sheet of heavy plastic, making sure there are no holes in the plastic. Select objects to be embedded. All sorts of materials may be used: twigs, grasses, yarns, bits of fabric, and tissue paper. Remember you are working "in reverse," that is, the objects you place down first will be the top layer of your completed work (see figure 14.16).

*(Figure 14.16) Objects to be embedded are being arranged facedown on piece of heavy plastic that, in turn, is on a piece of mat board on the work surface.*

When you are satisfied with the arrangement, begin covering the objects with paper pulp by pressing small amounts down around the objects (see figure 14.17). Continue until a fairly thick sheet of pulp has been formed. Press down firmly with a sponge, to remove excess water and to compact the pulp. Compacting may be assisted by rolling the surface of the sheet with a rubber brayer and sponging up the moisture squeezed out (see figure 14.18).

Cover work with another sheet of plastic and a second sheet of mat board. Carefully flip over the whole "sandwich," remove mat board and plastic, and inspect surface. Remove any material that you do not wish to remain or if you wish to leave only the impression of the object. Place work on a drying rack and turn over periodically until drying is complete (see figure 14.19).

*(Figure 14.17) Objects are covered with a fairly thick layer of pulp firmly pressed into place.*

*(Figure 14.19) Finished work is placed on shelf of drying rack.*

*(Figure 14.18) Layer of pulp is further compacted by rolling with a brayer and sponging to remove excess moisture.*

As drying progresses, the fibers of the paper will shrink and the embedded materials will be held firmly in place. The work will have a tendency to warp somewhat, which may be minimized by weighting the piece during final stages of drying. Some artists prefer to retain the warped quality for added interest. Because the works are somewhat three dimensional, they are effectively mounted in a deep frame of the shadow box type.

Another method for embedding is simply the reverse of the first method, in that the pulp layer is put down first and the objects to be embedded placed on the surface of the pulp and pressed in firmly. Sponge and roll as before and place finished work in the rack to dry. This method is somewhat simpler for beginners, because reverse visualization is not necessary as in the initial method described.

*Lamination*

Thin objects such as leaves, grasses, rope, feathers, and textured fabrics may be laminated between two sheets of paper. Materials to be laminated often work better if they are presoaked in water until damp. Do *not* soak tissues or fragile materials because they will discolor and/or disintegrate.

Prepare a fairly thick sheet of paper using the mold and deckle method as described. Couch this sheet onto a felt and place objects to be laminated on the couched sheet. Prepare another somewhat thinner sheet of paper and couch it directly over the first sheet and materials to be laminated. Press with a brayer, cover with another felt, apply pressure to remove excess moisture, and place laminated sheets to dry on the rack. (see figure 14.20).

*(Figure 14.20) Dried weeds and bits of string laminated between two sheets of paper.*

183

## Poured Pulp

A free approach in which fairly thin slurries of pulp in several colors are prepared and poured directly on the mould in adjoining shapes is shown in figure 14.21. The various pulps will intermingle, and if attention is paid to placement and color relationships, some interesting effects will be obtained. Pulps may be poured directly on the bare screen of the mould or onto a previously prepared thin sheet before it is couched from the mould.

## Casting with Pulp

The forms of various three-dimensional objects may be reproduced in paper very easily. The object or objects to be reproduced are arranged on a sheet of plastic and sprayed lightly with nonstick aerosol vegetable spray. Paper pulp is then applied to the objects, pressing the pulp down firmly (see figure 14.22). When pulp is dry enough to handle, remove it from the objects by lifting gently. A negative impression of the objects will be left in the paper.

*(Figure 14.21) Slurries of pulp are being poured directly on a mould to form a sheet of intermingled colors.*

*(a)*

*(b)*

*(Figure 14.22) (a) Scallop shell is being sprayed with nonstick vegetable spray. (b) Shell is covered with paper pulp, which is pressed down firmly.*

For casting positive impressions, first prepare a plaster mold of the object using standard methods outlined in ceramic texts. The prepared mold is then used by pressing paper pulp into the depression. Allowing it to dry and remove the casting from the mold as figure 14.23 illustrates.

## Papier-Collé and Collage
Scraps and damaged sheets of handmade papers having various textures and colors may be utilized to make papier-collés. Adhere them in a pleasing combination onto a piece of mat board with white glue or acrylic gel.

(a)

(b)

(c)

(d)

(Figure 14.23) (a) Plaster mold has been made from scallop shell. (b) Paper pulp is being pressed into mold. (c) Scallop shell, mold made from shell, positive and negative impressions in paper. (d) Finished shell motif made into a collage by mounting on a board in combination with tissue, cord, and actual shells.

Work slowly and let the papers themselves suggest the direction the design should take. When nonpaper materials, such as dried flowers, shells, and found objects, are incorporated into the design, the result is called a collage (see figure 14.24).

Students should study the many fine examples of works done with handmade paper in the books listed in the suggested reading list. Examples of student works are shown in figure 14.25.

Notes
1. For an excellent account of hand papermaking in Japan, see Timothy Barrett, *Japanese Papermaking: Traditions, Tools, and Techniques* (New York and Tokyo: Weatherhill, 1983).
2. Dard Hunter, *Papermaking: The History and Technique of an Ancient Craft,* 2d ed. (New York: Alfred Knopf, 1947); reprint (New York: Dover Publications, 1978).

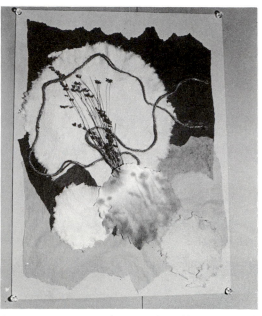

*(Figure 14.24) Student work: collage of handmade paper circles of various sizes, colored tissue, jute cord, and weeds.*

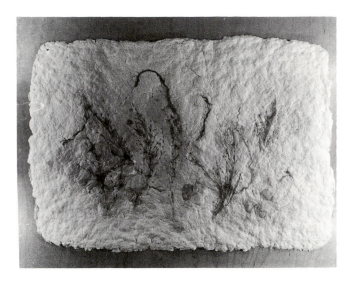

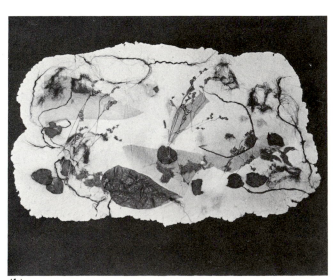

*(b)*

*(Figure 14.25) (a) Student work: free-form pulp sheet, colored areas with dyes, embedded grasses, frayed yarns. (b) Student work: free-form pulp sheet, embedded leaves, yarns, colored tissues.*

3. See *American Artist* (August 1977). Much of this issue is devoted to contemporary hand papermaking in America.
4. Very clear and easy to follow instructions for making moulds and deckles are to be found in Vance Studley, *The Art and Craft of Handmade Paper* (New York: Van Nostrand Publishing Co., 1977). 41–49.

*Suggested Readings*

*American Artist Magazine* (August 1977).

Barrett, Timothy. *Japanese Papermaking: Tradition, Tools, and Techniques.* New York and Tokyo: Weatherhill, 1983.

Heller, Jules. *Papermaking.* New York: Watson-Guptill Publications, 1978.

Hunter, Dard. *My Life with Paper: An Autobiography.* New York: Alfred Knopf, 1958.

———. *Papermaking: The History and Technique of an Ancient Craft.* 2d ed. New York: Alfred Knopf, 1947. Reprint. New York: Dover Publications, 1978.

Kern, Marna Elyea. *The Complete Book of Handcrafted Paper.* New York: Coward, McCann and Geohagen, Publishers, 1980.

Labarre, E. J. *Dictionary and Encyclopedia of Paper and Papermaking.* Amsterdam: Swets and Zeitlinger, 1952.

Loeber, E. G. *Dictionary and Encylopedia of Paper and Papermaking, Supplement.* Amsterdam: Swets and Zeitlinger, 1967.

*Papermaking: Art and Craft.* Washington, D.C.: Library of Congress, 1968.

Studley, Vance. *The Art and Craft of Handmade Paper.* New York: Van Nostrand, Reinhold, 1977.

Toale, Bernard. *The Art of Papermaking.* Worcester, Mass.: Davis Publications, 1983.

# 15 Printing

Printmaking is the process by which multiple identical copies of a design or pattern are produced on paper, fabric, or some other material from an original block into which the design has been cut with a tool. Printmaking (usually termed the *graphic arts*) may be classifed by technique into several general categories: *relief techniques* such as wood cut and linoleum cut; *intaglio techniques* such as etching, mezzotint, or engraving; *surface or planographic techniques* such as lithography and stencils; and *special techniques* such as monoprint and cliché-verre.

This chapter covers relief techniques and stenciling (known as silk screening), primarily because these can be simply done in the classroom and do not require special presses or other equipment for successful printing.

## Woodcuts

In relief printing techniques, a block of some material is cut with tools so that areas are left raised or *in-relief* on the block. When the block is inked and pressed onto a flat surface, the raised design is duplicated or *printed* onto the receiving surface.

Perhaps the earliest known instance of relief printing is found in the ancient Near East. Signet stones or seals carved with the name or emblem of some dignitary were used to stamp impressions onto official documents often written on clay tablets. This was, to be sure, a purely utilitarian use but technically can be considered printing. The *woodcut* technique of relief printing originated in China about the beginning of the first century A.D. Somewhat later, wood blocks were used in Egypt and India to impress designs onto textiles.

Printing processes were greatly facilitated by the invention of paper by the Chinese in A.D. 105, replacing such delicate materials as papyrus and silk as well as the more costly vellum and parchment. Woodcut prints on paper were being produced in China before A.D. 200 and in Japan somewhat later. The best known example of early mass production of prints from woodblocks on paper is the "million printed prayers" of the Empress Shotuku in A.D. 764. Japan had been victim of a widespread smallpox epidemic, and in order to drive out the evil demons responsible for the calamity, the empress ordered the printing of a million prayers, each to be enclosed in its own small wooden pagoda. The total number were distributed among ten Buddhist temples.[1]

The woodcut as an art form was practiced in China during the T'ang dynasty (618–907), and somewhat later the color woodcut appeared in Japan. The art of the woodcut came to Europe (particularly to Germany and the Netherlands) in the fifteenth century. Albrecht Dürer (1471–1528), for example, produced several great series of woodcuts: the *Apocalypse* (1498), the *Great Passion* (1500), and the *Life of the Virgin* (1504–1505). With the perfection of the process of etching in the early seventeenth century, the popularity of the woodcut declined somewhat, but was revived in Europe in the nineteenth century by several artists, including William Blake and Gustave Doré. Many modern artists have practiced the art, including Paul Gauguin and Ernst Barlach in Europe and Timothy Cole and Rockwell Kent in America.

The multicolor woodcut print evolved in Japan in the early eighteenth century with such artists as Masanobu and Harunobu, and reached its highest state of perfection in the nineteenth century with the work of Hokusai and Hiroshige. Japanese prints imported into Europe had a tremendous influence on the works of European artists, notably Manet, Van Gogh, and Whistler. A number of nineteenth century artists produced notable woodcuts, among them Gauguin, Munch, Schmidt-Rotluff, and Kollwitz. Following a long period of decline, the art of the woodcut in Japan was revived in the late 1920s and today, much of the world's finest graphic art, including numerous fine woodcuts, is coming out of Japan.

Blocks for woodcut prints are usually made by cutting with knives, gouges, or chisels into a slab of plank wood. Fine-grained hardwoods are preferable for precise cutting but the softer fruit woods and pine are also used, particularly when the artist wishes the wood grain to become a contributing factor in the design.

The *wood engraving* differs from the woodcut in that the wood used is an end grain block rather than a plank. Because the artist can cut in any direction without regard to how the grain runs, much more detailed designs are possible with wood engraving.

The same techniques used for making wood blocks have been adapted for use with blocks made of linoleum. Linoleum, invented by Frederick Walton in 1860, is a mixture of oxidized linseed oil and filler adhered to a backing of durable material, such as burlap. It was originated and widely used as a covering for floors and countertops. Small pieces of linoleum are often used in the classroom as a substitute for wood because the linoleum is much easier to cut, particularly for younger students. Picasso raised the linoleum block to respectability by making a series of very fine linoleum prints in the 1950s.

Both wood and linoleum blocks are used in the classroom for relief printing because they can be easily cut and simply printed by applying hand pressure with a baren or the back of a large wooden spoon. Contemporary graphic artists are reexploring the traditional methods, adding their own new and exciting innovative techniques and contributing to the production of tremendous numbers of relief prints in many media.

Because prints are relatively inexpensive (when compared to such works as paintings and drawings) and multiple editions are available, they are in demand by young collectors who are just beginning to buy original art. Even though prints are made in multiples, as long as they are printed from the original plate (after the beginning of the nineteenth century) and hand signed by the artist, they are considered originals.

Contemporary graphic artists usually prepare the block or plate themselves, and more often than not print it themselves, though not always. The artist decides at the outset how many copies of the print will be made. This is the *edition* size and, strictly speaking, once this number is reached, the plate or block is either destroyed or canceled by a strike across the surface with a tool. Prints are usually hand signed with pencil in the lower right corner and numbered in the lower left corner with a fractional designation. The number 10/50, for example, would indicate that the print is the tenth of an edition totalling fifty. Sometimes the title of the print is placed in the center between the artist's signature and the numerical designation.

During the preparation of the block, the artist will often pull trial proofs to check his or her progress. Sometimes these are more valuable than the final work because they are unique. Often the artist will also pull a number of prints for his or her own use before the regular edition is made. These are marked A/P and, ethically, should not total more than 10 percent of the total edition number. Some collectors search out and buy only artists' proofs.

In the case of prints made before the beginning of the nineteenth century, it is difficult to determine originality because artists did not always sign their prints and were sometimes prone to make additional copies of a work that had sold particularly well. Often one can find prints made from canceled (struck) plates. These are called *restrikes* and may or may not be valuable, depending on the reputation of the artist, the size of the restrike edition, and various other factors. In order to have some degree of assurance of the value of the print being purchased, the collector is wise to buy only from the artist or from a reputable dealer who will certify the authenticity of the print.

*Tools and Materials*
Basic tools and materials for preparing and printing wood are shown in figure 15.1. Almost any wood that is soft enough to be cut into may be used. Woods are classified as hardwoods, those that come from deciduous trees such as oak, maple, birch; softwoods, those obtained from coniferous trees such as pine, fir, and redwood; and fruitwoods, such as pear, cherry, apple and the like, though these are really a subclass of the hardwoods because they come from leaf-shedding trees. Generally speaking, the hardwoods have finer grain patterns and are thus more suitable for cutting fine details. The larger grained softwoods are more easily cut, considerably cheaper, and lend themselves to loose, open designs.

*(a)*

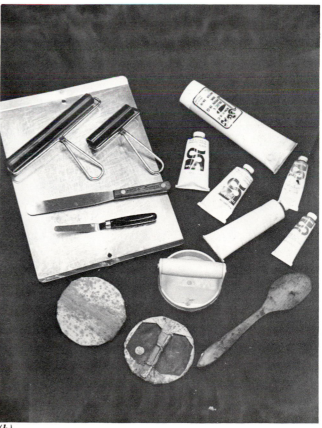

*(b)*

*(Figure 15.1) (a) Tools and materials for cutting wood-blocks. (b) Tools and materials for printing woodblocks and linoleum blocks.*

For classroom use, slabs of clear white pine planks may be obtained from a local lumber yard or special blocks of white wood or Philippine mahogany veneer may be ordered from a crafts supply house. These are available in various sizes, they cut well, and are relatively inexpensive. "Found" woods such as old weatherboards and pieces of bark or driftwood often have marvelously textured surfaces that may be inked and printed for their own beauty or incorporated into another design. Plywood is often used for larger prints though it has the disadvantage of splintering rather easily during cutting. Knots and other natural characteristics of wood can often be utilized to advantage by the printmaker.

Some printmakers use only a sharp knife, but because efficient use of the knife comes only through long experience, it is perhaps better for student use to invest in sets of wood cutting tools. These tools are made of steel blades set into hardwood handles. A set contains the various straight, V- and U-shaped gouges needed by the woodcut artist. Cutting tools must be kept very sharp so it is necessary to stop periodically and sharpen them.

Two types of sharpening stones are generally used—a flat stone having both medium and fine surfaces, and a slip stone with rounded edges (see figure 15.2). During use, both must be lubricated frequently with a good grade of oil.

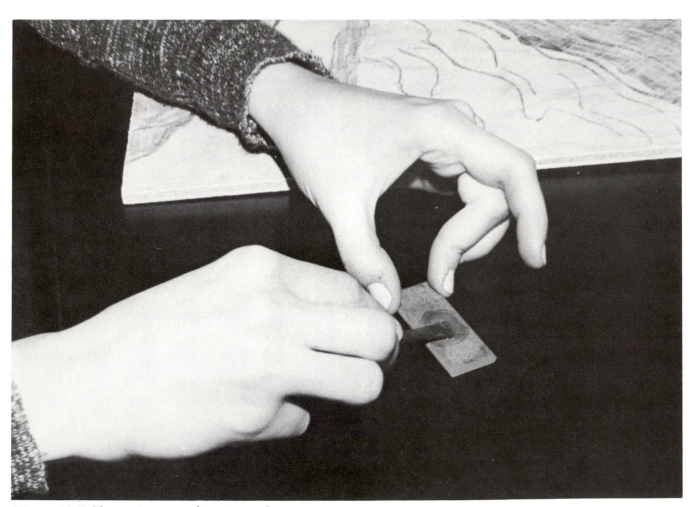

*(Figure 15.2) Sharpening a wood cutting tool.*

Sharpen tools with straight knife edges by holding the tool at a slight angle and rubbing with a circular motion, first one side then the other, on the oiled medium surface of the flat stone. The stone is then turned over and the process repeated with the fine surface of the stones. The edge of the blade is sometimes finished by rubbing it on a piece of leather.

To sharpen round gouge tools, begin with the outside curve, hold the tool at the natural angle of its bevel, and rub it on the oiled stone as directed in the preceding paragraph, at the same time rotating the wrist so that all portions of the curve are evenly sharpened. To do this properly requires some practice and is an essential operation to the woodcutter. Finish the inside curve with the curved edge of the slip stone by rubbing the oiled stone along the edge. To sharpen V gouges, rub both outside angles against the flat stone, as directed, while maintaining the proper angle of the bevel. When tools develop irregular cutting edges, they should be reground on a grindstone to remove all nicks, then resharpened as directed.

Inks for block printing may be either oil based or water based. Both are entirely satisfactory but for classroom use the water-base type may be more desirable because of easy cleanup. The inks come in tubes in a wide variety of colors and may be intermixed as desired. For use, the ink is squeezed out onto a slab of glass or sheet of metal where it can be manipulated with the palette knife to the proper consistency. A flat aluminum cookie sheet without sides makes an acceptable inking slab or palette.

Rubber rollers called *brayers* are used to roll the ink out on the palette and to apply an even film of ink to the surface of the block. Brayers vary in hardness or *shore,* depending on their purpose. A medium-hard brayer will be most useful in the classroom.

For transferring the ink from the block to the paper without a mechanical press, lay the printing paper facedown upon the inked block and burnish it with a tool of some sort, such as the back of a wooden spoon. Often the hand itself is used as the "burnisher." The most satisfactory tool and certainly the most

aesthetically pleasing to use is the Japanese *baren,* which consists of a circular pad of bamboo leaf about 5 inches in diameter, reinforced in the center, and having a twisted bamboo leaf handle. A commercial hand baren is also available.

Papers ranging from the fine handmade, 100 percent rag preferred by professional graphic artists to ordinary blank newsprint stock, and practically anything in between may be used for printmaking. The student should experiment with a variety. Papers vary considerably and such characteristics as composition, smoothness, thickness, softness, surface finish, and color tone will affect the appearance of the final print. For classroom use, a commercially available block print paper having a smooth, yet soft texture is very satisfactory. It is supplied in packages of one-hundred sheets and is more economical to purchase in the 18-by-24-inch size and cut it as desired. Various imported rice papers make handsome prints but are rather expensive for everyday classroom use.

*Designing for Woodcut*
In designing for woodblock printing, the student must keep in mind that the nature of the block itself will play a large part in the appearance of the finished print. Wood has grain; crisp edges often chip or break when the block is being cut; surfaces are often scratched or broken during the cutting process; sharp lines and perfect shapes are difficult to achieve. All these things mean that the woodcut simply does not lend itself to intricate, detailed designs. Once students understand and accept the fact that, indeed, this very thing gives a woodcut print its distinctive character, they can begin to design in such a way as to reconcile the simplicity and lack of delicacy inherent in the woodcut with their choice of subject matter so that both will work together to create a unified statement.

As Gerald Brommer puts it, "A delicate child's face would not be as suitable a subject as a rugged fisherman's craggy features, a small delicate animal not as suitable as a charging rhinocerous. Small flowers should give way to rugged trees, and gentle landscapes to rugged mountains or crashing surf."[2]

## Procedure for Making a Woodcut

There are several steps involved in creating a woodcut.

1. Choose a suitable design.
2. Sketch the design on the block. Remember that if the design is sketched on the block the resulting print will be reversed. If this matters, draw design first on paper with a soft pencil then turn it over and transfer it to the block by rubbing over the back with a soft pencil. Figure 15.3 illustrates the operation. By reversing the design on the block in this way, the final print will be just like the original drawing. It will help to visualize the final print if all areas that are to remain raised are painted in with a brush and India ink directly on the block. This will aid in more accurate cutting because, often when cutting by lines alone, students forget which areas are to remain and which are to be cut away.

(a)

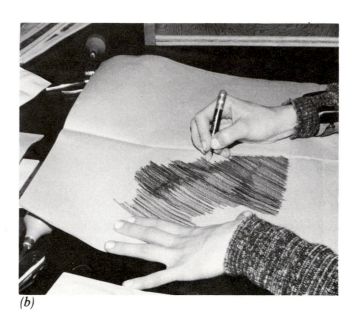

(b)

*(Figure 15.3) (a) Rough sketch for woodcut.
(b) Rubbing back of sketch with soft pencil to act as carbon paper. (c) Transferring design to woodblock. This will produce a print that is the reverse of the sketch.*

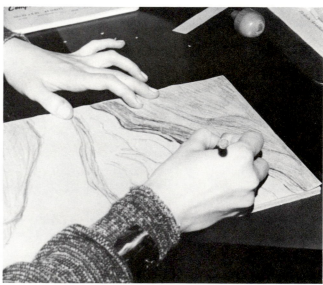

(c)

3. Cut design into the block leaving in relief (raised) all areas that are to be printed (see figure 15.4). Cutting will be greatly facilitated if a bench hook is used. This is designed so that the bottom projection hooks over one edge of the work table and the block being cut can be placed against the top projection. The left hand holds the block at the bottom and the right hand holds the cutting tool. *Always* cut away from the hand holding the block or a nasty cut could result if the tool slips.

4. Prepare ink by squeezing out a quantity onto the palette. Adjust color as necessary and work ink with the palette knife until it is well mixed and smooth.

5. Roll ink with the brayer to distribute it evenly on the palette (see figure 15.5). The ink should have a slightly "tacky" consistency. If ink is too thick, a few drops of water or turpentine (depending on whether water-base or oil-base ink is being used) may be added and mixed with the palette knife.

6. Dampen the block slightly with a wet sponge to prepare it to accept the ink more readily.

*(Figure 15.4) Cutting the design into the wood. Note that the block is held in place by the bench hook, and cutting is done away from the hand holding the wood in place.*

*(Figure 15.5) Ink is rolled with the brayer until the palette is evenly coated and the brayer is "charged" with a film of ink.*

7. Ink the block by rolling it with the charged brayer in several different directions as figure 15.6 shows.

8. When the block is inked, place a sheet of paper on it (see figure 15.7). The dimensions of the paper should be somewhat larger than the block.

9. Rub the back of the paper with the baren, applying even, firm pressure (see figure 15.8). Be sure to rub entire surface as evenly as possible.

10. Remove print from block by pulling up one corner (see figure 15.9).

11. Hang print to dry or place faceup in drying rack and continue printing entire edition, reinking the block between each pull. Theoretically, each pulled print should be identical to all the others in the edition. This is sometimes difficult to achieve when printing by hand because of minor differences in ink rolled on the block, nonuniformity of pressure, and the like. Again this is one of the charms of woodcut—that it is *not* a precise method.

*(Figure 15.6) Surface of lightly dampened block is rolled with the inked brayer to transfer even coating of ink to the block.*

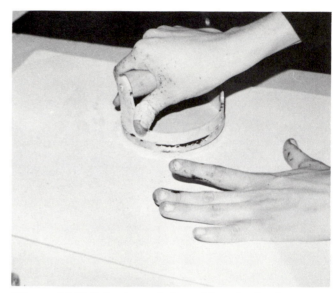

*(Figure 15.8) Print is made by rubbing back of paper with the baren.*

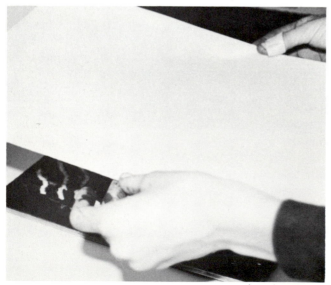

*(Figure 15.7) Sheet of paper is placed on surface of inked block.*

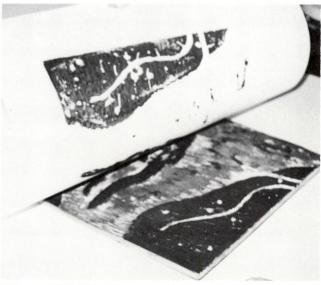

*(Figure 15.9) Print is removed from block.*

12. Clean surface of block with suitable medium, and wash all tools and equipment. Never allow ink to dry on tools or it will be difficult to remove, especially if oil-base ink is being used.

13. When prints are dry, sign and number them according to the system previously described. Prints, as any works on paper, are fragile and should be protected against damage. Unmatted prints should be stored flat with a sheet of thin paper between each one. Prints to be exhibited should be matted and framed under glass.

These instructions will, of course, result in a single color print. The making of a multicolor woodcut entails the cutting of a separate block for each color to be used, and printing these blocks in succession in such a way that they will be "in register" when they are printed. Registration is discussed in the following procedures for a two-color linoleum block print.

**Linocuts**

Tools and materials for linocuts are somewhat different than those for woodcut (see figure 15.10). Heavy-gauge battleship linoleum in a plain light color is best for use in making linocuts and may be obtained either from a floor covering dealer or ordered from an art supply house. Linoleum may be purchased in rolls or in cut pieces of various sizes. Twelve-by-twelve-inch pieces are a convenient size for the classroom. Linoleum may also be purchased premounted on a wood base for additional stability, but the convenience does not justify the additional expense except in special cases. Unlike wood, linoleum has no structure comparable to grain. It is smooth and flat, soft and pliable, and may be easily and quickly cut. Prints made from linoleum present color areas that are even and untextured, sometimes to the

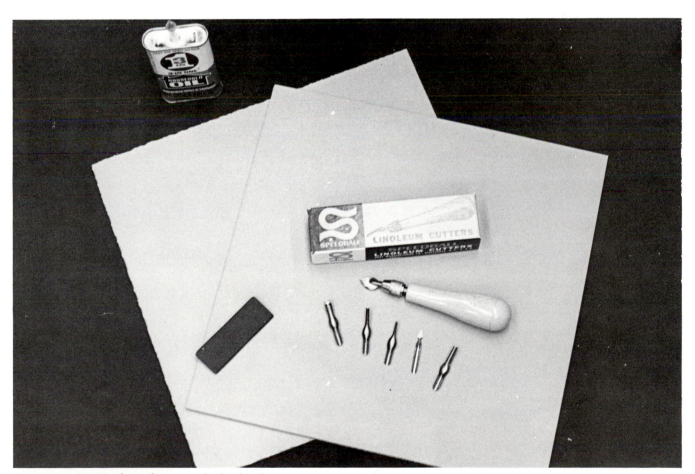

*(Figure 15.10) Tools and materials for linoleum cuts.*

point of being monotonous and impersonal. Properly handled, however, linoleum can be an exciting medium and certainly lends itself to far more detail than is possible with a woodcut (see figure 15.11).

Sets of linoleum cutting tools similar to those used for wood are available, but tools most commonly used are assortments of "push-type" blades that fit into a special screw chuck handle. Blades are made of high-quality steel and should be kept razor sharp. When cutting, use the bench hook and cut away from you as described in woodcuts section.

Inks, papers, brayers, palettes, and other printing equipment are exactly the same as those used for printing woodblocks.

There are various methods for printing blocks in register; the simplest of these involves the use of a register board. The base of the register board is made from a piece of smooth surfaced plywood ½ inch thick, cut to a convenient size. A board 20-by-20 inches will allow prints up to 16-by-16 inches to be printed. Pieces of stripping ½ inch thick and 2 inches wide are attached to the length of two sides, forming a right angle. Lines are ruled on the base board parallel to the two side strips exactly 2 inches in toward the middle. The lines form guides for placing the blocks to be printed and the side strips serve as paper guides.

*(Figure 15.11) Linoleum mounted on wood and cut into a design for a Christmas card. Print made from block is on the right. Note that the design is reversed when printed.*

*Procedure for a Two-Color Linocut Print*
There are several methods for arriving at multicolor linocut prints. The one described here involves cutting a separate block for each color to be printed, then printing the blocks in succession and in register.

1　Plan the design and draw it onto a sheet of paper the size you wish the finished print is to be. Color each area with magic markers or crayons.
2　Cut two pieces of linoleum *exactly* the same size and the size of the finished print. Linoleum may be cut with heavy scissors, but a more precise cut is obtained by using a paper cutter.
3　Tape the drawn design to the first block and trace all areas to be one color. Tape the drawn design to the second block and trace all areas to be the second color. These may be colored in on the blocks if desired to aid in cutting.
4　Cut each block carefully, leaving raised the areas that are to print (see figure 15.12). Proofs may be pulled to check progress, if desired. When both blocks are completely cut, print them in register as follows.
5　Prepare ink and pallete as for woodcuts. Prepare paper by cutting sheets exactly 2 inches larger all around than the block to be printed. For example, if the block is 6-by-12 inches, cut the paper 10-by-16 inches.
6　Select the block to be printed in the lighter color, turn it over, and apply several strips of masking tape to the back. The tape is doubled back on itself so there are two sticky sides (see figure 15.13).

*(Figure 15.12) Linoleum blocks cut with two different designs for two-color print.*

*(Figure 15.13) Apply strips of doubled over masking tape to back of block.*

7 Attach block to base of register board so that the lower left corner of the block fits exactly into the right angle of the drawn lines. Press down firmly to adhere block to the board (see figure 15.14).

8 Ink surface of the block with the ink charged brayer.

9 Place a sheet of paper so the edges of the paper fit exactly against the side strips as figure 15.15 illustrates.

10 Rub back of paper with baren to transfer ink from block to paper.

11 Remove print from block and hang to dry, or place faceup on the drying rack.

12 While prints from the first printing are drying, remove first block from register board and attach second block to the board as described previously. Be careful to place the second block in exactly the same position as the first by using the ruled guidelines.

13. Ink the block with the second color.

14. Run each dried, previously printed sheet through again, placing the paper edges exactly against the guide strips.

15. When prints are dry, sign and number them in the prescribed manner.

The secret of success in this method of printing in register is to measure the blocks precisely, trace the designs carefully, and make sure that blocks and paper are lined up exactly for each printing. Prints having more than two colors may be made by this method as long as a separate block is cut for each color.

*Other Approaches to Relief Printing*

While woodcut and linocut are the traditional ways of making relief prints, printing blocks may be prepared by a number of other ways as well. Technically, any surface with raised areas can be inked and used as a block to make a print, which gives rise to a number of possibilities.

*(Figure 15.14) Place first block on register board so the edges are exactly lined up with previously drawn guidelines.*

*(Figure 15.15) Place paper so it is lined up exactly with the sides of the register board.*

*Cardboard Prints* may be prepared in two ways.

1  A heavy sheet of cardboard may have designs cut into it with a mat knife. If successive layers of the cardboard are peeled away, certain areas will be left in relief to be inked and printed.

2  Shapes cut from cardboard may be glued to another sheet of cardboard until a pleasing design is obtained. All sorts of textures are possible by varying the types of board used for the cut shapes. This is really a type of *collagraph.* Cardboard plates are made more durable by brushing with shellac or spraying with several coats of clear acrylic.

*Collagraphs* result when a block is built up by glueing all sorts of materials to a firm backing to make a printing block. The name derives from the twentieth-century art form called collage, made popular by the artists of the cubist movement in France (see figure 15.16). The backing may be very heavy cardboard, thin masonite or plywood, or thin sheet metal. Various materials may then be glued to the surface to produce raised areas. Possibilities are cut or torn cardboard or paper, burlap, scraps of metal, bits of screen wire, shells, felt, leaves, flowers, bark, even hardened glue itself.

These are firmly attached with glue and flattened somewhat to the plate. When the glue is dry, spray the block with several coats of clear acrylic and allow to dry. The plate is inked with a brayer or with pads of fabric dipped into the ink. Portions of the inked surface may also be wiped away with a clean cloth to provide additional interest. When the plate is inked, lay a sheet of heavy, soft paper over the plate and apply very firm pressure with the hand, a baren or, soft rubber roller. If the paper is slightly dampened, it will be possible to press it down around the raised areas to achieve an intaglio effect.

Other possibilities for blocks are carved plaster, styrofoam, and sheets of Plexiglas. The latter is probably best cut into with motorized drills, burs, and grinding wheels because it is rather hard. Delicate effects, comparable to etching, can be achieved with a Plexiglas block, while plaster and styrofoam lend themselves to bold, strong forms.

Found objects such as weathered wood, rock surfaces, gears and cogs, machine parts, crumpled metal foil, dried plant life, bits of rope and twine, and the like may all be used as printing shapes in themselves or may be incorporated into other designs.

It should be evident from the foregoing material that the possibilities in woodcut and linocut printmaking are infinite and open up to the student a multitude of exciting avenues of exploration. The traditional methods presented should be learned, for they are basic; once mastered they can serve as a starting point for much creative thinking and experimental investigation. Indeed the constant discovery of new ways with prints makes this old craft an ever fresh and stimulating medium.

Example of a woodcut is shown in figure 15.17. A linocut is illustrated in figure 15.18 and a collagraph in figure 15.19.

*(Figure 15.16) Cardboard block (collagraph) made by gluing burlap, yarn, and dried grasses onto cardboard. Other textures and forms are obtained by glue buildup. Block is shellacked before use.*

*(Figure 15.17) Student work: woodcut.*

*(Figure 15.19) Student work: collagraph.*

*(Figure 15.18) Student work: linocut.*

## Silk Screen on Paper

Silk screen printing is a contemporary adaptation of the ancient Oriental process of stenciling. As currently used, the process involves the preparation of a stencil: drawing a pattern or design, placing the material from which the stencil is to be made over the pattern, and cutting away those areas that are to be printed. The stencil thus prepared is then adhered to a screen of tightly stretched silk, and the pattern is reproduced on any desired surface by forcing special inks, paints, or dyes through the cut out areas with the aid of a rubber squeegee.

Used for many years as a commercial process, particularly in the production of signs and posters, the silk screen printing process has been adopted and refined by many contemporary artists. During the past twenty to thirty years silk screening has gained the prestige of an art medium that is used widely. The name serigraph (seri meaning silk, graph meaning print) is usually applied to fine art silk screen prints.

Silk screening can be accomplished with fairly inexpensive equipment; it is a quick and easy method of duplicating a design on many varied surfaces, yet extremely complex patterns in almost unlimited forms and colors can be produced.

In the silk screen printing process, as presented in this section, a stencil is prepared from a nonporous material, such as paper or a plastic film, from which certain areas have been removed. The material, in turn, is attached to a tightly stretched screen of fine mesh silk. When this assembly is placed on the surface to be printed and paint or ink pushed across the surface with a rubber squeegee, the paint will be forced through the silk-supported film, where areas have previously been cut away, and deposited on the surface underneath.

### Tools and Equipment

The basic tools and equipment necessary for silk screen printing on paper are illustrated in figure 15.20. A list and description of each item follows.

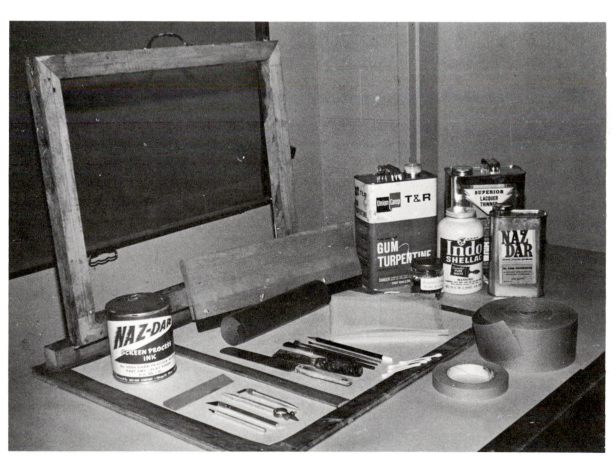

*(Figure 15.20) Equipment and materials for silkscreen printing on paper.*

1  The printing frame consists of a wooden frame made of well-seasoned 2-by-2-inch pine or fir, attached with removable pin hinges to a baseboard somewhat larger than the frame itself. The frame is easily constructed or may be purchased with silk already stretched on it. Convenient sizes for classroom use are 16-by-20 inches, 20-by-24-inches, and 24-by-30 inches.

2  Screen fabric may be any fine mesh, thin material, such as organdy, nylon, dacron, polyester, but silk is by far the most satisfactory. This may be fine quality Swiss silk or the less expensive American silk. Silk is graded according to the number of meshes per square inch from 2xx to 25xx. For general use, 12xx silk containing 125 meshes per square inch is a good choice. Silk is available in widths from 40 to 80 inches.

3  Although stencils may be prepared from any nonporous material, including ordinary paper or waxed stencil paper, a more durable and satisfactory material is a commercially available film, such as Naz-Dar "Nu Film amber standard," consisting of a layer of lacquer supported by a layer of waxed paper. In use, the design to be printed is cut through the lacquer layer, these areas peeled away from the backing paper and the remaining film adhered to the underside of the silk with a solvent that will soften the film so it sticks to the screen. The backing paper is then removed, leaving certain areas open for passage of the ink. Lacquer films are suitable for use with water- or oil-base inks; for lacquer-base inks, a special water-soluble film is used. Film stencils are especially useful for fine line designs or where sharp edges and fine details are needed.

4  Stencil knives consist of any small knives with a sharp blade. Several types are used, including the X-acto and Griphold general purpose stencil knives, the Griphold swivel blade cutter, and a parallel line cutter also by Griphold.

5  Arkansas stone is a fine hard stone for keeping stencil knives razor sharp.

6  Staple gun and staples are needed for attaching silk to the screen frame. Squeegees consist of a rubber blade about ⅜ inch thick, with a squared off edge, used for pulling the printing ink across the surface of the screen. The rubber blade is set into a wooden handle. Edges of the squeegee should be kept sharp by periodic sanding with garnet paper. Squeegees are available in any desired length and should be about 1 inch shorter than the width of the screen being used. When not in use, squeegees should be stored in such a manner that the rubber blade will not be damaged.

8  Spatulas of various widths and lengths, convenient for mixing inks and transferring the ink to the screen, are needed.

9  For routine use on paper, Naz-Dar Series 5500 screen process inks are recommended for silk screen ink. Other inks are available for a wide variety of effects.

10  A block-out medium recommended is Naz-Dar Watermask 2000, though a number of other materials such as glue or shellac may be used.

11  Naz-Dar film adhering liquid 2147 is used for Nu-Film amber standard. Manufacturers instructions should be followed for the film being used.

12  Solvents such as turpentine or mineral spirits for washing screens and lacquer thinner for removing stencil films from the screen are needed.

13  Ruler, compass, pencils, brushes, Q-tips, and other tools necessary for preparing drawings, stencils, and screens must be handy.

14  Any good grade of paper may be used in printing, including construction paper. Regular block print paper and the type known as "oatmeal" make good printing surfaces.

*Preparation of the Screen*

A number of steps are involved in stretching the silk.

1  Remove wood frame from backboard by withdrawing the hinge pins and lifting the frame away as figure 15.21 illustrates.

2  Cut silk, allowing about a 2-inch excess all around (see figure 15.22).

3  Beginning in the center of one side, bring silk over edge of frame and fasten with three staples placed about 1 inch apart (see figure 15.23).

4  Pull silk tight to opposite side and fasten with three more staples as shown in figure 15.24.

*(Figure 15.21) Lift frame away from backboard.*

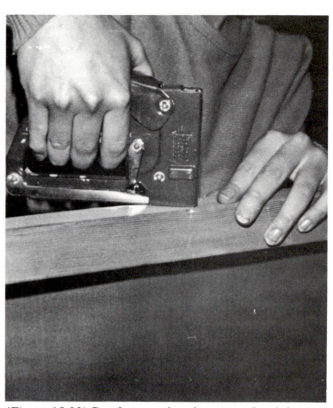

*(Figure 15.23) Staples are placed in one side of the frame in the center.*

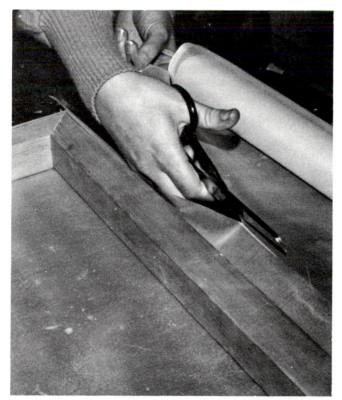

*(Figure 15.22) Silk is cut with a 2-inch margin left all around.*

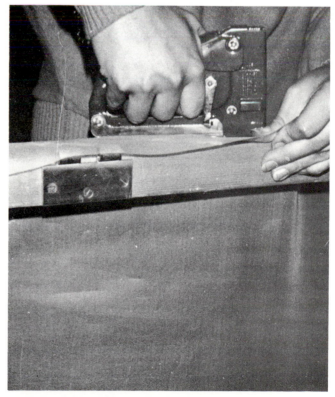

*(Figure 15.24) Silk is pulled tight and stapled to opposite side of frame.*

5 Repeat for the two ends. Working toward corners and alternating sides and ends, continue stapling until silk is completely stretched. Be sure silk is kept tightly stretched and free from wrinkles during the stapling process. Fold corners down and staple as figure 15.25 illustrates.

6 Trim away excess silk (see figure 15.26)

To prevent seepage of ink into the spaces between the silk and the frame, the screen must be taped on both sides with gummed kraft paper tape, 2 inches wide (see figure 15.27). Masking tape may be used but solvents used in washing the screen will dissolve the adhesive and loosen the tape, so it will have to be replaced frequently. The inside (ink well) of the frame is sealed by folding the tape in half and attaching one-half to the silk and one-half to the wood frame. The reverse side of the screen is taped in the same manner (see figure 15.28).

Paint all paper tape surfaces with a coat of white shellac and allow to dry thoroughly. Screen is then ready for use.

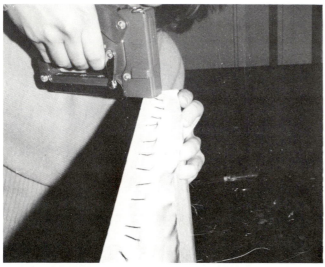

*(Figure 15.25) Silk has been stapled to frame and corners are being stapled. Note that staples are put in so they are vertical to the edges of the frame edges. This minimizes tearing when silk is stretched.*

*(Figure 15.27) Gummed paper strip is folded before being pasted to inside of frame.*

*(Figure 15.26) Excess silk is trimmed away.*

*(Figure 15.28) Outside of screen is taped with strips of gummed paper tape.*

### Preparing the Stencil

A full-size working drawing of the design to be printed is essential to serve as a guide for cutting the stencil as well as an aid for proper registering of various parts of a multicolor design. Dimensions of the drawing should be the same as the finished print desired. Cutting the stencil will be simplified if the drawing is colored with pencils or watercolors.

The silk screen printing process requires that the ink be passed through certain areas of the screen that have been left "open." Therefore, any areas not to be printed must be blocked out with some substance through which the ink will not pass. This may be accomplished with a block-out medium that can be painted directly onto the screen and allowed to dry. Commonly used block-out materials are glue, lacquer, shellac, or one of the commercial fillers. For classroom use, Naz-Dar Watermask 2000 is recommended for ease of application, diversity of obtainable effects, and convenience of removing from the screen with water. The block-out medium may be applied to the screen by brushing, sponging, spraying, slinging; or it may be pressed onto the screen from flat surfaces, such as paper shapes, that have been precoated with the medium. Each means of application will produce a somewhat different textured effect.

Another approach for painting or inking the screen may be used. A stencil, from which the areas to be printed have been cut out, may be attached to the screen; when paint is drawn across the screen, it will pass through these open areas and be resisted by all other areas. Stencils may be prepared from any good grade of thin nonabsorbent paper such as typing paper or regular waxed stencil paper. The paper should be transparent enough that the master drawing may be seen through it while the stencil is being cut. The completed stencil is attached to the screen with masking tape. A far more durable and satisfactory stencil may be cut from one of the commercially available stencil films, such as Naz-Dar Nu Film. Procedure for using this film is outlined next.

The working drawing is taped to the drawing board as figure 15.29 depicts. Those areas shown in black will be cut out and removed from the film. A piece of NuFilm somewhat larger than the drawing is taped directly over it onto the drawing board. Using a sharp stencil knife, cut and remove from the film all areas to be printed (see figure 15.30).

*(Figure 15.29) Working drawing is taped onto a drawing board.*

*(Figure 15.30) Areas of the film stencil which are to be printed are cut and removed. Try not to cut through the waxpaper backing.*

Be careful to cut in such a way that the knife goes only through the lacquer (colored) layer and not through the paper backing. Cut areas may be easily removed if you carefully lift one edge of a cut area and gently separate the film from the backing. If a multicolor design is being printed, a separate stencil must be cut in this same manner for each color of the design.

In order to attach the film stencil to the screen, several conditions are necessary: (1) the film must make close contact with the silk; (2) the lacquer layer must be softened just enough so it will stick to the screen, but not too much because it will dissolve; and (3) the film must be held firmly in place until the solvent evaporates and the film is adhered to the silk (see figure 15.31).

Numerous ways have been outlined in various manuals for accomplishing this step, but I have found them all to have serious drawbacks; so I developed the method outlined here, which is somewhat more time-consuming than certain others but gives completely satisfactory results. As shown in figure 15.31 the lacquer side of the film stencil is centered on the underside of the screen and held in place with the left hand that reaches around and behind the screen.

A Q-tip or a small brush is moistened with adhering liquid (Naz-Dar 2147) and touched to a small area of the film that is pressed firmly onto the silk from underneath and held in place until adhesion is complete. By working outward in this manner from the center to the edges, you can adhere the entire film to the silk. Care must be taken not to apply too much adhering liquid or "scrub" with the Q-tip because portions of the film will melt completely through. Should this occur, the resulting hole may be repaired with the Watermask liquid. Remove the paper backing from the film by carefully lifting one corner and peeling away slowly (see figure 15.32).

As the paper is removed, it should be inspected very carefully. If any small areas of film remain on it, adhere these by repressing the spot against the silk and applying a bit more adhering liquid. Block out any open spaces that remain between the edges of the film and the screen frame by brusing on a coat of Watermask over the whole area; allow this to dry and apply an additional coat on the reverse side (see figure 15.33).

Minor corrections may also be made on the film itself at the same time. Holding the screen up to the light, make sure no areas are open except those to be printed. Any pinholes in the film or surrounding area must be covered with Watermask, for the ink will pass through the smallest opening. Pay special attention to the areas next to the taped portion of the screen. When the Watermask is completely dry, reattach the screen to the backboard by replacing the hinge pins.

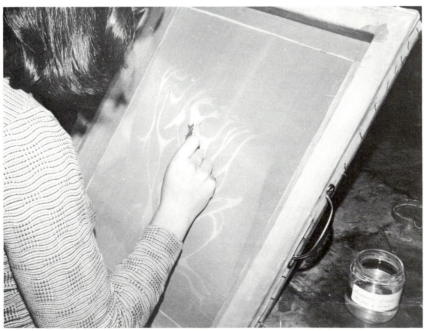

*(Figure 15.31) Stick film to the silk by applying adhering liquid with a Q-tip or small brush.*

*(Figure 15.32) When film is completely adhered, remove the waxpaper backing carefully by peeling it away.*

*(Figure 15.33) Watermask is applied to all areas not to be printed. A coat is applied to each side of the screen. Allow the liquid to dry between applications. Small pinholes will require patching with additional Watermask.*

## Making the Print

To be certain the printing paper is properly placed so that register is correct, place the original drawing under the stencil and move it around on the backboard until all cut out areas are lined up exactly with corresponding areas in the drawing (see figure 15.34). Carefully lift the screen so the drawing is not disturbed, and place two pieces of masking tape at right angles exactly adjacent to the corners of the drawing (see figure 15.35). Remove drawing, and replace with a sheet of the paper on which the print is to be made, making sure the corner of the paper fits exactly into the taped angle (see figure 15.36).

Carefully lower screen over paper. When making a multicolor print, line the film stencil for each color up with the original drawing in the same way as outlined for one color, thus ensuring that all colors will be in proper register. Select ink color to be used, mixing to obtain desired hue if necessary (see chapter 5 for information on color). Add to the ink a transparent base about one-third its quantity and mix well with a spatula. If a great deal of transparency is desired, up to 75 percent of transparent base may be added. Deposit a portion of the mixed ink across the top of the well in the screen frame as figure 15.37 shows.

*(Figure 15.34) Drawing is lined up perfectly with the cut out design in the film stencil.*

*(Figure 15.36) A sheet of printing paper is placed so the corner coincides exactly with the taped angle.*

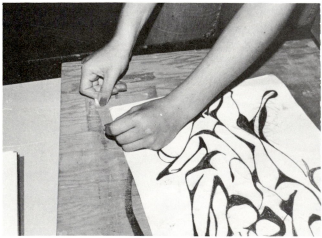

*(Figure 15.35) A corner of the drawing is marked by placing two pieces of masking tape at right angles. This step must be done carefully for the taped corner marks the placement of each sheet of paper to be printed.*

*(Figure 15.37) Printing ink is placed with a spatula along the top edge of the film.*

Select a squeegee that is about 1 inch shorter than the width of the screen well and position it at the top of the well. Then hold the squeegee at about a 45 degree angle while you pull it toward you, so the ink is drawn across the surface of the screen with the *sharp edge* of the squeegee, thereby forcing the ink through the openings in the stencil and onto the paper underneath (see figure 15.38).

Lift the frame and peel away the print, which is then hung up or placed in a rack to dry. Additional prints are made in the same manner. The finished student work is shown in figure 15.39.

As soon as the printing run is completed, place folded newspaper between the screen and the backboard and wash the screen thoroughly by pouring on turpentine and scrubbing with paper towels (see figure 15.40).

*(Figure 15.38) The squeegee held at an angle draws the ink across the film and forces it through the open areas onto the paper below, thereby making a print.*

*(Figure 15.40) Turpentine is poured on the screen to remove ink.*

*(Figure 15.39) Finished print titled "Dancers."*

Complete cleaning of the screen by removing Watermask with water and the film with lacquer thinner. With care, a well-prepared screen should last through many printings. Follow these five guidelines to protect your screen:

1 Never allow ink to dry on the screen because dry ink is practically impossible to remove and the screen openings will be permanently clogged.
2 Do not allow pencils, stencil knives, or other sharp objects to puncture the screen.
3 Inspect the screen by holding it up to light after each cleaning to be sure all traces of ink, Watermask, and film are removed.
4 Store screens attached to their backboards. A good way to store them is in a compartmented cabinet, with vertical partitions placed just far enough apart to accommodate the screen assembly standing on edge.
5 Periodically replace old tape with new, and reapply shellac.

Serigraphs may be designed to be printed in several colors; each color will require the preparation of a separate stencil. Each stencil is attached to a screen and printed successively so that all colors are in register on the final print. This is accomplished by lining up each stencil with the working drawing and placing the tape corner guides in the proper position each time as previously shown. Otherwise, the basic procedure is exactly the same as that already outlined for a single color print. Three stencils were cut for the three-color print shown in figure 15.41.

### Additional Methods of Stencil Preparation

While the paper, Watermask block-out, and cut film methods of stencil preparation are those most commonly used in my classes, several other techniques of stencil preparation should be mentioned.

Other block-out liquids: In addition to Watermask, several other liquids may be used as blockout materials. These are glue, shellac, and lacquer. They are usually applied directly to the screen in such a way that the desired design is left "open" on the screen. Take care to use a printing ink that will not dissolve the dried liquid while you are printing, and also use the proper solvent for cleaning the screen when the printing run is complete. Table 15.1 lists the block-out liquids and the inks and solvents used with each.

*Waxy materials:* A wax crayon or lithographic pencil may be used to draw directly on the silk screen. The wax fills the pores of the silk and all areas not so treated will print when ink is squeegeed across the screen. A water-base ink must be used because an oil-base ink

*(Figure 15.41) Print titled "Waterfall" made from three stencils, printed successively, each in a different color.*

**Block-out Liquids, Inks, and Solvents** (Table 15.1)

| Block-out Liquid | Ink | Solvent |
|---|---|---|
| Glue | Oil Base | For the ink, turpentine<br>For the glue, water |
| Lacquer | Water or oil base | For the ink, turpentine or water<br>For the lacquer, lacquer thinner |
| Shellac* | Water or oil base | For the ink, lacquer thinner<br>For the shellac, alcohol |

*Shellac is the least desirable of the block-out liquids, because dried shellac is extremely difficult to remove from the screen even with alcohol.

would dissolve the wax. After printing, wax may be removed from the screen with lacquer thinner or turpentine.

*Combination methods:* Several techniques may be combined to prepare the stencil. For example, a design may be drawn on the screen with wax crayons and the remainder of the screen covered with glue or Watermask. The crayon is then washed out with kerosene or turpentine, the screen allowed to dry, and prints made in the usual manner. The advantage of this method is that the design will be a positive print. Beautiful textural effects may be obtained when the waxy crayon is drawn across the silk. A commercial liquid called "tusche," which is sold for use in lithography, may be substituted for the crayon.

When doing a multicolor print, the stencil for each color may be prepared by a different method if desired. In the print shown in figure 15.42, the dune shape was printed through a paper stencil, the fence from a cut film stencil, the grass from a screen blocked out with Watermask (printed first in a dark green, then shifted slightly for a second printing in a lighter green), and the textured sky from a Watermask blocked out stencil.

*Photographic techniques:* A stencil may be prepared through the use of a photosensitive emulsion or film. The process is capable of producing detailed designs in exact facsimile, but requires, for best results, a darkroom and other special equipment. Because many schools do not have such equipment, the method is not emphasized in this text. Refer to the silk screen literature listed in the suggested readings and also to the manufacturer's instructions furnished with various commercially available film emulsions if you want to learn about this technique.

*(Figure 15.42) Print titled "Dunes" done by a combination of methods.*

Two variations that lead to interesting results are stencil shifting, and multicolor ink application to a single stencil. By shifting the same stencil to various positions on the sheet and printing in each new position, you can obtain a different effect. An example of student work is shown in figure 15.43.

## Silk Screen on Fabric

Human beings have used textiles for clothing and other purposes for thousands of years, and for much of that time, the surface of the fabric was probably embellished with some sort of decoration. Designs were often stamped or printed in shapes applied with flat stones, pieces of wood, or clay cylinders and colored with dyes obtained from natural materials such as berries, leaves, and earth pigments. Refer to chapter 10 on fabric dyeing for additional information on the history of dyes.

With the development of the screen process for printing in the early twentieth century and its subsequent adoption for many commercial uses, it was inevitable that the process would soon be modified for the decoration of fabrics. Handicapped at first by the fact that available inks usually left the fabric stiff, and

*(Figure 15.43) Student work: silk screen on paper.*

therefore unsuitable for clothing, designers were able to overcome this obstacle about 1940 when more suitable dyes were developed. The screen printing of fabrics, at first done by hand, has, of course, now been automated for commercial use. The additions of such refinements as the photographic preparation of screens and the use of fiber-reactive dyes has greatly increased the speed and reduced the cost of production, as well as resulted in products with brighter and more durable colors.

The studio craftsperson interested in hand-decorated textiles often uses the silkscreen process, especially if large quantities of fabrics are to be produced, because the screen process is much less laborious than block printing, for example, and has the capability for producing larger and more intricate designs as well.

*Tools and Materials*

Many of the tools and materials already described for silk screen printing on paper are used also for fabric printing. Please refer to that material. Principal differences are in the design of the screen frame, the type of inks used, the fabric, and the system of registration when printing (see figure 15.44).

Screen frames are designed without hinges and baseboards, because the frame must be picked up and moved around on the fabric while printing is done. Convenient sizes for studio use are 8-by-10 inch, 10-by-12 inch, and 12-by-16 inch. Silk is attached to the frame and the screen prepared for use exactly as for paper printing.

Various inks and dyes are available for use in fabric printing. The Naz-Dar 6000 series is a good all-around choice for studio use. Any fabric with reasonably smooth surface and firm weave may be used for screen printing. For student use, a cotton fabric such as Indian Head or Osnaberg is suitable. The fabric should be washed to remove sizing and ironed to eliminate wrinkles. Stencil film, knives, block-out media, adhering liquid, spatulas, and other tools are the same as those described for the paper process.

Designs that work best for fabric printing are usually those that may be repeated all over the surface of the fabric. Patterns may be as intricate as desired and may be multicolored, with a separate stencil being cut for each color used. The size of the motifs will depend to some extent on the dimensions of the cloth to be printed, as well as on the intended use of the finished fabric.

*Procedure*

Steps in the production of a length of fabric with repeat motifs in three colors is described. The student who provided the example planned that the fabric be used for a bed cover. Steps carried out in the same way as for paper printing are not fully illustrated in this section.

Make a full-size drawing for the design motif and plan color separation (see figure 15.45). Cut a film stencil for each color to be used, adhere these to the screens, and prepare screens for printing (see figure 15.46). Cover the work table with newspaper, and tape the washed and ironed fabric to it so the surface is smooth and taut (see figure 15.47).

*(Figure 15.44) Tools and materials for screen printing on fabric are different from those used for printing on paper.*

*(Figure 15.46) Screens prepared for three-color print on fabric.*

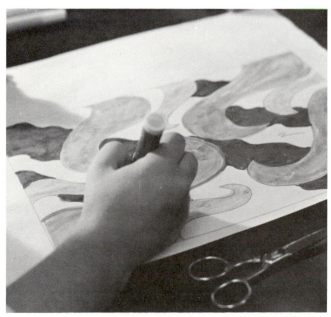

*(Figure 15.45) Drawing and color separation for three-color print.*

*(Figure 15.47) Fabric being stretched on work table that has been covered with newspaper.*

Because screened motifs are repeated all over the surface of the fabric, some system of registration for placement of the screens on the fabric must be worked out. The diagram shows several possible placements for frames measuring 8-by-12 inches on a 3-yard length of fabric, 48 inches wide (see figure 15.48). After the placement is decided on, the simplest means of registration is accomplished by placing the uninked screens on the fabric and making small dots with a soft pencil at the four corners of the frame as figure 15.49 illustrates.

Because the frame must not be put down with any portion of it covering a wet motif in the actual printing process, print the motifs by alternating the placement then go back and fill in other motifs when previously printed ones are dry. Therefore motifs one, three, five, seven, and so forth are printed first, and when these are dry, motifs two, four, six, eight, and so forth are printed. Print first color completely. It is well if two persons work together, one holding the screen firmly, the other pulling the squeegee (see figure 15.50). When all motifs in the first color are printed, remove fabric from table and hang up to air dry.

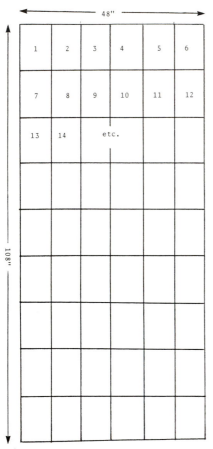

(Figure 15.48) Frame placement for repeat design of 54 motifs using an 8'' × 12'' printing frame, and printing all motifs.

Other placements may be worked out such as just printing odd numbered motifs or even numbered motifs, etc. for band effect; or odd numbers in row 1, even numbers in row 2, and so on for zig-zag effect. Placement may also be at random if desired.

(Figure 15.49) Markings being made for screen placement.

(Figure 15.50) Ink being forced through screen with squeegee.

To print remaining colors, attach fabric to table as before and repeat the procedure for printing the other colors. Once the first color has been printed, it is a simple matter to line up the other motifs visually because the film itself is transparent and the outlines of the first color may be easily seen.

When all printing is complete, remove fabric from work table and allow it to dry for at least twenty-four hours.

Colors must be "set" (made permanent) by ironing the fabric very slowly with a hot iron, first on one side then on the other. An alternate method is to place the fabric in a clothes dryer and tumble at high heat for thirty minutes. The finished piece is shown in figure 15.51. Another example of a printed fabric by a student is shown in figure 15.52.

*(Figure 15.51) Completed printed fabric.*

*(Figure 15.52) Student work: titled "Geometric."*

## Notes

1  A fascinating account of this event is to be found in chapter 3 of Professor Dard Hunter's *Papermaking: The History and Technique of an Ancient Craft,* 2d ed. (New York: Alfred Knopf, 1947); reprint (New York: Dover Publications, 1978).

2  Gerald F. Brommer, *Relief Printmaking.* (Worcester, Mass.: Davis Publications, 1970), 61.

## Suggested Readings

### Woodcuts and Linocuts

Bennett, Maggi, et al. *Printing without a Press.* Hollywood Fla.: Dukane Press, 1983.

Brommer, Gerald F. *Relief Printmaking.* Worcester, Mass.: Davis Publications, 1970.

Capron, Robin. *Introducing Abstract Printing.* New York: Watson-Guptill Publications, 1973.

Eichenberg, Franz. *The Art of the Print.* New York: H. N. Abrams, 1976.

Gilmour, Pat. *Artists in Print.* London: British Broadcasting Corp., 1981.

Gobartz, Norman. *Printmaking with Spoon.* New York: Reinhold Publishing Co., 1960.

Heller, Jules. *Printmaking Today: A Studio Handbook.* New York: Holt, Reinhart and Winston, 1972.

Johnson, Una E. *American Prints and Printmaker.* Garden City, N.Y.: Doubleday and Co., 1980.

Maxwell, William C. *Printmaking: A Beginning Handbook.* Englewood Cliffs, N.J.: Prentice-Hall, 1977.

Peterdi, Gabor. *Printmaking: Methods, Old and New.* New York: Macmillan, 1971.

Rothenstein, Michael. *Frontiers of Printmaking.* New York: Reinhold Publishing Co., 1966.

————. *Linocuts and Woodcuts.* New York: Watson-Guptill Publications, 1962.

————. *Relief Printing.* New York: Watson-Guptill Publications, 1970.

Russ, Stephen. *A Complete Guide to Printmaking.* New York: Viking Press, 1975.

Saff, Donald. *Printmaking: History and Process.* New York: Holt, Reinhart and Winston, 1978.

Shapiro, Cecile, and Lauris Mason. *Fine Prints: Collecting, Buying and Selling.* New York: Harper and Row, 1974.

Sotriffer, Kristian. *Printmaking, History and Technique.* New York: McGraw-Hill Book Co., 1968.

Watrous, James. *American Printmaking: A Century of American Printmaking.* Madison: University of Wisconsin Press, 1984.

Wenniger, Mary Ann. *Collagraph Printmaking.* New York: Watson-Guptill Publications, 1975.

### Silk Screen on Paper

Biegeleisen, J. I. and M. A. Cohn. *Silk Screen Techniques.* New York: Dover Publications, 1958.

Chieffo, Clifford, T. *Silkscreen as a Fine Art.* New York: Reinhold Publishing Co., 1967.

Kinsey, Anthony. *Introducing Screen Printing.* Cincinnati: Watson-Guptill Publications, 1968.

Lassiter, Frances, and Norman Lassiter. *Screen Printing: Contemporary Methods and Materials.* Philadelphia: Hunt Manufacturing Co., 1978.

Rainey, Sarita, and Burton Wasserman. *Basic Silkscreen Printing.* Worcester, Mass.: Davis Publications, 1971.

Schwalbach, Matilda V., and James A. Schwalbach. *Screen Process Printing.* New York: Van Nostrand, Reinhold, 1970. This work is perhaps the most sophisticated and complete of those listed and is highly recommended to the serious student of silkscreen printing.

Shokler, Harry. *Artist's Manual for Silkscreen Printmaking.* Greensboro, N.C.: Tudor Publishing Co., 1960.

Termini, Maria. *Silk Screening.* Englewood Cliffs, N.J.: Prentice-Hall, 1978.

### Silk Screen on Fabric

Ash, Beryl, and Anthony Dyson. *Introducing Dyeing and Printing.* New York: Watson-Guptill Publications, 1970.

Johnston Meda P., and Glen Kaufman. *Design on Fabrics.* New York: Van Nostrand, Reinhold, 1967.

Proctor, Richard M., and Jenifer F. Leu. *Surface Design for Fabric.* Seattle: University of Washington Press, 1984.

Proud, Nora. *Textile Printing and Dyeing.* New York: Reinhold Publishing Co., 1965.

Searle, Valerie, and Roberta Clayson. *Screen Printing on Fabric.* New York: Watson-Guptil Publications, 1968.

# 16 Stained Glass

Glass is a hard, usually transparent or translucent substance, composed of a mixture of flint (silica dioxide), alkaline flux (potash or soda), stablizier (limestone), coloring agents (metal oxides), and various other substances that give it special properties (for example, lead for density and sparkle, boron for electrical resistance, tin for opacity). The raw materials are heated in a special furnace to a high temperature until they melt and fuse together. The molten mixture may then be rolled into sheets or blown into various shapes. Early examples of glass made by hand have been found in Mesopotamia (circa 2000 B.C.) as well as in Egypt. The Egyptians are credited with making the first colored glass, the art eventually passing into Greece, Rome, and other parts of Europe. Small colored glass windows existed in some Christian churches as early as the fifth century A.D., as well as in some earlier Moslem structures. There also is evidence of glazed windows in Roman houses of the first century A.D.

The earliest known instance of the use of colored glass pieces put together with lead strips to form a window with a pictorial design is in the rebuilding of Rheims Cathedral in France in the late tenth century. Extensive use of stained glass in large windows was made possible during the twelfth century by Gothic architectural innovations, particularly the pier and flying buttress, which meant that the earlier massive walls of Romanesque architectural structure were no longer needed as weight-bearing elements. Gothic structures could be made lighter and taller and be pierced with large openings that could then be filled with brilliant facets of colored glass and ornate tracery.

Abbot Suger (chief advisor to both Louis VI and Louis VII of France) is credited by many art historians as being the "father of the Gothic style," because it was he who began rebuilding in 1140 the choir of the abbey church of St. Denis near Paris, bringing together in one building certain elements seen in various earlier Romanesque structures. In his own account of his plans for St. Denis, Abbot Suger speaks of the "miraculous light" entering through the "sacred windows," which symbolized for Suger the divine radiance of God and Christ as light of the world.[1]

In addition to furnishing illumination, pictorial stained glass windows in churches had an educational purpose, because scenes and figures from biblical history could be depicted and used as a "picture book" by the priest to illustrate and teach religious dogma, as well as moral lessons and events in the lives of Christ, the Virgin Mary, and the saints. Stained glass windows in a Gothic church also played an emotional role, creating a mystical, subdued atmosphere of light tinged with the many colors present in the windows.

Very little of the earliest stained glass still exists; some eleventh-century examples remain, notably the "five prophets" figure windows in Augsburg Cathedral, Germany, dating from 1050. The finest surviving examples of the twelfth and thirteenth centuries are those in Notre Dame de Paris. At Chartres, the famous window called "Notre Dame de la Belle Verriere" (Our Lady of the Beautiful Glass) miraculously survived the fire of 1194, which virtually destroyed the earlier cathedral begun in Romanesque times. Revived interest in stained glass crafting occurred in the nineteenth century in the work of William Morris (England) and Louis Comfort Tiffany (United States).

Several noted artists of the twentieth century have designed stained glass windows, including Henri Matisse (the Dominican nun's chapel at Vence, France), Georges Rouault (church in Plateau d'Assy, France), Graham Sutherland (new Coventry Cathedral, England), and Marc Chagall who designed twelve magnificent windows depicting the tribes of Israel for the synagogue of the Hadassah-Hebrew University Medical Center near Jerusalem.

The beauty of light filtering through stained glass has an almost universal aesthetic appeal, and a visit to a great Gothic cathedral such as Notre Dame de Chartres with its magnificent stained glass windows is a never to be forgotten emotional experience. Although few students will be able to acquire the facility and experience necessary to design and make such a masterpiece, it is quite possible to learn the simple techniques of stained glass crafting quickly and to create panels, lanterns, window inserts, mobiles, and other glass projects.

There are two basic approaches to stained glass crafting: the traditional method in which individual sections of glass are joined together with H-shaped strips of lead and the contemporary method of "wrapping" each section of glass in a narrow strip of copper foil and joining them with solder. The traditional leading approach is preferred for larger panels, especially for windows, where strength and durability are factors, but the foil technique is perfectly acceptable for smaller panels and various free-form projects. If the foil technique is properly carried out, it may be used for windows as well. Both methods are described here.

## Basic Tools and Materials

The basic tools and equipment necessary for stained glass crafting are illustrated in figure 16.1. A list and description of each item follows.

1  *A leading board* consists of a piece of plywood, ½ or ¾ inches thick, having perfectly square corners. The board is edged on two sides with a flat piece of molding or stripping, extending above the surface of the board by about ½ inch. The leading board serves as a working surface and aids in obtaining square corners when doing panels. For most student work, a board 24-by-24 inches is a convenient size.
2  *Soldering iron or gun* of the miniature sixty watt "industrial type" is satisfactory for studio work, and comes with a variety of tip sizes and shapes. Prior to its first use, a new tip should be "tinned" by heating; a small amount of flux is applied and the tip is rubbed in melted solder until it is completely coated. Keep soldering tips clean during use by rubbing the tip on a damp sponge periodically. The tip will eventually oxidize and must be cleaned with a stiff wire brush.
3  *A glazier's knife* is short and stocky with a curved blade sharpened on the outer edge of the curve. It is used with a rocking motion to cut lead came. A linoleum knife may be adapted by grinding down and sharpening the outer edge.
4  *Leading bar* is a piece of steel about 1-by-6-by-⅛ inches used between the hammer and the glass when a piece of glass is tapped into the channel of the lead came to avoid direct blows of the hammer on the glass or lead. A small block of hardwood is a suitable substitute.
5  *Hammer:* A fairly small, double-end (not clawed) tack hammer works well, although glazier's hammers are available.

6 *Glass cutters* such as the Fletcher "gold tip," Red Devil, or Craftsman "ball-end" types all work well. The ball-end variety is especially useful for tapping scored glass in the cutting operation. There is available a cutter with a carbide wheel that outlasts the ordinary cutters about five to one and is well worth the small extra expense. If the cutting end is kept immersed in a light oil, such as kerosene, it will remain sharp much longer.

7 *Ruler,* either 15 or 18 inches in length, is helpful in laying out designs and can act as a guide for cutting straight edges with the glass cutter. A wax or grease pencil, such as the Stabilo type, is useful for marking on glass.

8 *Grozing pliers* made especially for glaziers are available, but any pair of pliers with smooth, flush, fairly wide jaws may be used to remove tiny rough projections from the cut edges of the glass.

9 *Nails* about 1 inch in length, called small wire nails, are needed.

10 *Opening tool* consisting of any blunt wooden instrument, such as a boxwood tool used for modeling clay, may be used to open the channels in lead came. A tool can be made from a piece of ⅜ inch dowel rod. Some glass cutters are designed so the handle serves as a channel opener.

11 *Glazier's shears (Schablonenscheren)* are used for cutting patterns for traditional leading techniques and will automatically allow for the thickness of the "heart" of the lead came. They are expensive and not absolutely necessary, because a quite satisfactory substitute can be made by placing 1/16 inch thick cardboard or metal shim between two single edged razor blades and taping them together with masking tape.

12 *Circle cutter* is an instrument consisting of a cutting wheel set in the end of a rotating arm that is equipped with a movable suction cup. The cup is attached to the glass, the arm adjusted for any diameter from about 2 to 36 inches, and the arm swung around with sufficient pressure to score the glass.

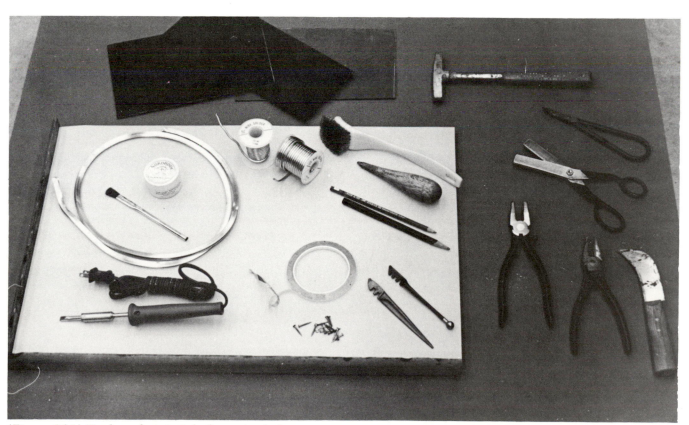

*(Figure 16.1) Tools and materials for stained glass.*

13 *A wood lathekin* or *metal burnisher* is needed for smoothing lead and foil seams.

14 *Cut running pliers* are a special pair for aiding in cracking glass along scored lines. They are less time-consuming than the tapping method but requires some practice for efficient use.

Materials necessary to stain glass are outlined next.

1 *Stained glass sheets* are available in a variety of sizes, types, and colors. For student work, 12-by-16-inch sheets are a convenient size. Several surfaces are available: plain (smooth surface), seedy (tiny air bubbles trapped inside), and rough, textured glass known as hammered or rippled. The plain and seedy varieties are easiest to cut. An assortment of colors should be ordered. Reds are more expensive than other colors.

2 *Came lead* are channeled lead strips, either H or U shape available in ⅛, ³⁄₁₆, or ¼-inch widths. The U shape is used on all outer perimeters of panels, the H shape for all other purposes. The crossbar of the H shape is called the "heart." Came usually comes in 6 foot long rolls, or lengths, and is used for traditional leaded glass.

3 *Rolls of copper foil tape* are backed with an adhesive and available in a variety of widths from ¼ inch and up. The tape is used in the foil technique in place of lead came.

4 *Solder* should be 60/40 solid (no core) type. Do not use acid or rosin core solder.

5 *Flux* made of commercial paste or liquid soft solder may be used. The purpose of the flux is to help clean the surface of the lead and to cause the solder to flow more readily. Oleic acid flux is easier to clean from the glass later on. Do not use hard solder (silver) flux.

6 *Glazier's putty* is used for filling joints between lead and glass. It is essential for windows or panels that will be exposed to the weather, but not absolutely necessary for small pieces that will be used indoors.

7 *Paper* of two types is needed; one, a lightweight drawing or layout paper used for making sketches, the other, a heavier kraft-type paper used for making patterns. Carbon paper is useful for duplicating patterns.

8 *Drawing tools* consist of rulers, pencils, compasses, drafting instruments, and drawing board.

An adequately lighted workbench of ample size, with an electrical outlet is essential. Space should be provided underneath for glass storage. A rack with narrow vertical partitions in which glass sheets can be stored on edge is ideal. A tool board mounted over the workbench is convenient. Coils and strips of lead may be stored flat in a box, or may be hung on pegs on the toolboard. A partitioned box is useful for storing smaller scraps of glass that might be usable later. Small scraps of glass may be collected in a box and used for glass mosaic or fused glass projects.

**Procedure for Traditional Leading Approach**
The procedure given is for a flat panel and may have to be modified somewhat for other projects. Make a sketch which may be anything from a rough doodle to a full-fledged drawing. When designing for stained glass, remember three things.

1 The work must be structurally sound, especially if a large panel is being planned. This means no extremely large sections of glass and no areas where too many leads come together at one point, making for a weak joint. Placement of leads should be planned in such a way that the piece is self supporting.

2 Conversely, individual pieces of glass should not be too small. Remember that a portion of each piece of glass will be covered with lead. If individual pieces are too small, the work will end up being all lead and no glass.

3 One does not really "cut" glass. It fractures along a prescored line; therefore, certain shapes are almost impossible to cut in one piece. For example, it would be difficult to cut an L-shaped piece of glass, as in figure 16.2, because the fracture line would tend to continue in the direction of the dotted lines. The L shape would have to be composed of two or more pieces of glass leaded together.

Make a full-size working drawing. After the design has been decided upon, the *cartoon* or full-size working drawing is made. Number and color code each separate section either by letters or by actually coloring in with pencils or watercolor paints. (see figure 16.3).

Make two patterns. This is done by tracing the working drawing onto two sheets of heavier paper with the aid of carbon paper. One pattern will be cut apart to make cutting guides for individual pieces, while the other will be used to lay out the glass after cutting to make sure all pieces are cut and accounted for (see figure 16.4).

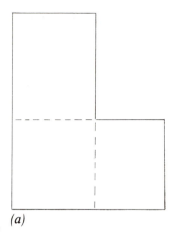

*(a)*

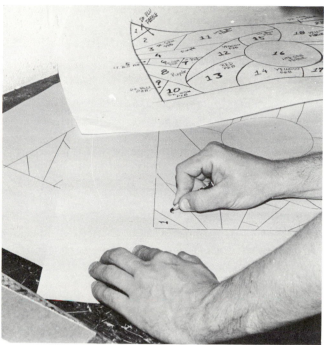

*(Figure 16.3) Two patterns made from original drawing.*

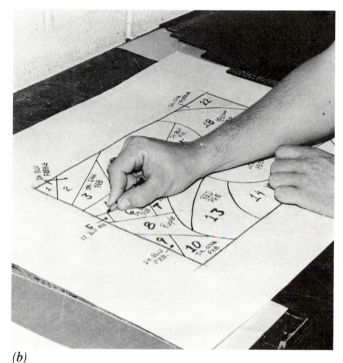

*(b)*

*(Figure 16.2) (a) The L-shaped piece shown would be impossible to cut in one piece because the fracture lines would continue as indicated by the dotted lines. Shape could be accomplished by cutting two or three pieces. (b) Full-size working drawing for small stained glass panel.*

*(Figure 16.4) One pattern is cut apart to make cutting guides for individual pieces.*

Be sure to number the sections of each pattern to correspond to the working drawing. The working drawing itself should be retained for later use in the leading step.

Cut the pattern as shown in figure 16.5. Using either glazier's shears or the razor blade assembly referred to earlier (and pictured in use), cut out each section of *one* of the patterns. The tiny portions of paper that curl away make allowances for the thickness of the heart of the lead. The use of regular scissors would not make this allowance, and the final assembly would not fit properly. Keep track of all pattern pieces. An excellent way to accomplish this is to fasten each piece as it is cut

to the corresponding section of the other pattern, using a dab of rubber cement or other temporary means.

Select a sheet of glass of the desired color and place one of the pattern pieces on top the glass. Allow about a ½-inch margin all around. Holding the pattern piece in place with one hand, grasp the cutter firmly in the other hand and, with the cutter held *perpendicular* to the glass, score the glass by following the pattern with uniform, moderately heavy pressure. The cutter should make a scratching sound on the glass and score an easily visible mark on top the glass (see figure 16.6). Turn the glass over, and holding the cutter loosely so that vibration occurs, tap with the ball end of the cutter along the scored line (see figure 16.7).

*(Figure 16.5) Method of cutting pattern with taped parallel razor blades to allow for thickness of lead cames.*

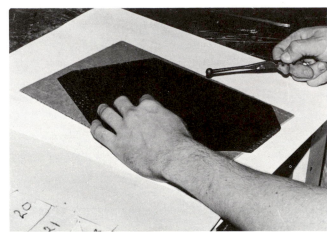

*(Figure 16.7) Tapping glass on reverse side with ball end of cutter to break glass.*

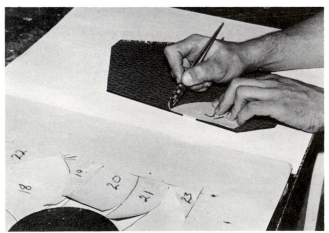

*(Figure 16.6) Scoring the glass with cutter to shape of piece to be cut.*

If tapping has been properly done, the section of glass will probably already have parted from the parent sheet; if not, this can easily be accomplished if you grasp the glass firmly on either side of the fracture and snap the pieces apart with a downward pull-apart motion (see figure 16.8).

Most beginners have some difficulty in learning to cut the glass shapes properly. This can be minimized by following the practice of scoring one edge at a time, breaking away that glass, then scoring the next edge, breaking that, and so on.

An alternate method to the "tapping" technique is the use of specially designed running pliers. When these pliers are placed on one end of a scored line and gently squeezed, they will "run" the break along the line and separate the glass easily (see figure 16.9).

Circles and irregularly shaped pieces of glass will have to be freed by scoring lines from several points out to the edge of the parent sheet, and following the same tapping procedure along these lines illustrated in figure 16.9.

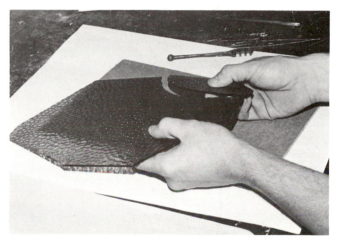

(Figure 16.8) Releasing cut piece from parent sheet with downward motion.

(a)

(b)

(Figure 16.9) (a) Running pliers are placed at one end of scored line so that mark on pliers is exactly lined up with scored line. (b) Handles of pliers are gently squeezed to separate two sections of glass.

The procedure for using the circle cutter to cut a circle of glass is shown in figure 16.10. The student should practice the various cutting steps on scrap glass until they are mastered, before attempting the first project. As each piece of glass is cut, lay it on the other pattern in its proper position and proceed in this manner until all necessary pieces for the design have been cut (see figure 16.11).

Edges of the cut pieces will sometimes be slightly irregular. In this event, they should be chipped away or "grozed" with the grozing notches on the cutter or with the glazier pliers. Minor irregularities will not matter because these will be covered with the came lead.

Prepare the lead by straightening and opening the came strips before using. To straighten a strip, place one end in a vise, grasp the other end firmly with the pliers, and exert a firm steady pull, which will stretch and

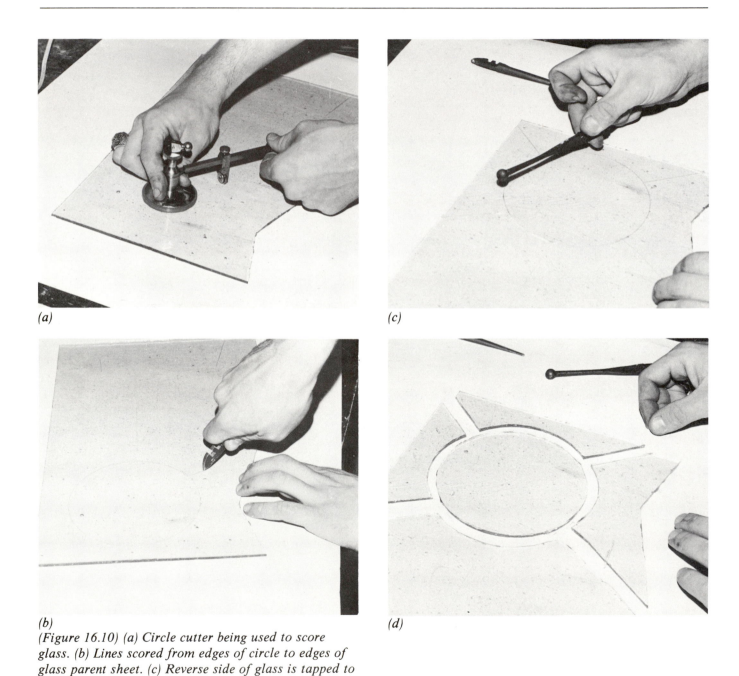

*(a)*

*(b)*

*(c)*

*(d)*

*(Figure 16.10) (a) Circle cutter being used to score glass. (b) Lines scored from edges of circle to edges of glass parent sheet. (c) Reverse side of glass is tapped to break glass. (d) Circle is released from glass sheet.*

straighten the strip. Now open the strip by drawing the wooden opening tool through the channel in the lead evenly along its length (see figure 16.12). The channel must be opened enough to receive the thickness of the glass, and a little to spare.

Assemble and lead the design. Place the leading board on the work table and tape the working drawing to its surface; be sure that the corner of the drawing is square with the corner of the leading board (see figure 16.13).

Using the glazier's knife with a gentle, rocking motion, cut two lengths of lead somewhat longer than the two sides of the panel. Because these will be the outer perimeters of the design, use the U-shaped lead. Place these strips inside the corner angle of the leading board, fitting the end of one piece of lead into the end of the other so they overlap. The first piece of glass is fitted into the channels of both strips and tapped firmly into place with the leading bar and hammer (see figure 16.14).

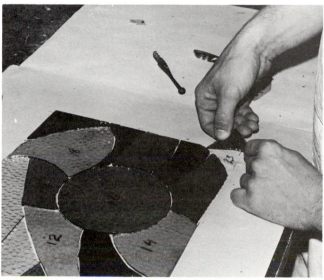

*(Figure 16.11) All pieces have been cut and laid out on second pattern.*

*(Figure 16.13) Working drawing is taped in corner of leading board to serve as leading guide.*

*(Figure 16.12) Channel in lead came is opened with tool.*

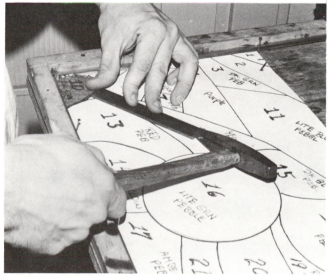

*(Figure 16.14) First piece of glass is put into place with aid of leading bar and hammer.*

Cut and fit the H-shaped pieces of lead for the other edges of the first piece of glass. All work is held in place with small wire nails that are removed as other pieces of glass are added (see figure 16.15).

From this point on, the assembly procedure is a matter of fitting in each piece of glass according to the working drawing, placing the lead properly, and continuing until all pieces are in place. Note especially the method of handling the glazier's knife in figure 16.16. When all pieces are in place and leaded, finish the remaining two sides of the panel with two lengths of U-shaped lead, as before. The completely leaded panel is then ready for soldering (see figure 16.17).

For a successfully constructed and well-leaded panel, the student should observe several precautions. The panel should be as sturdy as possible, which will be assured if each piece of glass is tapped firmly into place and held securely with small nails while work is in progress. Where one end of a lead strip meets another piece of lead there should be no gap; therefore angling the lead so it fits properly is often necessary. Remember that lead is very soft and must be handled carefully to prevent nicks and gouged places.

When the panel has been completely assembled and leaded, it must be joined by placing solder at every point where lead meets lead. Clean the tip of the soldering gun with a stiff brush, file, or piece of emery paper; plug the iron into the outlet; and when the iron is hot, tin the tip by rubbing it in a bit of solder until the solder melts and the tip is completely coated.

*(Figure 16.15) Additional pieces of glass are placed according to the pattern. Note use of nails to hold in place.*

*(Figure 16.17) Edges of the panel are leaded and held in place with nails.*

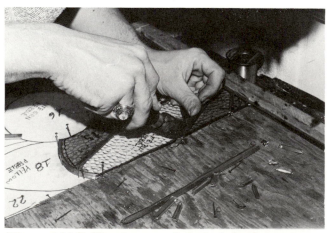

*(Figure 16.16) Showing use of glazier's knife to trim lengths of lead came.*

To solder a joint, first apply flux to the spot with a small brush. Then, holding the coil of solder in the left hand and the soldering iron in the right, heat the joint until the flux begins to sizzle; place the end of the solder on the joint and continue heating with a light rubbing motion until the solder melts and flows into a smooth, neat bond. Only a little solder is necessary. Remember that the melting points of the solder and lead are very close, and too much heat will melt a hole in the lead. The student should practice with scrap lead until the proper touch is learned. When all joints have been soldered, carefully turn the panel over and solder the reverse side (see figure 16.18).

Putty the work, if desired. Normally, small pieces of student work that will be used indoors are not puttied, but if a panel is to serve as a window insert or otherwise be exposed to the weather, or if it is fairly large, puttying is essential. Work the putty into all areas between the lead and the glass as shown in figure 16.19. Excess putty, flux, and other residue is removed by sprinkling the panel with glazier's whiting or plaster and scrubbing the whole surface with a stiff brush as shown in figure 16.20.

A photograph of the completed panel is shown in figure 16.21.

(Figure 16.18) All joints are soldered on one side of panel, then on the other.

(Figure 16.20) Panel is cleaned by using glazier's whiting.

(Figure 16.19) Panel is puttied to make it weathertight.

(Figure 16.21) Finished panel.

## Foil Method for Stained Glass

The foil technique for joining pieces of glass has been developed in the last few years and is being used by a growing numbers of glass artists. It utilizes a thin copper tape that comes in various widths and has an adhesive backing. The ¼-inch width is perhaps the most useful for general work. The foil technique can be accomplished with ease; is less expensive and time-consuming; and lends itself to all sorts of creative expressions, such as boxes, sculptural forms, free-form shapes, lamp shades, and the like. Soldering may be done without fear of melting the copper tape.

Procedure for a flat panel is described here. Make a sketch, full-size working drawing, and two patterns as outlined for the traditional method. The pattern is cut apart using ordinary scissors because it is not necessary to allow for the thickness of the heart of the lead came. Select the sheets of glass you want to use. When all glass necessary for the project has been cut, each piece of glass must be individually wrapped in strips of copper foil. Peel off a length of tape, allowing enough extra for a slight overlap (see figure 16.22).

Beginning in the center of one side of a piece of glass, apply adhesive side of tape making sure the edge is perfectly centered on the width of the tape, so there is an equal quantity on both sides. Fold down tape on either side, adhering it to the glass as figure 16.23

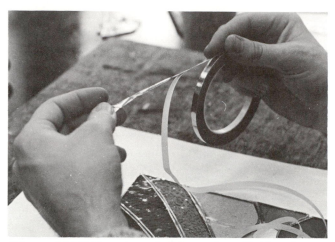

*(Figure 16.22) Tape is peeled from the roll. Tape has an adhesive on one side that allows it to stick to the edge on the glass pieces.*

*(a)*

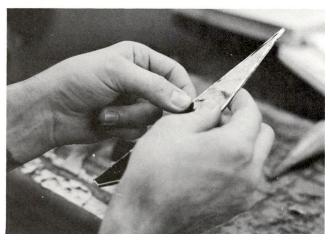

*(b)*

*(Figure 16.23) (a) Taping is begun in the center of one side of a piece of glass. (b) Tape is adhered to glass piece and folded down around edge.*

illustrates (you are making a channel for the edge of the glass). Turn corners neatly, and when tape is pressed down and adhered all around, go over all surfaces with the lathekin or burnisher to ensure good adhesion (see figure 16.24).

Continue until all glass pieces are wrapped. Assemble pieces according to the pattern, hold in place with nails, and tack with solder at all points where pieces touch as in the traditional lead method. Be sure to use flux so the solder will adhere properly. When all pieces are tacked in place, remove nails, flux all copper surfaces, and cover with solder. Foiled work is not cemented or puttied because doing so would damage the taped seams. Clean pieces with detergent and water or a commercial glass cleaner.

For extra strength, the outer edges of large panels may be covered with lead came to form a frame. This is especially desirable if the piece is to hang, because the foiled edges are not strong enough to support much weight. Rings for hanging may be made from 16 gauge brass or copper wire and attached to the upper corners of the panel. Completed work using the foil technique is shown in figure 16.25.

**General Notes**

Some glass workers prefer to make "floated" solder joints. This is accomplished by going back over the seams and applying a bit more solder, but holding the iron slightly above the seam so the solder will "rise" to meet the iron. The iron cannot be too hot or the process will not work. With practice, a good floated seam having a rounded convex contour will result, which gives the finished piece a more professional look. By applying the solder a little more heavily than usual, then touching down the tip of the iron at random and raising it quickly, you can produce textured seams.

You may darken or "antique" soldered seams by applying a solution of copper sulphate dissolved in *hot* water. Dissolve 2 ounces of the copper sulphate powder in 4 ounces of hot water, and apply with a brush to clean soldered seams. Some craftspeople add a few drops of hydrochloric acid or even vinegar to the mixture. Apply successive coats of the hot mixture until the desired effect is achieved. The treated solder will turn a brownish copper color, which may be buffed to a sheen with a cloth or very fine steel wool. Commercial mixtures for antiquing are also available. Untreated soldered seams will gradually darken with age, but may be brightened by periodic treatment with vinegar followed by polishing.

*(Figure 16.24) Tape is pressed down with wood lathekin on all surfaces.*

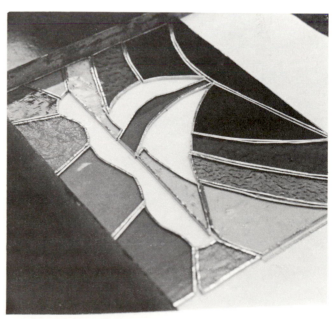

*(Figure 16.25) Completed work using foil technique. Note that the design motif is actually achieved through use of negative space.*

Although the craft of stained glass is not difficult, it does require patience and close attention to details such as measuring and cutting. The student should practice each step until proficiency is gained and should make a small panel by using both the traditional and foil methods before attempting a more ambitious project. Examples of student work are shown in figure 16.26.

*Note*
1 Erwin Panofsky, trans., *Abbot Suger on the Abbey Church of St. Denis and its Art Treasures* (Princeton, N.J.: Princeton University Press, 1946). *See also* H. W. Janson, *History of Art,* 2d ed. (Englewood Cliffs, N.J.: Prentice-Hall 1977), 283–86.

*Suggested Reading*

Chagall, Marc. *The Jerusalem Windows*. Text and notes by Jean Leymarie. New York: Braziller, 1962.

Duncan, Alastair. *Tiffany Windows*. New York: Simon and Schuster, 1980.

Duvall, Jean Jacques. *Working with Stained Glass*. New York: Thomas Y. Crowell Co., 1972.

Isenberg, Anita, and Seymour Isenberg. *How to Work in Stained Glass*. Philadelphia: Chilton, 1972.

Lee, Lawrence, George Seddon, and Frances Stephans. *Stained Glass*. New York: Crown Publishers, 1976.

Luciano. *Stained Glass Window Art*. Palo Alto, Calif.: Hidden House Publication, 1976.

Paterson, James. *Stained Glass*. London: Museum Press, 1968.

Reyntiens, Patrick. *The Technique of Stained Glass*. New York: Watson-Guptill Publications, 1967.

Sewter, A. *The Stained Glass of William Morris and His Circle*. New Haven: Yale University Press, 1974.

Wood, Paul W. *Stained Glass Crafting*. New York: Sterling Publishing Co., 1967.

*(a)*

*(b)*

*(Figure 16.26) Student work.*

# 17 Ceramics

Ceramics or pottery making is the process of creating objects from earth materials, which are subsequently heated to a high temperature to make them durable. The finished product, regardless of form, is usually called a *pot* and the process is *potting* or *pottery making.*

The major raw material is clay, formed by the geologic weathering of *feldspar rock;* therefore, clay exists in great abundance in nature. Chemically, clay is a mixture of the oxides of aluminum and silica, together with the oxides of iron, magnesium, titanium, and other elements. There are various types of clays, such as *earthenware, stoneware,* and *porcelain,* ranging in color from pure white to almost black. The color of clay depends primarily on the amount of *oxide of iron* and organic matter contained therein. Clay, when wet with the proper amount of water, is *plastic* and may readily be formed into various shapes. Clay may often be used just as it comes from the ground (*natural clay*), or several natural clays may be mixed together to form a *clay body.* Natural clay needs to be refined to remove small stones, twigs, and other undesirable materials.

As early as 5000 B.C. humans knew how to form clay into vessels by working the plastic material into shapes with the hands, pushing and pinching the clay, building the desired shape with coils of clay, or using a basket or other concave form to serve as a mold for the wet clay. These early clay forms were probably sun dried until hard, but it was soon discovered that by "burning" the pots in a fire a much harder, more durable product would result. Examples of such pots from Neolithic Mesopotamia and Egypt have been found.

The potter's wheel as a means for forming clay was in use in ancient Sumeria as early as 3500 B.C., in Egypt about 2800 B.C., and in Greece about 2500 B.C. Pottery making spread from these early beginnings to most areas of the world, becoming a "universal craft." In many cultures, such as Greece, China, Japan, and Scandanavia, the craft was developed into a fine art.

Museums abound with marvelous examples of Greek red- and black-figured vases dating from the sixth to fourth centuries B.C.; Chinese stoneware and porcelains from the T'ang ( A.D. 618–906), Sung (A.D. 960–1260), and Ming (A.D. 1368–1644) dynasties; and Japanese Raku tea ceremony vessels of the sixteenth century and painted semiporcelains of the nineteenth century. These works greatly influenced later European ceramics, particularly those of Scandanavia.

Such ceramics as Italian majolica, French faience, Sèvres and Limoges wares, Persian luster work, German Meissen porcelains, and works by the English potters Thomas Wheildon and Josiah Wedgewood are only a few other examples that are a part of the long and colorful history of pottery making. In America, a strong pottery making tradition has its roots in pre-Revolutionary domestic redwares, nineteenth century Rockingham pottery, and "china" dinnerware produced by such companies as Lenox in the twentieth century.

Contemporary pottery in America is often mass produced in factories, but the rise of the individual studio potter (about 70,000 at present) has meant an abundance of original fine one-of-a-kind pieces of all types. Such twentieth century potters as Otto and Gertrud Natzler, Henry Varnum Poor, Glen Lukens, Paul Soldner, Peter Voulkos, Maija Grotell, Harrison McIntosh, Ruth Duckworth, Bernard Leach, and Shoji Hamada, to name only a few, have made major contributions to pottery form, decoration, and glaze formulation.

Pottery making is taught in the schools at all levels, and many individuals of varying skills are involved with ceramics as a hobby. The high chemical, physical and thermal durability of fired clay makes it particularly suitable for such industrial uses as the manufacture of bath fixtures, water and sewerage pipes, building materials, such as bricks, floor and wall tiles, and many electrical applications. Ceramic technology is fast developing into an important science to explore the possibilities of clay in electronics and particularly to investigate Space Age demands for high-strength materials that will withstand extremes of thermal variation as well as unusual environmental conditions.

**Ceramic Process**

The ceramic process consists of the following steps:

1 *Preparation of the clay:* Clay may be purchased in the dry form and mixed with water for use, but in order to save time, a premixed clay body that comes in the moist form is often used. To this clay may be added a certain amount of *grog,* which is ground, fired clay. Grog adds strength, *porosity,* and textural interest to the clay. All air pockets must be worked out of the clay, which is accomplished by the process known as *wedging.*
2 *Formation of the clay:* The desired shape of a work can be performed by *hand-building methods* (slab, coil, drape, pinch), by *throwing* on the potter's wheel, or by *casting* into *molds* using liquid clay called *casting slip.*
3 *Drying:* To minimize strain, drying must take place slowly. When the clay is still wet but no longer pliable, it is at the *leather-hard* stage. During drying, *shrinkage* occurs, usually about 8 to 10 percent, though more or less may occur depending on the type clay being dried. A piece of formed, dried, unfired clay is called *greenware.* At this point the clay could be rewet and worked back into its original state.
4 *Cleaning and refining:* After forming and drying most pots will have some undesirable surface irregularities that may be removed by sanding, scraping, or sponging. Much of this may also be done at the leather-hard stage.
5 *First firing:* The dried pot is *fired* in a *kiln* to a temperature that corresponds to the *maturity point* of the clay being used. Temperature may range from about 1700° F to 2000° F (cones 08–02) for

earthenware, to about 2190° F to 2350° F (cones 4–8) for stoneware, or much higher for certain commercial applications. Kiln temperatures are measured by means of pyrometric cones, which are formulated to melt at certain temperatures and are accurate to within 5 degrees of the specified temperature. During the firing process, further shrinkage occurs and as well as certain *chemical changes,* which results in a hard, dense clay. Unglazed, fired clay is called *bisque,* and the first firing is known as the *bisque firing.*

6 *Glazing:* A glaze may be thought of as a *glass* coating on the surface of the clay. A mixture of glass-forming oxides called a glaze is applied to the surface of the pot. Upon firing, these oxides melt and form a glassy coating, which renders the pot smooth, nonporous, and of the desired color and texture. Glaze composition varies according to the properties desired. Because these properties develop during the firing, the appearance of the unfired glaze has little relation to the final fired appearance, therefore a *fired-color chart* must be used when selecting glazes. To prepare a glaze for use, the necessary dry ingredients are mixed with water and the resulting slurry applied to the surface of the pot by dipping, pouring, spraying, brushing, or any other convenient means.

7 *Second firing:* After the glazed pot is dry, it is placed in the kiln on *stilts* and fired a second time. The temperature of this firing depends on the maturity point of the glaze being used. Glazes may be formulated to melt (mature) over a wide range of temperature from about 1500° F to 2500° F (cones 013–14). The second firing is called the *glaze firing.*

There are, in general, four categories into which most ceramics can be placed or typed.

1 Pots as we know them: bowls, casseroles, vases, bottles, plates, cups, saucers, usually utilitarian, but also may be purely ornamental

2 Ceramic sculpture: heads, figures, free-form ornamental pieces
3 Architectural ceramics: murals, room dividers, walls, ornamental insets into the walls of buildings
4 Industrial ceramics

Another category may be added, the so-called "nonpots" that are an outgrowth of the dada or pop movement in the arts. The potter tries to make a form in which the pot itself has no practical use, except to exist as a form expressing an idea or as a purely decorative object.

Before proceeding with the actual building of a pot, the student should read extensively in the various books listed in the suggested readings at the end of this chapter.

**Methods of Forming Clay**
*Hand-Building*
Before beginning work, the clay must be wedged, that is, made free of all trapped air, and have grog worked into it. To fifteen pounds of clay is added one cup of grog and the whole mass worked with a kneading action until the grog is completely incorporated. For easier handling, the clay may be divided into two portions, with about half the grog worked into each portion. Eliminate air pockets by cutting through the clay mass, slamming the cut edges down on the wedging table, rekneading the mass, and continuing this procedure until no more pockets are visible when the lump is cut through. The clay is then ready for use and should be stored in a plastic bag to retain moisture (see figure 17.1). The tools used in ceramics and for hand-building or throwing on the wheel are shown in figure 17.2.

*Slab method:* The slab method entails construction of pots from flat slabs of clay that have been rolled to a uniform thickness. Many variations are possible, but for the first pot, I suggest a geometric shape of sufficient size that the hand can be gotten down into the pot while building is in progress.

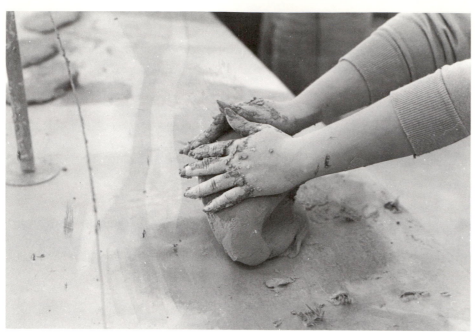

*(Figure 17.1) Wedging the clay. Moist clay is wedged by alternately kneading and cutting through the mass to expose air pockets. Wedging is continued until the lump is completely homogeneous. Grog may be worked in at this point if desired. Note wire for cutting down through the clay lump.*

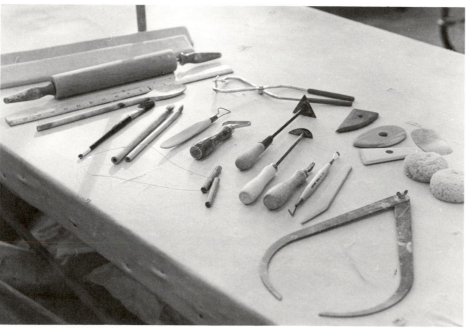

*(Figure 17.2) Tools used in hand-building and throwing on the wheel. Thickness sticks, rolling pin, ruler, paddle, brushes, wire loop tools, cutting wire, turning tools, calipers, sponges, throwing ribs, and glazing tongs. The tools are on a work table covered with canvas.*

Plan size and shape of pot to be made. For example, assume you are going to construct a rectangular weed pot or bottle with several necks, similar to the sketch in figure 17.3. The pot is to be 10 inches tall, 5 inches wide, and 3 inches deep. Therefore, for the sides you need two slabs 10-by-5 inches and two slabs 10-by-3 inches. For the top and bottom you need two slabs 5-by-3 inches. In cutting slabs for tops and bottoms always add 1 inch to the dimensions, so cut two slabs 6-by-4 inches.

Cover work table top with a piece of canvas or oilcloth with the cloth side up. On this, place a sizable lump of clay and roll it into a flat slab using the rolling pin. To minimize strain, roll in all directions, not just back and forth, turning the clay over at intervals to roll both sides. The final thickness of the clay slab should be approximately ⅜ inch. Accomplish this by placing the thickness sticks one on either side of the slab and continue to roll the clay until the ends of the rolling pin touch the sticks all the way along (see figure 17.4).

From the rolled slab, cut the necessary pieces to the desired size, measuring accurately with the ruler and using the right angle triangle to get square corners. Cut slabs with the needle end of the incising tool, being sure to hold it upright so the pieces will not have a beveled edge. As pieces are cut, place them flat on sheets of plywood making sure that all edges are straight. If you will need extra clay for necks, feet, handles or other additions, be sure to cut these pieces at the same time, because when a slab pot is put together, everything has to be the same degree of dryness. When all pieces are cut, cover the entire board with a sheet of plastic and set aside until the pieces are leather-hard (are firm enough to support their own weight).

When all cut pieces are leather-hard, begin construction of the pot by placing the slab that is to be the bottom of the pot down on a flat working surface. Move in about ½ inch from the edge and score the clay with the needle point tool. Score the bottom edge of one of the side pieces, apply clay slip to both scored areas, and attach the side piece to the bottom with gentle pressure and a slight rocking motion. Continue construction by attaching pieces one to the other to form the basic

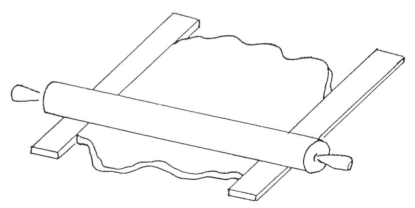

(Figure 17.4) Method of rolling uniform slabs with aid of thickness sticks and rolling pin.

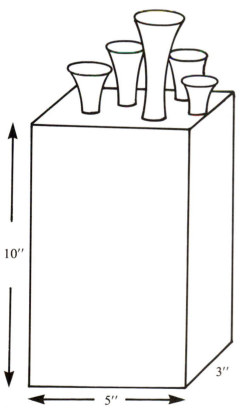

10″

3″

5″

(Figure 17.3) Plan for geometric weed pot to be constructed by the slab method of hand-building.

rectangular box shape, being sure that all edges fit together, are scored with the needle point, and joined with generous amounts of slip. Assure firmer joint by tapping the joined areas gently with a wooden paddle. Finish joints by applying a small coil of very soft clay along all points of contact and working it firmly into the adjoining clay. Figure 17.5 shows construction in progress, with one side and an end of the pot in place on the base.

When all four sides of the pot are in place and all interior work of joining seams is finished, attach the top piece by scoring the underside of the top and all edges along which the top is to fit; apply slip and also the extra coil of clay *before* the top piece is put into place. Join the top piece firmly by paddling until the excess clay oozes out all around. The form is now ready to receive the addition of necks, spouts, and handles. Finish by trimming off excess clay, scraping all surfaces to remove imperfections, and cutting a foot rim into the bottom. When the pot is finished, cover loosely with plastic and set aside to dry slowly.

Many variations of the slab technique are possible. Cut slabs may be joined into any geometric shape, slabs may be joined into cylindrical shapes, slabs may be folded around each other, torn into irregular shapes, or used in a free-form manner of construction. Browse in the literature for examples, and do not be afraid to experiment with your own pots.

*Coil method:* The coil method is perhaps the most ancient of all pottery making techniques, and entails construction of pots from coils of clay that have been rolled by hand to a uniform diameter. Round or oval pots of any size and shape are possible. The outside of the pot may be left with the coils showing or may be worked to a smooth finish.

Plan the size and shape of the pot to be made. Roll a small slab of clay somewhat thicker than usual and from this cut a circle of the proper diameter for the base of the pot. To roll coils, cover work table top with canvas or oilcloth. Roll a chunk of clay into a rough cylinder shape, place on tabletop, and form into a long

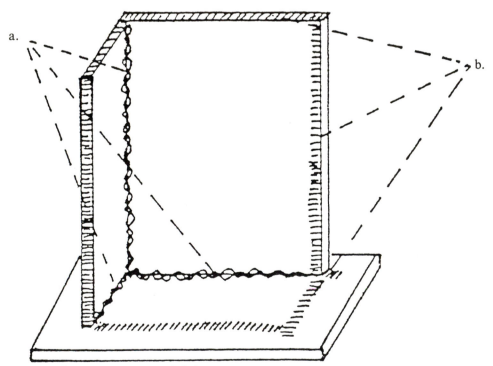

*(Figure 17.5) Construction of slab pot in progress.*
*(a) Extra clay and slip are applied for greater strength.*
*(b) Edges are scored.*

rope by rolling the clay with the *palms* of the hands until it elongates into a uniform coil about ½ inch in diameter. Clay must be very soft, hands must travel back and forth along the entire length of the coil while rolling, and even pressure must be exerted so ridges are not formed.

Start building by placing the coil of clay around the outside perimeter of the base until one complete round is formed. Break off the clay at this point and join the two ends by wedging the clay firmly together. Attach the coil firmly to the base by pushing some of the clay from the inside of the coil down into the base. When the first coil is firmly in place, continue building with additional coils in the same manner; make sure no joint is directly over the one before. Placement of coils depends on the shape of the pot being built.

In this manner, the walls of a coiled pot may be made to assume any shape desired. Outer surfaces of the coils may be left as is or smoothed one into the other. Insides of the coils are *always* worked into adjoining coils as building progresses, so the inside of the pot has a smooth solid surface. Pots are finished with sponging and scraping as necessary to refine the form.

It often helps to make a cardboard template of the profile of the pot being made so the shape can be checked during the building of the pot. If the clay is soft, no additional slip will be necessary to join coils together, though it may be used if desired. If large pots are made, larger coils must be used and the pot allowed to firm up at intervals so the clay will support its own weight.

*Pinch method:* You can form some pots by pinching a ball of clay into shape with the thumb and fingers of one hand while rotating the lump of clay with the other hand. This method lends itself to the making of small, open cup or bowl shapes; two pinch pots may be joined rim to rim to make a closed form or several pinch pots may be joined to make a multiple or "gang" pot.

Start with a ball of well-wedged soft clay about the size of a large orange or small grapefruit. Holding the ball of clay in the left hand, press the right thumb into the clay until it is about ½ inch from the bottom of the ball. With the thumb inside the ball of clay, the fingers outside and constantly turning the ball with the left hand, gently pinch the clay between the thumb and fingers until the walls of the pot begin to thin and rise. Always pinch from the bottom to the top, gradually working up when each level of clay has reached a uniform thickness, about ⅜ to ½ inch. Flatten the base of the pot by hitting it gently on the tabletop. The rim of the pot and the hands should be kept slightly moist while working so cracks will not develop.

Concentrate on giving the pot height rather than width. The tendency at first is to pull outward on the walls of the pot, thus flattening or flaring the walls, rather than making the desired cylinder shape.

When making two pots to be put together rim to rim, it is helpful to start with two balls of clay that are the same size. If cracks develop around the rim of the pot, it indicates that the clay is not moist enough. Cracks should be healed immediately by being rubbed with a finger moistened in water, or they will cause weak spots in the wall of the pot. When two pinch pots are joined rim to rim, the rims should be flattened, scored, and coated with slip. If necessary, extra clay may be added to the outside of the pot and worked in for extra strength. When making a "gang" pot (several joined together), score the spots where the pots touch, join with slip, and add extra clay to make a smooth transition from one pot to the other. In this way, the pots will look joined and not just stuck together; they will also be less apt to crack apart during the firing.

*Drape method:* The drape method is really an adaptation of the slab method and entails the formation of pots with rolled slabs of clay draped over or into preformed shapes. These draped forms are then joined or altered in some way to make pots.

*(Figure 17.6) Hand-built pots by the author. (a) Coil pot with slip and slung engobe decoration. (b) Two pinch pots joined at lip and shaped by hand; applied clay decoration and glazed surface. (c) Two draped forms joined at rims and paddled into shape; applied necks; overall rutile glaze. (d) Coil pot with three joined necks; incised decoration, tan rutile glaze. (e) Slab pot with applied cut slabs; green rutile glaze.*

*(f) Slab pot with paddled decoration achieved by striking the leather-hard pot with the edge of a stick; brown lustre glaze. (g) Slab weed pot with multinecks and brown rutile glaze; incised decoration. (h) Back "owl pot" formed by draping clay into papier-mache shapes in which fruit is shipped; hand-built neck; brown lustre glaze. (i) Tall slab pot with incised decoration; brown rutile glaze. (j) Large slab pot, overall gray-green glaze, and multiglaze decoration.*

All tools and materials listed for other hand-building methods plus a variety of preformed materials are needed for draping pots. Some possible materials are mixing bowls, styrofoam containers, cardboard tubes or cylinders, fruit or egg crate dividers, smooth stones, and plaster humps.

Select a form to be draped. If it is made of porous material, such as cardboard, no further preparation is necessary. If nonporous, such as glass, the surface to be draped must be covered with a thin sheet of plastic or damp paper towels to prevent the clay from sticking to the surface. Roll clay slabs following the procedure previously outlined. Slabs are then draped over convex forms or pressed into concave forms, with the fingers and a moist sponge used to make the slab conform to the shape selected.

If the shape is fairly shallow, one slab may be used but if the shape is fairly deep, the method works better if the slab is cut into portions, and the pieces placed into the form so that they overlap slightly, which will prevent excessive buckling of the clay. The overlapped pieces must, of course, be firmly joined together at the overlap point. Excess clay is trimmed away and the draped form allowed to become leather-hard, after which it may be removed from the form and modified in any desired fashion, such as with the addition of feet, rims, lips, or handles. Two identical bowl shapes may be joined rim to rim to make a closed bottle or vase shape that could be further modified if paddled to a different contour and enhanced with legs, necks, spouts or other interesting appendages.

The idea here is not simply to reproduce the form being used but to make the shape so obtained a point of departure to create a new form. A variation of this method is to roll the clay into small balls about 1 inch in diameter, pressing these into or onto the mold and joining each ball of clay firmly into the one(s) adjoining (see figure 17.6).

*Throwing on the Potter's Wheel*
Formation of pots on the wheel entails the shaping, with hands and fingers, of a lump of clay rotating on the head of a potter's wheel. Some wheels have a variable speed control; others are geared to operate at two speeds (which will be referred to as fast and slow).

Potter's wheel, *well-wedged soft* clay, sponges, various turning tools and ribs, trimming tools, wires, and lifters, are necessary tools and equipment. Some wheel heads are designed to accept a plaster bat that may be easily removed when a pot is finished. The bat should be moistened before use so the clay will stick properly. If too much water is used, the clay will slide off the bat during throwing. Be especially careful when wedging clay for throwing, because nonuniformity of the clay or the presence of air pockets will invariably cause failure. A pot may also be thrown directly on a metal wheel head, after which the pot is cut from the wheel head and transferred to a bat.

Throwing on the wheel involves a number of successive steps as shown in the illustrations in figure 17.7. The student should study these illustrations and accompanying instructions carefully and perform the steps over and over until they can be done with ease. Proficiency in throwing is gained only through practice, more practice, and still more practice over a period of several weeks.

Some helpful suggestions are:

1 For your first attempts, balls of clay about the size of a small grapefruit are recommended. As skill increases, larger lumps of clay may be used.
2 Keep the hands and clay lump moistened with water at all times, but be careful not to use too much water because this will weaken the walls of the pot and cause it to collapse.
3 Stand or sit comfortably at the wheel with elbows resting on the bracing bar, or held firmly at the sides. The arms must be kept from wobbling or else the hands will "float" on the clay lump and no work will be done.
4 *Think* about what you are trying to accomplish with each step and coordinate your hands to make the clay do what you want. *You must control the clay, not let the clay control you.*
5 Remember, your hands and fingers are your most useful tools. Ribs and turning tools are helpful at certain points, but do not become dependent on these to do jobs that are best done with the fingers.

*(Figure 17.7) Wheel-throwing. (a) A well-wedged lump of clay is thrown onto the wheel head with some force to make it stick. (If wheel head has a plaster bat rather than a metal head, the bat must be dampened so the clay will stick.) Moisten the clay lump with water. It is important that the clay and the hands be kept moist throughout the throwing process. Turn the wheel on (fast speed) and while the wheel head is turning, press down firmly with the hands to further adhere the lump and to begin to shape it into a smooth ball. This step is called "centering." Be sure the clay is in the exact center of the wheel head. Until this step is mastered it is of no use to try to throw a pot. With practice, however, centering is accomplished with little trouble. (b) With the arms braced on the edge of the splash pan and the hands interlocked, continue the centering process and gradually shape the clay into smooth mass with a slightly covexed top. Wheel is still on fast speed. (c) When lump is perfectly centered, the next step is to begin the "opening" operation. On fast speed, place the thumbs in the center of the lump; with the fingers riding on the sides of the lump, press firmly downward to within about an inch or less of the bottom of the clay lump. Be careful to exert even pressure, else the lump will be pulled off center. (d) Open the lump to the desired inner diameter by slowly pulling outward with the thumbs or fingers. The object is to have a low cylinder shape with fairly thick walls. (e) With the wheel speed on slow speed, begin raising the walls of the cylinder by placing the fingers of one hand inside and the fingers of the other hand outside the pot directly opposite the inner fingers. By making a number of successive passes in this manner, one can bring the walls to the desired thinness. A wooden throwing rib is being used to further thin and smooth the walls of the pot. (f) When the basic cylinder has been formed, the pot is given the desired contours and a lip is made to finish off the top of the pot. (g) To remove finished shape from the wheel head, stop the wheel; with the aid of the cutting wire, separate the bottom of the pot from the wheel head. Remove the pot from the wheel and set aside to dry to the leather-hard state. (h) When the pot is leather-hard, turn it upside down on the wheel head; being sure that it is in the exact center of the wheel, attach the pot with lumps of moist clay as shown. A foot rim is formed by removing excess clay from the bottom of the pot with the aid of various turning and cutting tools. When foot is complete, remove pot from wheel and set aside to dry completely prior to bisque firing.*

*(a)*

*(b)*

*(c)*

(d)

(e)

(f)

(g)

(h)

6 When finished a throwing session, clean the wheel, splash pan, back board, and all tools thoroughly. Scrape clay off bats and sponge clean (do not allow bats to become saturated with water because they will be useless for several days until they dry). Clean all tools and other equipment and replace on tool board (see figure 17.8).

**Design and Decoration of Pottery**

The form of a ceramic pot is strongly influenced by its intended use, (*form* follows *function*), by the qualities of the clay itself (*material*), and by the *method* used to construct the pot. In addition to these three influences, other points to be considered are center of interest, harmony of all elements, balance, repetition, and proportion. In short, the principles of good design that apply to all other art forms apply to pottery as well. Briefly stated then, a work of art has good design when it has *unity* with sufficient *variety* to make it interesting, and unity with variety is obtained through knowledge and use of the *elements of art* and the *principles of organization* (see chapter 5).

Surface decoration should be a part of and inseparable from the form of a pot. Often, a well-designed pot will require no other decoration, but if needed, there are many points in the process at which decorative treatments may be added.

*(Figure 17.8) Wheel-thrown forms bisque fired and left unglazed to serve as teaching models.*

Designs may be added to the clay in its wet state. Some possibilities are:

1 *Incising* (cutting) a design into the surface of the clay with various tools.
2 Texturing the surface of the clay slab by rolling it out on a rough surface such as burlap, or by pressing various textured objects (a pine cone or shell, for example) into the surface of the wet pot.
3 Sprigging (adding) extra clay to the surface of the pot. The added clay must be wedged firmly into the surface of the pot.
4 Stamping impressions into the clay. Make stamps by carving designs into a piece of hardened plaster or into clay, which is then bisque fired for durability.
5 Paddling the surface of the wet pot with wood sticks or bark-covered wood pieces to alter the shape of the pot and/or to give it texture.

In the leather-hard state, designs may also be added in a variety of ways.

1 Incising may be done.
2 *Sgraffito* techniques: The surface of the clay is covered with a layer of clay slip of a contrasting color and designs are scratched through the slip layer to reveal the color of the clay body underneath.
3 *Mishima* techniques: This is an Oriental inlay method wherein a design is incised into the surface of the leather-hard pot. The incised lines are then filled with clay slip of a contrasting color. When partially dry the surface is scraped flush.
4 Slip trailing: A plastic squeeze bottle fitted with a tip is filled with liquid clay slip that is squeezed onto the surface of the pot through the hole in the tip. This is a free technique and should be used discriminately.

Designs may also be incorporated into the work in the dry state, before firing. Such techniques include:

1 Application of coloring oxides: Thin water slurries of the various coloring oxides may be brushed onto the surface of the pot. When glazed over and fired, they will add color to the pot depending on the oxide used. For example, copper oxide will give green tones; cobalt oxide, blue tones; iron oxide, yellow or brown tones.

2 Wax resist techniques: A water-soluble wax emulsion is applied in patterns to the surface of the pot. When dry, the pot is brushed with a coloring oxide that will adhere to the unwaxed portion of the clay and be resisted by the waxed areas. Lines may also be incised through the waxed areas for additional interest before oxides are applied.

In the bisque state, designs may be added to the pottery with coloring oxides, wax resist techniques, and glazes (see section on glazes in this chapter).

**Firing**
At some point many thousands of years ago, primitive potters discovered that if their clay pots were heated to a fairly high temperature the clay would become hard and, thus, much more durable. Early methods of firing the pots consisted of a shallow hole or pit dug into the ground with the sun-dried pots being placed into the depression. Twigs and other dried organic matter were then placed over them and ignited. "Burning" the pots took several hours. More fuel was added as needed. These pit kilns could produce temperatures of about 1500° F (800° C). Somewhat later, potters developed a more efficient bank kiln by digging into a sloping bank of clay to form a chamber into which pots and fuel could be loaded. A hole into the top of the chamber served as a chimney and created an updraft capable of producing much higher temperatures.

Kilns of many types evolved through the centuries; photographs and descriptions of these may be found in the literature in the suggested reading. Modern studio kilns are constructed of metal-jacketed firebrick walls and are usually powered by electricity, though gas is sometimes used if reduction firing is to be done. The electric kiln is particularly suitable for the school studio because it is compact, simple and safe to operate, economical, and requires minimum maintenance.

Ceramic ware usually goes through two firings, the first or *bisque firing* in which the dry pots are fired to the maturity temperature of the clay being used and the second or *glaze firing* in which the bisqued or glazed pots are fired to the maturity temperature of the glazes being used. Tools and equipment consist of pots to be fired, electric kiln, pyrometric cones, kiln furniture (stilts, posts, shelves), kiln wash, asbestos gloves, and timer.

Loading the kiln is carried out in exactly the same manner for both types of firing, except that in the glaze firing pots are placed in the kiln on stilts so they will not stick to the shelves, and in the bisque firing pots may be set directly on the shelves and stacked one inside another. Kiln shelves should be coated with kiln wash so glaze drippings may be easily removed. Pots to be fired should be segregated according to height, with the shorter pots being placed into the kiln first because these are easier to post over. The taller pots should be placed near the top of the kiln because they require no posting (see figure 17.9).

The kiln is loaded at room temperature, the proper pyrometric cone placed in the automatic cutoff, and the kiln brought *slowly* up to the maturity temperature by manipulation of the various switch settings. After firing, the kiln is allowed to cool to room temperature before it is unloaded. The entire cycle usually requires about twenty-four hours, of which actual firing time will be eight to twelve hours depending on a number of variables. A typical bisque firing schedule is given in table 17.1.

**Bisque Firing Schedule** (Table 17.1)

| Length of Time (minutes) | Bottom Switch | Middle Switch | Top Switch |
|---|---|---|---|
| 30 | Low | | |
| 30 | Low | Low | |
| 30 | Low | Low | Low |
| 30 | Medium | | |
| 30 | Medium | Medium | |
| 30 | Medium | Medium | Medium |
| 30 | High | | |
| 30 | High | High | |
| 30 | High | High | High |

*Note:* Lid of kiln is propped open approximately 2 inches during the *water-smoking* period.

*(Figure 17.9) Kiln loaded, ready for bisque firing. Note use of shelves and posts to allow total utilization of the kiln capacity.*

Continue firing with all switches on high and lid partially open until kiln shows a dull red heat inside and no more moisture is escaping. This will require about three to four hours. Close lid, insert peephole plugs, and allow kiln to fire until maturity point is reached and the automatic cutoff tripped. (Automatic cutoff devices are practically foolproof, but for safety's sake follow the practice of always having someone on hand to make sure the automatic cutoff has operated properly.) If the kiln has no automatic cutoff device, cones are placed in front of the peephole and observed periodically until they begin to bend, indicating that maturity point has been reached.

Pyrometric cones are small triangular cones of clay formulated to melt at a specific temperature. They were developed by a ceramic engineer named Edward Orton, and are accurate to within plus or minus 5 degrees. Cones are available for a wide range of temperatures and are placed in the kiln to measure firing temperature or, more specifically, maturity temperature. For most studio firing, the following cones are used:

- Bisque (stoneware clay)    cone 6    2291° F  (1255° C)
- Bisque (earthenware clay)    cone 02    2098° F  (1148° C)
- Bisque (Raku)    cone 05    1944° F  (1062° C)
- Glaze (low fire)    cone 05    1944° F
- Glaze (high fire)    cone 6    2291° F

Temperatures given are for small Orton Standard Pyrometric cones. When large cones are used, temperatures are somewhat lower.
For maximum efficiency in kiln operation, the kiln should be fired with a full load each time. The practice is followed of accumulating dried pots for bisque firing and glazed pots for glaze firing on the firing racks and when enough pots have accumulated, the kiln is loaded.

During the firing process, the clay goes through several stages. First, any traces of physical moisture evaporates at about 350° F. Beginning at about 950° F, chemically combined water and organic matter begins to leave the clay. It is during this "water-smoking" period that the clay shrinks, because the clay particles are being drawn more closely together. Beginning at about 1750° F, a chemical change begins in which crystals of alumina silica ($3 Al_2O_3SiO_2$), called mullite, are formed. These crystals give fired clay its high strength. It is extremely important that firing be done slowly and carefully to allow ample time for the necessary changes to occur. Carelessness at this point can result in defective pots as well as possible damage to the kiln.

Firing procedures described thus far are for *normal* or *oxidation firing* in which adequate oxygen is present for the process to continue. When a part of the firing cycle is carried out with a lessened amount of oxygen present, free carbon or carbon monoxide is formed in the kiln. The carbon monoxide will combine with the metallic oxides in the clay and/or glaze, resulting in the formation of colors that cannot otherwise be obtained. This *reduction firing* is usually carried out in a gas-fired kiln in which the burners can be adjusted to provide the oxygen-starved atmosphere needed. Reduction firing should be done only where there is adequate ventilation, ideally out of doors, so noxious fumes can be harmlessly dispelled.

**Glazes and Glazing**
A glaze consists of three basic types of ingredients. These are:

1  A glass former consisting of silica (flint, quartz).
2  A flux to lower the melting point of silica. Lead compounds, alkaline compounds (borax), soda ash and colemanite are low fire fluxes. Whiting (calcium carbonate) is a high fire flux.
3  A refractory element consisting of alumina compounds hardens the glaze.

Various coloring oxides are added to obtain specific colors. The most common of these are copper oxide (greens), cobalt oxide (blues), iron oxide (yellows to browns), and manganese dioxide (browns, purples, and black). For special properties other chemicals may be added; for opacity, tin oxide or zirconium oxide; for matte (dull) glazes barium or aluminum compounds; and for mottled (antique) effects, rutile.

There are many types of glazes: low fire glaze (alkaline and lead), high fire, ash glaze, frit glaze, crackle glaze, matte glaze, reduction glaze, crystalline glaze, salt glaze, and slip glaze. Each of these has its own particular characteristics. Several million different glaze effects are possible with all the glaze types available, the variations in additives, and the variations in firing.

During the past one hundred years, potters specializing in scientific glaze formulation have done much careful and thorough research into materials and methods used in compounding glazes. A large body of literature exists recording results of such research. The serious student of ceramics should consult such material to obtain a background in glaze formulation. For classroom use, however, the problem of glaze formulation may be simplified with the practice of preparing a number of so-called base glazes, to which may be added the proper amount of coloring oxide mixed with water and used to glaze pots. Because the color and properties of glazes develop during firing, it is necessary to have a fired color chart. The final appearance of a glaze depends on a number of variables, such as thickness of application, firing conditions, and shape of pot on which it is applied, so the small glazed chips are to be considered approximations only. Type of clay will also effect glaze colors, so test sample should be on the clay body being used.

The chart in table 17.2 makes use of several base glazes with appropriate coloring oxides added as indicated. We have seen that a glaze requires three elements, a glass former (silica), a flux, and a hardner. These elements are obtained from a number of common materials because it is uneconomical to use pure oxides. Figure 17.10 illustrates a glaze chart of fired samples. Let us discuss some common materials used in glaze formulations.

**Base Glazes with Coloring Oxides** (Table 17.2)

|  | + 0.5% CoO | + 1% CoO | + 2% CuO 1% CoO | + 3% CuO | + 3% FeO | + 7% FeO | + 3% MnO$_2$ | + 5% MnO$_2$ 2% CuO 2% CoO |
|---|---|---|---|---|---|---|---|---|
| *Base A: Transparent Gloss* | A-1 | A-2 | A-3 | A-4 | A-5 | A-6 | A-7 | A-8 |
| *Base B: transparent matte* | B-1 | B-2 | B-3 | B-4 | B-5 | B-6 | B-7 | B-8 |
| *Base C: opaque matte* | C-1 | C-2 | C-3 | C-4 | C-5 | C-6 | C-7 | C-8 |
| *Base D: opaque gloss* | D-1 | D-2 | D-3 | D-4 | D-5 | D-6 | D-7 | D-8 |
| *Base EG: rutile gloss* | EG-1 | EG-2 | EG-3 | EG-4 | EG-5 | EG-6 | EG-7 | EG-8 |
| *Base EO: rutile matte* | EO-1 | EO-2 | EO-3 | EO-4 | EO-5 | EO-6 | EO-7 | EO-8 |
|  | *Glaze F: copper blue* | *Glaze G: gunmetal* | *Glaze H: brown lustre* | *Glaze J-1: Albany slip glaze* | *Glaze J-2: white matte glaze* | *Combination J-1 and J-2: "iron spot" glaze* |  |  |

*To use chart: Select glaze wanted from fired sample. Find base glaze to use in far left column. Read amount of coloring oxide across top. Coloring oxides used are CoO (cobalt oxide), CuO (copper oxide), FeO (iron oxide), MnO$_2$ (manganese dioxide).*

*Feldspar* is a mineral made up of an alkaline portion (sodium, potassium, or calcium), alumina, and silica. It is used as a flux (usually in high fire glazes) and as a source of alumina and silica in glazes of all types (potash feldspar's formula is $K_2O \cdot Al_2O_3 \cdot 6SiO_2$).

*Clay* can be China clay, ball clay, kaolin, and many more. "Pure" clay, as such, rarely exists in nature, there usually being present traces of impurities such as iron and other minerals. Clay is used as a source of alumina and silica in glazes (kaolin's formula is $Al_2O_3 \cdot 2 SiO_2 \cdot 2H_2O$).

*Flint* is pure silica ($SiO_2$) and used to obtain the necessary silica in a recipe when not enough is supplied by the feldspar and clay in the formula.

*Lead* is the principal *flux* in low fire glazes. It may be in the form of white lead ($2PbCO_3 \cdot Pb(OH_2)$) or red lead $Pb_3O_4$). Remember that raw (unfritted) lead is extremely poisonous and great care must be taken not to breathe lead dust or get it into the mouth from brushes and other things. Students *must* use an aspirator (face mask) when weighing out and compounding glazes containing lead. Lead glazes should not be used for dishes and food containers because food acids could dissolve out enough free lead from the glaze to make it dangerous.

*Borax* ($Na_2O \cdot 2B_2O_3 \cdot 1 OH_2O$) is used as a flux in alkaline glazes. Borax is soluble in water, therefore, it is usually fritted before use but may be used as is, provided the glaze is used immediately after compounding. Alkaline glazes are desirable because of certain colors such as turquoise blues and greens, which are not usually obtained in lead glazes.

*Whiting* is calcium carbonate ($CaCO_3$), which is used as a flux in *high fire* glazes and as a source of calcium oxide in any glaze where necessary.

*Colemanite or Gerstley borate* ($2CaO \cdot 3B_2O_3 \cdot 5H_2O$) is a source of boron and has the advantage of being insoluble in water. Colemanite is used as a flux. In combination with rutile, it adds a broken mottled quality to glazes.

*Rutile* is an ore consisting primarily of titanium dioxide plus iron impurities. It produces glazes with a mottled, broken surface and is sometimes referred to as "antique" glazes.

*Zinc oxide* ($ZnO$) is used as a flux and can also produce a matte glaze in higher concentrations. In low concentrations, zinc oxide gives a smooth, even quality to glazes.

*(Figure 17.10) Student selects glaze from chart of fired samples.*

*Tin oxide* ($SnO_2$) is used as an opacifier in glazes.

*Zircopax* is a silicate of zirconium ($ZrO_2 \cdot SiO_2$) and is used as a substitute for tin as an opacifier. Zircopax requires about twice as much to do the same job that tin does, but is much cheaper than tin oxide.

*Barium oxide* is used primarily to produce matte glazes.

Metal oxides are used to impart color to glazes. The common ones are as follows:

1  Copper compounds produce greens, blue greens.
2  Cobalt compounds produce blues.
3  Manganese compounds produce purples or browns.
4  Iron compounds produce tan to brown tones.
5  Chromium compounds produce green colors.

Various oxides are often combined to produce subtle color variations. For example, cobalt and copper together will produce blue-green tones; manganese, copper, and cobalt will produce blue-blacks, sometimes with a metallic sheen; iron and manganese together will produce a metallic lustre appearance; iron and copper together will produce olive greens. Formulations given in table 17.3 will produce a group of low fire (cone 05 maturity) glazes suitable for applying to stoneware or earthenware bisque. These formulas, used by me for years, have been found to work well in classroom situations and provide a wide range of colors and effects. All weights are in grams and amounts are for 1000-gram batches. Dry ingredients are weighed carefully and sifted together several times to ensure mixing.

### Formulations for Low Fire Glazes (Table 17.3)

Glaze A: transparent, glossy, lead formula

| | |
|---|---|
| White lead | 450 grams |
| Whiting | 120 grams |
| Feldspar | 200 grams |
| Kaolin | 70 grams |
| Flint | 160 grams |

Glaze B: transparent, matte, borosilicate formula

| | |
|---|---|
| Colemanite | 300 grams |
| Feldspar | 450 grams |
| Zinc oxide | 50 grams |
| Barium carbonate | 60 grams |
| Kaolin | 40 grams |
| Flint | 100 grams |

Glaze C: opaque, matte, borosilicate formula

To glaze B add 100 grams of tin oxide or 200 grams zircopax.

Glaze D: opaque, glossy, lead formula

To glaze A add 100 grams tin oxide or 200 grams zircopax.

Glaze EG: gloss, rutile (antique)

To glaze D add 66 grams of rutile.

Glaze EO: opaque, matte, rutile (antique)

To glaze C add 60 grams of rutile.

Specialty glazes

Glaze F: copper, blue-black*

| | |
|---|---|
| Soda ash | 180 grams |
| White lead | 300 grams |
| Zinc oxide | 20 grams |
| Feldspar | 240 grams |
| Flint | 180 grams |
| Tin oxide | 50 grams |
| Copper carbonate | 20 grams |
| Copper oxide | 10 grams |

Glaze G: gunmetal*

| | |
|---|---|
| Soda ash | 170 grams |
| White lead | 270 grams |
| Zinc oxide | 20 grams |
| Feldspar | 220 grams |
| Flint | 170 grams |
| Tin oxide | 50 grams |
| Copper carbonate | 100 grams |

Glaze H: brown lustre*

| | |
|---|---|
| White lead | 580 grams |
| Feldspar | 130 grams |
| Kaolin | 40 grams |
| Flint | 160 grams |
| Manganese carbonate | 60 grams |
| Red iron oxide | 30 grams |

"Iron spot" glaze (two parts)

| | | |
|---|---|---|
| Part 1 | Albany clay | 500 grams |
| | Red lead | 500 grams |
| Part 2 | White lead | 524 grams |
| | Zinc oxide | 40 grams |
| | Feldspar | 318 grams |
| | Kaolin | 49 grams |
| | Ball clay | 45 grams |
| | Flint | 24 grams |
| | Tin oxide | 100 grams |

To use, apply part 1 heavily to bisque pot, then apply one or more coats of part 2 over. Effect obtained will vary depending on thickness of application but will be white with tan to brown mottling. Part 2 used alone makes a very good opaque white matte glaze.

*Used without addition of more coloring oxide.
*Note: Wear an aspirator when weighing and mixing lead compounds.*

When mixing glazes, refer to the fired color chart in table 17.2 and select the glaze you want to use on a specific pot. The chart indicates which glaze base you need to use. Weigh out 100 grams of the base glaze (more for a large pot), and add the proper amount of coloring oxide. If the chart indicates the addition of 3 percent copper oxide, add 3 grams to the 100 grams of base glaze. Mix with enough water to make a slurry, which will be about the consistency of heavy cream. *Shake* well (shaking works better than stirring) and apply to the pot after it has been lightly sponged with a damp sponge to remove dust, finger marks, and other foreign material.

Generally, apply three coats of glaze if you are brushing it on. There are a number of ways in which liquid glaze can be applied to a pot. For the inside of a pot into which a brush will not reach, pour the glaze in, slosh it around, and pour it out again. Glaze for pouring should be made somewhat thinner than for other uses. Glaze may also be poured over the outside of pots for special effects. Glazes are sometimes sprayed onto the pot, particularly in commercial applications. By far the most common method of glaze application is to brush it on the pot. Using the wide glazing brush, saturate it thoroughly with glaze and brush a coat on the pot. Do not try to brush the glaze out too thin or you will have starved spots. Allow this coat of glaze to dry for a few minutes (it will lose the shiny surface appearance), apply a second coat, allow to dry, and apply a third coat. Set on shelf to dry and await firing.

Students always ask how thick a coat of glaze is, which is a question that cannot really be answered. You must learn by experience and by using common sense. Too little glaze will result in a starved pot; too much glaze will probably run excessively and flow off the pot onto the kiln shelves. One glaze may be applied over another for special effects and some surprises; experiment and

see what happens. If you use more than one glaze on a pot, just be sure they have enough contrast to show up and that the total application is three coats, or in some cases, four at most.

**Raku Techniques**
During the past twenty years or so, American potters have become extremely interested in the ancient Oriental technique of pottery making known as Raku. Raku pottery has been a treasured part of Japanese culture and philosophy for over three hundred and fifty years. In order to understand the veneration in which Raku ware is held, one must consider certain Oriental concepts derived from ancient practices of sharing sacred offerings in Shinto worship. The Shinto forces and forms of nature are modified by Zen Buddhist principles of *wabi* (simple, plain, to find beauty in things that are "nothing"), *sabi* (appreciation of the rustic and imperfect), *shibui* (impeccable taste), and *fura* (harmony of the self with the spirit of beauty in nature). Thus, in the Raku bowl with its lack of symmetry, rough pitted glazes, soft colors, and spontaneous, often accidental effects of a creative process largely undominated by the crafter, we find the perfect expression of understated yet profound beauty combined with practical utility.

For the contemporary potter whose training emphasizes symmetrical shapes, smoothly glazed surfaces, and strict control of techniques, a study of Raku can lead to a new and deeper feeling for materials, a closer understanding of one's relation to the natural environment, and a more sensitive appreciation of the soul or spirituality with which the artist-potter must imbue his or her work lest it become merely an exercise in technical facility.

Raku ware originated in Japan about 1566 when Sen-no-Rikyu, the greatest of all tea masters, recognized in the work of Chojiro, a potter of Korean ancestry working in Kyoto, those qualities of beauty and simplicity most desirable for Cha-no-yu (tea ceremony) vessels. Rikyu commissioned Chojiro to make tea bowls for his personal use. These bowls, enhanced by Rikyu's approval, were greatly sought after by other tea masters and tea ceremony devotees. The shogun (war lord) Hideyoshi was particularly pleased with Chojiro's work and presented him with a gold seal bearing the engraved ideograph *Raku,* meaning contentment, pleasure, and enjoyment.

The descendants of Chojiro, comprising some fourteen generations, have continued to use the seal or variations to mark their wares. Japanese critics consider that Raku ware reached its finest state of perfection with the work of Donyu (1599–1656), third potter in the line, though bowls by any member of the line are highly prized by collectors. Not only were tea bowls produced by the Raku process but also incense containers, tea jars, flower vases, water jars, and other tea ceremony vessels as well.

Other famous potters working in the Raku tradition were Ogata Kenzan (1663–1743), considered by many to be Japan's greatest ceramic artist; Hon'ami Koetsu (circa 1558–1637), a pupil of Donyu, the third Raku; and potters of the kiln located at Horaku, established in 1820. Works of the latter were often ornamented with decorative designs.

A variety of methods are used in Japan for making Raku pots but, generally speaking, the basic procedure is as follows. To a white or buff firing clay is added a quantity of grog (fired, powdered clay) to increase porosity and reduce subsequent thermal shock. Bowls are formed by hand into two basic shapes, the taller winter bowl and the shorter, more shallow summer bowl. After drying, the bowls are fired to about 950° C (cone 08–06), usually in a small wood or charcoal fired updraft kiln built into the side of a hill.

The fired (bisque) bowls are glazed by being dipped or brushed with a low fire glaze in a free manner. The foot and bottom of the bowl is left unglazed. Glazes are usually formulated with lead and traditionally are of three types: (1) brownish-black, which is the most common; (2) a reddish-orange; and (3) a thick white. Occasionally the ware may be decorated with a free brush design using various metal oxides, those of iron (yellows), cobalt (blues), and copper (greens) being most common.

When the glaze is dry, the bowls are refired in a reduction atmosphere. The kiln is carefully watched. When the glaze appears molten, the bowl is withdrawn from the kiln with tongs and allowed to cool in the open air. Sometimes, the red-hot bowl may be plunged into a tub of water to hasten cooling and to "freeze" the molten glaze. The surface of the resulting soft-quality glaze is covered with tiny cracks that gradually fill with tea and become watertight, acquiring in the process the highly priced patina of use and age. Marks made by the tongs in the red-hot glaze are considered desirable and add greatly to the value of the pot.

For classroom use, the technique as outlined is followed but with several modifications. Pots are made by hand or on the potter's wheel. Glazes are compounded with borate rather than lead because the borate formulations are more safely used by students. Pots are fired in a studio electric kiln in an oxidation atmosphere. Immediately after firing the red-hot pot is locally reduced by being thrust into a covered receptacle containing leaves, straw, sawdust, or other combustible material then allowed to remain for several minutes. This "smoking" leads to many subtle variations in the color and surface appearance of the glaze, comparable to those obtained by no other procedure. Glazes often take on a magnificent iridescence due to the reduction of the metallic oxides present, and it is not uncommon in cases where copper oxide is present to obtain areas of pure metallic copper.

In the usual process of producing pottery, much emphasis is placed upon uniformity of shape, smoothness of surface, uniform application of glazes, perfect execution of designs, and elimination of any irregularity. Firing is strictly controlled, with the temperature of the kiln being brought slowly to the point of maturity, then just as slowly back to room temperature so the ware will suffer no undue thermal shock. It is easy to see why the potter, normally subjected to such rigid control, escapes with such pleasure to the Raku process in which the sense of immediacy and personal involvement in the entire process, the sense of oneness with the philosophy behind it, together with the pleasing and often unexpected results, make Raku one of the most exciting and rewarding experiences.

Any clay body suitable for pottery may be used for Raku, provided about 20 to 30 percent coarse grog (ground fired clay) is worked into the moist clay. The addition of grog makes the clay more porous and better able to withstand the extremes of thermal shock encountered in the process. A buff or red firing clay often produces more interesting effects than a white firing body. Commercial low fire glazes may be used, but because Raku is such a "personal" process it is far better to make your own glazes.

Some formulas that I have found to work well are given in table 17.4.

**Formulations for Raku Glazes** (Table 17.4)

*Transparent gloss glaze:*

| | |
|---|---|
| Gerstley borate (colemanite) | 800 grams |
| Feldspar | 200 grams |

*Semimatte white glaze:*

| | |
|---|---|
| Gerstley borate (colemanite) | 600 grams |
| Kaolin | 400 grams |
| Silico (flint) | 200 grams |

*Terracotta red glaze:*

| | |
|---|---|
| Gerstley borate (colemanite) | 500 grams |
| Borax | 500 grams |
| Copper carbonate | 100 grams |
| Iron oxide | 30 grams |

*Blue glaze*

| | |
|---|---|
| Gerstley borate (colemanite) | 500 grams |
| Borax | 500 grams |
| Cobalt oxide | 10 grams |
| Rutile | 30 grams |

*Engobe*

Sometimes, the potter wishes to cover portions of the pot with a white undercoat before applying glazes or brushed designs. Such an undercoat or *engobe* is made as follows:

| | |
|---|---|
| Colemanite (Gerstley borate) | 300 grams |
| Kaolin | 300 grams |
| Flint | 300 grams |

To make any of the Raku glazes, weigh ingredients and mix together thoroughly. To use, mix with water and brush on pots that are allowed to dry before firing.

Pots are fired until the glaze is molten, then withdrawn from the kiln with tongs and immediately thrust into a vessel containing some combustible material such as dried leaves, straw, paper, sawdust, or any organic matter. A large metal garbage can with a lid works very well. The combustible material will immediately catch fire on contact with the red-hot pot. Keep hands and face away from flames, which will subside as soon as the container is covered. Pots are left in this low oxygen (reduction) atmosphere for periods ranging from a minute to five minutes or more. Unglazed clay will turn black if the pot is smoked for long periods. The smoke will also penetrate cracks in the glazed surface, producing a beautiful crackled network.

As noted, areas of pure copper may be obtained on the surface of the pot under certain conditions. The chances for achieving this effect are best if thin layers of a slurry of copper oxide in water is built up between layers of glaze, finishing with a layer of oxide, firing until the glaze is just melted and smoking for a short period (5–10 seconds). Raku is a marvelously free approach to ceramics that allows for all manner of experimentation and creative innovations. As such it has a special appeal for students.

The craft of ceramics presents many possibilities, which makes it impossible to cover the subject adequately in one chapter. A full list of suggested readings is included at the end of the chapter. Students wishing to know more about ceramics should study a number of these references.

Each student should set certain standards of self-evaluation, looking critically at every pot produced, asking such questions as "Did I accomplish what I set out to do?" "Is this the best effort of which I am capable?" "How could I improve the design of this pot?" Then and only then should the decision be made to retain those pots that are considered good and discard those that do not measure up. To see a student take the hammer to a poor pot is an extremely healthy sign, for it means that he or she is developing discrimination and not following the "I made it, therefore I must keep it" theory.

**Suggested Readings**

Ball, Frederick C. *Decorating Pottery with Clay, Slip and Glaze.* Columbus, Ohio: Professional Publications, 1967.

————. *Making Pottery without a Wheel.* New York: Reinhold Publishing Co., 1965.

Bitters, Stan. *Environmental Ceramics.* New York: Van Nostrand, Reinhold, 1976.

Blandino, Betty. *Coiled Pottery: Traditional and Contemporary Ways.* Radnor, Pa.: Chilton Book Co., 1984.

Cameron, Elisabeth, ed. *Potters on Pottery.* New York: St. Martin's Press, 1976.

Campbell, Donald. *Using the Potter's Wheel.* New York: Van Nostrand, Reinhold, 1978.

Charleston, Robert J., ed. *World Ceramics, An Illustrated History.* Secoucus, N.J.: Chartwell Books, 1977.

Clark, Garth. *American Potters: The Work of Twenty Modern Masters.* New York: Watson-Guptill Publications, 1981.

Colbeck, John. *Pottery: Techniques of Decoration.* New York: Van Nostrand, Reinhold, 1983.

Conrad, John W. *Ceramic Formulas: The Complete Compendium.* New York: Macmillan, 1973.

———. *Contemporary Ceramics Techniques.* Englewood Cliffs, N.J.: Prentice-Hall, 1979.

Chandler, Maurice Henry. *Ceramics in the Modern World.* Garden City, N.Y.: Doubleday and Co., 1968.

Dodd, Arthur Edward. *Dictionary of Ceramics* New York: Philosophical Library, 1964.

Fraser, Harry. *Glazes for the Craft Potter.* New York: Watson-Guptill Publications, 1974.

Hannah, Frances. *Ceramics: Twentieth Century Design.* New York: Dutton, 1986.

Hamilton, David. *Van Nostrand Reinhold Manual of Pottery and Ceramics.* New York: Van Nostrand, Reinhold, 1974.

Honey, William Bowyer. *The Ceramic Art of China and the Far East.* London: Faber and Faber, 1945.

Hopper, Robin. *The Ceramic Spectrum: A Simplified Approach to Glaze and Color Development.* Radnor, Pa.: Chilton Book Co., 1984.

Kenny, John B., *Ceramic Design.* Radnor, Pa.: Chilton Book Co., 1963.

———. *The Complete Book of Pottery Making.* 2d ed., Radnor, Pa.: Chilton Book Co., 1976.

Lane, Peter, *Studio Ceramics.* Radnor, Pa.: Chilton Book Co., 1983.

Leach, Bernard H. *A Potter's Book.* New York: Transatlantic Arts, 1948.

———. *The Potter's Challenge.* New York: Dutton, 1975.

Lynggaard, Fenn. *Pottery: Raku Technique.* New York: Van Nostrand, Reinhold, 1973.

Munsterberg, Hugo. *The Ceramic Art of Japan.* Rutland, Vt.: C. E. Tuttle Co., 1964.

Nelson, Glenn C. *Ceramics: A Potter's Handbook.* 5th ed. New York: Holt, Rinehart and Winston, 1984.

Nigrosh, Leon I. *Claywork: Form and Idea in Ceramic Design.* Worcester, Mass.: Davis Publications, 1975.

Norton, Frederick H. *Ceramics for the Artist Potter.* Reading, Mass.: Addison-Wesley Publishing Co., 1956.

Peterson, Susan. *Shoji Hamada: A Potter's Way and Work.* New York: Harper and Row, 1974.

Preaud, Tamara. *Ceramics of the 20th Century.* New York: Rizzoli International Publications, 1982.

Priolo, Joan B. *Ceramics by Coil.* New York: Sterling Publishing Co., 1976.

———. *Ceramics by Slab.* New York: Sterling Publishing Co., 1973.

Rada, Pravoslav. *Book of Ceramics.* London Spring Books, n.d.

Rawson, Philip S. *Ceramics.* London and New York: Oxford University Press, 1971.

Rhodes, Daniel. *Clay and Glazes for the Potter.* rev. ed. Radnor, Pa.: Chilton Book Co., 1973.

———. *Pottery Form.* Radnor, Pa.: Chilton Book Co., 1976.

———. *Kiln: Design, Construction and Operation.* Radnor, Pa.: Chilton Book Co., 1968.

Ruscoe, William. *Sculpture for the Potter.* New York: St. Martin's Press, 1975.

Seegar, Nancy. *A Ceramist's Guide to the Safe Use of Materials.* Chicago, Ill.: School of the Arts Institute of Chicago, 1984.

Speight, Charlotte. *Hands in Clay: An Introduction to Ceramics.* Sherman Oaks, Calif.: Alfred Publishing Co., 1979.

Winter, Thelma F. *The Art and Craft of Ceramic Sculpture.* New York: John Wiley and Sons, 1973.

Woody, Elsbeth S. *Pottery on the Wheel.* New York: Farrar, Straus and Giroux, 1975.

Zakin, Richard. *Electric Kiln Ceramics: A Potter's Guide to Clays and Glazes.* Radnor, Pa.: Chilton Book Co., 1981.

# Part 3    *Professional Portfolio*

*A selection of photographs of works by contemporary, professional craftspeople working in a variety of crafts are presented in part 3.*

# 18 Craftspeople at Work

In the last twenty years, we have seen a tremendous increase in the numbers of people professionally engaged in making fine objects in all areas of the crafts. These dedicated artists, highly trained and experienced in both the technicalities and aesthetics of their work, have been largely responsible for changing the attitudes toward crafts of reviewers, galleries, museums, and the general public, many of whom for years considered works in such media as fiber, paper, metal, clay, and glass to be secondary to the "fine arts" of drawing, painting, and sculpture. Crafts were designated as functional, utilitarian, the so called "domestic arts." Today, however, one has only to visit a large crafts fair, a crafts museum, any of the numerous shops that show and sell fine crafts, or simply leaf through current issues of *American Crafts*[1] or other magazines devoted to the arts to realize that contemporary craftspeople are going far beyond such traditional attitudes and are producing works in which "concept" and "idea" are just as important as process and deserve consideration as aesthetic expressions, as much as painting or sculpture.

The professional craftsperson may work as a full-time studio artist, may combine studio production with teaching or some other occupation, or may have set up a combination studio/shop as a business venture. In any case, it is of vital importance to the professional craftsperson to obtain as much exposure for his or her work as possible by exhibiting in gallery or museum shows, by placing work in crafts shops and art centers, and by utilizing every opportunity to get the attention of designers, buyers, critics, museum people, and those of the general public who love beautiful things and appreciate fine craftsmanship. Information regarding opportunities for exhibiting crafts as well as calendars of current exhibitions may be found in *American Crafts* as well as in *The Crafts Report*.[2]

Certainly the need to draw attention to one's work is of vital concern to the craftsperson, especially one who is in the process of building a reputation for the quality of his or her work. There are numerous avenues for building a following; a beginning is often made by renting display space in a local, state, or regional crafts fair. These are usually held annually and may be small or large in scope. They may be open to anyone wishing to pay the booth rental fee or may be strictly juried with acceptance based on high standards of craftsmanship and design. These shows gradually build up a devoted following of patrons who know they can depend on finding beautiful, well-crafted works and meet the people who create them. Some of these fairs, over a period of years, have gained national reputations, attracting the best contemporary craftspeople displaying their work to thousands of visitors, including dealers who come to select fine work for sale in their shops and galleries.

American Craft Enterprises, the marketing arm of the American Crafts Council, sponsors several regional exhibitions each year in various parts of the United States: Baltimore, Maryland in the winter, West Springfield, Massachusetts, in the early summer, and San Francisco, California, in the late summer.[3] These shows have grown from modest beginnings; now they may exhibit the work of some seven hundred craftspeople during a single week, attract wholesale buyers and retail customers from many states, and generate millions of dollars of income for the craftspeople whose work is on display (see figure 18.1).

*(Figure 18.1) View of portion of a crafts show sponsored by American Craft Enterprises. Photo by George Post. Photo courtesy of American Craft Enterprises.*

Many professionals, in addition to exhibiting in regional fairs, place their work in crafts shops and galleries. With the revival of the crafts tradition in America and with an increased awareness of the value of crafts as fine art, it is not surprising that there are few cities of any size that do not have at least one shop where quality professional crafts may be found for sale. These shops are often owned either by a professional craftsperson or by someone with a great interest in good design, in fine craftsmanship, and in presenting the fine art of crafts in the buying public (see figure 18.2).

(a)

(b)

*(Figure 18.2) (a) Portion of salesroom. Signet Gallery, Charlottesville, Virginia. (b) Portion of salesroom. Virginia Handcrafts, Lynchburg, Virginia.*

Dealers make it a point to attend the large crafts fairs. With a keen appreciation for high quality-crafts and practical knowledge of what their patrons will buy, they select pieces for their shops. Works may be taken on a consignment basis, or as some dealers prefer, they may be purchased outright. In any case, the craftsperson can earn a living, the craftsperson and the dealer have the satisfaction of knowing that they have made a positive contribution to keeping the American crafts movement going, and the general public is enriched by the availability of beautiful crafts to use in their homes and give as gifts. Many museums not only show and sell fine handcrafted objects in their shops but also mount periodic exhibitions of the work of individual and/or groups engaged in the crafts.

Students of the crafts should avail themselves of every opportunity to visit crafts fairs, shops, museums and galleries; to meet and talk to craftspeople; and if these are not readily available, to study examples of good crafts in books and magazines.[4]

A number of works by contemporary professional craftspeople are shown in this chapter. These have been photographed in several shops, galleries and homes through the courtesy of the shop and private owners; in the studios of the craftspeople; and in the gallery at Lynchburg College; during annual crafts shows. With each photo, a brief biographical sketch and statement of concept have been furnished by the craftspeople themselves.[5]

**Karen Adachi**
**Handmade Paper**
"For the past few years, I have focused on paper as a means to break through the familiar rectangular shape. By taking the same process of breaking down various fibers to the beginning stage of pulp, I can manipulate the various forms to create continuous motion. Color and texture are also controlled by adding dyes, pigments, various fibers, metallics, and bamboo to the glutinous fiber before shaping takes place."

Karen Adachi was born in Los Angeles and now lives and has her studio in Santa Cruz. She has a B.F.A. degree from Long Beach State University. While in college, she became interested in ceramics and was a studio potter for the next few years. An interest in Oriental brush painting, which she used to decorate her pots, led Karen to study and work in the art of handmade paper. Her work is exhibited in selected galleries throughout the country (see figure 18.3).

*(Figure 18.3) Karen Adachi: "Kimona." Handmade paper collage.*

**Michael and Christina Adcock**

"As a basket weaver and a potter, we saw great potential in combining the media of clay and fiber, and have been able to manifest our ideas into an harmonious union of the two. Clay and fiber are not only mutually compatible but each enhances the qualities of the other. We attempt always to reveal the natural beauty of the materials while adhering to a simplicity of formal design."

Michael Adcock holds degrees in art history and ceramics from the University of California at Santa Cruz. He has been a successful studio potter for over ten years and teaches ceramics in the Santa Barbara City College extension program.

Christina Adcock studied art at the University of California and has woven baskets for ten years, experimenting with a variety of materials and techniques. In 1980 she lived with the Papago Indians in Arizona, studying traditional weaving skills and techniques. She has been active in a program at the Santa Barbara Natural History Museum to revive the woven arts of the Chumash Indians, and teaches part time at the Braille Institute in Santa Barbara.

The Adcocks live in Santa Barbara, and their work has been widely shown and featured in a number of publications (see figure 18.4).

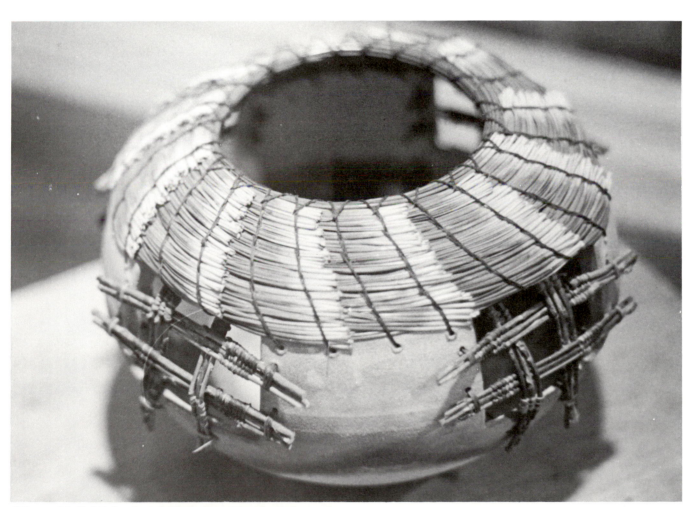

*(Figure 18.4) Michael and Christina Adcock: Raku and fiber bowl.*

**Gwendolyn Orsinger Anderson ("Orsini")**
**Enamels**

"Despite thirty-one years of enameling, I am still excited about the beauty and the color, as well as the mystery of what goes on in the kiln. It is magic!

"Enamelists forever balance on a tight-rope: we are the 'gamblers' of the art world, for unlike other art forms, we are never truly in *complete control* of our medium. The Fire Gods are the actual Masters because, due to a shift of twenty-five degrees in temperature or a mistiming of FIVE SECONDS in the glowing kiln, we can destroy forty hours of labor! It is this very 'unpredictability' that makes enameling so fascinating and so frustrating. Thus the serious enamelist must possess unlimited patience and be willing to accept depressing failure along with joyful success."

Gwen Anderson who signs her enamels "Orsini" (after a twelfth-century ancestor) teaches enameling workshops throughout the eastern United States. Her work has been exhibited in eleven solo exhibitions and has won thirteen first place awards in national exhibitions. She is listed in several *Who's Who* volumes, including *Who's Who in American Art, Who's Who in American Women,* and *Two Thousand Women of Achievement* (Great Britain). Orsini lives in Burke Centre, Virginia, for six months of the year and in Wellington, Florida for six months. She has a studio in the Torpedo Factory Art Center in Alexandria. Gwen makes periodic trips abroad to study the works of craftspeople in other countries and has just recently returned from such a trip to Russia (see figure 18.5).

*(Figure 18.5) Orsini (Gwen Anderson): Left, top, Aztec prince, cloisonne. Bottom, Marathon, cloisonne. Right, Persian rug, champleve. All pieces owned by Terry D. Sumey.*

**Sandra Bowden**

"I see the physical earth as a celebration by the Creator. I paint the earth's beauty and truth and to me, this is a reflection of God. I speak of comfort drawn from the earth and those things it has revealed to man, as well as the mystery of all that is still to be discovered. Semiabstract landscapes inspired by the Book of Psalms and its poetic references to the earth, give a feeling of archaic secrets rediscovered."

Sandra Bowden, a native of New England, lives with her husband and two children in Clifton Park, New York, where she works from a studio in her home. She has a degree from the State University of New York and has studied at the Massachusetts College of Art, Berkshire Christian College, and the College of St. Rose. Sandra Bowden has had numerous one-woman shows throughout the United States, Canada, and Israel. Her work is in the collections of IBM, Holiday Inn International, United Jewish Appeal, Vatican Museum of Contemporary Art, and the Judaic Heritage Society, as well as in many churches and synagogues (see figure 18.6).

*(Figure 18.6) Sandra Bowden: "Sinai I and II," dyptich collograph with handmade paper. Circles are 19" × 19".*

**Jack Brubaker**

"Seeing forged steel as a plastic medium like clay and hot glass, I am trying to use blacksmithing as a direct spontaneous medium capable of serving functional needs and creative expression."

Jack Brubaker combines a solid technical knowledge of forging and a creative approach to design. His new work includes one-of-a-kind sculptural and collectable pieces and large architectural pieces. He has experimented with combining steel and glass as in his weathervanes, kenetic sculptures, and hanging lamps.

Studying printmaking with Rudi Pozzatti and photography with Henry Holmes Smith, Brubaker received a Master of Fine Arts degree from Indiana University in 1968. Prior to that, Brubaker studied metalsmithing with Berry Merrit and John Marshall at Syracuse University where he graduated cum laude in 1966, receiving a Bachelor of Fine Arts degree.

Jack Brubaker resides in rural Brown County, Indiana, with his wife, Susan Showalter, and their infant daughter, Laura, on a 112-acre farm. Well known in the field of blacksmithing, Brubaker has exhibited in over thirty national juried, invitational, and solo exhibitions. He teaches his craft on local, state, national, and international levels. Brubaker was recently president of the Artist Blacksmith Association of North America (ABANA). Presently he is liaison from ABANA to the British Artist Blacksmith Association and is active in other local, state, and national arts organizations. The author of magazine articles on blacksmithing, Brubaker has also produced audiovisual programs about traditional and contemporary crafts.

His work was featured in the August/September 1984 issue of *American Crafts* magazine (see figure 18.7).

*(Figure 18.7) Jack Brubaker: "14-Arm Chandelier." Hand-forged steel and brass (34 inches tall). Photo by Sidney Sander.*

## Jane Campbell

"I studied in Richmond, Virginia, at Virginia Commonwealth University, near the Virginia Museum, which has a good collection of Fabergé. Fabergé was one of the finest goldsmiths that ever lived, famous for his jeweled Easter eggs that come apart and have surprises inside. Ever since that time, I have wanted to make beautiful, precious things to delight and amaze people.

"I didn't get to this point overnight; I've been working in metal for fourteen years so it pretty much does what I want now. About six years ago I assigned myself the task of making jewelry that would fit on a base for display, because I needed some showpieces and was no longer challenged by jewelry alone. The boxes with wearable lids were the result [see figure 18.8].

"Early boxes had simple lids that were just pins you lifted off to wear, then the idea for the necklaces with the chains already attached and hidden inside came all at once. Now I've made boxes with earring tops, cufflink tops, and ring tops; and just last year I had a major breakthrough where the hinge pins are wearable too, and major pieces have secret compartments with matching rings or earrings inside. The best pieces make several jewelry outfits or are his and her sets."

Jane Campbell is a native of Rochester, New York, and now lives in Cambridge Springs, Pennsylvania, where she and her husband, a potter, have a successful business, The Factory Studios. Jane has a B.F.A. from Virginia Commonwealth University (Richmond). Her work has been exhibited at all the major crafts festivals as well as in fine galleries across the United States. She has received a number of first place and best of show awards, most recently first place in jewelry at the St. Augustine Arts and Crafts Festival, March 1986. In addition to her unique boxes, Jane also designs and sells a line of production jewelry.

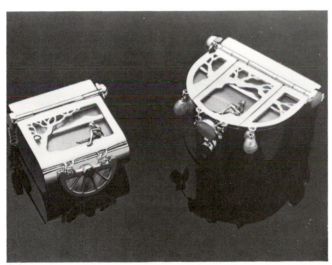

*(a)*

*(b)*

*(Figure 18.8) Jane Campbell. (a) Boxes with wearable lids. Left, flat rectangle necklace lid, 2-by-1½-by-¾ inches high. Right, triple lid arch, necklace, and earrings, 2-by-2-by-1¼ inches high. Shell, amethyst, opal, tourmaline, pearls, sterling. (b) Flat rectangle necklace lid box shown open; pendant length 5 inches. Abalone, mother of pearl, opal, tourmalines, pearls, sterling.*

**Barbara Cornett**

"I am excited by color, texture, and form. Fiber has been a constantly challenging medium for my art. The technical aspects can be tedious and overwhelming, but the added dimension of the textural material makes it all worthwhile for me. This has also led me toward sculptural pieces as well as flat wall pieces. Space is a very strong concern for me and the architectural or environmental setting for a piece is very important."

Barbara Cornett lives in Lynchburg, Virginia. She holds a B.A. in studio art from Randolph-Macon Woman's College, Lynchburg, Virginia, and has done graduate study in fibers at Skidmore College, Saratoga Springs, New York, and at the University of Tennessee, Knoxville. She has studied with Jack Lenor Larsen at the Haystack School of Arts and Crafts, Deer Isle, Maine. Barbara has exhibited her work nationally and abroad, and she has completed commissions for works which hang in corporate buildings in New York, Richmond, Roanoke, and Lynchburg. She teaches fiber arts part time in local colleges and designs handwoven fashions for small shops (see figure 18.9).

*(a)*

*(b)*

*(Figure 18.9) Barbara Cornett: fibers. (a) "Inner Space." Sisal and copper wall hanging 9-by-12 feet. (b) "Fiberstruction." Felted tubes and chrome.*

## Virginia Irby Davis
## Glass and Metal Constructions

"Upon seeing my work for the first time, many people comment on the wide variety of media and styles in evidence. It is true that I am interested in exploring many media and techniques and I find that the change from one to another helps to prevent the periodic 'creative slump' to which artists are subject. Moving from painting to metal to glass to photography, etc., presents an ever fresh challenge, which is tremendously stimulating to me. My themes are often taken from nature and my long-standing absorption with the radial (mandala) motif shows up again and again. Light through colored glass and the effects of the torch on metal appeal strongly to my aesthetic sense and I am fascinated with the element of texture. These interests together with my love for mechanical manipulation and working with tools furnish the inspirational motivation in my search for creative personal expression. Being a Virgoan, however, I tend to seek perfection, and thus, have been completely satisfied with very few of my efforts!"

Virginia Irby Davis, author of this text, has been a professor of art at Lynchburg College, Virginia, since 1968. Her degrees include a B.S. in chemistry and English from Roanoke College, a B.A. in studio art and art history from Randolph-Macon Woman's College, and a M.Ed. in education from Lynchburg College. She has studied at the Art Students League (New York), at the University of Georgia, and was a protégé of the late Peter Williams with whom she studied ceramics, sculpture, and metal construction.

Virginia Davis has exhibited in group and one-person shows in Lynchburg, Roanoke, Danville, Bath County, and Virginia Beach, as well as in Winston Salem, and Atlanta. Her work is represented in a number of collections. Her travels to study art have included Europe, Mexico, Greece, Iran, and Haiti (see figure 18.10).

(a)

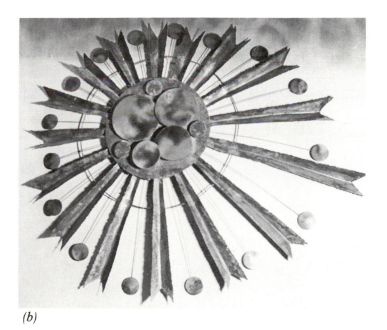

(b)

*(Figure 18.10) Virginia I. Davis. (a) "Radial variation #18." Stained glass, copper, brass, lead. Owned by Lynchburg College, Virginia. Photographed from backside to show method of construction. (b) "Radial Variation #4." Copper, brass, enamel. Collection of the author.*

**Michael Elkan**

"The great beauty of nature's jewels—gold, silver, diamonds, pearls—is hidden in the beginning in their rough state. So it is with the wood we work, the pearls of the forest. Our object is to take this wood with all its history; to learn its ways and make it into things of natural beauty, functionally organic. At our home/studio near Silver Creek Falls in the foothills of the Oregon Cascades, we work surrounded by the trees from which we get our inspiration. Like the creek, energy flows naturally, is absorbed, and our work is a reflection of this process. We use mostly Oregon woods, such as Oregon bigleaf maple burl. The wood is the most important element, and each individual piece really does tell us how to work or cut it."

Michael Elkan was born in Philadelphia and spent his early working years in the clothing business designing knitwear, much of which appeared in well-known trade publications and national magazines. Tiring of the pressures of city life, Michael and his wife Sharon moved to Oregon, where they built a home and studio in Silverton and began working with wood burls (see figure 18.11).

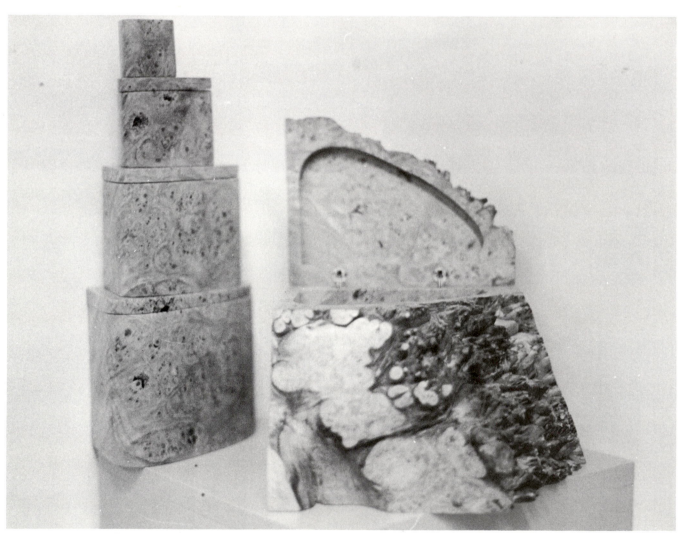

*(Figure 18.11) Michael Elkan: Oregon birdseye maple burl boxes.*

**Karen Engelke**
**Stained Glass**

"The emotional impact of a stained glass window is exhilerating to me—so alive, so dynamic, constantly changing with the sun and wind outside. Glass can be powerful, solid, and chunky as in slab glass, or infinitely graceful and liquid as in the finest hand-blown antique glass. Since not everyone can place a stained glass window, I started making stained glass boxes, which I see as small jewels which sparkle and catch the light. While my windows are abstract and subtle and can lead to creative contemplation by the viewer, the boxes make people smile when they see them and that gives me great satisfaction."

Karen Engelke, Schenectady, New York, was apprenticed to Rose Wellings-Crispin of Long Island for three years, learning design and construction of full-sized leaded windows. Since that time, she has worked on her own for nine years, producing windows, mirrors, and boxes. She has developed a strong wholesale following for her work in New York, Maryland, and Virginia, and has produced work for Eli Lilly, Bendix Corporation, and Kaiser Permanente. Karen has taught stained glass classes in continuing education programs and at the Schenectady Museum.

*(Figure 18.12) Karen Engelke: stained glass and mirror.*

**Stephen Fellerman**
**Glass**

"There is a great challenge in going into the studio every morning and doing a high-level, quality piece with freshness. I try to make certain that each piece has something special going for it. It's a combination of repetition and spontaneity that makes for a successful piece. Glass has a great tradition of being collected and bought. I try to be original, but I use some of the traditional things which a broad base of collectors can relate to. My work is designed to catch the eye and give the beholder a sense of magic in that the luster of the glass is everchanging."

Stephen Fellerman graduated from Pratt Institute in 1972. He was introduced to glass blowing at the Sausalito Art Center in California. After establishing his studio in Kent, Connecticut, he won prizes and awards of distinction at the Washington Square Outdoor Art Festival, the Miami Beach Festival of the Arts, and the Show at Rhinebeck.

In 1976 his work was displayed in "Contemporary Art Glass": '76 at Lever House in New York City.

Fellerman in 1977 attained prominence as a finalist in the Fragile Arts glass competition. In 1980 and 1981 Fellerman's glass was exhibited in Wippon Gakki's, Yamaha-sponsored "American Glass Now II and III." In 1981 the Indianapolis Museum of Art featured his glass in a one-man show, and in the same year he was commissioned by ITT to do a limited edition special design vase for corporate directors and executives. In 1982 Fellerman was honored by the governor of Connecticut with an exhibition in the governor's residence.

Glass by Stephen Fellerman now graces many corporate, gallery, and private collections, including the permanent collection of the Chrysler Museum in Norfolk, Virginia.

In 1986 he was chosen by the Connecticut Commission on the Arts for its first artist showcase at Bradley International Airport, New Terminal Building Gallery and in September of 1986 his glass was featured in a one-man show at Saks Fifth Avenue (see figure 18.13)

*(Figure 18.13) Stephen Fellerman: blown glass vase with iridescent lusters.*

**Jody Fine**

"In doing my work, I attempt to combine technique, form and function—and if that won't work I do it anyway. Mostly it's hard work, but that's not why I do it."

Jody Fine attended Bard College, New York, and the University of California at San Diego and Los Angeles, as well as California State University at Sonoma. Mr. Fine has conducted numerous workshops and demonstrations and has served as teaching assistant at the Pilchuck School in Washington State and as guest artist at Penland School in North Carolina. Jody Fine's work has been exhibited widely all over the United States and abroad, including shows at America House, Tenafly, New Jersey, the Museum of Art in Seattle, and the Craft International show in Japan. Jody Fine's work is represented in many private collections as well as in the Corning Collection, Corning, New York, and at the Smithsonian Institution. He currently maintains a studio and business in Berkeley (see figure 18.14).

*(Figure 18.14) Jody Fine: bowl with swirl decoration. Blown glass.*

**Diane Gabriel**

"My goal is to produce a body of work which expresses commitment to the beauty of truth of the human experience as I know it in my lifetime. My favorite pieces evolve from joy, sorrow, and personal conflicts. I am drawn to communication and creativity in many forms; I am not committed to any one media and technique, which is secondary to expression. For the past ten years, I have owned and operated a business, producing my designs in fabric sculpture wearables and accessories."

Diane Gabriel, a native of New York City, lives now in Burlington, Vermont. She holds a degree from Goddard College, and has also studied at the Art Students League, at Carnegie Mellon, and the Parsons School of Design. She received an individual artists grant from the Vermont Council on the Arts in 1977 and 1978. Her work has been shown in a number of crafts exhibitions and galleries. She has taught fiber arts to both adults and children (see figure 18.15).

*(Figure 18.15) Diane Gabriel: "Pegasus." Soft sculpture.*

**Barbara Grenell**
**Fibers**

"The warmth and receptiveness of fiber caused me to choose it as the medium with which to express my images of the landscape. Although not literal, my work is influenced by the mountain landscape surrounding my home and studio and by my sketches and drawings from travels in other areas. Developing each tapestry from preliminary drawings, I custom dye all the yarns myself with permanent fiber reactive dyes on a variety of cotton and woolen yarns. When you use an eccentric tapestry technique, then the natural Belgian linen warp becomes a visible element which unifies and softens the colors and images."

Barbara Grenell lives and works in Burnsville, North Carolina, in a mountaintop studio built by her husband, who is also her business associate. She studied art at the Philadelphia College of Art and was a scholarship student at Penland School where her interest in weaving became intensified because of her introduction to natural dye making. After art school, Barbara was apprenticed in New York City to Mark Frank, who was in the process of becoming one of America's greatest sculptors. After moving to North Carolina in 1969, she received a National Endowment for the Arts fellowship and used the grant to study the Navajo and Hopi techniques for natural dyeing in Arizona and New Mexico.

Today, Barbara Grenell's work is located throughout North America and is included in the collections of Banker's Trust, the Library of Congress, the Fine Arts Museum of the South, R. J. Reynolds Industries, IBM, Capitol City Broadcasting, and General Electric (see figure 18.16).

*(Figure 18.16) Barbara Grenell: Fibers. "Evening Hills." 54-by-54 inches. Owned by Lynchburg College.*

**Mary and Doug Hancock**

"Being able to share our love for the cultures and relics of the past through the jewelry is extremely rewarding. It provides us with a marvelous excuse to travel, to see the places we want, and to discover new ideas we can utilize in our work. It has also been an amazing vehicle for meeting the most incredible people. Getting to know them has been as important and exciting to us as knowing that they enjoy wearing our jewelry."

The idea for developing a line of jewelry based on Indian artifacts and themes from the Americas began during the years Doug was an archeologist in Central America. Frustrated at not being able to use any of the artifacts Doug was excavating from Mayan sites in the Guatemalan jungle, Mary befriended a Mayan Indian who later gave her the head of a clay figurine he had found in a nearby cornfield. With it, she made her first choker.

Out of this beginning, the Hancocks developed their business, The Mummy's Bundle, specializing in the creation of a line of "ancient-looking" jewelry, which is now displayed and sold in fine shops all over the United States (see figure 18.17). The Hancocks live and work in Sedona, Arizona.

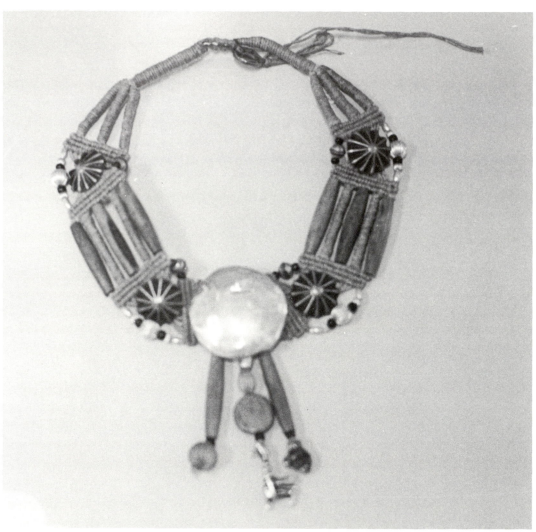

*(Figure 18.17) Mary and Doug Hancock: necklace.*

**Russell Kagan**

"My work reflects a constant testing of limits—a seeking of new boundaries. When I throw large forms on the wheel, I pull the form to the limit of its support system. My desire is to create the illusion of a free-floating yet powerful vessel. When I Raku fire, I strive for that *ultimate* color. My vessels are inspired by classic shapes of the past: Greek amphora, Southwest Indian water jugs, and the large clay and metal vessels used by the Spanish Armada in shipping."

Russell Kagan left a business career to explore the techniques and aesthetics of clay, and after five years of study became a studio potter in 1975. He lives and has his studio in a country setting in Hartford, Wisconsin.

Russell Kagan's work is included in many museums, corporate and private collections, and has been shown in group and one-person shows all over the world, including the American Crafts Festival at Lincoln Center in New York and America House in Tenafly, New Jersey. He is represented by nearly one hundred galleries throughout the United States, the Orient, South America, and the Middle East, and his work has been pictured in such publications as *Ceramics Monthly, The Guild: A Source Book of American Craft Artists,* and the *New York Times Magazine*. Kagan has received thirty-eight best of show, best of clay, and best in crafts awards in regional juried art festivals (see figure 18.18).

*(Figure 18.18) Russell Kagan: Raku/clay. Three Raku and enamel pots.*

**Ina Kozel**

"In 1976 I went to Kyoto, Japan, to study silk kimono dyeing, yuzen, batik, and stencil dyeing with Japanese masters; it was here that my art career turned in the direction of dyed garments because of the impact of the kimono. The kimono, which combined unabashed beauty, impeccable craft, and functional service, turned my attention to garments. The sensuality of color on silk, the sculptural softness of silk covering the body, the surface design's ability to enhance the structure of the garment are the elements which intrigue me as I work."

Ina Kozel lives part of the year in Monterey, but spends most of her time in her studio in Oakland, California. She has a degree in art from Cleveland Institute of Art and Western Reserve University, and has traveled and studied extensively in Southeast Asia, Europe, and Japan.

Her work has been written about in numerous publications, including three times in *American Craft*. Exhibited widely in the United States and abroad, Ina's work was included in the 1985 Asia tour, "American Art to Wear," sponsored by the American Crafts Museum and the United States Information Service. Most recently, she has turned her attention to the completion of a number of major architectural commissions in Georgia, Florida, and Texas. In 1985 her work "Fanfare" consisting of ten units, each 10-by-15 feet, was installed in the four-story atrium of the Interfirst Plaza in Dallas (see figure 18.19).

*(Figure 18.19) Ina Kozel: hand-painted silk kimono.*

**Richard Lane**
**Ceramics**
"Over the years, the pottery has gradually become square and rectangular and secondary to the surface design for which it is the format."

Richard Lane of Santa Barbara, California, has a B.A. from the California College of Arts and Crafts, Oakland. He also studied ceramics at University of California at Santa Cruz and University of California at Santa Barbara, after which he worked as a production potter for Santa Barbara Ceramic Design. He opened his own studio in 1979. Richard Lane feels that his work is influenced by Japanese pottery known as "Oribe ware," produced during the Momoyama period, 1573–1615 (see figure 18.21).

**Mimi Layne**
"I approach my work with an open mind, not wishing to limit myself. Thus, one body of work may include people and environments in surreal or humorous settings; another series may be flowing, organic and have a feminine quality; yet another may be more masculine, geometric and often symbolic. Environmental influences, photographs, and human experiences are my major sources of inspiration. My goal is to bring into tangible existence that which has been unmanifest and latent, both visually and psychologically. I consider my work to be an exploration and I derive great joy in seeing it evolve from concept to completed work."

Mimi Layne lives in Standardsville, Virginia. She holds a B.A. in studio art from the University of Virginia, and has done graduate work in glass at Arrowmont School of the Arts and Crafts and at Virginia Commonwealth University. Her work has been widely exhibited, and she received the first place award for glass in the Art Quest '86 National Art Competition sponsored by Parsons Gallery in New York City. Mimi teaches glass and metal sculpture in the Artists Workshop Series at the Virginia Museum (see figure 18.20).

*(Figure 18.20) Mimi Layne: glass. "Progression." Window hanging with bevels.*

*(Figure 18.21) Richard Lane: slab platter with tree and hills design. Fifteen-inch square.*

**Janet Marshman**

"I began creating masks as gifts for family and friends. They were so well received that I decided to make the masks to sell. I use all sorts of feathers and often combine them with other materials such as bark, lace, sequins, raffia, fur, dried flowers, and anything else that strikes my fancy. Each mask is individually designed and the design usually develops as I work. The fun thing about masks is that they provoke all sorts of comments and that they will change in character according to who is wearing them. When not being worn, a mask can become a decorative accessory for a room."

Janet Marshman was born in Pennsylvania and lives now in Harrisonburg, Virginia. Largely self-taught, she has exhibited her masks in many crafts shows and won several first place awards. She has lectured at James Madison University and is currently working with two galleries in New Orleans to promote her masks (see figure 18.22).

*(Figure 18.22) Janet Marshman: feather mask. Ostrich, silver pheasant, golden pheasant feathers.*

**John F. Nygren**
"A three-weeks course in glass at Penland taught me the basics of glass; beyond that I am self-taught. I enjoy developing my own techniques which become the vocabulary for my conversation with glass. I work alone in the studio and enjoy the company of the natural world in the garden outside my studio door."

John Nygren was born in Big Springs, Nebraska. He lives now in Walnut Cove, North Carolina, and has maintained a studio there since 1969. Mr. Nygren has a B.F.A. degree from the University of Nebraska at Lincoln and an M.F.A. from Cranbrook Academy of Art, Bloomfield Hills, Michigan.

He has exhibited his work in major shows all over the United States, as well as in Canada, Italy, and West Germany. John Nygren's glass is in many collections, including the Corning Museum of Glass, the Smithsonian Institution, the R. J. Reynolds Corporate collection, and the University of Texas at El Paso. His work was featured in the portfolio section of the August/September 1986 issue of *American Craft* (see figure 18.23).

*(a)*

*(b)*

*(Figure 18.23) John Nygren. (a) "Spring Sunrise" vessel. Glass, 1986. Photo courtesy of Smith, Weller, Smith. (b) "Flying Lizard." Glass, 1986. Photo courtesy of Smith, Weller, Smith.*

**Nancy Ramsey**

"I discovered clay in 1973 at a community recreation class where I was attempting temporary escape from two preschoolers. With the help of an artist friend, I prepared enough original, albeit primitive, work to enter a local crafts show in early 1974. Instant success, to my amazement! My goal is to create pottery pieces with which people can identify. Some pieces have a practical function, almost all are whimsical. It is a real challenge to try to translate ideas—sometimes really strange ones—into pottery."

Nancy Ramsey is a native of California, now living in Woodbridge, Virginia. Trained as a microbiologist, she has metamorphosed into a "potter-sculptor-craftsperson." She maintains a studio in northern Virginia, which employs another potter and three assistants. She shows her work in several large juried crafts shows and is represented by a number of galleries and shops (see figure 18.24).

**Julia Ricciardi-Vansell**

"My baskets have evolved from my having always worked as an artist/craftsperson, and attempting to incorporate creativity in everything I do. I want to make an affordable yet individual piece of art which will serve to bridge the gap between the artist and the public. My baskets seem to work this way. I very much enjoy the sculptural aspects of basket weaving."

On a remote farm nestled in the foothills of Niles Canyon, near Fremont, California, Julia Ricciardi creates unique baskets synthesizing her concept for color and sculptural form. Julia holds a B.A. degree in art from San Francisco State University and is currently working on her M.F.A. at San Jose State University. She taught ceramics in England in 1983, where she became involved in the study of textiles and the English methods of mixing colors and dyeing materials. These experiences, combined with her background in ceramic sculpture, inspired her to begin creating colored sculptural baskets. Julia's husband, Bryan Vansell, a ceramic artist, often helps create the unusual basket handles from distinctive branches and vines (see figure 18.25).

*(Figure 18.24) Nancy Ramsey: "Fountain and Dragons." Clay.*

*(Figure 18.25) Julia Ricciardi-Vansell: two baskets with dyed elements.*

**Gil Roberts**
**Jewelry**
"I had been woodworking for about twelve years, carving and sculpting commissioned work, when in 1980 I began combining precious metals with small wooden inlayed pieces. Gradually the metals and gemstones lured me away from wood and I started working with jewelry. Recently I have been traveling to mines in this country and abroad searching for unique one-of-a-kind pieces to incorporate into my jewelry."

Gil Roberts lives in the southwestern Virginia town of Pilot. He is currently working toward a gemnologist's degree and shows his work at crafts fairs and galleries in the eastern and central United States (see figure 18.26).

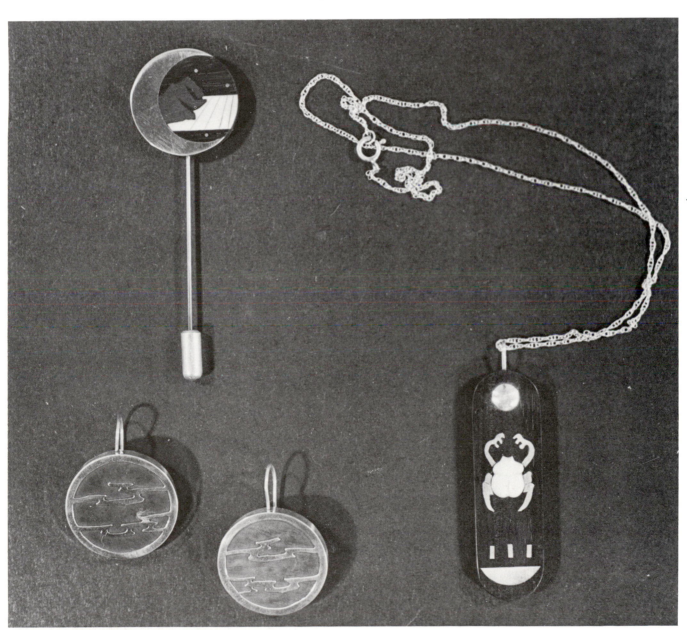

*(Figure 18.26) Gil Roberts: jewelry. Upper left, "Moonscape." Sterling stick pin with wood inlay. Lower left, sterling and wood earrings. Right, scarab necklace of ebony and turquoise.*

**David R. Rogers**
**Wood**

"I enjoy creating things from wood and I no doubt have definite concepts, goals, and a working philosophy, but I find it very difficult to put them into words. It is enough for me that I can put them into my work for others to use and enjoy."

David Rogers studied furniture design and construction at Virginia Commonwealth University and has a B.F.A. degree from that institution. He has worked as a furniture designer and engineer for two furniture manufacturers. He also designs and makes furniture and wood boxes in his spare time (see figure 18.27).

**Shirley Rosenthal**

"The challenge in enamels for me has been to work on a larger scale than generally associated with the medium. My works are usually one-of-a-kind pieces or very limited editions. My latest commission was for a 22-foot wall in the lobby of Moog, Inc., an aerospace industry in East Aurora, New York."

Self-trained as an enamelist, Shirley Rosenthal has worked professionally in the medium since 1964. She maintains a studio in Williamsville, New York, and accepts architectural commissions in addition to smaller wall pieces. She has taught at the Kenan Center, Lockport, New York, and as artist-in-residence at Artpark, Lewiston, New York. She annually exhibits in

*(Figure 18.27) David Rogers: two boxes with lids. Walnut wood.*

the large juried shows such as Wintermarket in Baltimore and the Northeast Craft Fair in Rhinebeck (see figure 18.28).

## Bernie Rowell

Bernie Rowell has been professionaly producing fiber art for residential and commercial and interiors for seven years. Her canvas collage works combine a stitchers' skill with rich painted surfaces. Canvases are cut, woven, torn, pleated, and layered to achieve three-dimensional textures. Geometric shapes interact with smoothly modulated color. Iridescent and metallic paints in combination with sewn line drawings add detail interest to these one-of-a-kind works.

Born in Lansing, Michigan, Bernie Rowell lives now in Knoxville, Tennessee, where she maintains a working studio/gallery. She attended Michigan State University, University of Tennessee, and Arrowmont School of Crafts. Ms. Rowell has taught children and adult art classes at the East Lansing Arts Workshop, the New Prospect Craft Center, Maryville College, and at Arrowmont School of Crafts in the elderhostel program. Her textile designs for clothing, accessories, and soft sculpture have been featured in *Needlework for Today, Needle and Thread*, and *Handmade*. She has exhibited widely and has received a number of awards (see figure 18.29).

*(Figure 18.28) Shirley Rosenthal: "Best Friends." Enamel on metal, 16-by-20 inches.*

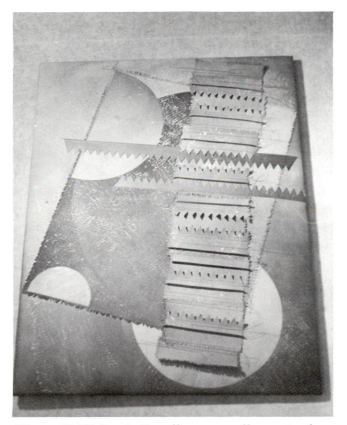

*(Figure 18.29) Bernie Rowell: canvas collage, mixed media, textile.*

**John Shedd**
**Pottery**

"I attempt in these works to control and manipulate color in clay. Because of this emphasis on color, the forms, of necessity, must be of simple line and easy to construct. While weight and physical structure are considerations, the overriding concern will be the illusion of surface depth and graphic distancing. Give me the difficulty inherent in pigment limitations at high temperature and let me play with those ranges to bring animation to a frozen, stony surface. Let me work with the variations of natural glaze materials and reduction firings to bring to that animation a richness unobtainable in any other media."

John Shedd received his B.F.A. in ceramics from Rockford College in Illinois and his M.F.A. in ceramics from Rochester Institute in New York. From 1977 to 1979 he managed a production pottery in South Carolina. Mr. Shedd and his wife Nina Gelardi, also a ceramic artist, originated Clayphernalia Gallery in 1979. It adjoins their studio in a two-hundred-year-old converted mill in Rocky Hill, New Jersey.

John Shedd was featured as one of six craftspersons who participated in the film "My Craft, My Life" by public television. John and the Clayphernalia studio were the subjects of a report on WOR television, "New Jersey People." Shedd has exhibited his work in many juried and invitational shows, and in 1984 the New Jersey Designer Craftsmen Organization selected one of his porcelain vases to be presented to Mayor John Lynch of New Brunswick (see figure 18.30).

*(Figure 18.30) John Shedd: large platter, two vases.*

**Gertrude Shook**
**Fiber Sculpture**

"My present work with sculptural fiber forms is derived from a long-time interest in the fiber arts of macramé, coiling, and weaving. It is an experimental technique, combining paper "ropes" with fibers such as jute and wool. I hope to expand the idea into larger pieces, perhaps environments for children to play in. My work is largely unplanned and is allowed to grow in whatever direction my fancy dictates at the moment. My goal is to use my God-given curiosity to create beauty from whatever source, wherever I am."

Gertrude Shook, Keysville, Virginia, has studied art at Longwood College (Farmville, Virginia) and with a number of private instructors. She has attended World Craft Council workshops in Canada and Mexico. Travels abroad have brought her in contact with the work of craftspeople in Greece, England, and Belgium. Her work has been shown in many juried exhibitions and has won a number of awards. Gertrude executes commissions for interior decorators and has taught at Southside Community College and at Longwood College. She also teaches private workshops all over the state of Virginia (see figure 18.31).

*(Figure 18.31) Gertrude Shook: experimental fiber sculpture.*

**Karl Stephenson**

"I have always enjoyed the work of the late Hans Coper and perhaps some of his influence has rubbed off on my work. I am always trying to incorporate other materials and motifs into clay which are not expected, hence the cloth ears on the sheep; besides ceramic ones would break off and wouldn't be as much fun!"

Karl Stephenson studied at Loughbrough Art College in England, specializing in ceramic design and processes. He now lives in Seattle, where his firm, Bergschrund and Company, produces designs in porcelain cast from original molds (see figure 18.32).

**Henry P. Summa**

"The Fire Works is glassblowing, and much more. It is an approach to art and life that focuses my creative energy into transformation. The tremendous energy in fire that can melt steel, mature ceramics, liquify sand into glass, has captured me. I find myself returning again and again to fire: welding, Raku, stoneware, and now free-blown glass, for me the most beautiful and exciting.

"To blow glass beautifully, I must be totally centered; feel the life force flowing from my solar plexus. This centering, combined with a mastery of basic glassblowing techniques, is what I know as the dance of

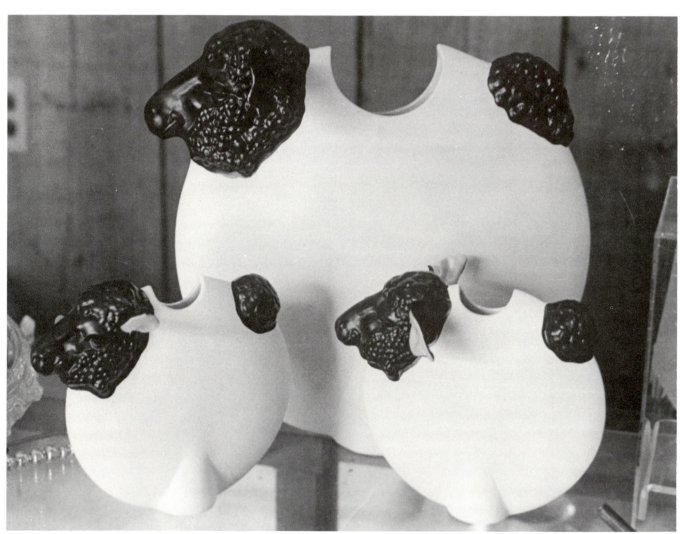

*(Figure 18.32) Karl Stephenson: "Sheep family."*
*Porcelain with cloth ears.*

glass. From this center I spin outward into the glass, giving it solidarity, fixing it in time and space. These pieces are solidified energy from this dance in glass."

Henry Paul Summa was born July 28, 1949, in Bremerhaven, Germany. He has lived in Germany, Turkey, India, and various parts of the United States. After training in ceramics at Monterey Peninsula College, his interest turned to glassblowing, and he apprenticed himself for a short period at the Glory Hole Glassworks in Santa Fe, New Mexico, before organizing

his own studio near Woodstock, New York. While in New York, he taught several intensive glass workshops and exhibited twice in the annual Southern Tier Arts and Crafts Show in Corning, New York. He returned to New Mexico in the summer of 1974, and has established his studio in the Rio Grande river valley halfway between Santa Fe and Taos, near Velarde. His work can be seen in galleries in Arizona, California, Colorado, Connecticut, Florida, Hawaii, Illinois, Kansas, Louisiana, Maryland, New Mexico, New York, Pennsylvania, Texas, Vermont, Virginia, Washington and Washington, D.C. (see figure 18.33).

*(Figure 18.33) Blown glass bowl, decanter, and tumblers.*

**Thelma Twery**

"I work in a variety of media, including painting in oil, acrylic, and watercolor; printmaking in collagraph, etching, and various relief media; and drawing. The subject and expressive intent are what determine my choice of medium for a particular work or series of pieces. This involvement with many different media also relates well to my teaching of art, since I feel that the broader my experiences, the better able I am to be open to the various needs and interests of my students.

My work is figurative, but with much attention to design relationships in each piece. I enjoy doing landscapes, which focus on cloud formations and trees, but my dominant interest has been in the human face as a mask and as an expressive symbol which mirrors the individual's search for greater self-awareness."

Chairperson of the art department and associate professor of art at Lynchburg College, Thelma Twery has also taught at Governor's School for the Gifted (for Virginia high school students), numerous teachers' workshops in art in Lynchburg city schools, and adult art classes at the Lynchburg Fine Arts Center. She has been recipient of fellowship grants to Yaddo, an artist's retreat in Saratoga Springs, New York, the Virginia Center for the Creative Arts in Sweet Briar, Virginia, and the Mednick Memorial Grant from the Virginia Foundation for Independent Colleges.

Thelma has exhibited widely in solo and group shows in Virginia and North Carolina, and her work has been chosen for traveling shows by the Virginia Museum and the Virginia Center for the Creative Arts. She has studied at Carnegie Institute of Technology (Carnegie-Mellon University in Pittsburgh); Showhegan School of Painting and Sculpture, State University of Iowa, University of Georgia, Printmaking Workshop in New York City, New York University, and the Art Students' League, as well as traveled and studied in France and Italy (see figure 18.34).

*(a)*

*(b)*

*(Figure 18.34) Thelma Twery. (a) "Past is Present." Photo silkscreen. (b) "Masquerade." Linocut.*

## Peter Wreden

"My jewelry is an outgrowth of my previous experience as a sculptor and began when I designed and made a necklace for my wife, which received many compliments. Since that time I have concentrated on jewelry, fashioning contemporary pieces from sterling, gold, and mixed metals. I have learned that people appreciate the different and unusual and, while some of my pieces may be similar, no two are identical. My goal is to produce 'sculpture' to wear."

Peter Wreden lives and operates a studio/shop/gallery in Roanoke, Virginia. He received his art training at the Art Students League in New York and at the École National Superior des Beaux Art, Paris. Before turning to jewelry, he worked as a designer and art director for several firms in Virginia and New York. Peter Wreden's work is in many public and private collections and he exhibits regularly in craft shows from Massachusetts to Florida (see figure 18.35).

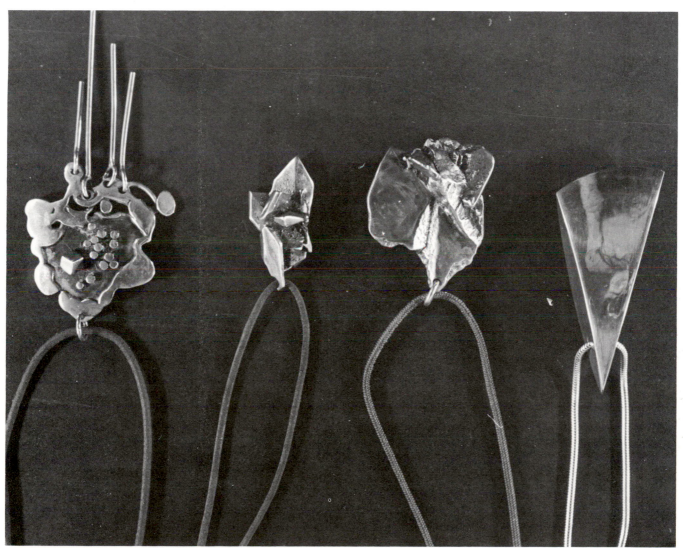

*(Figure 18.35) Peter Wreden: Four pendants from the authors' collection.*

Names and addresses of craftspeople included in the professional portfolio:

Karen Adachi
702 Monarch Way    Santa Cruz, CA 95066

Michael and Christina Adcock
P.O. Box 31109    Santa Barbara, CA 93130

Gwendolyn Orsinger Anderson ("Orsini")
5906 Wood Sorrel Court    Burke Centre, VA 22015

Sandra Bowden
237 Moe Road    Clifton Park, NY 12065

Jack Brubaker
RR 2, Box 102A    Nashville, IN 47448

Jane Campbell
The Factory Studios
228 Church Street    Cambridge Springs, PA 16403

Barbara Cornett
1542 Club Drive    Lynchburg, VA 24503

Virginia I. Davis
1082 Timberlake Drive    Lynchburg, VA 24502

Michael Elkan
22364 N. Fork Road    Silverton, OR 97381

Karen Engelke
1791 Central Parkway    Schenectady, NY 12309

Stephen J. Fellerman
RR 1, Box 104, RT 7    Kent, CT 06757

Jody Fine
1800 Fourth Street    Berkeley, CA 94710

Diane Gabriel
211 Hinesburg Road S    Burlington, VT 05401

Barbara Grenell
1132 Hall's Chapel Road    Burnsville, NC 28714

Doug and Mary Hancock
The Mummy's Bundle    Box 2038
Sedona, AZ 86336

Russell Kagan
6900 Sconfinato    Hartford, WI 53027

Ina Kozel
4701 San Leandro Street    Oakland, CA 94601

Richard Lane
433 Elsueno Road    Santa Barbara, CA 93110

Mimi Layne
SR 33, Box 24W    Standardsville, VA 22973

Janet E. Marshman
Rt. 4, Box 43    Harrisonburg, VA 22801

John F. Nygren
Rt. 1, Box 140    Walnut Cove, NC 27052

Nancy Ramsey
2600 Woodfern Court    Woodbridge, VA 22192

Julia Ricciardi-Vansell
P.O. Box 2062    Fremont, CA 94536

Gil Roberts
P.O. Box 7    Pilot, VA 24138

David R. Rogers
Rt. 1, Box 432 AB    Coleman Falls, VA 24536

Shirley Rosenthal
67 Fenwick Road    Williamsville, NY 14221

Bernie Rowell
5002 Kingston Pike    Knoxville, TN 37919

John Shedd
200 Washington Street    P.O. Box 276
Rocky Hill, NJ 08553

Gertrude Shook
Rt. 2, Box 202    Keysville, VA 23947

Karl Stephenson
Bergschrund & Co.
309 S. Cloverdale Street C-26    Seattle, WA 98108

P. Summa
P.O. Box 67    Velarde, NM 87582

Thelma Twery
397 Woodland Avenue    Lynchburg, VA 24503

Peter Wreden
415 King George Avenue    Roanoke, VA 24016

Notes

1 *American Crafts* (formerly *Crafts Horizon*) published bimonthly by the American Crafts Council, 401 Park Avenue South, New York, NY 10016.

2 *The Crafts Report* is published monthly by the Crafts Report Publishing Co., 700 Orange Street, Wilmington DE 19801. This journal contains much information of interest to professional craftspeople, teachers, students, and those who use crafts in any way.

3 Information concerning these shows may be obtained from American Craft Enterprises, P.O. Box 10, New Paltz, New York, NY 12561.

4 A representative listing of shops, museums, galleries, and crafts fairs may be found in appendix A.

5 I am indebted to the craftspeople whose work is shown as well as to several owners of fine crafts shops: Penny Bosworth, The Signet Gallery, Charlottesville, Virginia; Bob Leiby, The Crafters' Gallery, also in Charlottesville; Frances Harris, Virginia Handcrafts, Inc., Lynchburg, Virginia; and Andy Williams, Gallery 3, Roanoke, Virginia. I am also grateful to those collectors who allowed me to photograph work owned by them.

# Appendix A

**Craft Shops and Galleries**

There are to be found throughout the United States numerous galleries and shops that exhibit and sell the works of professional craftspeople. Only a few of these are listed here; others may be found in the pages of arts and crafts magazines, trade papers, newspapers, and in the yellow pages of telephone directories. The Craftmarket Listing © contains lists of over fifteen thousand shops, galleries, and other outlets that carry fine crafts. Information may be obtained from the publishers, Francisco Enterprise, 572 143rd Street, Caledonia, MI 49316.

Albertson-Peterson Gallery, Inc.
329 Park Avenue South    Winter Park, FL 32789

The Allrich Gallery
251 Post Street    San Francisco, CA 94108

Alter/Associates, Inc.
122 Cary Avenue    Highland Park, IL 60035

America House Gallery
24 Washington Street    Tenafly, NJ 07670

Bellas Artes
301 Garcia at Canyon Road    Santa Fe, NM 87501

The Best of Everything Ltd.
12211 River Road    Potomac, MD 20854

Beyond Horizons
7050 Third Avenue    Scottsdale, AZ 85251

The Blue Streak
1723 Delaware Avenue    Wilmington DE 19806

Bri'on and Company
8702 Keystone Crossing    Indianapolis, IN 46240

Emphasis on Maine
36 Main Street    Bridgton, ME 04009

Folk Art Gallery
4138 University Way    NE Seattle, WA 98105

Gad-Fly
215 S. Union Street    Alexandria, VA 22314

Gallery Eight
7464 Girard Avenue    LaJolla, CA 92037

Gallery Fair
Kasten and Ukiah Streets    Mendocino, CA 95460

Gallery of Contemporary American Crafts
91 Union Street    Newton Centre, MA 02159

Gallery 3
213 Market Street    Roanoke, VA 24011

Katie Gingrass Gallery
714 N. Milwaukee Street    Milwaukee, WI 53202

Glass Arts Collaborative, Inc.
36 Newbury Street    Boston, MA 02116

The Glass Gallery
4931 Elm Street    Bethesda, MD 20014

Great American Gallery
1925 Peachtree Road    Atlanta, GA 30309

Habatat Galleries
28235 Southfield Road    Lathrup Village, MI
48076

Habatat Galleries
1090 Kane Concourse    Bay Harbor Islands, FL
33154

Hand Workshop
1812 W. Main Street    Richmond, VA 23220

Hibberd McGrath Gallery
Box 815    Keystone, CO 80435

Hickory Street Gallery
Kapalua Bay Hotel    Kapalua, Maui, Hawaii

Cameron's
University Mall    Chapel Hill, NC 27514

Carlyn Gallery, Inc.
1145 Madison Avenue    New York, NY 10028

Clay and Fiber
N. Pueblo Road    Taos, NM 87571

Clay Phernalia Gallery
200 Washington Street    Rocky Hill, NJ 08553

Cobb Lane Gifts
1 Cobb Lane    Birmingham, AL 35205

Contemporary Crafts
3934 S.W. Corbett Avenue    Portland, OR 97201

Contemporary Images
14027 Ventura Boulevard    Sherman Oaks, CA
91423

Crafters' Gallery
RFD 12, Box 97    Charlottesville, VA 22901

The Craft Shop
Piedmont Craftsmen, Inc.
411 N. Cherry Street    Winston-Salem, NC
27101

Cross Creek Gallery
3835 Cross Creek Road, space B    Malibu, CA
90265

G. H. Dalsheimer Gallery, Ltd.
336 N. Charles Street    Baltimore, MD 21201

DBR Gallery
13111 Shaker Square    Cleveland, OH 44120

Delmano Gallery and Studio
11981 San Vincente Boulevard    Los Angeles, CA
90049

Helen Drutt Gallery
1721 Walnut Street    Philadelphia, PA 19103

Editions Limited Gallery, Inc.
Lafayette Square    St. Louis, MO 63104

Holsten Galleries
Elm Street    Stockbridge, MA 01262

Holsten Galleries
206 Worth Avenue    Palm Beach, FL 33480

Incorporated Gallery
1200 Madison Avenue    New York, NY 10128

Kurland/Summers Gallery
8742A Melrose Avenue    Los Angeles, CA 90069

Latitudes
68 Greenwich Avenue    Greenwich, CT 06830

Maurine Littleon Gallery
3222 N Street NW Georgetown Court
Washington, DC 20007

Lodestone Gallery
1237 Pearl Street    Boulder, CO 80302

Mariposa Gallery
113 Romero, NW    Albuquerque, NM 87104

Maple Hill Gallery
367 Fore Street    Portland, ME 04101

Meredith Gallery
805 N. Charles Street    Baltimore, MD 21201

National Craft Showroom
11 E. 26th Street    New York, NY 10010

Netsky Gallery
3107 Grand Avenue    Coconut Grove, FL 33133

Louis Newman Galleries
322 N. Beverly Drive    Beverly Hills, CA 90210

Shelia Nussbaum Gallery
358 Milburn Avenue    Milburn, NJ 07041

Anne O'Brien Gallery
1701 Pennsylvania Avenue NW, suite 101
Washington, DC 20006

One Step Up Gifts
323 Romany Road    Lexington, KY 40502

Peddlers
2826 Piedmont Avenue    Duluth, MN 55811

Perception Galleries
2631 Colquitt    Houston, TX 77098

The Platypus
2120A Cumberland Avenue    Knoxville, TN 37916

The Private Collection
21 E. Fifth Street    Cincinnati, OH 45202

Private Stock Gallery
1612 Westport Road    Kansas City, MO 64111

Joan Robey Gallery
2701 E. Third Avenue    Denver, CO 80206

Rock House Gallery
1311 West Abram    Arlington, TX 76013

Running Ridge Gallery
301 E. Ozai Avenue    Ozai, CA 93023

Running Ridge Gallery
640 Canyon Road    Santa Fe, NM 87501

Esther Saks Gallery
311 W. Superior Street    Chicago, IL 60610

Carol Saunders Gallery
927 Gervais Street    Columbia, SC 29201

Ree Schonlau Gallery
511 S. Eleventh    Omaha, NE 68102

Showcase Gallery
169 Main Street    Cold Spring Harbor, NY 11724

A Show of Hands
506 Amsterdam Avenue    New York, NY 10024

Signature
Village Market Place    Hyannis, MA 02601

Signature
Dock Square, North Street    Boston MA 02109

The Signature Shop Gallery
3267 Roswell Road NW    Atlanta, GA 30305

Signet Gallery
212 Fifth Street NE    Charlottesville, VA 22902

16 Hands
119 W. Washington    Ann Arbor, MI 48104

Snyderman Works and Galleries
317–319 South Street    Philadelphia, PA 19147

Swan Gallery
132 S. 18th Street    Philadelphia, PA 19103

Hodges Taylor Gallery
227 N. Tryon Street    Charlotte, NC 28202

Ten Arrow Gallery/Shop
10 Arrow Street    Cambridge, MA 02138

Evelyn Todd Gallery
Dover Place, 83 Washington Street    Dover, NH
03820

Torpedo Factory Art Center
101 N. Union Street    Alexandria, VA 22314

Sylvia Ullman American Crafts Gallery
13010 Woodland Avenue    Cleveland, OH 44120

Vermont State Craft Center
Frog Hollow    Middlebury, VT 05753

Virginia Handcrafts, Inc.
2008 Langhorne Road    Lynchburg, VA 24501

Wallengren, USA
72 Thompson Street    New York, NY 10012

Westminster Gallery
132A Newbury Street    Boston, MA 02116

Whichcraft
52 Vose Avenue    South Orange, NJ 07079

Willing Heart Gallery
615A E. Sixth Street    Austin, TX 78701

Zimmerman Saturn Gallery
131 2nd Avenue, N.    Nashville, TN 37207

# Appendix B

**Crafts Museums**

Numerous art museums present periodic temporary exhibitions of crafts, some display crafts as a part of their permanent collection, and many feature and sell works of regional craftspeople in their shops. Other museums are devoted primarily to collecting the best examples of the work of past and present artisans as well as the crafts of various regions. A representative list of these is given here. For a comprehensive listing of over 6,200 museums of all types in the United States, refer to *The Official Museum Directory* published by the American Association of Museums, 1055 Thomas Jefferson Street NW, Washington, DC 20007, and the National Register Publishing Company, 3004 Glenview Road, Wilmette, IL 60091.

American Craft Museum
40 W. 53rd Street   New York, NY 10036

Brookfield Craft Center
Route 25   Brookfield, CT 06804

California Crafts Museum Ghirardelli Square
900 North Point   San Francisco, CA 94188

Contemporary Crafts Assn.
3934 SW Corbett Avenue   Portland, OR 97201

Craft & Folk Art Museum
5814 Wilshire Boulevard   Los Angeles, CA 90036

Crafts Museum
11458 Laguna Drive   Mequon, WI 53092

Fine Arts Gallery of the University of the South
Georgia Avenue   Sewanee, TN 37375

Folk Art Center
Milepost 92 Blue Ridge Parkway   Asheville, NC 28815

Hammond Museum
　　Deveau Road (Route 124)　North Salem, NY
　　10560

Institute of American Indian Arts
　　1369 Cerillos Road　Sante Fe, NM 87501

The Jones Gallery of Glass and Ceramics
　　Douglas Mountain Road　East Sebago, ME 04029

Liberty Village Arts Center & Gallery
　　Box 269, Main Street　Chester, MT 59522

Mattye Reed African Heritage Center
　　N.C.A. & T. State University　Greensboro, NC
　　27411

Mexican American Cultural Heritage Center
　　2940 Singleton Boulevard　Dallas, TX 75212

Mississippi Crafts Center
　　Natchez Parkway　Ridgeland, MS 39157

Museum of American Treasures
　　1315 E. 4th Street　National City, CA 92050

Museum of Oriental Cultures
　　426 S. Staples Street　Corpus Christi, TX 78401

Ohio Ceramic Center
　　State Route 93　Crooksville, OH 43731

The Old Stone House
　　3051 M Street NW　Washington, DC 20007

Piedmont Craftsmen, Inc.
　　300 S. Main Street　Winston-Salem, NC 27101

Renwick Gallery of the National Museum of American
Art, Smithsonian Institute
　　Pennsylvania Avenue at 17th Street　Washington,
　　DC 20560

Sauder Museum Farm & Craft Village
　　Star Route 2　Archbold, OH 43502

Southwest Craft Center
　　300 Augusta Street　San Antonio, TX 78205

Steppingstone Museum
　　461 Quaker Bottom Road　Havre De Grace, MD
　　21078

Worcester Craft Center
　　25 Sagamore Road　Worcester, MA 01605

# Appendix C

**Suppliers**

Most cities of any size have one or more outlets where crafts supplies may be purchased. Larger quantities for school or professional use are more economical when ordered from large general supply houses or companies that specialize in supplies for specific crafts. The list given here are those suppliers of which I know or have done business with and is by no means a complete list. More sources can be found in the various books listed in this work with each craft. Another valuable source for names of suppliers as well as for a wealth of other interesting information is the crafts section of *The Next Whole Earth Catalog,* Stewart Brand, ed., New York: Random House, 1981.

*General Suppliers:*
(Almost all supplies needed for the crafts covered in this work may be obtained from one or more of these firms.)

Dick Blick Co.
   Box 1287   Galesburg, IL 61401

Chaselle Arts & Crafts
   9645 Gerwig Lane   Columbia, MD 21046

Nasco Arts & Crafts
   901 Janesville Avenue   Fort Atkinson, WI 53538

Nasco West
   1524 Princeton Avenue   Modesto, CA 95352

Sax Arts & Crafts
   P.O. Box 2002   Milwaukee, WI 52301

Sax Arts & Crafts (east)
   P.O. Box 2511   Allentown, PA 18001

Suppliers for specific crafts:

*Enameling Supplies*
American Art Clay Co.
    4717 W. 16th Street    Indianapolis, IN 46222

Thomas C. Thompson Co.
    P.O. Box 127    Highland Park, IL 60035

*Glass Arts*
S. A. Bendheim Co.
    122 Hudson Street    New York, NY 10013

Blenko Glass Co.
    Milton, WV    25541

Glass-Art
    P.O. Box 2404    Santa Fe, NM 87501

Kokomo Opalescent Glass Co.
    Box 809    Kokomo, IN 46901

Nervo Distributors
    650 University Avenue    Berkeley, CA 94710

Whittemore-Durgin
    Box 2065    Hanover, MA 02339

*Graphic Arts*
Advance Process Supply Co.
    400 N. Noble Street    Chicago, IL 60622

Craftools, Inc.
    1 Industrial Road    Woodbridge, NJ 07075

Naz Dar Co.
    1087 N. Branch St.    Chicago, IL 60622

Screen Process Supplies Mfg. Co.
    1199 E. 12th Street    Oakland, CA 94606

Speed Ball Inks
Hunt Manufacturing Co.
    1405 Locust Street    Philadelphia, PA 19102

Standard Screen & Supply Co.
    15 W. 20th Street    New York, NY 10011

Ulano Products Co.
    610 Dean Street    Brooklyn, NY 11238

*Fiber and Fabric Arts*
Crafts Yarns
    603 Mineral Springs Avenue    Pawtucket, RI 02862

Dharma Trading Co.
    P.O. Box 1288    Berkeley, CA 94701

Frederick J. Fawcett, Inc.
    129 South Street    Boston, MA 02111

Fibrec, Inc.
    2815 18th Street    San Francisco, CA 94110

Lily Mills Co.
    Shelby, NC    28150

School Products Co.
    312 E. 23rd Street    New York, NY 10010

The Yarn Depot
    545 Sutter Street    San Francisco, CA 94102

*Jewelry/Metalcraft*
Allcraft Tool & Supply Co.
    215 Park Avenue    Hicksville, NY 11801

Art Jewelers Supply Co.
    43 W. 47th Street    New York, NY 10036

W. H. Curtin Co.
    P.O. Box 606    Jacksonville, FL 33033

W. H. Curtin Co.
    P.O. Box 1491    New Orleans, LA 70113

W. H. Curtin Co.
    1812 Griffin Street    Dallas, TX 75202

Jewelry Distributing Co.
    315 West 57th Street    Los Angeles, CA 90013

Rio Grande, Albuquerque
    6901 Washington, NE    Albuquerque, NM 87109

Southwest Smelting & Supply Co.
    P.O. Box 1298
    118 Broadway    San Antonio, TX 78206

*Papermaking*
Frank Davis Co.
   P.O. Box 231   Cambridge, MA 02139

Dieu Donne Press & Paper
   3 Crosby Street   New York, NY 10013

Gold's Artworks, Inc.
   2100 N. Pine Street   Lumberton, NC 28358

Twinrocker Papermaking Supplies
   RFD 2   Brookston, IN 47923

Michael John Verlangieri
   790 Santa Barbara Drive   Claremont, CA 91711

*Shop Tools and Hardware*
Brookstone Co.
   Dept. C River Road   Worthington, MA 01098

U.S. General
   100 Commercial Street   Plainview, NY 11803

*Ceramics*
American Art Clay Co.
   4717 W. 16th Street   Indianapolis, IN 46222

A.R.T. Studios
   921 Oakton Street   Elk Grove, IL 60007

Capitol Ceramics, Inc.
   2174 S. Main Street   Salt Lake City, UT 84115

Creek-Turn Pottery
   Route 38   Hainesport, NJ 08036

Minnesota Clay Co.
   8001 Grand Avenue   S. Bloomington, MI 55420

New England Ceramic Supply
   P.O. Box 151   Waltham, MA 02154

Seattle Pottery Supply
   400 E. Pine Street   Seattle, WA 28122

Western Ceramic Supply
   1601 Howard Street   San Francisco, CA 94103

Westwood Ceramic Supply
   14400 Lomitas Avenue   City of Industry, CA
   91744

# Glossary

**annealing**   In metal working, the process of restoring malleability to a piece of work that has been "work-hardened" through working with the metal. Heating the piece to a dull red heat and cooling by dropping into water or a pickling solution, realigns the molecules of the metal and restores its working properties.

**appliqué**   Designs or patterns made of one material and fastened to another. Widely used in stitchery and other fiber arts.

**artist's proof**   A term in printmaking indicating a trial proof "pulled" from the block while it is being cut. This is done at intervals to check the artist's progress.

**baren**   A round pad, usually made of a bamboo leaf, stretched over a firm backing to which a handle has been attached. The baren is rubbed over the back of the paper that has been laid over an inked block in order to transfer the design to the paper.

**batik**   A resist process, originated in Indonesia, for decorating fabric. Areas of the cloth are successively blocked out with melted wax and dyed. True batik is characterized by a network of fine lines produced when the dye penetrates cracks in the wax.

**bench hook**   Small wooden platform used to aid in the cutting of wood and linoleum blocks. One end has a flange pointing downward, which hooks over the edge of the work table, and the other has a flange pointing upward, against which the block being cut may be rested to prevent slipping.

**bench pin**   A jeweler's tool consisting of a piece of hardwood into which a V shape has been cut. The pin is attached to the workbench and used to support a piece that is being sawed, drilled, or otherwise worked on.

**bisque (biscuit)**   In ceramics, a term meaning clay that has been fired once, resulting in a dense, hard, and durable product.

**block-out medium**   Any material such as glue, starch, shellac, tusche, or a commercial water-base masking compound that, when applied to a silk screen, will dry and block out areas of the screen.

**brayer** A hard rubber cylinder to which a handle has been attached in such a way that the cylinder revolves. The brayer is used to roll printing ink to the proper consistency on the palette and to transfer the film of ink to the surface of the block.

**bubbling or arcing** A term in weaving, meaning to incorporate a bit more weft yarn into each pass than actually needed to relieve tension and prevent the work from becoming too tight.

**butterfly** A bundle into which long individual cords are made and secured with a rubber band in such a way that cord is released as knotting progresses in macramé.

**canvas embroidery** Needlework done on a backing of mesh canvas rather than on a woven fabric; for example, needlepoint, bargello.

**casting** The process of making shapes by pouring some fluid substance, such as molten metal, liquid, or clay into a mold.

**ceramics** The art of making pottery from clay, which is then fired in a kiln to make it durable.

**champlévé** Decorative enameling technique whereby a design is carved or gouged into a metal surface, filled with enamel, and fired. The raised areas serve to contain the enamel as well as form the outline of the design.

**clay** Raw material for pottery; formed by the geological weathering of feldspathic rocks. When moist, clay is plastic and may be formed with the hands or in molds.

**cloisonné** Decorative enameling technique whereby thin metal strips or cloisons are attached to a metal base to outline design areas, which are then filled in with enamels and fired; brought to a high state of perfection by the Chinese.

**coiling** Contemporary adaptation of a basketry technique in which a fiber core or rope is wrapped with yarn and the resulting wrapped core used to make containers or sculptural works; also a method of hand-building pottery.

**collage** Art work made by gluing various objects such as bits of paper, cloth, twigs, shells, and the like onto a firm backing; a favorite technique of the early cubists.

**collograph** Printmaking technique utilizing a block that has been prepared by gluing various textured substances to the surface of a backing material. The block is inked and printed as for other relief printing methods.

**coloring oxides** Various metals exist in their oxide forms and as such are used to impart color to enamels, glazes, and other fired substances. Most common of these are copper oxide ($CuO$) for green colors, cobalt oxide ($Co_2O_3$) for blue color, iron oxide ($FeO$) for tans, yellows, and browns, manganese dioxide ($MnO_2$) for browns and purples, and chromic oxide ($C_2O_3$) for greens. Colors obtained will depend upon the formulation and concentration of the oxide included.

**color wheel** A system of color analysis based on primary, secondary, and teritary hues. It is a simple means of understanding such terms as complementary colors, color schemes, color modulation, and other properties of color.

**components of art** Subject matter (what the work is about); form (how the work is organized); content (what the work means, its statement). The components are usually very much interrelated, particularly form and content.

**couching** Method of removing wet paper sheets from the mould by pressing the mould upside down onto a dampened felt or blanket and gently rocking the mould to transfer the sheet to the felt.

**counterenamel** Enamel applied and fired to the reverse of a metal piece to protect the surface, provide decoration, or prevent flat panels from warping.

**crackle enamels** Special mixtures that are applied over previously fired base coats of enamel. When the piece is refired, a network of crackles develop, which allows the base coat to show through.

**design** The ordered arrangement of the various elements in a work of art, resulting in a unified statement with enough variety to give the work interest.

**double weave** Woven fabric with two layers, accomplished by warping both sides of the weaving frame; technique widely used in woven sculpture and other three-dimensional fiber work.

**dyes** Any substance used to impart color to another substance. Dyes may be naturally derived from plants and animals (indigo, madder, cochineal) or minerals (ochre, chromium, cobalt) or may be synthesized from various coal tar substances such as benzene or aniline.

**edition** The predetermined number of prints made from a particular block. Prints are numbered using a fractional system. For example, if a print is numbered 26/100, this means the print is number 26 of a 100-print edition.

**elements of art** Basic visual tools used by the artist to make a statement. These are line, value, texture, color, and shape. In three-dimensional works, mass and space are also included.

**emery** A powdered mixture of silicon carbide and magnetite used for removing deep scratches from metallic surfaces; usually used with buffing wheels powered by a motor.

**enamels** Finely ground, glasslike materials that may be fused onto the surface of various metals (copper, silver, gold) to impart color and design.

**fiber** Threadlike parts of various organic and inorganic materials; a filament; includes threads, yarns, cords, and ropes of wool, cotton, linen, hemp, and synthetic materials such as rayon, nylon, and acrylic; used in all types of fiber construction such as weaving, coiling, stitchery, macramé, or combinations thereof (called the "fiber arts").

**finishing** Final step in any craft process; for example, filing and polishing of metals in jewelry making; hemming and backing of a stitchery panel; cleaning the surface of a mosaic or piece of stained glass.

**fire-scale** Heavy oxidation that forms on the surface of metals, particularly on copper, when heated to a high temperature; sometimes forms interesting patterns that may then be covered with transparent glazes or enamels to become part of the decorative design of the work.

**firing** The process of subjecting certain substances such as clays, glazes, and enamels to high temperatures in a kiln in order to cause melting of glazes or to make clay hard and durable. During normal firing, the kiln contains an ample supply of oxygen (oxidation firing). Reduction firing occurs when there is insufficient oxygen in the kiln.

**floated joint** In glass crafting, technique of achieving slightly convex soldered seams. This is accomplished by holding the soldering iron just slightly above the seam, so the melted solder will "rise" to meet the iron.

**flux** One of a number of substances used in ceramics and enameling to aid in the melting and flowing of other materials. For example, rosin acts as a flux in soldering; borax is used as a flux in low fire glazes.

**foil tape** A narrow tape made of copper, having an adhesive on one side and used with solder to put stained glass work together. The technique of using foil has largely replaced the use of lead came.

**found objects** Discarded or junk materials widely used by artists and craftspeople in the twentieth century to add interest to their work; technically known as "assemblage."

**fritting** A process of melting together various chemicals, cooling the molten mass by pouring it into water, and grinding the resultant mass to a fine powder. In ceramics, fritting is used extensively in the preparation of glazes with lead because the process not only makes the mixture more homogeneous but also renders the lead nontoxic. Fritted glazes or enamels are substances that have been prepared in this manner.

**glaze** In ceramics, a smooth glasslike coating on the surface of pots that protects the clay, makes it waterproof, and often adds color and decorative design.

**graphic arts** Those arts and crafts concerned with the multiple copies of a design from a "block" of some sort. These include *relief* techniques (woodcut); *intaglio* techniques (etching); *surface* or *planographic* techniques (lithography); and special techniques such as monopoint and cliche-verre.

**grissaille** A monochrome painting in shades of gray on the surface of enamels or in stained glass work.

**grout** A mixture of cement or plaster and water used to fill in the cracks between tesserae in mosaic techniques.

**grozing** In glass crafting, the removal of tiny rough projections from the cut edges of glass with special wide-jawed pliers known as grozing pliers.

**gum arabic (gum acacia)** A sticky mixture made with dried ground leaves of the acacia plant and water; used for adhering dry enamel to curved or slanted metal surface.

**hand-building** In ceramics any method of forming clay into shapes with the hands; for example, slab, coil, pinch and drape methods.

**jewelry** Any ornament meant to be worn, such as a ring, brooch, bracelet, or necklace; usually, but not necessarily, made of metal such as gold, silver, or bronze, and often set with precious or semiprecious stones.

**kiln** A furnace or oven built with insulting firebrick enclosed in a metal jacket and powered by electricity or fuel; used for burning, baking, or drying something. These are used extensively in enameling procedures and in the production of ceramics.

**kiln furniture** Various aids needed in the process of firing: posts, stilts, shelves, trivets, and triangles are used in loading the kiln and supporting the objects to be fired.

**knotting board**   A thick rigid piece of wallboard to which foundation cords may be attached and work may be pinned while macramé knotting is in progress.

**lead came**   Lead strips in H or U shapes having channels and used for putting stained glass work together. A traditional method still used for larger pieces; now largely replaced with the foil technique.

**leather-hard**   Clayware in the semidry state. There is enough moisture still present that the clay is slightly pliable; it may be easily cut or carved and pieces may still be easily joined together.

**linoleum print (linocut)**   Relief print made from a block of linoleum into which a design has been cut; the block is then inked and printed by pressure onto paper or other material.

**linters (cotton linters)**   A by-product of the textile industry; the short cotton fibers remaining on the seed after the ginning process are removed with a special machine called a linter. These cotton fibers are then used for the making of paper and for other purposes.

**loom**   Device used in weaving for holding the warp in place and under tension. This may be as simple as a wooden frame or as complicated as the huge mechanical looms used in commercial operations.

**luster**   Any substance that imparts a shiny, metallic, irridescent appearance to the surface of a glazed ceramic pot or piece of enamel work.

**macramé**   The art of knotting threads or cords into patterns to make decorative or utilitarian objects.

**matte**   Term used to characterize any material (particularly glazes and enamels) having a dull, nonshiny surface.

**mold**   A hollow shape into which molten or fluid materials may be poured in order to form a casting.

**mosaic**   A decorative technique consisting of small pieces of colored glass, ceramic tile, stones, or other materials, fitted together on a suitable foundation. The small pieces (tesserae) are set in a mastic or cement and the interstices filled with grout.

**mould and deckle**   A two-part frame used to make paper sheets. The mould is a wooden frame, the top of which is covered with a fine mesh screen of brass or fiberglass. The deckle is a separate open frame that fits down over the mould to produce a feathered or deckled edge on the wet paper sheet.

**papier-collé**   A collage made by using only bits and pieces of paper or items made from paper.

**patina**   A surface appearance achieved on metal by treating the metal with some substance, such as liver of sulphur, copper sulfate, or a commercial liquid. In time, a natural patina will form on the surface of most metals through oxidation; for example, the green patina that forms on copper and bronze when exposed to the weather.

**pickling**   Process of cleaning metals by immersing them in a solution of acid or other chemical. Particularly used in metal crafting to remove oxidation from the surface of the metal either prior to or after soldering or brazing.

**plain or "tabby" weave**   The most common of all weaves consisting of simply passing the weft thread alternately over and under every other warp thread (under one, over one).

**post**   A papermaking term meaning a stack of alternate felts and sheets that is then subjected to pressure to remove excess water.

**principles of organization**   Various means used by the artist to control the elements of art. These are balance, rhythm, harmony, repetition, proportion, dominance, economy, contrast, and movement.

**printing inks**   Inks or paints formulated especially for use in the graphic arts. These inks come in a wide variety of types and colors; both water base and oil base and are usually much thicker than writing inks.

**pulp**   Paper fibers that have been "beaten" or shredded, mixed with water, and readied for making sheets of handmade paper; sometimes called "half-stuff."

**pyrometer**   An instrument consisting of an indicator dial and a thermocouple used for measuring very high temperatures in kilns.

**pyrometric cone**   In ceramics, a series of triangular cone shapes made from clay and designed to melt at various temperatures; used to measure the internal temperature of a pottery kiln during firing.

**Raku**   A ceramic process originated in Japan to produce vessels used in the tea ceremony. It differs from regular ceramics in that the clay is highly grogged; glazed ware is placed in a red-hot kiln, removed as soon as the glaze melts, and thrust into a container of combustible materials to "smoke" the pot in a reduction atmosphere.

**registration**   The exact fitting together of design parts and colors in a multicolor print. Because multicolor prints require use of several different blocks, some system must be devised to ensure that the parts will line up perfectly. For classroom use, the simplest method is that described in the text.

**resist work** Various decorative techniques, such as batik and tie-dye, in which certain areas of the fabric are "blocked out" with wax, starch, glue, or bound with cord so the dye cannot penetrate and color those areas.

**restrike** Additional prints made from a printing plate from which the original edition has already been pulled; strictly speaking, not an ethical procedure, especially if the later edition is not labeled as being restrikes.

**rouge (red rouge or jeweler's rouge)** Powdered ferric oxide used in the fine polishing of metallic surfaces in jewelry making. There is a special *white rouge* for white metals such as silver and aluminum.

**running pliers** A glass crafter's tool designed to aid in the cutting and breaking of glass. When placed properly at one end of a scored line and slight pressure exerted, the glass breaks easily and cleanly.

**serigraph** A print (usually on paper) made by means of the silk screen process.

**sgraffito** An Italian word referring to a decorative design scratched through a top layer of plaster, paint, slip, or enamel to reveal a contrasting material or color underneath.

**shed stick** In weaving, a long, narrow stick of thin wood used to raise alternate warp threads to form a shed so the needle or bobbin bearing the wool may be quickly passed through.

**silk screen** A frame over which a very fine-mesh silk fabric has been stretched. A stencil cut from a special lacquer film is adhered to the screen and the assembly used to print a design onto various surfaces by squeezing ink through the openings with a squeegee. Prints so made are called "serigraphs."

**sizing** A preparation of glue, gum, starch, or gelatin with water; used to make fabric or paper less penetrable by liquids or to provide stiffening. For example, handmade paper is "sized" with gelatin to make it suitable to paint on.

**tesserae** Small pieces of glass or marble used in mosaic work; technically one that has four corners but generally applied to any small fragment of material.

**tie-and-dye** A method of fabric dyeing whereby parts of the cloth are bound tightly with cord or twine and placed in a dye bath. The bound portions will resist the dye and remain the original color of the fabric.

**tripoli** A light colored, soft stone that is powdered and used for polishing metallic surfaces.

**weaving** A fiber art consisting of the interlacing of sets of threads at right angles to each other to form cloth or fabric; may be a simple or plain weave or may have intricate multicolor patterns. Vertical or lengthwise threads are called the "warp" and horizontal or crosswise threads are called the "weft" or "woof."

**wedging** In pottery making, the process of kneading moist clay to make it more plastic and homogeneous; sometimes includes the working of grog (finely ground fired clay) into the moist clay to give it more porosity and strength.

**wheel-throwing** In ceramics, the process of forming clay into shapes with the aid of the potter's wheel.

**woodcut** Relief print made from a wooden block into which a design has been cut; the block is inked and printed by pressure onto paper or some other material. A slab of plank wood is usually used for the block, and the grain of the plank becomes a part of the design. A wood engraving is also a relief print made from a woodblock, but the block is prepared from end grain wood.

# Index

## A

Albers, Josef, 7
*American Crafts* (magazine), 7
Art Education, 11–18
  evolution in the curriculum, 12–15
  objectives of crafts, 15–17
  teaching arts and crafts, 19–25, 59–61
    evaluation and grading, 24–25
    objectives, 20–23
    qualifications, 20
    standards, 23
  value of crafts in, 11–12
Arts and Crafts Teacher, The, 19–26

## B

Basic Design for Crafts Students, 33–50
Batik, 90–95
  crayon, 94
    materials, 94
    procedure, 94
    tools and equipment, 94
  history, 90
  procion dye process, 91–94
    materials, 91
    procedures, 92–94
    tools and equipment, 90–91
Bauhaus, The, 6, 7
Bayeux Tapestry, 125

## C

Ceramics, 233–54
  design and decoration, 244–45
  firing, 245–47
  glazes and glazing, 247–51
    application, 251
    basic ingredients, 247
    coloring with oxides, 248
    formulations, 250
    materials used in, 249–50
  hand building, 235–41
    coil method, 238–39
    drape method, 239–41
    pinch method, 239
    slab method, 235–38
  history, 233–34
  materials, 233, 247–50
    clays, 233
    glazes, 247–50
  procedures
    general outline, 234–35

raku, 251–53
tools and equipment, 236
wheel throwing, 241–44
Coiled Basketry, 69–75
  history, 69
  materials, 70
  procedure, 70–74
  tools and equipment, 70
Color, 45–46
  color properties, 46
    hue, 46
    intensity, 46
    value, 46
  color schemes, 46
  color spectrum, 45
  color wheel, 45
  simultaneous contrast, 46
Crafts
  definitions, 3–4
  evolution, 4–6
    American revival (1920's), 7, 57
    art nouveau influence, 6
    Bauhaus, Germany, 6
    colonial America, 6, 57
    Greece, 4
    Industrial Revolution, 5
    Middle Ages, 5
    nineteenth century revival, 5
    Paleolithic era, 4
    Renaissance, 5
  history (*see listings of individual crafts*)
  philosophy, 3–4
  use for the elderly and handicapped, 64
  use in recreation, 61
  use in schools, 19–25, 59–61
  use in therapy and rehabilitation, 63
  value of, xi
Crafts and Creativity, 27–32
Crafts and Society, 3–9
Crafts and the Art Education Program, 11–18
Crafts Fairs, 8
Crafts Guilds, 5
Craftsmen
  evolution (*see* Crafts, evolution)
Crafts Museums
  American Crafts Museum, 7
  listing, Appendix B, 299–300

Crafts Organizations
  American Craft Enterprises, 8, 258
  American Crafts Council, 8
  Southern Highlands Handicraft Guild, 7
Crafts Program
  organization of, 51–56
    considerations, 51
    materials and supplies, 56
    purpose, 51
    tools and equipment, 55
    workshop set-up, 53–55
Crafts Publications, 7
Crafts Schools, 7
Crafts Shops and Galleries
  America House, 7
  listing, Appendix A, 295–98
Crafts Suppliers
  listing, Appendix C, 301–3
Crafts Terminology
  listing, Glossary, 305–9
Crafts Today, 57–66
Creativity
  definition, 29
  measuring, 30
    I.Q. tests, 27
    Torrance Tests of Creative Thinking, 30
  research of, current, 31
  research of, early, 27–29
  stages of, 30

## D

Design
  approach to original design, 48–49
  art components, 34
    content, 34
    form, 34
    subject matter, 34
  elements of art, 35–46
    color, 45–46
    line, 36–38
    shape, 43–44
    texture, 39–41
    value, 42–44
  principles of organization, 47
    balance, 47
    dominance, 47
    economy, 47

movement, 47
proportion, 47
rhythm, 47
translation of design to art object,
    schematic diagram, 35
Dewey, John, 14

## E

Eaton, Allen H., iv
Enamels on Metal, 77–87
history, 77–78
materials, 79–80
procedures
    champlévé, 84
    charging, dry, 83
    charging, wet, 83
    cloisonné, 84
    counterenameling, 82
    crackle enamels, 86
    firing, 81
    foil techniques, 83
    grisaille, 84
    luster techniques, 83
    methods of application, 80
    painting techniques, 83
    separation enamel, 86
    sgraffito, 83
    stenciling, 82
    threads and lumps, 83
tools and equipment
    firing, 78–79
    preparation and application, 79

## F

Fabric Dyeing, 89–102
dyes, natural, 89
dyes, synthetic, 89
history, 89
Fiber Techniques, 103–45. *See also*
    Weaving; Macramé;
    Stitchery
history, 103

## G

Glossary, 305–9
Gropius, Walter, 7

## H

History of Crafts. *See listing of
    individual crafts*

## I

Itten, Johannes, 6

## J

Jewelry, 147–61
design, 159
history, 147–48
materials, 148

procedures
    findings, 158
    finishing, 157
    sheet metal, 154–55
    soldering, 155–57
    stone setting, 158–59
    texturing, 158
    wire jewelry, 151–53
tools and equipment, 149–51

## K

Klee, Paul, 6

## M

Macramé, 114–24
basic knots, 119–22
    diagonal hitch, 120
    double half-hitch, 120
    Josephine knot, 122
    lark's head, 119
    overhand knot, 122
    sennit, 122
    square knot, 120
finishing, 123–24
history, 114–15
materials, 116–17
Moholy-Nagy, Laszlo, 7
Morris, William, 6
Mosaics, 163–70
history, 163–64
materials, 164–65
procedures
    direct method, 166–69
    indirect method, 170
tools and equipment, 165–66

## O

Organizing a Crafts Program, 51–56

## P

Papermaking, 171–87
history, 171–72
materials, 174
procedures, additional, 181–86
    casting with pulp, 184–85
    embedding, 181–83
    lamination, 183
    papier-colle and collage, 185–86
    poured pulp, 184
procedures, basic, 174–80
tools and equipment, 172–73
Printing, 189–218. *See also* Relief
    Printing; Silk Screening
Professional Portfolio, 260–93. *See also
    listing of artists included
    below*
Adachi, Karen, 260
Adcock, Michael and Christina, 261
Anderson, Gwendolyn (Orsini), 262
Bowden, Sandra, 263
Brubaker, Jack, 264

Campbell, Jane, 265
Cornett, Barbara, 266
Davis, Virginia I., 267
Elkan, Michael, 268
Engelke, Karen, 269
Fellerman, Stephen J., 270
Fine, Jody, 271
Gabriel, Diane, 272
Grenell, Barbara, 273
Hancock, Doug and Mary, 274
Kagan, Russell, 275
Kozel, Ina, 276
Lane, Richard, 277
Layne, Mimi, 277
Marshman, Janet, 278
Nygren, John F., 279
Ramsey, Nancy, 280
Ricciardi-Vansell, Julia, 280
Roberts, Gil, 281
Rogers, David R., 282
Rosenthal, Shirley, 282
Rowell, Bernie, 283
Shedd, John, 284
Shook, Gertrude, 138, 285
Stephenson, Karl, 286
Summa, Henry P., 286–87
Twery, Thelma, 288
Wreden, Peter, 289

## R

Relief Printing, 189–202
linoleum cuts, 197–202
    materials, 197–98
    procedures, 199–201
    tools and equipment, 198
other methods, 200–202
woodcut, 189–97
    design, 193
    history, 189–90
    materials, 191–93
    procedures, 194–97
    tools and equipment, 191–93
Rousseau, Jean-Jacques, 14

## S

Shahn, Ben, 34
Silk-Screening, 203–18
fabric base, 214–17
    materials, 214
    procedures, 215–17
    tools and equipment, 214
paper base, 203–13
    materials, 204, 213
    procedures, 204–12
        making the print, 210–12
        preparation of the screen,
            204–6
        preparation of the stencil,
            207–9
    tools and equipment, 203–4

Stained Glass, 219–32
  history, 219–20
  materials, 222
  procedures, 222–32
    foil method, 230–32
    traditional method, using lead
      cames, 222–29
  tools and equipment, 220–22
Stitchery, 125–45
  contemporary stitchery, 126–45
    appliqué, 129
    bargello, 130–32
    crochet, 132–33
    description, 126
    finishing, 142–43
    knitting, 134–36
    materials, 128
    needlepoint, 129–30
    quilting, 134
    soft sculpture, 137–41
    tools and equipment, 127–28

  history, 125
  traditional stitchery, 125–26
    embroidery, 125–26

*T*

Teaching Crafts, xiii
  state requirements, xiii
    state of Virginia, xiii
Tie and Dye, 95–101
  history, 95
  materials, 95–96
  procedures, 97–101
  tools and equipment, 95–96
Tiffany, Louis Comfort, 6–7
Torrance, E. Paul, xi, 30
  roles for teaching creativity, xii

*W*

Weaving, 103–14
  back-strap loom weaving, 113
  card loom, 113
  history, 103–4

Inkle loom, 113
materials, 112
multiple harness loom, 113
procedures
  additional weaves, 108–10
  basic weaves, 104–8
  color changes, 106
  dovetailing, 106
  Egyptian knot, 108
  finishing, 113
  ghiordes knot, 108
  interlocking, 106
  rya knot, 110
  slit technique, 106
  soumak knot, 108
  tabby weave, 104–6
sculptural weaving, 114
tools and equipment, 110–11
Webb, Aileen Osborne (Mrs. Vanderbilt),
  7